DARK PASSAGES
OF THE BIBLE

DARK PASSAGES
OF THE BIBLE

ENGAGING SCRIPTURE WITH
BENEDICT XVI & THOMAS AQUINAS

MATTHEW J. RAMAGE

THE CATHOLIC UNIVERSITY OF AMERICA PRESS
WASHINGTON, D.C.

Library of Congress Cataloging-in-Publication Data
Ramage, Matthew J.
Dark passages of the Bible : engaging scripture with Benedict XVI
and Thomas Aquinas / Matthew J. Ramage.
pages cm.
Includes bibliographical references and index.
ISBN 978-0-8132-2156-4 (pbk. : alk. paper)
1.Bible—Criticism, interpretation, etc.
2. Bible—Hermeneutics.   3. Benedict XVI, Pope, 1927–
4. Thomas, Aquinas, Saint, 1225?–1274.
5. Catholic Church—Doctrines.   I. Title.
BS511.3.R36 2013
220.6—dc23   2013012085

CONTENTS

ACKNOWLEDGEMENTS

Before recognizing the many individuals who have directly contributed to this book, I must begin by acknowledging the debt of gratitude I owe to our Holy Father, Pope Benedict XVI, for his commitment to the enterprise of a biblical exegesis that is at once thoroughly critical and thoroughly faithful to Christ's church. The inspiration for this work in its present form came from Benedict's encouragement of scholars to help the faithful approach the "dark" passages of the Bible in a way that elucidates their meaning in light of the mystery of Christ.

As the first stages of this book were developed in my dissertation at Ave Maria University, I first extend my heartfelt gratitude to my director, Gregory Vall, who introduced me to Ratzinger's "Method C" proposal, meticulously examined and critiqued my dissertation, patiently taught me Hebrew when I had only one eye with which to read it, and offered a stellar witness of a family man who strives unabashedly to do serious scholarly exegesis within the heart of the church. I thank all my theology and classics professors from Ave Maria, in particular Fr. Matthew Lamb, Jeremy Holmes, and Michael Waldstein, who served on my dissertation board. The many insights I gained through conversations with Roger Nutt and discussion groups with Fr. Joseph Fessio, SJ, were also invaluable for this endeavor. I likewise benefited tremendously from the tutelage of Matthew Levering and Michael Dauphinais of the Aquinas Center at Ave Maria University. Many of the translations I was commissioned to prepare by the Aquinas Center served an important role in establishing the Thomistic foundations of the present work.

Although the first pages of this book were written at Ave Maria, many of the ideas it contains germinated some years earlier. I therefore thank those who mentored me at the University of Illinois, Msgr. Stuart Swetland and Dr. Kenneth Howell. These men first awoke in me the desire to be a Catholic intellectual, to read the works of the fathers, and to have a profound encounter with God's living and active word. I would be remiss not to mention also the work of the Fellowship of Catholic University Students through whose ministry I first began to read and ask deep questions of the Bible on a consistent basis, as well as the Apostles of the Interior Life whose spiritual direction and friendship have been a mainstay in my life for over a decade. My colleagues in philosophy and theology at Benedictine College—all of whom are united in their dedication to the pursuit of the truth within the heart of the church—are also a pillar of strength in my academic life. I thank James Madden in a particular for thoughtful conversations which strengthened this work and helped to refine its philosophical foundations. A word of gratitude is also due to Jane Schule and the Benedictine College library staff for their dedicated work, without which I would never have had access to the raw materials necessary for this project.

Finally, I would never been able to undertake this project without the total, continued support of my family, especially my wife and parents. My mom and dad raised me in the Catholic faith, taught me the importance of the church and her Magisterium, and provided an environment where the discussion of genuine, critical questions was seen as a way to fall more deeply in love with God. My wife, Jen, has contributed more to this book than I can express, from changing diapers and cooking while I read and wrote, to proofreading the entire manuscript, to serving as a formidable "devil's advocate" to cross-examine my words. I dedicate this book to her, to my parents, and to my children. I pray that the present endeavor will contribute to their good and to the realization of Pope Benedict's vision for the New Evangelization as the church seeks to reawaken a vital encounter between the faithful and God through the medium of his word.

"HOW CAN *THAT* BE IN THE BIBLE?"

"How can *that* be in the Bible?" This question arises time and again in the minds of Christians who undertake serious study of the written word of God. When believers pose this question, often the more pressing issues of life cause them to forget about it before they are able to arrive at a satisfactory answer. Others pose it, do some investigation, and eventually have to set it aside for want of a satisfying response. Some even lose their faith over it. Nevertheless, the history of biblical exegesis is replete with attempts to reconcile contentious texts with sound Christian doctrine.

Many of these endeavors have proven to be powerful and fruitful. As a result, Christians who profess the doctrines of biblical inspiration and inerrancy tend not to bat an eye at the psalmist's frequent association of Yahweh with "the gods." We typically do not consider the possibility that the psalmist meant this literally, that his portrait of the divine nature might entail elements of polytheism which differ from or even contradict our own belief in the triune God. Indeed, in light of divine revelation, we now know the "gods" of which the psalmist speaks are not gods at all but rather demons or inanimate objects we choose over and against the one true God.

This vindication of the truth and unity of scripture intuitively rings true to the faithful Christian ear, but traditional interpretations often prove less convincing to believers today. When Psalm 137 declares blessed those who dash Babylonian infants against rocks, it simply does not suffice to insist that the author is not really referring to infant humans at all but rather to nascent sins that believers must "dash" before they spawn and grow into full-fledged vices. There is something true, beautiful, and important in this interpretation that preserves the unity of the biblical message concerning God's love, but in the eyes of many it falls far short of accounting for the sheer amount of development we observe when comparing the moral teaching of the Old Testament to Christ's new commandment of love.

With the advent of historical-critical scholarship in the early modern period, once widely accepted Christian interpretations like the ones described above have been seriously and sometimes radically called into question. Whereas readers in times past interpreted scripture in such a way as to highlight its unity and stress its harmony, modern scholars typically have no problem acknowledging development, diversity, and even apparent contradictions within the biblical message. As fruitful as certain traditional responses have proven to be, the challenges and insights of modern scholarship are simply too great to write off as inventions of godless academicians.[1] Nor can we overcome these problems solely by following the typical approach of conservative theologians today, an approach which consists largely in elucidating the tradition of ecclesiastical dogma on the inspiration and inerrancy of scripture. While this work is vital, one of the greatest weaknesses among theologians who strive to follow the Magisterium of the Catholic Church is that we tend to theologize about scripture without having scripture's most challenging texts before our eyes.

It is therefore necessary that we add to our theologizing an inductive dimension which takes into account not only ecclesiastical

---

1. As evangelical exegete Kenton Sparks points out, too often conservative Christians mistakenly dismiss historical-critical scholarship and the problems it raises due to an assumption that these problems are not real but rather the mere result of spiritual weakness on the part of biblical critics. For Sparks's critique and response to this view, see his *God's Word in Human Words: an Evangelical Appropriation of Critical Biblical Scholarship* (Grand Rapids, Mich.: Baker Academic, 2008), 303–8. Here he observes that "there are no substitutes for good critical skills, nor for a healthy relationship with God." (306.)

dogma but also the most difficult texts of scripture and the best insights modern research has to share concerning them. All this will keep us honest and purify our faith. It will force us to dig deeper than ever in our attempt to reconcile traditional dogma with the concrete challenges we encounter in the Word of God. We will therefore ask poignant questions: What does the Church really mean when she teaches that Sacred Scripture is "inspired" by God? How can one explain that the Bible is "without error" in the face of the myriad concrete objections of modern scholars? The present volume aims to elucidate a theology of scripture, a systematic account of the nature of scripture that will give Christians the principles and examples they need to answer precisely these kinds of questions and to apply those answers to the most challenging texts in the biblical canon.

Benedict XVI's much anticipated apostolic exhortation *Verbum Domini* and the second volume of his book *Jesus of Nazareth* were both published in the midst of the present volume's composition. Having already laid this book's foundations on the exegetical principles set out in the writings of Benedict over the past decades, it was thrilling to see the pope's new works reiterate many of his same central ideas in a new context.[2] Of particular significance was the fact that Benedict now directly called on scholars to help the faithful grapple with the most challenging texts of scripture. In a section of *Verbum Domini* entitled "The 'Dark' Passages of the Bible," Benedict recalls the instances of violence and immorality narrated in the Bible and exhorts scholars to address these problems by keeping in mind the historical rootedness of divine revelation, in particular the fact that God's plan to educate mankind was realized only slowly and indeed in spite of our resistance. As this passage is among Pope Benedict's most recent statements directly relevant to the present project, it merits to be cited in full:

In discussing the relationship between the Old and the New Testaments, the [2008 Synod of Bishops meeting on the theme of *The Word of God in the Life and Mission of the Church*] also considered those passages in the

---

2. Note that I have opted for the convention of referring to the one man Ratzinger/Benedict as "Benedict" throughout this book even in writings antedating his pontificate.

Bible which, due to the violence and immorality they occasionally contain, prove obscure and difficult. Here it must be remembered first and foremost that *biblical revelation is deeply rooted in history. God's plan is manifested progressively* and it is accomplished slowly, *in successive stages* and despite human resistance. God chose a people and patiently worked to guide and educate them. Revelation is suited to the cultural and moral level of distant times and thus describes facts and customs, such as cheating and trickery, and acts of violence and massacre, without explicitly denouncing the immorality of such things. This can be explained by the historical context, yet it can cause the modern reader to be taken aback, especially if he or she fails to take account of the many "dark" deeds carried out down the centuries, and also in our own day. In the Old Testament, the preaching of the prophets vigorously challenged every kind of injustice and violence, whether collective or individual, and thus became God's way of training his people in preparation for the Gospel. So it would be a mistake to neglect those passages of Scripture that strike us as problematic. Rather, we should be aware that the correct interpretation of these passages requires a degree of expertise, acquired through a training that interprets the texts in their historical-literary context and within the Christian perspective which has as its ultimate hermeneutical key "the Gospel and the new commandment of Jesus Christ brought about in the paschal mystery." I encourage scholars and pastors to help all the faithful to approach these passages through an interpretation which enables their meaning to emerge in the light of the mystery of Christ.[3]

The key hermeneutical principle guiding our quest in this book is taken directly from writings of Benedict like the one we read above: problematic texts in the Bible can be adequately addressed only if we take seriously the fact that "God's plan is manifested *progressively* and it is accomplished slowly, *in successive stages* and despite human resistance." According to Benedict, God patiently and gradually revealed himself to his people in order to "guide and educate" them with the ultimate end of "training his people in preparation for the Gospel."

The above text from Pope Benedict echoes the words of the Second Vatican Council's *Dei Verbum* and the later *Catechism of the Catholic Church*. As the Catechism eloquently states: "The divine plan of revelation ... involves a specific divine pedagogy: God com-

---

3. Benedict XVI, *Verbum Domini*, 2010, §42 (emphasis Benedict's). Cited hereafter as *VD*.

municates himself to man gradually. He prepares him to welcome by stages the supernatural revelation that is to culminate in the person and mission of the incarnate Word, Jesus Christ."[4] Throughout the course of this work, the case will be made that a sound and satisfying Christian reading of Sacred Scripture must take to heart the divine pedagogy, the reality that the pages of scripture manifest the gradual teaching method by which God led his chosen people to the fullness of truth in Christ. We will see that the hermeneutic of divine pedagogy is precisely the bridge that enables one to reconcile the unity of scripture traditionally emphasized by Christian exegetes with the development, diversity, and apparent contradictions observed by modern scholars. For the hermeneutic of divine pedagogy affirms that scripture has a unity in light of the fact that it proceeds from God's one wise educational plan for mankind and communicates God himself to man.

At the same time, this hermeneutic is comfortable with development and diversity within scripture. While Pope Benedict acknowledges that these are the natural consequences of a divine plan which unfolded gradually over time in accordance with man's capacity to receive it, he is intent on demonstrating that apparent contradictions in scripture are precisely that—apparent. He explains that this is the case because the Bible is a "living organism" that developed as a result of the "process" of God's gradual revelation: "The Bible is the condensation of a *process of revelation* which is much greater and inexhaustible.... It is then part of a living organism which, through

---

4. *Catechism of the Catholic Church,* translated by United States Catholic Conference. (Washington, D.C.: Libreria Editrice Vaticana, 1994), §53. Cited hereafter as *CCC.* I have cited the Catechism here because of its clarity and conciseness, but the Catechism itself is summarizing the Second Vatican Council constitution *Dei Verbum* §15. For other magisterial statements of the divine pedagogy, see Pius XI, *On the Church and the German Reich* [*Mit brennender sorge*], *1937,* §15 and *Lumen gentium, 1964,* §9, which explains Israel's relationship with God in terms of gradual instruction: "[God] therefore chose the race of Israel as a people unto Himself. With it He set up a covenant. Step by step He taught and prepared this people, making known in its history both Himself and the decree of His will and making it holy unto Himself. All these things, however, were done by way of preparation and as a figure of that new and perfect covenant, which was to be ratified in Christ, and of that fuller revelation which was to be given through the Word of God Himself made flesh."

the vicissitudes of history, nonetheless *conserves its identity*."[5] The following selection of Benedict's Old Testament exegesis further elucidates this dynamic process and pinpoints the key which enables us to make sense of it:

The Bible is thus the story of God's struggle with human beings to make himself understandable to them over the course of time; but it is also the story of their struggle to seize hold of God over the course of time.... The whole Old Testament is a journeying with the Word of God. Only in the process of this journeying was the Bible's real way of declaring itself formed, step by step.... For the Christian the Old Testament represents, in its totality, an advance toward Christ; only when it attains to him does its real meaning, which was gradually hinted at, become clear. Thus every individual part derives its meaning from the whole, and the whole derives its meaning from its end—from Christ. Hence we only interpret an individual text theologically correctly ... when we see it as a way that is leading us ever forward, when we see in the text where this way is tending and what its inner direction is.[6]

Benedict emphasizes that the Bible is the story of a twofold struggle: God's struggle to "make himself understandable to them over the course of time," and the people of God's struggle to "seize hold of God over the course of time." He describes this familiarization between God and man as a journey of faith, arguing that "only in the process of this journeying was the Bible's real way of declaring itself formed, step by step." Once again, we are presented here with Benedict's own articulation of the divine pedagogy. The message of the Bible becomes clearer as salvation history progresses and man acquires an increasing ability to penetrate the divine mysteries. Ultimately, however, the whole Old Testament is "an advance toward Christ," and as such its real meaning becomes clear only in light of

---

5. Benedict XVI, "Sources and Transmission of the Faith," *Communio* 10, no. 1 (1983): 28.

6. Benedict XVI, *In the Beginning: A Catholic Understanding of the Story of Creation and the Fall*, translated by Boniface Ramsey (Grand Rapids, Mich.: Eerdmans, 1995), 10–11. See also Benedict's *Jesus of Nazareth* (New York: Doubleday, 2007), where he explains that the process of the Bible's formation was "not linear ... but when you watch it unfold in light of Jesus Christ, you can see it moving in a single overall direction." According to Benedict and his "Christological hermeneutic," Christ is "the key to the whole" of Scripture. (xix.)

him who is its end. The pope therefore argues that exegetes interpret individual texts correctly only when they "see in the text where this way is tending and what its inner direction is."

Benedict's revealing interview *God and the World* likewise illumines this point in a striking way. It is noteworthy that in this work Benedict contrasts Islam and Christianity precisely on the issue of whether the scriptures exhibit development. Contrasting Islam's belief that the Koran was dictated directly to Muhammad by God, he observes that the books of the Bible "bear the impression of a history that [God] has been guiding," since they were composed and developed over a thousand years, mediated by "quite different stages of history and of civilization."[7] As in the two texts just discussed, so here he explains, "The Bible is not a textbook about God and divine matters but contains images with perceptions and insights in the course of development, and through these images, slowly and step by step, a historical reality is coming into existence."[8] If the Christian cannot turn to a given page of the Bible for the fullness of revealed truth, then where can he find it? "The level on which I perceive the Bible as God's Word is that of the unity of God's history.... In our Christian reading of it, we are more than ever convinced, as we said, that the New Testament offers us the key to understanding the Old."[9] The idea I wish to convey by sampling these works of

7. Benedict XVI, *God and the World* (San Francisco: Ignatius Press, 2002), 151–52 (emphasis added).

8. "Let us compare Holy Scripture with the Koran, for example. Moslems believe that the Koran was directly dictated by God. It is not mediated by any history; no human intermediary was needed; it is a message direct from God. The Bible, on the other hand, is quite different. *It is mediated to us by a history, and even as a book it extends over a period of more than a thousand years.* The question of whether or not Moses may have been a writer is one we can happily leave to one side. It is still true that the biblical literature grew up over a thousand-year history and thus moves through quite different stages of history and of civilization, which are all reflected in it. In the first three chapters of Genesis, for instance, we meet with a quite different form of culture from what came later, or in the exilic literature, or in the wisdom literature, and then finally in the literature of the New Testament. It becomes clear that God did not just dictate these words but rather that *they bear the impression of a history that he has been guiding; they have come into being as a witness to that history.*" Ibid. (emphasis added).

9. Ibid., 153 (emphasis added). Benedict again goes on to speak of the "process of collective development" and the "many stages of mediation" by which the biblical

Benedict on the importance of a divine pedagogy hermeneutic is summarized well in a fourth work, *Introduction to Christianity*, in which he states quite simply, "Anyone who wishes to understand the biblical belief in God must follow its historical development from its origins with the patriarchs of Israel right up to the last books of the New Testament."[10] In the end, our ability to appreciate the dynamics of God's gradual teaching method in scripture is the key to ascertaining the meaning of challenging texts in the biblical canon and in turn to developing a sound theology of scripture that accurately grasps the nature of biblical inspiration and inerrancy.

In view of achieving this understanding, the ensuing chapters will unfold in the following manner. In chapter 1 we will begin with a brief survey of the types of problems which a modern, historical-critical reading of the Bible reveals. The first part of the chapter is devoted to important problems concerning the biblical canon and the physical text of scripture, that is, the manuscripts by means of which the scriptures have come down to us today. Here readers will grapple with how any claim to biblical inspiration can be justified given the many problems posed by a critical examination of extant manuscripts. The chapter will also introduce to the reader three important themes which run throughout the Bible, all of which are greatly illumined by the hermeneutic of divine pedagogy: the nature of God, the nature of good and evil, and the afterlife. We will provide concrete examples within each of the above themes in order to lay bare their respective problems.

The issues that emerge from this brief survey can be boiled down to two: First, significant developments occurred within Israelite and Christian theology over the millennia, and the scriptures testify to this growth. The essential issue here is that the scriptures present us with Israelites and Christians living later in history who

---

books gradually were able to "bring the history of God's people and of God's guidance to verbal expression."

10. Benedict XVI, *Introduction to Christianity* (San Francisco: Ignatius Press, 2004), 116. It is illuminating to read the entire chapter from which this citation is taken, as in it Benedict traces the roots of Israel's monotheism as it developed throughout the Old Testament period.

acknowledge certain truths that those who lived earlier did not. The question therefore arises: how can scripture be inerrant if in certain areas it does not contain the fullness of revealed truth? Second, granted the fact that certain parts of scripture do not explicitly teach the fullness of truth known by Christians today, there remains a second—and more problematic—difficulty for us to address: the fact we sometimes observe biblical texts making statements that seem plainly to contradict the teachings of other texts. This is especially problematic when later texts seem to constitute regressions rather than developments with respect to texts written earlier in the course of divine revelation.

Cognizant of these two great problems that lie before the reader of scripture, chapter 2 will lay the foundation for a faithful and robust theological response. Here we will spell out Pope Benedict's "Method C" hermeneutics proposal which he began articulating almost two decades before becoming pope. This schema will provide the basis for our later work of grappling with the challenging themes introduced above in light of the divine pedagogy. Put briefly, Benedict argues that if today's exegete is to make sense of the problems in scripture he must have recourse to both ancient and modern methods of interpretation. The ancient, patristic-medieval method (which he calls "Method A") is vital because it provides us with something so many modern exegetes lack: an approach to the biblical text which is based on faith and seeks to build up the church. Within our discussion of Method A exegesis, we will need to summarize the theological principles which govern biblical interpretation within the Catholic Church. These include, above all, the doctrines of inerrancy and inspiration which speak to the nature of scripture itself. In addition, there is the importance of having recourse to the traditional four senses of scripture and to the guidelines of the Catholic magisterial teaching as expounded in such sources as *Dei Verbum* and the later Catechism: to interpret individual scriptural passages in light of scripture as a whole, to read scripture in light of the church's entire living tradition, and to bear in mind the analogy of faith. Here we will explore the divine pedagogy in more detail, emphasizing its nature as sacred teaching and paying particular attention to the "condescension" whereby God came down to mankind and taught us by means of our own feeble human words.

With these general principles in place, we will introduce the essential features of the modern, historical-critical method ("Method B"). With his positive appraisal of historical-critical exegesis, Pope Benedict has sometimes scandalized the Catholic faithful who tend to reject this method outright due to the fact that many scholars practice it with a bias against the miraculous and even against the Christian faith in general. The pope, however, argues that the Method B approach must be an essential component in faithful biblical exegesis today. In particular, in this work it will enable us to ask deep questions—and entertain corresponding answers—which faithful exegetes of the past did not tend to raise.[11] Indeed, many of the problems introduced in chapter 1 are recognizable precisely thanks to evidence garnered by Method B exegesis. Method B is able to do this because it provides us with scientific tools for ascertaining the meaning of biblical texts which even the brightest of ancient thinkers simply did not possess. In later chapters we will draw on these resources to spell out chapter 1's problems in no uncertain terms. For the present, suffice it to note that Method B and Method A both have their strengths and weaknesses. Our work will entail sorting these out in the attempt to synthesize the two into a "Method C" which later can be applied to specific texts in scripture.

Having surveyed problematic themes within Scripture in chapter 1 and elucidated Benedict's Method C exegesis proposal in chapter 2, in the next two chapters we will be in a position to explore more precisely how a Method C approach to scripture might operate. Here we will show that St. Thomas Aquinas's theology provides the proper basis for carrying out Benedict's exegetical proposal. In-

11. On the subject of asking deep questions that challenge our Christian faith, it is instructive to read Brennan C. Pursell's book *Benedict of Bavaria: An Intimate Portrait of the Pope and His Homeland* (North Haven, Conn.: Circle Press, 2008). In the present volume, we will be joining Pope Benedict in asking demanding questions concerning highly debated issues with direct relevance to the foundations of our Christian faith. A helpful piece on the subject by Tom Hoopes can be found at www.ncregister.com/blog/benedict_radical_questioner.

deed, Pope Benedict himself has explicitly connected his exegetical program with that of Aquinas. In his recent volume *Jesus of Nazareth*, for example, the Holy Father explained that Aquinas's work is not a "Life of Jesus" or a "Christology," but rather that his treatise on the life of Christ in the *Summa* is "closer to my intention" and that with this work "my book has many points of contact."[12] Though privy to modern tools for elucidating the words of scripture, Benedict identifies with Aquinas in his patient attentiveness to God's word and his desire to put believers in touch with the mystery of Jesus, his "figure and message."[13]

In the section of his Erasmus Lecture entitled "Basic Elements of a New Synthesis," Benedict expounds at greater length on one such point of contact: the importance of Thomas's thought for helping believers encounter Christ through his word. In contrast with a Kantian "ready-made philosophy," Aquinas's "open philosophy" is "capable of accepting the biblical phenomenon in all its radicalism" by admitting that a real encounter of God and man is witnessed in history—and made possible today—by the scriptures.[14] For Benedict, a "critique of the critique" requires a rejection of the false presuppositions of those who would exclude *a priori* God's ability to speak through human words. Aquinas's exegesis, deeply rooted in

12. Benedict XVI, *Jesus of Nazareth: Holy Week: From the Entrance into Jerusalem to the Resurrection*, translated by Philip J. Whitmore (San Francisco: Ignatius Press, 2011), xvi. It is significant that here Benedict approvingly refers to two "excellent studies" of the person of Jesus which are thoroughly historical-critical and controversial to some readers: Joachim Gnilka, *Jesus of Nazareth: Message and History* (Peabody, Mass: Hendrickson Publishers, 1997); John Meier, *A Marginal Jew: Rethinking the Historical Jesus* (New York: Doubleday, 1991). He also refers the reader to the "especially important" work of Marius Reiser, *Bibelkritik und Auslegung der Heiligen Schrift: Beiträge zur Geschichte der biblischen Exegese und Hermeneutik* (Tübingen: Mohr Siebeck, 2007).

13. Ibid.

14. Benedict XVI, "Biblical Interpretation in Conflict: On the Foundations and the Itinerary for Exegesis Today," in *Opening Up the Scriptures: Joseph Ratzinger and the Foundations of Biblical Interpretation*, edited by José Granados, Carlos Granados, and Luis Sánchez-Navarro (Grand Rapids, Mich.: Eerdmans, 2008), 23. Note that there are three different published editions of Benedict's Erasmus Lecture in the English language alone. Although I have used a different version elsewhere in the manuscript, this one is appropriate to cite here as it reveals more explicit connections with Aquinas than the other version of the text.

the Catholic tradition with its conviction that the boundary of time and eternity is permeable, allows for the Bible to be what the church has always claimed it to be: the word of God in human words.

A second point of contact between Benedict and Aquinas is pivotal for the work of chapter 3. The key here lies in Aquinas's and Benedict's mutual recognition of how essential it is to grasp the Christological teleology of salvation history. Thomas serves as a "counter-model" to the Kantian approach mentioned above, for he presupposes that the action of divine providence guided salvation history to its destination in Christ. Christ is therefore "the unifying principle" of history "which alone confers sense on it," and God's action gradually leading his people towards Christ is "the principle of the intelligibility of history."[15]

Chapter 3 will thus elucidate Aquinas's "theology of the history of revelation," in which he is able to show the unity of scripture (emphasized by Method A exegesis) while acknowledging the significant developments (emphasized by Method B exegesis) observable as God gradually prepared his chosen people to welcome the coming of Christ. We will use Aquinas's thought in the effort to account for the first major difficulty raised by chapter 1's historical-critical observations: the fact that not all portions of scripture explicitly teach the fullness of revealed truth Christians expect to find in the Bible. We will see that, according to St. Thomas, the *substance* of the Judeo-Christian faith did not change throughout the course of salvation history even though there was a development or increase in the *number* of truths believed by the faithful as God gradually taught them about himself in preparation for the coming of Christ, who alone revealed the truth in its fullness. Aquinas's framework illumines the phenomenon of development within scripture, thus making it possible to defend the inerrancy of early biblical texts which fail to explicitly display a clear conception of the divine oneness (Theme 1), an understanding of evil consonant with Christian doc-

---

15. Ibid., 24, n. 37. Benedict here is citing Maximino Arias Reyero, *Thomas von Aquin als Exeget: Die Prinzipien seiner Schriftdeutung und seine Lehre von den Schriftsinnen* (Einsiedeln: Johannes Verlag, 1971), 106; cf. "Biblical Interpretation in Conflict," 23, n. 35.

trine (Theme 2), or hope for the resurrection of the dead (Theme 3). Later in the book we will return to these problematic biblical themes and apply Aquinas's thought to them, but in this chapter our task will be simply to elucidate his theological principles.

In chapter 4 we will continue our exploration into how a Method C approach might operate, now with respect to the second major difficulty raised through the observations of chapter 1. Here our concern is the problem of apparent contradictions within the biblical canon, specifically the reality that later biblical texts make statements that appear to stand in direct opposition to the teachings of earlier texts. In this chapter, we turn from Aquinas's theology of the *history* of revelation elucidated in chapter 3 to his theology of the *act* of revelation. Although not aware of many of the challenging issues raised in this book, Aquinas again is able to provide principles we can appropriate in responding to them. Here we will see that examining what takes place when God reveals truth to a prophet is precisely what enables one to make sense of apparent contradictions in the scriptures. Specifically, with the help of Aquinas's theology we will be able to show that passages in which the sacred authors seemingly contradict one another or what Christians know to be true today do not in fact contain errors. For from the perspective of Aquinas, the truth of scripture depends on what its authors intend to affirm or teach, and if a given passage appears to contain something contradictory then the exegete must seek within this passage an aim beyond that of definitively teaching an erroneous point of view.

Most importantly, Aquinas's work bids us to consider the spiritual sense of scripture. In this lies scripture's ultimate aim. This is crucial because, at the end of the day, even if Method C exegesis is able to account for all objections to the inspiration and inerrancy of scripture, this explanation itself does not necessarily bring the believer to an encounter with the word of God—which is the divine author's deepest purpose in composing the scriptures. As we will see in the final chapters of this work, it turns out that the Christian's spiritual encounter with scripture provides a final and definitive key for elucidating a sound theology of scripture.

As an illustration of this point, in *Verbum Domini* Pope Benedict has drawn on Aquinas, who himself cites Augustine to emphasize the importance of the spiritual sense and the reality that "it is impossible for anyone to attain to knowledge of that truth unless he first have infused faith in Christ" since "the letter, even that of the Gospel, would kill, were there not the inward grace of healing faith."[16] In the Erasmus Lecture Benedict speaks to this at greater length:

> To discover how each given historical word intrinsically transcends itself, and thus to recognize the intrinsic rightness of the rereadings by which the Bible progressively interweaves event and sense, is one of the tasks of objective interpretation. It is a task for which suitable methods can and must be found. In this sense, the exegetical maxim of Thomas Aquinas is much to the point: "The task of the good interpreter is not to consider words, but sense."[17]

In contrast with those whose methodologies focus solely on the "words" of scripture, Benedict shares with Aquinas the conviction that the words of scripture were meant to be "re-read" over time, to point beyond themselves to a reality revealed through them but which transcends them.[18] In this way, their rich teaching on the senses of scripture, while giving due attention to its words, also points beyond the words so as to show that even scripture's "darkest" and most problematic passages may put believers in touch with Christ. The text in its wholeness, Benedict says, must become *Rabbenu*, "our teacher."

Having considered at length Method C's principles as anticipated and exemplified in the work of Aquinas, in the book's final two chapters we will instantiate these principles by applying them to challenging passages from each of the themes introduced in chapter 1. The goal here is to synthesize the strengths of faithful and practical patristic-medieval exegesis (Method A) with the tools and findings of historical-critical exegesis (Method B). Our first task for treating each of the themes in question will be to take up the tools

16. *Verbum Domini*, 29; cf. *ST* I–II, q. 106, a. 2.

17. Benedict XVI, "Biblical Interpretation in Conflict," 26 (emphasis added), citing Thomas Aquinas, *In Matthaeum*, XXVII, n. 2321. Benedict cites Aquinas three times in this work. Cf. *Verbum Domini*, 37.

18. For the reality of revelation being broader than the Bible see Benedict XVI, "Biblical Interpretation in Conflict," 26 and *Verbum Domini*, 16.

associated with Method B with the goal of laying bare the respective problems introduced briefly in chapter 1. Our effort towards a solution to these problems will then proceed as follows. First, we will employ Aquinas's principles in light of historical-critical observations in order to illumine the literal sense of problematic biblical texts. Countering objections to the inerrancy and inspiration of these texts, we will attempt to search out intentions of their human authors, ascertain their place within the canon of scripture, and elucidate their role within the divine pedagogy as God used them to teach the people of Israel about himself. Second, we will consider these same problematic texts in light of the divine author's ultimate purpose in composing them. Here we come to an investigation of the spiritual sense of the texts, asking what all we have ascertained thus far has to teach us today. As part of this quest, we will seek to show that the pedagogy by which God gradually taught his chosen people as a whole, throughout history, has an additional dimension: the divine author of scripture has used his word to teach not only the nation of Israel and the church of the past but also to teach individual members of the faithful still today.[19] As Benedict indicates, Christians may be privy to the fullness of revelation in a way our "elder brethren" of the Old Testament epoch were not, but the ancient truths taught therein "are of course valid for the whole of history, for all places and times" and "always need to be relearned."[20]

It is vital that our hermeneutic emphasize this twofold character of the divine pedagogy, as it encapsulates the two components that go into Method C exegesis and provides a bridge between them. For

19. This second dimension of the divine pedagogy is eloquently described in *Dialogue and Proclamation* by the Pontifical Council for Inter-Religious Dialogue, (1991). "[The Church] takes her lead from divine pedagogy. This means learning from Jesus himself, and observing the times and seasons as prompted by the Spirit. Jesus only progressively revealed to his hearers the meaning of the Kingdom, God's plan of salvation realized in his own mystery. Only gradually, and with infinite care, did he unveil for them the implications of his message, his identity as the Son of God, the scandal of the Cross. Even his closest disciples, as the Gospels testify, reached full faith in their Master only through their Easter experience and the gift of the Spirit. *Those who wish to become disciples of Jesus today will pass through the same process of discovery and commitment.*" §69 (emphasis added).

20. Benedict XVI, *God and the World*, 154.

on the one hand, even the most problematic of biblical texts have a definite literal sense. That is to say, their human authors had some pedagogical purpose in mind when they composed them for their original audience. Method B acknowledges this in an eminent way, and one who wants to do Method C exegesis must attend to it. Meanwhile, these same texts signify something in addition to the original intended meaning of their human authors: namely, they signify realities in the lives of believers today who meditate on these texts in order to gain the knowledge and strength they need to faithfully endure the strife that is human life, suffering, and death. Method A exegesis describes this further meaning of Scripture in terms of a spiritual sense that surpasses any conscious intention on the part of their original authors. In his own turn, a Method C exegete will be such insofar as he seeks out this spiritual sense and shows that it is not merely one among many possible readings of scripture but rather the *telos* for which the literal was composed in the first place and the key that discloses the logic of the divine pedagogy at work therein. By doing this, Method C exegesis does not deny the importance of the literal sense—upon which the spiritual is founded—but in light of the divine pedagogy it allows us to show how the literal sense opens up into spiritual senses that touch the lives of believers in every age. The following is an apt summary of Benedict's twofold approach to the divine pedagogy and his attitude toward how the believer ought to approach scripture's "dark" passages:

If I only read the Bible in order to see what horrible bits I can find in it, or to count up the bloodthirsty bits, then of course it won't heal me. For one thing, the Bible reflects a certain history, but it is also a kind of path that leads us in a quite personal way and sets us in the right light. If, therefore, I read the Bible in the spirit in which it was written, from Christ … in faith, then indeed it has the power to transform me. It leads me into the attitude of Christ; it interprets my life to me and changes me personally.[21]

By attempting to following Benedict in his attempt to facilitate a spiritual encounter with Christ teaching his people in the "problematic" texts of Scripture, our project thus will have completed perhaps its most significant and urgent task.

21. Benedict XVI, *God and the World*, 155.

CHAPTER 1

THE BIBLE'S PROBLEMS

Responding to the question of how the extremely bleak book of Ecclesiastes made it into the biblical canon, Peter Kreeft has written that there is nothing more meaningless than an answer without its question—and Ecclesiastes is in the Bible precisely because it provides the question to which the rest of the Bible is the answer.[1] The solutions proposed in the present work would likewise be meaningless if we did not first survey some of the problems in biblical exegesis today. The goal of this chapter is to elicit in the minds of readers questions such as "How can *that* be in the Bible?" and "How can the Bible be the inspired and inerrant word of God if the evidence presented here is true?" After arousing this wonder at the text of scripture in the present chapter, we will be in a better position to suggest a meaningful theological response in the chapters that follow.

THREE CHALLENGING BIBLICAL THEMES

The following pages introduce the reader to some of the greatest challenges a Christian must face in his quest to vindicate the truth of Sacred Scripture. To this end, I will be using the same method I employ in the university classroom where I group the Bible's problems into three major themes which run throughout the canon,

---

1. Peter Kreeft, *Three Philosophies of Life* (San Francisco: Ignatius Press, 1989), 19.

each of which poses unique difficulties. What immediately follows here is a survey of the problems bound up with these themes; at the end of this book we will revisit them and offer a solution in light of the hermeneutical principles laid out in subsequent chapters.

Theme 1: The Nature of God

It is foundational to the Christian faith that our God is the one and only divine being in existence. Just as we saw above in the case of the afterlife, however, scripture as a whole does not paint the uniform view of God's nature that Christians tend to assume. An authority no less than Pope Benedict himself takes it as an obvious given that ancient Israelites once believed in the existence of Sheol as well as in the existence of multiple deities. Taking up both of these issues in the same breath, he writes, "The official religion of Israel ... no more denied all existence to Sheol than, at first, it denied the existence of other gods than Yahweh."[2] Whereas the previous section explored problems bound up with the biblical portrait of the afterlife, in this section we will address scriptural evidence which seems to contradict orthodox Christian teaching concerning the nature of God, in particular his oneness.[3]

Let us begin with the issue of whether the Bible paints a unified portrait of God's oneness. Monotheism is at the heart of the Judeo-Christian tradition, and it is rightly touted as one of our religion's unique and great contributions to civilization. To be sure, the Old Testament gives us many clear declarations of Israel's monotheistic faith, as we will see later in this work. However, what concern us at this point are those times when the Israelites seem to have accepted as a matter of course the existence of multiple divine beings; for, if

2. Benedict XVI, Eschatology: Death and Eternal Life, translated by Michael Waldstein (Washington, D.C.: The Catholic University of America Press, 1988), 83–84.

3. Important historical-critical sources whose evidence is drawn upon in this section include: Brendan Byrne, "Sons of God," vol. 6, The Anchor Bible Dictionary, (herein after cited as ABD), edited by David Noel Freedman (New York: Doubleday, 1992.), 156–59; Jarl Fossum, "Son of God," ABD, vol. 6, 128–37; F. W. Horn, "Holy Spirit," translated by Dietlinde Elliott, ABD, vol. 3, 260–80; Carol Newsome, "Angels," ABD, vol. 1, 248–53; John Scullion, "God (OT)," ABD, vol. 2, 1041–48; Terrence Fretheim, "Word of God," ABD, vol. 6, 961–68.

this indeed is the case, one would be hard pressed to find a more salient challenge to the inerrancy of scripture's teaching. We witness the subtle presence of this view in passages like the following from the book of Exodus:

But Pharaoh said, "Who is the Lord, that I should heed his voice and let Israel go? I do not know the Lord, and moreover I will not let Israel go." Then they said, "The God of the Hebrews has met with us; let us go, we pray, a three days' journey into the wilderness, and sacrifice to the Lord our God, lest he fall upon us with pestilence or with the sword" (Ex 5:2 3).[4]

Here it is interesting to consider how Moses and Aaron reply to Pharaoh, "The God of the Hebrews has met with us." It is not far-fetched—indeed it is common—to see in this statement the assumption that Yahweh (translated "the Lord" in the RSV) is the God of the *Hebrews* alone, that is to say one specific divine being among others who also exist but are simply worshiped by nations other than Israel. This would be consonant with Yahweh's command forbidding the worship of foreign deities, "I am the Lord your God, who brought you out of the land of Egypt, out of the house of bondage. You shall have no other gods before me" (Ex 20:2–3). Again, this statement does not claim that other gods are unreal but rather that they are not to be *worshiped* by the people of Israel. In the eyes of Moses, Israel's worship of Yahweh is something the nation should be proud of, for the gods of the neighboring nations are simply not as close to their subjects as Yahweh is to the people of Israel: "For what great nation is there that has a god so near to it as the Lord our God is to us, whenever we call upon him?" (Dt 4:7)

If the above sketch is correct, it clearly presents us with a problem; for both faith and reason inform Christians that only one God exists, but here we seem to have the Old Testament assuming the existence of more than one God. Of course, there are multiple ways we could explain this statement without accepting such an interpretation: Moses could be speaking of "the God of the Hebrews" merely as a way of relating better to Pharaoh, and the "other gods"

4. Unless otherwise noted, all biblical citations in this work are from the Revised Standard Version (hereafter RSV).

described in the First Commandment could simply refer to created physical or spiritual idols. The question, however, is whether these alternative explanations satisfactorily account for the evidence. This problem will come into much sharper focus as we begin to adduce other trace evidence of polytheism in ancient Israel.

Several passages in the Psalms have a similar feel to the former in that they appear to be concerned with demonstrating Yahweh is the *greatest* among the many gods that exist. For example:

> There is none like thee among the gods, O Lord,
> nor are there any works like thine (Ps 86:8).

> For the Lord is a great God,
> and a great King above all gods (Ps 95:3).

> For great is the Lord, and greatly to be praised;
> he is to be feared above all gods (Ps 96:4).

> For thou, O Lord, art most high over all the earth;
> thou art exalted far above all gods (Ps 97:9).

> For I know that the Lord is great,
> and that our Lord is above all gods (Ps 135:5).

> O give thanks to the God of gods,
> for his steadfast love endures for ever (Ps 136:2).

As usual, the Christian tradition has various ways of interpreting the "gods" described in these passages. The gods could be idols, or even angels as the later tradition came to understand them. While such explanations are theoretically possible, a more thorough examination of the biblical data reveals their shortcomings and makes many question their credibility. At the same time, the fact that these passages speak of multiple gods does not mean simply that ancient Israelite religion was polytheistic. Indeed, scholars of religion in the Ancient Near East often describe these passages as an expression not of polytheism but of "henotheism" or "monolatry." Henotheistic systems are those which acknowledge the existence of multiple gods yet see all but one as unworthy of worship.

If ancient Israel embraced a henotheism akin to other nearby Canaanite religions, it would not be surprising to see it closely bound up with the ancient Canaanite conception of a "divine council," a royal court in heaven headed by a king with divine beings as his counselors, political subordinates, warriors, and agents. Indeed, as Jarl Fossum states, "The Israelites took over the Canaanite concept of an assembly of gods under the supremacy of El, even designating Yahweh as the 'master in the great council of the holy ones.'"[5] In the following texts we are introduced to the "heavenly beings" who comprise this council:

> Ascribe to the Lord, O heavenly" beings,
> ascribe to the Lord glory and strength (Ps 29:1).

> God has taken his place in the divine council;
> in the midst of the gods he holds judgment (Ps 82:1)

> For who in the skies can be compared to the Lord?
> Who among the heavenly beings is like the Lord,
> a God feared in the council of the holy ones,
> great and terrible above all that are round about him?
> (Ps 89:6–7)

> For who among them has stood in the council of the Lord
> to perceive and to hear his word,
> or who has given heed to his word and listened?
> … But if they had stood in my council,
> then they would have proclaimed my words to my people,
> and they would have turned them from their evil way,
> and from the evil of their doings (Jer 23:18,22).

The members of the divine council spoken of here, sometimes called "gods," or "holy ones" (a term referring to divinities in ancient Ugarit) and other times "sons of the gods" or "sons of God," preexisted the creation of the material world. Brendan Byrne explains the rationale for the term "sons" being applied to the members of Yahweh's divine council:

The use of the expression "sons of God" (more correctly, "sons of the gods") with reference to heavenly beings does not imply actual progeny of God (or the gods) but reflects the common Semitic use of "son" (Heb. *ben*) to denote membership in a class or group. "Sons of the gods," then, designates beings belonging to the heavenly or divine sphere. Such allusions to a plurality of divine beings, occurring especially in the Psalms and related poetic litera-

5. *ABD*, vol. 6, 129.

ture, represent a stage when Israel's Yahwism found room for a pantheon in many ways similar to Canannite models (cf. the literature of Ugarit). In the Bible, however, these beings are clearly subordinate to Yahweh, forming his heavenly court or divine council.[6]

The "sons of God" of the Old Testament enjoyed special powers such as the ability to intervene in the world's affairs. We see this in the case of Satan in the book of Job and in the mythological Nephilim or "giants" in the book of Genesis:

Now there was a day when the sons of God came to present themselves before the Lord, and Satan also came among them. The Lord said to Satan, "Whence have you come?" Satan answered the Lord, "From going to and fro on the earth, and from walking up and down on it." (Jb 1:6–7)

> Where were you when I laid the foundation of the earth …
> when the morning stars sang together,
> and all the sons of God shouted for joy? (Jb 38:4,7)

When men began to multiply on the face of the ground, and daughters were born to them, the sons of God saw that the daughters of men were fair; and they took to wife such of them as they chose.… The Nephilim were on the earth in those days, and also afterward, when the sons of God came in to the daughters of men, and they bore children to them. These were the mighty men that were of old, the men of renown. (Gn 6:1–2, 4)

In the above texts it is shown that the "sons of God" have the ability to test humans and, strangely, to intermarry with them. Other passages present us with more subtle echoes of the divine council's activity and deliberation among its members:

Then God said, "Let us make man in our image, after our likeness" (Gn 1:26).

Then the Lord God said, "Behold, the man has become like one of us, knowing good and evil; and now, lest he put forth his hand and take also of the tree of life, and eat, and live for ever" (Gn 3:22).

Come, let us go down, and there confuse their language, that they may not understand one another's speech (Gn 11:7).

And I heard the voice of the Lord saying, "Whom shall I send, and who will go for us?" Then I said, "Here am I! Send me" (Is 6:8)

---

6. *ABD*, vol. 6, 156.

We have already observed that the divine council was typically thought to be headed by a king who was served by subordinate divine beings in their various roles. The Old Testament appears to maintain remnants of this polytheistic tradition, especially in the Genesis narrative of man's creation and original sin. God says, "Let us make man in our image," "Man has become like one of us," and "Let us go down," while in Isaiah he asks "Who will go for us?" Once again, Christians have various means by which to deny traces of polytheism here (for example, stating that God is speaking with the "royal we" or that the "us" refers to the persons of the Trinity). The question is whether these explanations hold up when we honestly confront all the trace evidence of polytheism in the Old Testament.

The issue of polytheism becomes all the more acute when we acknowledge the probable dependence of Genesis on other, much older myths of creation and flood from the ancient Near East. The book of Genesis was written no earlier than the thirteenth century B.C. (the time of Moses, who was traditionally held to be the author of Genesis), and current scholarship indicates Genesis was most likely redacted by multiple authors over a period of centuries (between 900 and 400 B.C.). However, Babylon's polytheistic creation myth *Enuma Elish*—with the like of which the people of Israel would almost certainly have been familiar—dates to the second millennium B.C. Scholars possess tablets of the *Enuma Elish* which date to the seventh century B.C., meaning the story is likely several centuries older than Genesis. While there are significant theological differences between the creation account of Genesis 1–2 and the *Enuma Elish*, both operate within the same cultural milieu, share concepts, and at points even narrate their stories in the same order (the "waters," creation of heaven and earth followed by creation of the heavenly bodies and of man, etc.). Similarly, the flood narrated in Genesis 6–9 has close parallels in much more ancient polytheistic myths with which the Israelite authors of Genesis would have been familiar. For instance, we possess copies of *Gilgamesh* dating to the first half of the second millennium B.C. (though the story itself may date as early as the middle of the third millennium B.C.) and copies of *Atrahasis* dating to the seventeenth century B.C. What is the most probable and logical explanation for the similarities between Genesis and these other myths? It is conceivable that these parallels are purely coincidental, but as Kenton Sparks states, "The most sensible explanation for the similarities is that the pentateuchal authors [of Genesis] borrowed some of their materials from the ancient world."[7]

Returning to the Bible's divine council and the identity of its individual members, we find traces in various places, but perhaps some of the most interesting are those which seem to interchange "The Lord" with subordinate agents such as his *dabar* or "word" (used over 600 times in the Old Testament) and *ruach* or "spirit" (used forty-six times in the Old Testament). Here, however, we will consider a few examples of confusions between the God of Israel and his divine messenger or "angel" (מַלְאָךְ):

Then *the angel of God* said to me in the dream, "Jacob," and I said, "Here I am!" And he said, "Lift up your eyes and see, all the goats that leap upon the flock are striped, spotted, and mottled; for I have seen all that Laban is doing to you. *I am the God* of Bethel, where you anointed a pillar and made a vow to me. Now arise, go forth from this land, and return to the land of your birth" (Gn 31:11–13).

And *the angel of the* Lord appeared to him in a flame of fire out of the midst of a bush; and he looked, and lo, the bush was burning, yet it was not consumed. And Moses said, "I will turn aside and see this great sight, why the bush is not burnt." When *the Lord* saw that he turned aside to see, *God called to him out of the bush*, "Moses, Moses!" And he said, "Here am I" (Ex 3:2–6).

And *the angel of the* Lord appeared to [Gideon] and said to him, "The Lord is with you, you mighty man of valor." And Gideon said to him, "Pray, sir, if the Lord is with us, why then has all this befallen us? And where are all

---

7. Kenton Sparks, *God's Word in Human Words: An Evangelical Appropriation of Critical Biblical Scholarship*, (Grand Rapids, Mich.: Baker Academic, 2008), 97. On the subject of the Bible's dependence on more ancient myths from the Near East, see ibid., 97–99; Peter Enns, *Inspiration and Incarnation* (Grand Rapids, Mich.: Baker Academic, 2005), 23–56; Peter Enns, *The Evolution of Adam: What the Bible Does and Doesn't Say about Human Origins* (Ada, Mich.: Brazos Press, 2012); Victor Matthews and Don Benjamin, *Old Testament Parallels: Laws and Stories from the Ancient Near East* (New York: Paulist Press, 1991). Creation and the Flood are by no means the only parallels that can be drawn between the Pentateuch and other ancient Near Eastern literature. One can also find parallels to the Fall, the tower of Babel, and Yahweh's crushing of sea monsters, to name a few.

his wonderful deeds which our fathers recounted to us, saying, 'Did not the Lord bring us up from Egypt?' But now the Lord has cast us off, and given us into the hand of Mid'ian." *And the Lord* turned to him and said, "Go in this might of yours and deliver Israel from the hand of Mid'ian; do not I send you?"... *And the angel of God* said to him, "Take the meat and the unleavened cakes, and put them on this rock, and pour the broth over them." And he did so. Then the angel of the Lord reached out the tip of the staff that was in his hand, and touched the meat and the unleavened cakes; and there sprang up fire from the rock and consumed the flesh and the unleavened cakes; and the angel of the Lord vanished from his sight. Then Gideon perceived that he was the angel of the Lord; and Gideon said, "Alas, O Lord God! For now I have seen the angel of the Lord face to face." But *the Lord* said to him, "Peace be to you; do not fear, you shall not die." (Jgs. 6:11–23).

On that day the Lord will put a shield about the inhabitants of Jerusalem so that the feeblest among them on that day shall be like David, and the house of David shall be *like God, like the angel of the Lord*, at their head (Zec 12:8).

Then he showed me Joshua the high priest standing before the *angel of the Lord*, and Satan standing at his right hand to accuse him. And *the Lord* said to Satan, "*The Lord* rebuke you, O Satan! The Lord who has chosen Jerusalem rebuke you! Is not this a brand plucked from the fire?" (Zec 3:1–2)

Here we observe that the Israelites were not privy to a clear distinction between Yahweh and his divine messenger. In the first passage, the "angel of God" appears to Jacob but subsequently tells him "*I am* the God of Bethel." In the second, it is the "angel of the Lord" who initially appears to Moses, but then "the Lord" sees him and "God" calls to him from the bush. In the third, "the angel of the Lord" appears to Gideon, but all of a sudden the narrative tells us "And *the Lord* turned to him" and spoke. This interchange between the Lord and his messenger continues throughout this selection from the book of Judges. The fourth text from the prophet Zechariah contains an appositive that appears to explicitly identify "God" with "the angel of the Lord." Finally, the other text from Zechariah is noteworthy because it presents us with "the angel of the Lord," "the Lord," and Satan. The high priest stands before the angel of the Lord, but then it is the Lord himself rather than his "angel" who goes on to rebuke Satan. Also interesting here is the fact that the Lord speaks to Satan in the third person ("And *the Lord* said to Satan, "*The Lord* rebuke you, O Satan!"), an odd construction if Zechariah is truly reporting the words of the Lord. As we have noted above, Christians enjoy many different ways of interpreting these challenging passages in such a way as to preclude a literal reference to the existence of multiple divine beings or a confusion between "the angel of the Lord" and Yahweh himself. However, we should sincerely ask whether these explanations face the real problem or not. It is also worth noting that Pope Benedict appears to assume an identification between "the angel of the Lord" and Yahweh himself. While the pope does not address the issue in depth, he does make some comments on those times in the Old Testament when the "angel of the Lord" appears in human form.[8] Concerning the last two of these theophanies, he writes:

> In each case the "angel of the Lord" is recognized only at the moment of his mysterious withdrawal. Both times a flame consumes the food-offering as the "angel of the Lord" disappears. The mythological language expresses, on the one hand, the Lord's closeness as he reveals himself in human form, and, on the other hand, his otherness, as he stands outside the laws of material existence.[9]

From Benedict's language, it is clear he understands that these apparitions of "the angel of the Lord" are "mythological" expressions of the mystery of God's own "closeness" to man and his "otherness" in relation to the material world. This identification has been depicted beautifully in Rublev's icon of the Trinity, in which the three angels who visited Abraham are connected with the three persons of the Trinity.

In order to fully appreciate the evidence presented thus far that ancient Israelite religion was not strictly monotheistic, it is once again important to recall that the patriarchs grew up within the context of the broader religious landscape of the ancient Near East. Indeed, the book of Joshua informs us that Israel's ancestors were polytheists:

8. Cf. Gn 18:1–33; Jgs 6:11–24; 13; Jo 5:13–15.
9. Benedict XVI, *Jesus of Nazareth: Holy Week: From the Entrance into Jerusalem to the Resurrection*, translated by Philip J. Whitmore (San Francisco: Ignatius Press, 2011), 267.

And Joshua said to all the people, "Thus says the Lord, the God of Israel, Your fathers lived of old beyond the Euphra'tes, Terah, the father of Abraham and of Nahor; and they served other gods.... Now therefore fear the Lord, and serve him in sincerity and in faithfulness; put away the gods which your fathers served beyond the River, and in Egypt, and serve the Lord. And if you be unwilling to serve the Lord, choose this day whom you will serve, whether the gods your fathers served in the region beyond the River, or the gods of the Amorites in whose land you dwell; but as for me and my house, we will serve the Lord" (Jo. 24:2,14–15).

In the broader context of this passage, we clearly observe that Joshua is not asserting that there are no other gods but simply that Yahweh alone among them is worthy of Israel's worship. The reason Israel should follow Yahweh and not some other god is because it was *he* who brought them out of the land of Egypt and into the Promised Land. One can hardly overemphasize Joshua's statement that Abraham's own father Terah "worshiped other gods." For it is easy for Christians to fall into the trap of assuming that the chosen people have always professed the same fundamental elements of the faith as Christians, minus Christ and the Trinity. However, the commonly-used names Elohim and Adonai (which we translate "God" and "Lord," respectively) are themselves both plural forms in biblical Hebrew, indicating they once likely referred not to one God but to many gods. Indeed, the terms could just as well—and indeed even more naturally if they were not accompanied by singular modifiers—be translated "gods" and "lords." Another subtle but important clue to consider is the fact that over a dozen names for God are scattered throughout the Pentateuch, some of which initially may have referred to other gods before being subsumed by Israel as titles for their God.[10] This ancient association of Israel's God with the gods of the nations could help us account for the mythological tone we sometimes encounter in stories of Yahweh thundering, lightning, and crushing sea monsters.[11]

---

10. These include the commonly used Yahweh, Adonai, and Elohim as well as El, Ha-El, El-Elohe-Yisra'el, El-Bethel, El-Berith, El-Olam, El-Elyon, El Shaddai, El Elyon Shaddai, El Roi, Pahad-Yitzak, and Abir-Yakob.

11. See Is 51:9–10; Is 27:1; Hb 3:8–11; Na 1:3–6; Jb 26:12; Pss 74:14; 89:10; 104:26 for images of Yahweh crushing mythological sea monsters and Ex 19:16–19; 20:18; Ps 18:14;

Taking all this evidence into account, Peter Enns concludes that ancient Israelite religion at its inception did not look very different from the religions of the nations that were its neighbors:

> We must not allow our modern sensitivities to influence how we understand Israel's ancient faith. *We may not believe that multiple gods ever existed, but ancient Near Eastern people did.* This is the religious world within which God called Israel to be his people. When God called Israel, he *began* leading them into a full knowledge of who he is, but he started where they were.[12]

The difference between Israel's faith and that of her neighbors lay in God's plan for Israel and his gradual revelation to the people. For the moment, however, the problem still remains of how we are to explain that the inerrant word of God sometimes appears to affirm the existence of multiple deities. All this is not even to mention the various difficulties involved when it comes to defending against claims that the New Testament's portrayal of Christ and the Trinity itself is polytheistic. However, for the purpose of this study we will confine our discussion to the more obvious problems involving God's oneness in the Old Testament.

When it comes to defending the unity of biblical revelation, it is difficult to think of a more poignant problem than the ambiguity regarding God's oneness that we have seen above; yet this is by no means the only problem Christians must face with respect to scripture's depiction of the divine nature. Divine immutability, the attribute of God indicating that his perfect nature cannot suffer change, is also at stake in this discussion. Leaving aside any issues regarding the human nature of Jesus, his growth in wisdom (cf. Lk 2:52), and his lack of knowledge regarding certain realities (cf. Mt 24:36), the Old Testament appears to affirm that God learns new things in his divine nature and even changes his mind. A handful of passages will suffice to illustrate this problem:

> The Lord saw that the wickedness of man was great in the earth, and that every imagination of the thoughts of his heart was only evil continually.

Jb 37:5; Am 1:2; Hb 3:11 for mythological imagery of Yahweh thundering and lightning from the heavens.

12. Enns, *Inspiration and Incarnation*, 98.

And the Lord was sorry that he had made man on the earth, and it grieved him to his heart. So the Lord said, "I will blot out man whom I have created from the face of the ground, man and beast and creeping things and birds of the air, for I am sorry that I have made them." (Gn 6:5–8)

And the Lord repented of the evil which he thought to do to his people (Ex 32:14).

And Samuel did not see Saul again until the day of his death, but Samuel grieved over Saul. And the Lord repented that he had made Saul king over Israel (1 Sm 15.35).

When they had finished eating the grass of the land, I said, "O Lord God, forgive, I beseech thee! How can Jacob stand? He is so small!" The Lord repented concerning this; "It shall not be," said the Lord (Am 7:2–3).

And God sent the angel to Jerusalem to destroy it; but when he was about to destroy it, the Lord saw, and he repented of the evil (1 Chr 21:15; cf. 2 Sm 24:16).

[The angel of the Lord] said, "Do not lay your hand on the lad or do anything to him; for now I know that you fear God, seeing you have not withheld your son, your only son, from me" (Gn 22:12).

In the first passage, we discover that God is "sorry" and "grieved" over his creation of man, odd sentiments to behold in an omniscient being who presumably would foresee man's sin even before his creation. In the next several cases, God changes his mind or "repents" regarding a prior decision whether at the instigation of Moses's or Amos's intercession, Saul's faithlessness, Abraham's faithfulness, or simply of his own initiative. Again, the problem here is that, if God really is the perfect being we take him to be, then by definition he cannot learn new truths or change his mind as these passages claim. The last example is drawn from the famous account of Abraham's faith that would have him sacrifice his firstborn son Isaac. According to the narrative, the "angel of the Lord" has to *learn* that Abraham is faithful. "Now I know that you fear God," he says. Once in possession of this knowledge, the angel of the Lord can now release Abraham from the command to slaughter his son. Of course, the faithful Christian may well point out that in this last passage it is not the Lord who learns but rather the *angel* of the Lord. However, as we have seen above, this only creates more problems upon closer examination of the nature of this "angel" of the Lord. This is but one of many illustrations of how difficult it is to establish a biblical account of God's nature that accords with orthodox Christian doctrine today.

As a final note before turning to our next theme, there are other issues concerning the nature of God which one could address more thoroughly although we have only treated the issues of divine oneness and immutability here. For example, one has to contend with challenging evidence that presents us with *sophia* or "lady wisdom" who appears as a quasi-divine, *feminine* figure in the book of Proverbs and the very late book of Wisdom.[13] Christians also have to reckon with Old and New Testament passages that intimate feminine traits in Yahweh himself.[14] Our pope has offered helpful suggestions for confronting this issue in *Jesus of Nazareth*, but he does not claim to have definitively solved the conundrum. The "feminine" dimension of God in scripture only adds fuel to the fire of texts which challenge the uniform portrait of the divine nature most Christians expect out of the Bible.[15]

13. For Lady Wisdom (Σοφία), see especially Prv 1; 4:13; 7:27; 8; 9:1–6 and Ws 7–8.

14. In the Old Testament, see Dt 32:18 ("the God who gave you birth"); Ps 22:10 (which appears to compare God to a midwife); Ps 131:2 ("like a child quieted at its mother's breast"); Is 42:14 (where God cries out as a woman in labor); 46:3; 49:15 ("Can a mother forget her infant?"); 66:13 ("As a mother comforts her son …"); Nm 11:10–12; Hos 13:8 ("like a bear robbed of her cubs"); Gn 1:2 (where the Spirit hovers over creation as over a brood); Ps 17:8; 36:7; 57:1; 61:4; 91:1,4; Is 31:5 (shelter in the shadow of God's wings); Jb 38:29 (which contains the image of a divine "womb"). For the New Testament, see Mt 23:37; Lk 13:34 (Jesus sighs, "How often would I have gathered your children together as a 'hen'"); Acts 17:28 (states that "in him we live, move, have our being"); 1 Cor 3:1–3; 1 Pt 2:2 (calls us "babes in Christ" and speaks of "spiritual milk"); Jn 1:13 (speaks of Christians being "born of God"; 3:5 ("born of water and the Spirit"). Moreover, on three occasions in his first volume of *Jesus of Nazareth*, 139, 197, 207, Pope Benedict observes that the New Testament's depiction of Jesus's "compassion" (cf. Lk 7:13, for example) is intimately bound up with the feminine imagery, particularly the Hebrew notion of a mother's womb (*rahamim*).

15. Benedict XVI, *Jesus of Nazareth*, 139–40. After treating the issue of whether or not the Old Testament presents us with a God who is not only our Father but also our "mother," the pope concludes that "we cannot provide any absolutely compelling arguments" for not praying to God as mother; however, he observes that "while there are fine images of maternal love, 'mother' is not used as a form of address for God." The sobriety of Benedict's conclusion is a testimony to his great humility as an exegete and pastor: he teaches the fullness of Christian truth while willingly acknowledging the presence of myriad difficulties and challenges to it.

Theme 2: The Nature of Good and Evil

Having just raised the question of how God could "repent of evil" puts us in the perfect position to tackle our next set of problems which concern how the Bible deals with the phenomenon of evil, particularly the questions of whether God can do or command evil and what role Satan plays in our evil actions. This is a critically important area, for even Christians who are willing to acknowledge the subtle issues regarding history and science in the Bible commonly assume that the sacred page presents a unified account when it comes to matters of faith and morals. The problems we have touched thus far have dealt with the "faith" issues of the afterlife and God's nature. Our next topic concerns what is typically referred to as "morals."[16] Below, we will explore the question with several series of statements which acutely frame the problem:

[Yahweh] blotted out every living thing that was upon the face of the ground, man and animals and creeping things and birds of the air; they were blotted out from the earth. Only Noah was left, and those that were with him in the ark (Gn 7:23).

At a lodging place on the way the Lord met him and sought to kill him (Ex 4:24).

And that night the angel of the Lord went forth, and slew a hundred and eighty-five thousand in the camp of the Assyrians; and when men arose early in the morning, behold, these were all dead bodies (2 Kgs 19:35).

At midnight the Lord smote all the first-born in the land of Egypt, from the first-born of Pharaoh who sat on his throne to the first-born of the captive who was in the dungeon, and all the first-born of the cattle (Ex 12:29).

These first passages raise the simple question: how can a good God directly kill off the human beings he once lovingly created? This applies both to the flood account in our first passage as well as to Yahweh's

---

16. Important historical-critical sources whose evidence is drawn upon in this section include: Neil Forsyth, *The Old Enemy: Satan and the Combat Myth* (Princeton, N.J.: Princeton University Press, 1987); Elaine H. Pagels, *The Origin of Satan* (New York: Vintage Books, 1996); Victor Hamilton, "Satan," *ABD*, vol. 5, 985–89; Duane Watson, "Devil," *ABD*, vol. 2, 183–84; Foerster, "διάβολος," Theological Dictionary of the New Testament (hereafter *TDNT*) 2:71–81.

attempt to kill Moses (or Moses's son, as some have interpreted it) in the second passage. The first case of God killing off practically the entire human race is difficult for many Christians to accept: only Noah and those with him in the ark survived the flood, which means that countless women and children were killed as a result of God's action. At least the author gives us a reasonable explanation: "The Lord saw that the wickedness of man was great in the earth, and that every imagination of the thoughts of his heart was only evil continually. And the Lord was sorry that he had made man on the earth, and it grieved him to his heart" (Gn 6:5–6). In the second scenario, the Lord has just called Moses to lead his people out of slavery, and then turns around and seeks to kill his chosen messenger—quite the opposite of what one would expect from a God who loves his people and remains faithful to them even in the midst of their sins. In the second and third texts we have the Lord and his "angel" slaying Israel's enemies. It is often argued that these individuals were guilty and therefore deserving of death, but to many Christians there remains something odd about God slaying 185,000 Assyrians during the night and smiting the children of Egypt. Were these children culpable and deserving of death? There are many ways to go about arguing this point, but the issue is whether God's action is consistent with Christian doctrine today. The type of question one could pose here is: would we place our trust in a God who went around and deliberately killed babies?

Other times in the Bible we are scandalized not because God himself kills people but rather because he commands humans to kill—sometimes brutally and mercilessly—other humans:

Moreover I swore to them in the wilderness that I would scatter them among the nations and disperse them through the countries, because they had not executed my ordinances, but had rejected my statutes and profaned my sabbaths, and their eyes were set on their fathers' idols. Moreover I gave them statutes that were not good and ordinances by which they could not have life; and I defiled them through their very gifts in making them offer by fire all their first-born, that I might horrify them; I did it that they might know that I am the Lord (Ez 20:23–26).

When the Lord your God brings you into the land which you are entering to take possession of it, and clears away many nations before you, the Hit-

tites, the Gir'gashites, the Amorites, the Canaanites, the Per'izzites, the Hivites, and the Jeb'usites, seven nations greater and mightier than yourselves,
and when the Lord your God gives them over to you, and you defeat them;
then you must utterly destroy them; you shall make no covenant with them,
and show no mercy to them (Dt 7:1–2).

But in the cities of these peoples that the Lord your God gives you for an
inheritance, you shall save alive nothing that breathes, but you shall utterly destroy them, the Hittites and the Amorites, the Canaanites and the
Per'izzites, the Hivites and the Jeb'usites, as the Lord your God has commanded (Dt 20:16–17).

And the Lord our God gave him over to us; and we defeated him and his
sons and all his people. And we captured all his cities at that time and utterly destroyed every city, men, women, and children; we left none remaining (Dt 2:33–34; cf. 3:6; Jo 6:21).

And [Saul] took Agag the king of the Amal'ekites alive, and utterly destroyed all the people with the edge of the sword. But Saul and the people
spared Agag, and the best of the sheep and of the oxen and of the fatlings,
and the lambs, and all that was good, and would not utterly destroy them;
all that was despised and worthless they utterly destroyed (1 Sm 15:8–9).

The first of these passages offers us an explanation of Israel's woes
from a God's-eye point of view. God intentionally "gave them statutes that were not good" and "ordinances by which they could not
have life." He "defiled them … making them offer by fire all their
first-born" in order that they might come to know and accept his
lordship. Regardless of the good end which the narrator puts before
us, the glaringly obvious problem is that the text says God actually
made the Israelites destroy their own children. Any Christian moral
theologian worth his salt will teach us that a good end or intention
does not justify the use of intrinsically evil means, which to all appearances is what is described in this passage.

The other texts above present us with "the ban," Israel's total war-
fare commanded by Yahweh in order to govern the chosen people's
conduct in their invasion of Canaan. God specifically commands
the Israelites to "utterly destroy" the land's inhabitants and to "show
no mercy" toward them. In the second text it is clear that his order
is to "save nothing alive that breathes." As we read in Moses's narration within the third selection, the Israelites "utterly destroyed"

every city they defeated, including the men, women, and children *of the towns*. To make this problem all the more stark, in the final text we observe God's anger at King Saul for *not* "utterly destroying" every living being among the cities he invaded. Saul had "destroyed all the people with the edge of the sword"—presumably including women and children—but because he failed to kill King Agag and all the animals, God rejects him from being king over Israel (1 Sm 15:23). These texts are even more explicit than those cited in the prior series, and they present us with a slightly different problem: here it is not God himself who is said to have performed the killing but rather human beings whom he commands to kill other human beings. Many of those killed—in light of Christianity's moral standards today, at least—were innocent. In a nutshell, the problem could be framed as follows: if he were witnessing this sort of behavior today, what Christian would not unhesitatingly call it murder, even genocide? It is also worth mentioning in this connection a pair of troubling texts which, while not explicitly linking the killing of children with God's orders, are nonetheless very disturbing:

> Samaria shall bear her guilt,
> because she has rebelled against her God;
> they shall fall by the sword,
> their little ones shall be dashed in pieces,
> and their pregnant women ripped open (Hos 13:16).

> O daughter of Babylon, you devastator!
> Happy shall he be who requites you
> with what you have done to us!
> Happy shall he be who takes your little ones
> and dashes them against the rock! (Ps 137:8–9)

The first of these passages is a prophecy from Hosea in which he describes what will befall the people of Israel as a result of their rejection of God. Though not as problematic as the subsequent text, it provides the imagery and context to help us understand just what the psalmist means when he declares blessed the man who "dashes" the Babylonian children against the rock. In doing this, the Israelites are exacting revenge against their oppressors for what Hosea had correctly predicted would be done to them. Again, here it is not God who explicitly commands evil behavior such as we have seen in other passages, but many people are rightly disturbed by a sacred author inspired by God and writing the word of God who yet appears to be unchecked in his approval of horrific behavior. The revenge endorsed by the psalmist cannot be condoned on the basis of the New Testament or church teaching today.

The ensuing group of passages deals with a different, peculiar dimension of the problem of evil within the Bible. Here we are not dealing with the problem of God killing or commanding others to kill, but rather with God deliberately interfering with human free will by sending wicked spirits among them:

Now the Spirit of the Lord departed from Saul, and an evil spirit from the Lord tormented him (1 Sm 16:14; cf. 18:10; 19:9).

And God sent an evil spirit between Abim'elech and the men of Shechem; and the men of Shechem dealt treacherously with Abim'elech (Jgs 9:23).

And Micai'ah said, "Therefore hear the word of the Lord: I saw the Lord sitting on his throne, and all the host of heaven standing beside him on his right hand and on his left; and the Lord said, 'Who will entice Ahab, that he may go up and fall at Ramoth-gilead?' And one said one thing, and another said another. Then a spirit came forward and stood before the Lord, saying, 'I will entice him.' And the Lord said to him, 'By what means?' And he said, 'I will go forth, and will be a lying spirit in the mouth of all his prophets.' And he said, 'You are to entice him, and you shall succeed; go forth and do so.' Now therefore behold, the Lord has put a lying spirit in the mouth of all these your prophets; the Lord has spoken evil concerning you" (1 Kgs 22:19–22; cf. 2 Chr 18:21ff).

The first two texts speak of an "evil spirit" sent by Yahweh in order to disrupt the affairs of men. It is unclear precisely who this "spirit" is; but the fundamental problem is to account not only for how God could allow evil but could actually will evil upon someone—regardless of whether he is a friend or foe. In the third text, God put a "lying spirit in the mouth of all these your prophets," apparently with the end of setting King Ahab up to fall.

Although we would be hard pressed to find someone more evil than the man duped by God in the above scenario, the question still remains whether Christians today can exonerate a God who lies to his creatures and sends evil spirits among them in order to set them up for destruction. It is also important to grapple with the challenge of a God who directly hardens the hearts of individuals, as we see in the following texts:

And the Lord said to Moses, "When you go back to Egypt, see that you do before Pharaoh all the miracles which I have put in your power; but I will harden his heart, so that he will not let the people go" (Ex 4:21; cf. 9:12; 10:1,20, 27; 11:10; 14:8).

For it was the Lord's doing to harden their hearts that they should come against Israel in battle, in order that they should be utterly destroyed, and should receive no mercy but be exterminated, as the Lord commanded Moses (Jo 11:20).

So then he has mercy upon whomever he wills, and he hardens the heart of whomever he wills (Rom 9:18).

What then? Israel failed to obtain what it sought. The elect obtained it, but the rest were hardened, as it is written, "God gave them a spirit of stupor, eyes that should not see and ears that should not hear, down to this very day" (Rom 11:7–8).

The first verse cited is one of many in a series which narrate the dialectic of Moses and Pharaoh as Yahweh tries to get his people freed from slavery in Egypt. At certain points the narrative goes on to indicate that God directly "hardened the heart" of Pharaoh. Since Moses was appointed with the specific end of leading God's people out of slavery, it is mysterious that this same God would subsequently harden Pharaoh's heart, "so that he will not let the people go." In any event, for the purpose of our investigation the issue here is not *why* God hardens Pharaoh's heart but rather how we can justify God's apparent interference with human free will in the person of Pharaoh. It is likewise difficult to justify Joshua's account of God hardening the hearts of Israel's enemies for the purpose of setting them up to be "utterly destroyed" and "exterminated." In this passage which ties together the theme of killing with the theme of hardening, the reader is presented with a God who apparently sets people up, against their will, in order that they might be massacred. For many people, such a description might seem little different from that of a god who drugs someone and then places him in the driver's seat of a car about to head over a cliff. The same type of problem appears in a less dramatic but perhaps all the more troubling manner in the final two passages from St. Paul. In Romans 9–11, the apostle draws on concepts from Isaiah to explain that Israel's rejection of Christ was due to God's hardening their hearts. This is troubling because it is one thing to say the Old Testament presents us with theological problems, but readers of the New Testament naturally expect to see its teaching line up with modern standards of orthodox doctrine.

Before concluding this introductory survey of theological problems within scripture, there remains a final issue for us to consider, namely Satan's role in relation to evil. Many Christians are not aware that there are only scant references to Satan in the Old Testament, and even when he does appear his role and identity is not the same as what we gather from the New Testament. We have already drawn from Zechariah 3:1–2 and Job 1–2, two of the four Old Testament texts that reference the figure of the celestial "accuser" or הַשָּׂטָן in Hebrew. In Zechariah, הַשָּׂטָן appears as a member of the divine council. He is not precisely equivalent to the fallen angel "Satan" as we know him today; rather, his function in the heavenly courtroom is to accuse Joshua, the high priest. In Job, הַשָּׂטָן is also described as one of the "sons of God" who, though inferior to Yahweh, is granted license to torture the book's protagonist. It is unclear whether הַשָּׂטָן in Job is a legitimate member of the divine council or rather an intruder from the outside, for God asks him: "Whence have you come?" and Satan replies, "From going to and fro on the earth, and from walking up and down on it" (Jb 1:7).

Whatever the case may be, Satan is not identified as the "devil" here or in much of the Old Testament. The temptation narrative of Genesis 3, for instance, does not mention the devil or Satan. This identification was made later in the New Testament, where St. John narrates that "the great dragon was thrown down, that ancient serpent, who is called the Devil and Satan" (Rv 12:9). Nor do the early strata of the Old Testament depict Satan as the cause of death (Ws 2:24), the "god" of this world (2 Cor 4:4; cf. Jn 12:31; Eph 2:2), the "tempter" (Mt 4:3; 1 Thes 3:5; 2 Cor 11:3), "father of lies" (Jn 8:44), and "enemy" (Mt 13:19,39) of God's people. Much less is הַשָּׂטָן recognized as Satan in the book of Numbers, the third text in scripture where he appears. This passage tells us that "God's anger was kindled" at Balaam, and "the angel of the Lord took his stand in the way as his adversary" (Nm 22:22). It is important to observe that the "adversary" described here is in no way inimical to God and in fact appears to be a good angel acting on God's own behalf—quite a different view from what most Christians would expect of Satan.

The only text in the Old Testament where the word Satan serves as a proper name for an antagonistic celestial being is 1 Chronicles 21:1. Here, the chronicler pinpoints Satan as the cause of David's unlawful act of numbering Israel: "Satan stood up against Israel, and incited David to number Israel." It is of the utmost importance to realize that this is the only place in the Old Testament where שָׂטָן is mentioned without the definite article "the" (ה). *Satan* is therefore not merely a title for the prosecuting attorney of the heavenly court, but rather a unique celestial being. The picture painted here much more closely resembles that which Christians typically have in their minds when pondering the role of Satan. He "incites" us to evil and is therefore a cause of our evil actions. However, even this passage which would appear to be the most promising of all Old Testament texts presents us with difficulties in terms of reconciling it with Christian doctrine. For it is common knowledge today that the works 1–2 Chronicles were composed well after and 1–2 Samuel and 1–2 Kings and retold their stories. The two histories, 1–2 Chronicles and 1–2 Samuel, run parallel, and often lengthy passages match up nearly word for word. With this in mind, it is highly instructive to compare 1 Chr 21:1, cited above, with the parallel text 2 Sm 24:1, which states: "Again the anger of the Lord was kindled against Israel, and he incited David against them, saying, 'Go, number Israel and Judah.'" The difference between the two texts is clear: 1 Chronicles tells us that Satan was the cause of David's evil action, whereas 1 Samuel indicates Yahweh is its cause. Why do these two texts read differently? Many scholars suggest that the chronicler's adaptation of 1 Samuel was a piece of political propaganda, aimed at exonerating King David for his bad decision by placing the blame on a celestial power who acted upon David without his consent.[17]

---

17. For example, see Sparks, *God's Word in Human Words*, 101–4 and 126–29. Other evidence for political propaganda in Chronicles can easily be adduced. For example,

The Christian should really feel the force of the argument at this point. On what basis do Christians hold their beliefs about Satan and his role in our evil actions? Can we trust biblical history when it appears to contain, at best, pious but deliberate variations or, in a worse case, perhaps even lying propaganda? This final issue ties together the theme of evil discussed in the Bible with other important themes, themes we could address in a lengthier volume. For example, we could address issues of the trustworthiness of Israelite historiography. Breaking down the Bible's divergent histories, we might ask how a document seemingly riddled with historical errors and overt alterations of the sort discussed above could be considered anything but the mere feeble words of men.

We could also examine the related and sometimes apparently tenuous relationship between the Old and New Testaments. Further, we could ask why Jesus and the early church made such a great enemy of Satan, a figure who plays so small a role in the Old Testament. Like the Old Testament, the New Testament itself contains divergent histories and even employs different words to denote the figure we commonly call Satan. In 2 Cor 6:15, St. Paul calls him Be'lial, and in Mt 12:24 Jesus and the Pharisees speak of Be-el'zebul, "the prince of demons." Rv 12:9 alone identifies "the ancient serpent" of the Garden of Eden with "the great dragon" who is called "the Devil" and "Satan." If we look back to the Old Testament, we see still more demonic names: Tb 3:8 introduces the demon Asmodeus, and Hos 9:7–8 appears to speak of the demon Mastema, but in neither case is it clear who these figures are or how they are related to Satan.

---

when one compares 2 Sm 5:21 ("And the Philistines left their idols there, and David and his men carried them away.") with its parallel in the later 1 Chr 14:12 ("And they left their gods there, and David gave command, and they were burned"), he has to ask at least two questions. First, why did the chronicler make that change? To many it appears that the chronicler, wanting to make David look good, deliberately changed the text so as to make it appear that David obeyed God's command to destroy the idols of his enemies. Second, if this explanation is even plausible, it begs the question of how portions of the Bible which apparently contain outright factual distortions can be considered inerrant. The principles established in the following chapters will enable us to address precisely this type of question.

Theme 3: The Afterlife

The theme of the afterlife is treated last here and will be explored in the greatest depth at the end of the entire book, precisely because in it we find ample, clear evidence that challenges a fundamental article of the Christian faith, namely hope for the resurrection of the body. This is an important topic because too many Christians who have great faith in the Resurrection do not realize just how significant this doctrine is—that it is radical and unique in the history of world religions, developing late even in the history of the people of Israel itself. It is easy for Christians to fall into the trap of thinking that since we believe in the resurrection of the body, the whole of Sacred Scripture must explicitly teach the same doctrine. In reality, however, there is little evidence for this position in scripture itself. If anything there is evidence that Old Testament doctrine on the afterlife is quite diverse and that even the New Testament is not utterly uniform in its depiction of the hereafter. However, for the purpose of this study we will largely prescind from issues within the New Testament and focus on the more obvious problems present within the Old Testament, in which certain writers went so far as to deny altogether the reality of life after death for man. We will now survey examples of such denials, beginning with the work of the prophet Isaiah.

Although we will have occasion to observe later that the "Isaiah Apocalypse" (Is 24–27) seems to indicate hope for an afterlife in a few places, the book is far from unanimous in its view on the matter. For example, the prophet proclaims:

> They are dead, they will not live;
> they are shades, they will not arise;
> to that end thou hast visited them with destruction
> and wiped out all remembrance of them (Is 26:14).

It is important that we be familiar with the context of the above citation. In the previous verse he had just observed that "other lords besides thee have ruled over us." Thus the "they" who will not live or arise has "other lords" as its antecedent. This makes the verse much more palatable to the Christian who might otherwise see in it a blanket denial of the possibility of the afterlife. On the other hand, this verse still falls short of teaching the fullness of Christian truth vis-à-vis the afterlife. For here the dead are depicted as mere "shades" (רְפָאִים), a term which elsewhere in the Old Testament clearly refers to the hopeless and ever-roaming inhabitants of the netherworld. In light of Christ's teaching, however, we today are privy to knowledge of man's immortality—that even those who do evil continue to live a bodily existence after their death as they come forth to the "resurrection of judgment" (Jn 5:29). In the Old Testament period exemplified here by Isaiah, no clear distinction was made between the resurrection of the righteous to heaven and the resurrection of the evil to hell or "Gehenna." Indeed, in this period we do not find much evidence of hope in a resurrection at all, not even for the righteous.

Turning to another text of Isaiah we catch a clearer glimpse of how Israelites of the period tended to view life after death. Reporting the words of King Hezekiah, Isaiah writes:

> For Sheol cannot thank thee,
> death cannot praise thee;
> those who go down to the pit cannot hope
> for thy faithfulness (Is 38:18).

Here we find one of myriad biblical references to the ancient Israelite belief in the netherworld (Heb. שְׁאוֹל; Gk. ᾅδης) which for centuries was generally accepted as the lot of the dead. Like others living in cultures of the ancient Near East, ancient Israelites believed that persons continued to exist in some form after their death. The Old Testament describes that deceased human spirits all "went down" through watery passages into a gloomy land below the earth, called Sheol. Like a cistern, Sheol was far removed from the land of the living and even from God himself. It was considered to be a land of "darkness"[18] aptly depicted through the synonyms "pit,"[19] "earth,"[20] "grave,"[21] "cistern" or "dungeon,"[22] and "Abaddon" or "destruction."[23]

---

18. Cf. Jb 17:13, 10:21; Ps 88:7,12.

19. Cf. Ps 16:10; Jb 17:13–14; Is 38:17–18; Jn 2:3–7.

20. Ps 88:12, 143:3.   21. Cf. Ps 88:5, 11; Jb 10:19.

22. Cf. Is 5:14; 38:18; Ez 31:16; Pss 30:4; 88:4–5; Prv 1:12. For a more thorough presentation of the abode of the dead as it was viewed in ancient Israel, see Theodore J. Lewis, "Dead, Abode of the," *ABD*, vol. 2, 101–5.

23. Cf. Ps 88:11; Jb 26:6; Prv 15:11.

Dead souls would be trapped in this place indefinitely, devoid of all thanksgiving, praise, and—most importantly—hope. For, having crossed the chasm and descended to the underworld, they entered a world sealed off by locks and gates: the "gates of death."[24] The "gates of death" prevented anyone from ever returning to the land of the living and to communion with the Lord.[25]

As Pope Benedict observed, in a work written while he was still a cardinal, in his own work on the subject the ancient view of Sheol described above remained dominant in Israel until around the time of Christ. At this point in time, Israelites began to view Sheol as the place where not all individuals, but rather the ungodly alone, suffered the fate of eternal separation from God.[26] Describing the use of the Greek term Hades in the New Testament, W. D. Davies and Dale Allison write, "By the first century there was a tendency to think of Hades or certain sections of it as an underworld peopled not by the dead in general but by *the ungodly dead*, as well as by demons and evil spirits."[27] This notion appears in the parable of Lazarus in Luke 16. Here, Jesus indicates that Hades is clearly reserved as "a place of torment" for the unjust rich man, whereas Lazarus was carried off by angels to the "bosom of Abraham." However, Je-

24. L. Wächter, "Sheol," translated by Douglas W. Stott, *Theological Dictionary of the Old Testament* (hereafter *TDOT*) 14: 245. The expression "gates of death" and other related expressions appear frequently in the Old Testament: "Have you entered into the springs of the sea, or walked in the recesses of the deep? Have *the gates of death* been revealed to you, or have you seen the gates of deep darkness?" (Jb 38:16–17); "I said, In the noontide of my days I must depart; I am consigned to *the gates of Sheol* for the rest of my years. I said, I shall not see the LORD in the land of the living" (Is 38:10–11); "Be gracious to me, O Lord! Behold what I suffer from those who hate me, O thou who liftest me up from *the gates of death*" (Ps 9:13); "They loathed any kind of food, and they drew near to *the gates of death*" (Ps 107:18).

25. "The general view is that Yahweh has nothing to do with the deceased and that the latter have no community with him." Wächter, "Sheol," *TDOT* 14:246.

26. See Benedict XVI, *Eschatology*, 119–23, where he describes how Israel gradually began to see the just and unjust as separated after death. Benedict analyzes biblical images and compares them to how the afterlife is portrayed in various apocryphal works of inter-testamental Jewish literature, in particular the book of Enoch (c. 150 B.C.), the fourth Book of Ezra (c. 100 A.D.), and the works of the community at Qumran.

27. W. D. Davies and Dale C. Allison, *A Critical and Exegetical Commentary on the Gospel According to Saint Matthew* (Edinburgh: T.&T. Clark, 1988), 633.

sus does not clarify the relationship between Hades and Gehenna, the ever-burning garbage heap outside of Jerusalem elsewhere employed in the New Testament as an image for everlasting punishment (cf. Mt 5:22; Lk 12:5; Jas 3:6; etc.). The presence of both of these terms only further complicates the Bible's portrait of the afterlife, for the teaching of Jesus himself does not square precisely with what Christians who take the terms "heaven," "hell," and "purgatory" for granted might expect.

Returning to the Old Testament's portrayal of Sheol as a shadowy place forever barred off from the presence of God, in those parts of the Old Testament that testify to this view one also observes the belief that the dead "shades" exerted power over the living and even communicated with them. As Wayne Pitard explains:

> There is evidence that many Israelites thought that the dead continued to play an active role in the world of the living, possessing the power to grant blessings to their relatives and to reveal the future. This was done through the process of necromancy, the consultation of the dead by a medium, and related practices, which appear to have been quite popular in Israel.[28]

Pitard observes that Israel's pre-exilic practice of necromancy does not figure prominently in the Old Testament because it was eventually repudiated and denounced as heterodox.[29] However, one account of an illicit necromantic session has been preserved in the Bible, the story of Saul's consultation of the witch at Endor:

> When Saul saw the army of the Philistines, he was afraid, and his heart trembled greatly. And when Saul inquired of the Lord, the Lord did not answer him, either by dreams, or by Urim, or by prophets. Then Saul said to his servants, "Seek out for me a woman who is a medium, that I may go to her and inquire of her." And his servants said to him, "Behold, there is a medium at Endor." So Saul disguised himself and put on other garments,

28. Wayne Pitard, "Afterlife and Immortality," in *The Oxford Companion to the Bible*, edited by B. M. Metzger and M. D. Coogan (New York: Oxford University Press, 1993), 16. See also the discussion of the Rephaim in Benedict XVI, *Eschatology*, 80–81.

29. As he shows, a few passages from the late eighth to sixth-century prophetic and legal literature illumine the matter since they attack wrongheaded popular notions about the dead. See Lv 19:31; 20:6, 27; Dt 18:10–14; Is 8:19–20. These passages show that much work had to be done by Yahweh in terms of correcting Israel's early misconstrued notions about the afterlife, a process of teaching that took time.

and went, he and two men with him; and they came to the woman by night. And he said, "Divine for me by a spirit, and bring up for me whomever I shall name to you." ... Then the woman said, "Whom shall I bring up for you?" He said, "Bring up Samuel for me." When the woman saw Samuel, she cried out with a loud voice; and the woman said to Saul, "Why have you deceived me? You are Saul." The king said to her, "Have no fear; what do you see?" And the woman said to Saul, "I see a god coming up out of the earth." He said to her, "What is his appearance?" And she said, "An old man is coming up; and he is wrapped in a robe." And Saul knew that it was Samuel, and he bowed with his face to the ground, and did obeisance. Then Samuel said to Saul, "Why have you disturbed me by bringing me up?" Saul answered, "I am in great distress; for the Philistines are warring against me, and God has turned away from me and answers me no more, either by prophets or by dreams; therefore I have summoned you to tell me what I shall do." (1 Sm 28:5–8, 11–15)

In this passage, Saul sees the Philistine army encamped against him, and he beseeches God for help using every licit means possible. When God refuses to answer him through these sanctioned means, Saul turns to a medium and asks her to bring the spirit of Samuel up from the dead for him. For the purposes of our work, the relevant issue at stake in this passage is not whether or not Saul should be practicing necromancy; rather, the problem lies in the fact that the passage portrays the witch's activity as efficacious; she actually *succeeds* in conjuring up the spirit of the godly Samuel from Sheol, and Saul has a discussion with him. The passage is powerful and problematic because it unabashedly assumes the view of Sheol described above. While not denying the reality of life after death for man, it presents a strange picture that is difficult to reconcile with Christian teaching on the subject.

The view of Sheol found in Isaiah and 1 Samuel 28 is even more prevalent and pronounced in the book of Psalms. The following texts testify not merely to King Hezekiah's struggle with the phenomenon of death but rather to the struggle of an archetypal man of faith, namely David. As is typical of the psalmist's mode of exposition, many of the problematic areas below are framed in the form of questions. As questions, they do not represent categorical denials of the afterlife, yet they are telling descriptions of the psalmist's worldview since the Hebrew construction he employs clearly expects a negative response from God.[30] It is easier to feel the weight of this problem when one puts himself in the place of the agonizing psalmist while reading the following texts:

> Turn, O Lord, save my life;
> deliver me for the sake of thy steadfast love.
> For in death there is no remembrance of thee;
> in Sheol who can give thee praise? (Ps 6:4–5)

> What profit is there in my death,
> if I go down to the Pit?
> Will the dust praise thee?
> Will it tell of thy faithfulness? (Ps 30:9)

> What man can live and never see death?
> Who can deliver his soul from the power of Sheol? (Ps 89:48)

The questions posed in these texts seem to deny that God is present to those who inhabit the netherworld. In death no one remembers the Lord, and no one can praise him. There is no profit in death, and no one has the ability to deliver the soul which has descended to Sheol. As if this picture were not stark enough, the following is even more so:

> For my soul is full of troubles,
> and my life draws near to Sheol.
> I am reckoned among those who go down to the Pit;
> I am a man who has no strength,
> like one forsaken among the dead,
> like the slain that lie in the grave,
> like those whom thou dost remember no more,
> for they are cut off from thy hand.
> Thou hast put me in the depths of the Pit,
> in the regions dark and deep ...
> Dost thou work wonders for the dead?
> Do the shades rise up to praise thee? [Selah]
> Is thy steadfast love declared in the grave,
> or thy faithfulness in Abaddon?

30. If a Hebrew author expects a "Yes" answer to his question, he typically uses the Hebrew form הֲלֹא (translated best as "Do not ... ?") rather than הֲ ("Do ... ?"), which is used commonly here and expects a negative response. Thus when we encounter questions such as "Do the shades rise up to praise thee?" we should understand the psalmist's tacit reply to be, "Of course not!"

Are thy wonders known in the darkness,
   or thy saving help in the land of forgetfulness? (Ps 88:3–6, 10–12)

This last psalm is especially powerful for the haunting images it uses to name the reality of the netherworld: "Sheol," "the Pit," "regions dark and deep," "the grave," "Abaddon (destruction)," "the darkness," and "the land of forgetfulness." Also troubling is its depiction of the soul who draws near to death: like "the shades" who inhabit Sheol, he is "full of troubles," "has no strength," "like one forsaken among the dead," "like the slain," "like those whom thou [God] dost remember no more," "cut off from thy [God's] hand." Here again, the psalmist asks God a series of questions to which the expected answer is clearly "No": "Dost thou work wonders for the dead?"; "Do the shades rise up to praise thee?". At first glance this psalm thus appears to be a work of despair and nothing more; God has nothing to do with the dead, and there is no hope that he ever will change this state of affairs. Later we will have occasion to respond to the question of how such a hopeless text can be in the Bible.

Whereas we have seen that the psalmist typically framed his denials of hope for the afterlife in the form of questions, the book of Job often takes a more straightforward—and therefore perhaps all the more disturbing—approach to the issue:

> As the cloud fades and vanishes,
> so he who goes down to Sheol does not come up (Jb 7:9).

> As waters fail from a lake,
> and a river wastes away and dries up,
> so man lies down and rises not again (Jb 14:11).

> For when a few years have come
> I shall go the way whence I shall not return (Jb 16:22).

Unlike the psalmist, in these passages Job does not couch his doubt in the form of questions: he who descends to Sheol "does not come up." A man lies down in death and "rises not again." Job believes that he will soon go the way of all flesh and "not return" to life. Apparently these denials are factual descriptions of what Job takes to be the lot of the dead, and for this reason they seem even more difficult to reconcile than the psalmist's bleak questioning. For, even if his questions displayed only the slightest glimmer of hope for the afterlife, the fact remains that a problematic question is not the same as a problematic denial.[31]

The book of Sirach is interesting to examine on this subject as it combines both questions and outright denials on the topic of life after death:

> Who will sing praises to the Most High in Hades,
> as do those who are alive and give thanks?
> From the dead, as from one who does not exist,
> thanksgiving has ceased;
> he who is alive and well sings the Lord's praises.
> How great is the mercy of the Lord,
> and his forgiveness for those who turn to him!
> For all things cannot be in men,
> since a son of man is not immortal (Sir 17:27–30).

> My son, let your tears fall for the dead,
> and as one who is suffering grievously begin the lament.
> Lay out his body with the honor due him,
> and do not neglect his burial ...
> Do not give your heart to sorrow;
> drive it away, remembering the end of life.
> Do not forget, there is no coming back;
> you do the dead no good, and you injure yourself.
> "Remember my doom, for yours is like it:
> yesterday it was mine, and today it is yours."
> When the dead is at rest, let his remembrance cease,
> and be comforted for him when his spirit is departed
> (Sir 38:16,20–23).

As in the case of several passages cited above, here the sacred author begins with a question ("Who will sing praises ... ?") which apparently expects the answer "No one." He then proceeds to make plain denials of life after death for man: "From the dead, as from one who does not exist, thanksgiving has ceased," and "a son of man is not immortal." In the second passage, he continues this thread with the admonition, "Do not forget, there is no coming back [from death]." In light of this, he advises, "When the dead is at rest, let his remembrance cease."

With this we come at last to the most melancholic of all bibli-

---

31. Here it is worth noting one passage in which the psalmist himself casts his doubt in the form of a denial rather than a question. He tells the Lord: "Look away from me, that I may know gladness, before I depart and be no more!" (Ps 39:13).

cal works concerning man's hope for life after death: the book of
Ecclesiastes, also known as Qoheleth (its Hebrew name). Ecclesiastes is well known for its gloomy view that all in life is הֶבֶל or "vanity,"
but often Christians fail to appreciate the seriousness of this claim
which, while repeated throughout the book, is made especially clear
in certain places:

> For the fate of the sons of men and the fate of beasts is the same; as one
> dies, so dies the other. They all have the same breath, and man has no ad-
> vantage over the beasts; for all is vanity. All go to one place; all are from the
> dust, and all turn to dust again (Eccl 3:19–20).

> For the living know that they will die, but the dead know nothing, and they
> have no more reward; but the memory of them is lost.... Whatever your
> hand finds to do, do it with your might; for there is no work or thought or
> knowledge or wisdom in Sheol, to which you are going (Eccl 9:5, 10).

It is hard to imagine a more categorical denial of life after death
than what we find here. The fate of man and the beasts is precisely
the same; everything comes from dust and everything shall turn
to dust again. In contrast to what Christians tend to assume, this
book makes no mention of rising from the dust; it is the final resting
place of man and beast alike. In this state, the dead "know nothing,
and they have no more reward; but the memory of them is lost." *You*
are going to Sheol, Ecclesiastes reminds his reader. Therefore it is
best to enjoy the present life while possible, "for there is no work or
thought or knowledge or wisdom in Sheol, to which you are going."

After reading the texts introduced in the above pages, it is no
wonder that after the dust clears from the Old Testament period one
still has to reckon with the fact that the New Testament portrays two
powerful rival camps—the Pharisees and the Sadducees—who disagree on the question of whether there will be a resurrection at the
end of time. The evidence above helps explain why the Sadducees so
adamantly denied hope in the resurrection. A successful defense of
biblical inspiration must be able to deal with the problem presented
by people like the Sadducees who base their rejection of Christianity on the observation that doctrines so fundamental to Christians
as the resurrection of the body do not always appear explicitly in a
large portion of the writings Christians hold to be inspired by God.

TWO PROBLEMS THAT ARISE IN LIGHT
OF METHOD B'S OBSERVATIONS

As intriguing and worthy of treatment as these last issues may be, our effort in the present volume remains modest. As Pope Benedict stated with regard to his *Jesus of Nazareth*, it is even more true that this work represents only the beginning of an effort to adequately articulate a theology of scripture. In line with the exploration we have already begun, this work will continue to focus on what directly concerns the nature of God, the nature of good and evil, and the afterlife, since these are all clearly issues of "faith and morals." To be sure, Catholicism teaches that the entirety of scripture is inerrant and not merely those parts which bear upon faith and morals. However, these problems are particularly crucial because Christians who hold divergent opinions vis-à-vis what the Bible intends to teach in matters of science and history typically agree in their expectation that the Bible "gets it right" when it comes to matters directly concerning Christian doctrine (faith) and behavior (morals). What, then, is the Christian to make of the discrepancies described in this chapter, and why do they seem to be glossed over today? How can the Bible be God's word if it is rife with problems in so many areas? Can we trust what the church teaches us concerning the nature of God, the nature of good and evil, and the afterlife if the foundations of our knowledge in these areas appear so tenuous? If we wish to offer a credible vindication of the Catholic doctrines of biblical inspiration and inerrancy, these are the type of questions we have to ask ourselves today.

For the sake of brevity and clarity, our brief survey of theological problems in the Bible can be boiled down to two essential issues that will be addressed in the following chapters: First, in our investigation thus far we have drawn from evidence throughout the Bible and not just from one theological school or one historical period. Given this data, it is clear that significant developments occurred within Israelite and Christian theology throughout the course of the Bible's composition. The Bible's later declarations of Yahweh's oneness are a far cry from earlier texts which accept the existence of

a heavenly council of divine beings. Late Judaism's hope for resurrected immortality seems quite distant from the earlier view that all
deceased souls went to Sheol. The chronicler blames Satan for an
evil deed which had been attributed to Yahweh himself in the earlier
text of 2 Samuel. The fundamental challenge here is that the scriptures present us with inspired authors living later in history who
write in a markedly different fashion concerning God, evil, and the
afterlife in comparison with their predecessors. Our first question
therefore arises: how can scripture be inerrant if in certain areas it
does not contain the fullness of revealed truth known by Christians
today?

Moreover, granted the fact that certain parts of scripture do not
explicitly teach the fullness of truth known by Christians today, a
second—and more problematic—difficulty demands our attention:
the fact that we sometimes observe biblical texts making statements
that seem plainly to contradict the teachings of other texts. This is especially problematic when later texts seem to constitute regressions
rather than developments with respect to texts written earlier in the
course of divine revelation. When we consider a historical-critical
dating of the biblical corpus, it is apparent that the Bible's theology does not always develop in a linear fashion; it does not progress ever closer toward the fullness of truth as we would naturally
expect. Ecclesiastes, for instance, wrote centuries after the prophets
began to exhibit hope for resurrected immortality, yet he still could
not accept their claim that God will vindicate the just man on the
other side of death. How is this not a manifest contradiction of the
Catholic doctrines of biblical inspiration and inerrancy? In the following pages, we will provide the principles for a robust solution to
precisely such questions.

Before turning for the moment from our considerations of problematic texts in the Bible, it is important to address a possible objection to all the arguments produced above. From time to time in the
following pages we will observe that Christians enjoy many ways of
addressing challenges to particular biblical texts. The believer may
therefore rightly ask: what is the point of all this effort to develop a
new hermeneutic when it is conceivable that every problem raised

by historical criticism can be answered independently on the basis of already available explanations? As we mentioned earlier in this chapter, this very question itself must be answered with another question, namely whether traditional explanations are not only *conceivable* but are also *sensible* and *plausible* for believers today. The Method C exegete, one who accepts the best of historical criticism and desires to meet Christ in the scriptures, must have the ability to assess the body of biblical evidence as a whole, an effort which entails much more than merely answering individual problems as they arise. In other words, the Method C exegete will take into account the *cumulative force* of the evidence adduced thus far, asking whether certain standard explanations account for the deeper fact that problematic statements concerning God's nature, the nature of good and evil, and the afterlife appear not merely in one text but throughout the Old Testament. The Method C exegete will have certitude that the problems he observes are real precisely because of the sheer amount of evidence pointing in their direction.

Pope Benedict and John Henry Newman both have helpful contributions to make on this point. The pope is very open in his recognition that historical criticism does not yield infallible conclusions. He states, "We must be clear about that fact that historical research can at most establish high probability but never final and absolute certainty over every detail."[32] If the Method C exegete follows Newman, he will find similar ideas confirming that the insufficiency of certain traditional Christian biblical interpretations cannot be proven deductively and beyond the shadow of a doubt. According to Newman, however, when it comes to matters of religion such as the inspiration of scripture, the proper method by which to arrive at certitude is through "accumulated probabilities."[33] Newman most fully elucidates the meaning of this expression in his *Essay in Aid of a Grammar of Assent*, as when he says: "The real and necessary method" for arriving at certitude lies in the "cumulation of proba-

32. Benedict XVI, *Jesus of Nazareth*, 104.

33. John Henry Newman and Charles Kingsley, *Newman's Apologia Pro Vita Sua, The Two Versions of 1864 & 1865; Preceded by Newman's and Kingsley's Pamphlets* (London: H. Frowde, 1913), 292.

bilities, independent of each other, arising out of the nature and circumstances of the particular case which is under review."[34] Applying Newman's wisdom to this book and its concern with the nature of God, the nature of good and evil, and the afterlife, we acknowledge that the gravity of the problems we have observed is fully recognizable only in light of the cumulative force of the biblical evidence. It is for this reason that we dwelt at length on the problems and drew from a wide variety of biblical texts which exemplify them. None of these questions admits of a simple answer. Each one must be dealt with patiently if we are to form reasonable conclusions that both acknowledge the real issue at hand and approach it in a spirit of faithful confidence. In this confidence we may now turn to Pope Benedict and seek to articulate his vision for approaching the Bible's greatest problems.

34. John Henry Newman, *An Essay in Aid of a Grammar of Assent* (New York: Clarendon Press, 1985), 230. The following words of Newman are also helpful: "None of these questions, as they come before him, admit of simple demonstration; but each carries with it a number of independent probable arguments, sufficient, when united, for a reasonable conclusion about itself." Ibid., 232.

CHAPTER 2

BENEDICT'S "METHOD C" PROPOSAL AND CATHOLIC PRINCIPLES FOR BIBLICAL INTERPRETATION

Having highlighted many of the significant problems concerning the text and contents of the Bible, we can now begin to lay the theological foundation for a robust response that takes seriously the claims of the previous chapter and yet maintains a deep faith in the truth of scripture. In view of achieving this end, we will look to Benedict's "Method C" hermeneutics proposal for guidance, seeking to elucidate the principles found therein so we can later apply them to the various problems that arise within text of scripture.

At the conference following his Erasmus Lecture in New York City in 1988 Pope Benedict, who was then prefect of the Congregation for the Doctrine of the Faith, argued convincingly that today's exegetes must have recourse to both ancient and modern methods of interpretation if they are to make sense of the problems in scripture. He called upon exegetes to develop a new, fuller hermeneutical method that makes the truth of scripture more evident by synthesizing the best of ancient (patristic-medieval) and modern (historical-critical) exegesis:

You can call the patristic-medieval exegetical approach Method A. The historical-critical approach, the modern approach ... is Method B. What I am calling for is not a return to Method A, but a development of a Method

C, taking advantage of the strengths of both Method A and Method B, but cognizant of the shortcomings of both.[1]

Benedict's program aims to incorporate insights from both the patristic-medieval method, which tends to emphasize the unity and truth of scripture, and the historical-critical method, which often observes development, diversity, and apparent contradictions therein. The synthesis of these two approaches in the present work aims to draw us closer to a sound reading of scripture's most difficult texts by showing that a unity underlies the development and diversity within scripture that came about as a result of the divine pedagogy.

To be sure, entire volumes could be written just on the question of what constitutes a particular hermeneutical method, ancient or modern. It would be a very difficult task since there is no single "method" followed unilaterally by all others of a particular epoch or school. With Benedict one can, however, identify two basic sets of principles held by modern scholars which distinguish them from their patristic and medieval counterparts. As Gregory Vall explains:

> Strictly speaking, we are dealing not with two specific "methods" but two general approaches. A series of basic principles unites the work of exegetes as diverse as Origen and Chrysostom, Bernard of Clairvaux and Thomas Aquinas, so that we may speak of a single dominant patristic-medieval approach to exegesis, which Cardinal Ratzinger has labeled "Method A." When we turn to consider those biblical commentators whose work falls under the umbrella of "historical-critical" exegesis, the diversity of specific methodologies is perhaps even greater. But in this case too, fundamental principles of exegesis shared by these scholars may be identified, justifying the label "Method B."[2]

Before we can employ Benedict's synthesis of methods to help address problems within scripture, in this chapter we need to outline

1. Benedict's words are taken from a summary and transcript of the discussion following his lecture. See Paul T. Stallsworth, "The Story of an Encounter," in *Biblical Interpretation in Crisis: The Ratzinger Conference on Bible and Church*, edited by Richard John Neuhaus (Grand Rapids, Mich. Eerdmans, 1989), 107–8. Benedict's lecture "Biblical Interpretation in Crisis: On the Question of the Foundations and Approaches of Exegesis Today" is printed in ibid., 1–23.

2. Gregory Vall, "Psalm 22: *Vox Christi* or Israelite Temple Liturgy?" *The Thomist* 66 (2002), 176, n. 2.

the principles which Vall alludes to as distinctive of Method A and Method B exegesis, beginning with Method A.

FIRST PRINCIPLES OF METHOD A: INSPIRATION, INERRANCY, AND THE FOUR SENSES OF SCRIPTURE

Christians who practice traditional patristic-medieval exegetical methods and are at least indirectly acquainted with historical-critical scholarship are often struck—and disenchanted—by the failure of their historical-critical counterparts sometimes to appreciate one key trait, the role of faith in exegesis. The question at hand here is whether we should approach the biblical text through the eyes of faith and with the goal of building up the church, or whether we should above all treat the Bible "scientifically," endeavoring to analyze it in an objective, disinterested manner. On this point, Method A exegetes of both past and present steadfastly follow the Christian tradition in emphasizing the former, faith-based approach, whereas some Method B exegetes of the modern period feel no obligation to adhere to the guidelines of the Christian theological and exegetical tradition. If the question of faith's role in the interpretation of scripture is the most striking feature which distinguishes ancient and modern exegetical approaches, it is proper that we begin by summarizing the theological principles which govern our understanding of the nature of scripture and its interpretation within the Catholic faith.[3]

The first principal point of Catholic doctrine in this matter regards the inspiration of scripture. The *locus classicus* for this dogma is 2 Tm 3:16, where St. Paul writes, "All scripture is inspired by God

3. This book assumes Catholic theological principles, but I would like to express my hope that it will be of benefit to all Christians who seek greater understanding of their faith even as I draw largely from works in the Catholic theological tradition. Catholics certainly have benefited from Evangelical Christians in this regard, and some of them have made endeavors similar to mine. For example, in his *Living and Active: Scripture in the Economy of Salvation* (Grand Rapids, Mich.: Eerdmans, 2002), Telford Work seeks to articulate the nature of Sacred Scripture through what he calls a "bibliology." While I have not chosen to adopt that term, it does encapsulate the scope of the present project.

and profitable for teaching, for reproof, for correction, and for training in righteousness, that the man of God may be complete, equipped
for every good work." St. Paul's original Greek word θεόπνευστος,
which we translate "inspired," literally means "God-breathed." This
term indicates that the scriptures issue from God himself, from his
breath, his word. As *Dei Verbum* articulates, God himself authored
all of Sacred Scripture: "The books of both the Old and New Testaments in their entirety, with all their parts, are sacred and canonical
because written under the inspiration of the Holy Spirit, they have
God as their author and have been handed on as such to the Church
herself."[4] Just as the Holy Spirit guided the composition of the New
Testament, so the "the Spirit of Christ" was at work in the production of the Old Testament, so that the Bible contains everything God
wanted written for the sake of man's salvation, and nothing more.[5]

According to the Catholic tradition, God chose to achieve the
end of educating Israel in divine realities by humbling himself or
"condescending" to men. As one might explain it in Thomistic
terms, God the principal author of scripture ennobled humans as
secondary or instrumental authors so they could cooperate as true
authors in the composition of the scriptures. These human authors were not puppets in God's hands, but neither were they self-
sufficient in the process of composing scripture. It was a work which
entailed the full use of the faculties and gifts of scripture's human
authors, put to use in order that God's own ineffable words might be
put into human words which his people could understand. In order
to describe this dynamic, *Dei Verbum* thus employs the Christological analogy: "The words of God, expressed in human language, have
been made like human discourse, just as the Word of the eternal
Father, when He took to Himself the flesh of human weakness, was
in every way made like men."[6] By keeping this Christological anal-

4. Second Vatican Council, *Dei Verbum, 1965,* §11. Cited hereafter as *DV*; cf. *CCC*
§105.

5. 1 Pt 1:10–11; cf. *DV* §11. For more on a Thomistic view of the dual authorship
of Scripture, see the thorough discussion in Paul Synave and Pierre Benoit, *Prophecy
and Inspiration: a Commentary on the Summa Theologica II-II, Questions 171–178* (New
York: Desclée Co., 1961), 93–145.

6. *DV* §13; cf. *CCC* §101; Pius XII, Promotion of Biblical Studies, [*Divino afflante*

ogy in mind throughout the course of this work, we may maintain
a mean between the various opposing theories of scriptural inspiration proposed over the centuries.[7] For as true human discourse,
scripture was not merely "dictated" by God to passive human instruments who blindly wrote down what God wanted them to
write. At the same time, as true divine discourse the inspiration of
scripture does not merely consist of a "subsequent approbation" by
which God later accepted as his own various human writings which
he had no hand in composing.[8] Furthermore, the church acknowl-

---

Spiritu], *1943*, §37. Cited hereafter as *DAS*. As regards the role of the Christological
analogy in maintaining a sound "Chalcedonian" doctrine of inspiration, see also Mary
Healy, "Behind, in Front of ... or Through the Text? The Christological Analogy and
the Last Word of Biblical Truth," in *Behind the Text: History and Biblical Interpretation*,
edited by Craig Bartholomew, C. Stephen Evens, Mary Healy, and Murray Rae (Grand
Rapids, Mich.: Zondervan, 2003), 181–95. Healy observes that the Christological analogy ultimately has roots in the patristic period (e.g., Origen's comparison of scripture to
the flesh of Christ). As she puts it, there exists a kind of "Monophysite" exegesis wherein, as ancient heretics denied Christ's human nature, the exegete "downplays or ignores
the human factors that went into the composition of the biblical text." Ibid., 191. On the
other hand, Healy notes that the more typical form of modern scholarship is "Nesto-
rian." She writes, "Such an approach deliberately and methodologically considers the
text as a purely human reality and superimposes the divine only as a second operation
after the crucial exegetical judgments have already been made." Ibid, 192. According to
Healy, as the ecumenical council of Chalcedon recognized Jesus's true divinity and true
manhood, so a "Chalcedonian form of exegesis" seeks to do justice to both the human
and divine aspects of Sacred Scripture. See also Denis Farkasfalvy's treatment of the
Christological analogy in his *Inspiration and Interpretation: A Theological Introduction
to Sacred Scripture* (Washington, D.C.: The Catholic University of America Press, 2010),
230–35. It is important for the present study that Farkasfalvy extends the Christological
analogy and suggests: "The 'divine pedagogy' and 'condescension' of which the anti-
Marcionite Church Fathers (beginning with Irenaeus) spoke, mostly in defense of the
imperfections of the Old Testament, must be extended to all of Scripture.... Just as
Jesus 'grew in age and wisdom' from infancy to maturity as a human being, each book
of the Bible had a true process of formative development." (232.)

7. See James Tunstead Burtchaell, *Catholic Theories of Biblical Inspiration since
1810: A Review and Critique* (London: Cambridge University Press, 1969), where the
author describes at length the various theories of scriptural inspiration proposed in the
Catholic Church over most of the past two centuries. A few examples of such theories
are mentioned in this section.

8. See Thomas Aquinas, *De veritate*, q.11, a.1 ad 6. (Unless otherwise noted, citations to Aquinas's smaller works are from www.corpusthomisticum.org/iopera.html.
All of these writings can be found in *S. Thomae Aquinatis Opera Omnia: ut sunt in Indice Thomistico, additis 61 scriptis ex aliis medii aevi auctoribus*, edited by Robert Busa, 6

edges that God is the author of scripture in its entirety. The Christological analogy leaves no room for the proposition that some parts of the body of scripture (the "primary or religious" elements) are of God and others ("secondary or profane" elements) are merely of man.[9] God is the principal author of all Sacred Scripture, and yet he chose free human instruments to actively participate in his authorship throughout its entire process. Attention to this mysterious interplay of divine and human activity will be of capital importance in the chapters that follow.

The second significant point of Catholic teaching on the nature of scripture concerns its inerrancy. The fact that scriptures were inspired and authored by God—who can neither lie nor deceive—necessitates that they contain no error. This constant tradition of the church was repeated once again at the Second Vatican Council:

> Therefore, since everything asserted by the inspired authors or sacred writers must be held to be asserted by the Holy Spirit, it follows that the books of Scripture must be acknowledged as teaching solidly, faithfully and without error that truth which God wanted put into sacred writings for the sake of salvation.[10]

This teaching is pivotal for the present investigation, whose goal in effect is to better understand how this sentence from the Second Vatican Council applies to some of the most contentious texts within the biblical canon. For if all of scripture is inerrant, then even the darkest and most confusing passages of scripture are also inerrant, and a robust Catholic theology of scripture must account for their existence in such a way that preserves this understanding. In other words, if a portion of scripture appears to state something that is difficult to reconcile with what we know today through such avenues as philosophy, science, and Christian theology, it nevertheless must

---

vols. [Stuttgart-Bad Cannstatt: Frommann-Holzboog, 1980]). Also see Matthew Lamb's discussion in Aquinas's *Commentary on Saint Paul's Epistle to the Ephesians*, translated by Matthew Lamb (Albany, N.Y.: Magi Books, 1966), 261, n. 29.

9. Benedict XV, *On St. Jerome* [*Spiritus Paraclitus*], 1920, §19. This is the terminology used by the Holy Father in 1920 to describe the errors of those in his day who attempted to narrow the inspiration of scripture to matters of the "religious" realm. Cf. Leo XIII, *On the Study of the Holy Scripture* [*Providentissimus Deus*], 1893, §20.

10. *DV* §11.

be believed to convey something true. The challenge for today's Christian is to discern with the church what precisely is being proposed as true in scripture.

Given that Method A considers all of Sacred sacred to be the inspired and inerrant word of God, it ought not to come as a surprise that God's voice resounds in unique ways through the various portions of the sacred page. This brings us to a third point undergirding Catholicism's traditional view of scripture: its teaching on the "voice" of scripture and its "four senses." Accomplished human authors are not the only ones who craft their literary works to contain multiple layers of meaning; God himself authored Sacred Scripture in such a way that it can be read on multiple levels. In certain parts of scripture God teaches man about himself in a direct way. For example, as Method A exegetes understand, the pre-incarnate Word was openly at work in ancient Israel teaching the people about himself in order to prepare them for his coming as a man. As Pope Benedict reminds us, for Method A it is the voice of the pre-incarnate Word of God, the *vox Christi*, who speaks in the Psalms; it is he who is foretold in prophecy; it is he who is present in the types of the patriarchs.[11] So strong is their sense of the divine voice that in many cases Method A exegetes consider such Old Testament realities to be spoken more directly in reference to Christ than to the nation or individuals in Israel that the human author of scripture probably intended to describe in his work. An instance of this can be seen in Aquinas's discussion of Psalm 30, a psalm attributed to King David. The verse in question reads: "O Lord, thou hast brought up my soul from Sheol, restored me to life from among those gone down to the Pit." St. Thomas comments:

This cannot be literally understood of David, because he was not dug up from Sheol when he wrote this Psalm. It can be understood of him meta-

11. In his second volume of *Jesus of Nazareth*, translated by Adrian J. Walker (New York: Doubleday, 2007), Benedict writes: "Augustine offered a perfect explanation of this Christian way of praying the Psalms—a way that evolved very early on—when he said: it is always Christ who is speaking in the Psalms—now as head, now as the body.... Yet through him—through Jesus Christ—all of us now form a single subject, and so, in union with him, we can truly speak to God." (146–47.)

phorically, as if he was freed from mortal peril. But it is literally understood of Christ, whose soul was drawn out of Sheol by God.[12]

According to St. Thomas, Christ is not merely foreshadowed in Psalm 30. The subject of the psalm is not primarily David or any anonymous author of the psalm; rather, in this case the literal sense—that fundamental meaning intended by an author to be signified by his words—is Christ himself. For Method A exegetes, Christ is both he of whom the Old Testament speaks and he who speaks in the Old Testament.

As seen above in the case of Psalm 30, sometimes Method A views the literal sense of Old Testament passages in direct reference to Christ. At other times, however, Method A recognizes that the obvious meaning of a text is not Christological and that such a meaning is only attained by searching out its "spiritual sense." For example, according to its literal sense the word ἔξοδον—which means "departure" in Greek—signifies that historical event whereby the children of Israel departed from bondage in Egypt in the late second millennium B.C. The spiritual sense, then, arises whenever things signified by words themselves have a signification.[13] In this case, a look to the spiritual sense reveals that the event denoted with the word "exodus" itself signifies something, namely the "exodus" of Jesus as he departed this world through his Passion and death and attained new life in the Resurrection.[14] There is also the "exodus" of the Christian believer when he dies to his old way of life and rises to new life with Christ in baptism.[15] And there is the "exodus" that

12. Thomas Aquinas, *In psalmos Davidis expositio*, super Psalmo 29 (my translation). Note that the numbering of St. Thomas's commentary differs from the standard numbering of Psalms in the RSV.

13. Thomas Aquinas, *Summa Theologica* [*Summa theologiae*] translated by the Fathers of the English Dominican Province (Westminster, Md.: Christian Classics, 1981), I, q.1, a.10. (Hereafter, *ST*)

14. Narrating the Transfiguration event, the Gospel of Luke states that Jesus "appeared in glory and spoke of his departure (ἔξοδον), which he was to accomplish at Jerusalem" (Lk 9:31).

15. Even when not using the Greek term ἔξοδον, the New Testament conveys this meaning of spiritual exodus in various ways. See St. Paul's description of Christian freedom with imagery of liberation from slavery, which he leads into by showing that Christians enter through baptism into the mystery of Christ's own suffering, death, and

Christians hope to make when they, too, depart from their life on earth and enter into heavenly glory.[16]

According to the tradition espoused by Method A exegetes like St. Thomas and maintained throughout church history to the present day, the spiritual sense itself is subdivided into three senses: the allegorical, moral, and anagogical.[17] In this way, a given passage of scripture may speak to any or all of four things, one in a literal and three in a spiritual manner. As a medieval couplet cited in the Catechism has it, "The Letter speaks of deeds; Allegory to faith; The Moral how to act; Anagogy our destiny."[18] Thus, to return to the example of the Exodus, four realities are signified by this word: the deliverance of Israel in the Exodus event itself (literal sense); Christ's exodus whereby he passed through death into the resurrection (allegorical sense); the exodus of the Christian believer who dies to his old self through baptism (moral sense); and, the believer's exodus from death into eternal life on the Last Day (anagogical sense).

Resurrection: "Do you not know that all of us who have been baptized into Christ Jesus were baptized into his death? We were buried therefore with him by baptism into death, so that as Christ was raised from the dead by the glory of the Father, we too might walk in newness of life" (Rom 6:3–4). See also 1 Cor 10:1–2, where St. Paul implies that Israel's passage through the sea was a type of Christian baptism: "I want you to know, brethren, that our fathers were all under the cloud, and all passed through the sea, and all were baptized into Moses in the cloud and in the sea." St. Augustine confirms this interpretation in his discussion of Old Testament signs in chapter 20 of his *On the Catechising of the Uninstructed* [*De catechizandis rudibus*], translated by S. D. F. Salmond, in vol. 3, *Nicene and Post-Nicene Fathers, First Series*, edited by Philip Schaff (Buffalo, N.Y.: Christian Literature Publishing Co., 1888).

16. This anagogical sense of exodus seems to be at work in the book of Revelation where St. John sees a portent in heaven of those who had conquered the beast and who "sing the song of Moses, the servant of God, and the song of the Lamb, saying, 'Great and wonderful are thy deeds, O Lord God the Almighty! Just and true are thy ways, O King of the ages!'" (Rv 15:3)

17. Thomas Aquinas, *ST*, I, q.1, a.10; cf. Aquinas's treatment of the "four-fold way of interpreting Sacred Scripture" in his *Scriptum super Sententiis*, q.1, a.5; cf. *CCC* 115–19. As Henri de Lubac does well to point out, this four-fold schema itself was the product of centuries of development with regard to the church's theology of the spiritual sense, and during this time other related schemas have been propounded. Cf. Henri de Lubac, *Medieval Exegesis, vol. 1, The Four Senses of Scripture*, translated by Marc Sebanc (Grand Rapids, Mich.: Eerdmans, 1998), 1–39.

18. *CCC* §118.

METHOD A AND THE CANON: THE PIVOTAL ROLE OF
SACRED TRADITION AND THE MAGISTERIUM

Having reviewed Method A's foundational principles regarding the nature of scripture and the various modes by which it speaks to us, it is instructive to take a closer look at the pivotal role played by sacred tradition and the Magisterium—the church's official teaching office comprised of the bishops throughout the world in union with the Roman Pontiff—in establishing the authoritative canon and interpretation of scripture accepted by Method A exegetes. Here we must first confront a potential challenge concerning the question of where the "real" and authoritative Bible is to be found if no extant autograph (original copy) of it survives today. In other words, the issue to be asked of Method A is: how can believers have any confidence that the Bibles they read and hear proclaimed in their own language faithfully transmit God's revelation given that they represent a mixed bag of variant textual traditions, the result of one group of (non-inspired) scholars translating the work of another group of (non-inspired) scholars whose "critical edition" the former trusted to have reproduced the original biblical text as accurately as possible?

For a Christian community whose faith is based on the Bible alone, this question might appear to defy a rational answer. Method A exegetes in communion with the Catholic Church, however, have long held a very simple and profound understanding of this issue: believers have always had and always will have access to the "true" Bible because the Bible is not primarily found in any specific written document or record in the first place but rather *in the heart of the church*. As Pope Benedict puts it, "The Scripture emerged from within the heart of a living subject—the pilgrim people of God—and lives within this same subject. The People of God—the Church—is the living subject of Scripture; it is in the Church that the words of the Bible are always in the present."[19]

Like Mary who treasured the mystery of Christ in her heart (cf.

19. Benedict XVI, *Jesus of Nazareth*, xx–xxi.

Lk 2:19,51), Christian believers as a whole treasure the memory of God's word in their hearts, ceaselessly pondering its mystery and searching out its authentic meaning in accordance with the mind of Christ [20] This memory preserved in the church dates back to well before the scriptures were written, a crucial point to take into account since the church's life was not always bound up with the written records we have since come to enjoy. For example, as the eminent scholar Yves Congar tells us, "The Eucharist was celebrated and administered without waiting for [the Scriptures] to be written.... The Church could not wait until the critics were agreed among themselves: she had to live."[21] Important as scripture is, Catholics are aware that there has always existed a reality prior to it, a memory which was alive and present to the early Christians and which enabled the heart of the church to pulse even before the canon of scripture was complete. As Pope Benedict puts it:

> The seat of all faith is, then, the *memoria Ecclesiae*, the memory of the Church, the Church as memory. It exists through all ages, waxing and waning but never ceasing to be the common situs of faith. This sheds light once again on the question about the content of faith.... The Church is the locus that gives unity to the content of faith.[22]

In continuity with the Holy Father's words, Christians today must take seriously the living reality of the church's memory if we wish to maintain that the early church faithfully preserved divine revelation while lacking the written scriptures.

These last statements push the previous paragraph's question regarding the "location" of the Bible back a step. For even if we grant Method A its premise that scripture is not primarily located in any physical text, we still have to ask: where, then, is this reality called the "Church's heart" on which the scriptures are supposedly writ-

---

20. Cf. *CCC* §113. The Catechism refers here to Origen, whom Benedict XVI also cited in his April 23, 2009 address to participants in the plenary assembly of the Pontifical Biblical Commission: "Sacred Scripture is written in the heart of the Church before being written on material instruments." Cf. Origen, *Homilae in Leviticum*, 5,5.

21. Yves Congar, *The Meaning of Tradition* (San Francisco: Ignatius Press, 2004), 22–24.

22. Benedict XVI, *Principles of Catholic Theology: Building Stones for a Fundamental Theology* (San Francisco: Ignatius Press, 2009), 23–24.

ten? Earlier, we described the heart of the church in terms of the Christian community's continual reflection on God's word, but now we can address this reflective practice in greater depth. The heart of the church, the Mystical Body of Christ, is the heart of Christ himself whom Christians encounter through the entirety of the church's sacred tradition present even when the physical text of scripture is absent. *Dei Verbum* underscores the importance of sacred tradition in the following words:

> There exists a close connection and communication between sacred tradition and Sacred Scripture. For both of them, flowing from the same divine wellspring, in a certain way merge into a unity and tend toward the same end.... Consequently it is not from Sacred Scripture alone that the Church draws her certainty about everything which has been revealed. Therefore both sacred tradition and Sacred Scripture are to be accepted and venerated with the same sense of loyalty and reverence. Sacred tradition and Sacred Scripture form one sacred deposit of the word of God, committed to the Church.[23]

Sacred tradition, a source of revelation not limited to writing, comprises the deposit of God's word along with Sacred Scripture. It is venerated with the same reverence as the scriptures, but what, concretely, is contained within sacred tradition? As Congar has shown, "Tradition comprises the holy scriptures, and, besides these, not only doctrines but things: the sacraments, ecclesiastical institutions, the powers of the ministry, customs and liturgical rites—in fact, all the Christian realities themselves."[24] The realities mentioned in Congar's list come together to form the dynamic, lived experience of the Christian who through his regular encounter with them develops a sense for the "pulse" of the church's heart. When one considers the evidence indicating that the scriptures were typically written down decades or even centuries after the period they relate to their audience, it is easy to see that what we know today as the Bible is itself part of this much broader tradition, a tradition which preexisted the Bible and preserved the memory of God's word until it could be documented in written records. Indeed, in stating that

23. *DV* §§9–10; cf. *CCC* §§80–82.
24. Cf. Congar, *The Meaning of Tradition*, 13ff.

"the whole of Scripture is nothing other than Tradition," Pope Benedict indicates that the Bible simply *is* sacred tradition crystallized in its privileged, written form.[25] He describes this process of crystallization using the evocative image of generation and "birth." Extending the Christological analogy and applying it to the provenance of the scriptures, he writes: "As the word of God became flesh by the power of the Holy Spirit in the womb of the Virgin Mary, so Sacred Scripture is born from the womb of the church by the power of the same Spirit."[26]

Recent magisterial documents like Benedict's *Verbum Domini* cited above are replete with other images and expressions which shed light on this relationship between scripture, tradition, and Christ whose heart we encounter through them. A central idea therein is that the Word of God contained in tradition and scripture bears witness to the Word of God *the person* and enables believers to encounter him in a revelatory experience that cannot be exhaustively described in written words. For example, the Catechism cites St. Bernard of Clairvaux in describing Christianity as being not a "religion of the book"—a religion limited to God's written word—but rather a religion of the living Word of God, Jesus Christ, whom scripture and tradition make present to us.[27] Citing the same words of St. Bernard, *Verbum Domini* elucidates the analogical nature of the word of God and additionally speaks of a "symphony of the word," a "polyphonic hymn" by which the Word reveals himself to man in his person, in scripture, and in nature.[28] Of particular note is the pope's statement, "Although the word of God precedes and exceeds sacred Scripture, nonetheless Scripture, as inspired by God, contains the divine word (cf. 2 Tm 3:16) 'in an altogether singular way.'"[29] This word of God which precedes and exceeds scripture is none other than Jesus Christ as he has made himself knowable through sacred tradition.

The idea that the Word of God preexists, exceeds, and is served

25. Benedict XVI and Vittorio Messori, *The Ratzinger Report: An Exclusive Interview on the State of the Church*, translated by Salvator Attanasio and Graham Harrison (San Francisco: Ignatius Press, 1985), 160.

26. *VD* §19.   27. Cf. *CCC* §108.
28. Cf. *VD* §7.   29. *VD* §17.

by scripture was articulated by Pope Benedict XVI, even before he became a Cardinal, decades ago in his work *Revelation and Tradition*. Concerning the revelation of the Word, he wrote, "Revelation means God's whole speech and action with man; it signifies a *reality* which scripture makes known but which is not itself simply identical with scripture. Revelation, therefore, is more than scripture to the extent that reality exceeds information about it."[30] In the more recent *Verbum Domini* we find an expression which sheds light on the meaning of the pope's repeated statements to the effect that revelation exceeds scripture. He writes, "Indeed, the word of God is given to us in sacred Scripture as an inspired testimony to revelation; together with the Church's living Tradition, it constitutes the supreme rule of faith."[31] Although the language of "testimony" or "witness" has certainly been used by some to convey a very low view of scripture, the terminology is extremely valuable for those Christians because it conveys the truth that the scriptures are the word of God and yet also have the subservient role of testifying to the *person* of the word, not exhausting the reality of the second person of the Trinity but serving as a means to make available his revelation to mankind. The excelling majesty of Christ's revelation can be no more fittingly described than it is at the end of St. John's Gospel: "But there are also many other things which Jesus did; were every one of them to be written, I suppose that the world itself could not contain the books that would be written" (Jn 21:25).

Granted that Sacred Scripture witnesses to the revelation of Jesus Christ and that it emerged out of the more ancient tradition described above, this still leaves unresolved the question: how can a Method A exegete justify the origin of the biblical canon in the early church, that is to say the fact that some books were deemed "the word of God" and other, ostensibly very similar books were not. The short answer to this question is that it hinges on the existence of a teaching authority instituted by Jesus himself, one invested with the

---

30. Karl Rahner and Benedict XVI, *Revelation and Tradition* (New York: Herder, 1966), 35.

31. *VD* §18.

power to make infallible determinations such as the establishment of the biblical canon. A more in-depth explanation involves the recognition that the Magisterium was able to know and declare which books constituted the biblical canon as a result of her contact with the tradition already alive in the heart of the church [32] Since the Bible itself does not explicitly define the canon, it was incumbent upon the bishops and pope to search the various forms of tradition to make their determination. In particular, Pope Benedict tells us that "a book was recognized as 'canonical' if it was sanctioned by the Church for use in public worship.... In the nascent Church, the reading of Scripture and the confession of faith were primarily liturgical acts."[33] In other words, the bishops saw that the best guarantee of a particular text's inspiration was the constant tradition of the church solemnly proclaiming the contents of the text over the centuries.

In addition to this all-important criterion, considered in sanctioning texts in the church's liturgy, the bishops also examined and evaluated lists of books found in the writings of church fathers dating from the second century A.D. up to the time of their promulgations in local councils beginning in the late fourth century. Writing near the end of the fourth century, St. Athanasius provides the most ancient witness to a New Testament canon of twenty-seven books, though his list lacks the Old Testament deuterocanon. Soon thereafter, St. Augustine offered an authoritative list containing all the books present in Catholic Bibles today, at which time discussion regarding the extent of the canon was for all intents and purposes closed in the Western church. At this point Augustine's canonical list of forty-six Old Testament and twenty-seven New Testament books took on official ecclesiastical status as it was adopted and promulgated at the regional councils of Hippo (393 A.D.), Carthage III (397 A.D.), and Carthage IV (419 A.D.), and affirmed by a letter of Pope Innocent I in 405 A.D. The later ecumenical councils of Florence (1442 A.D.) and Trent (1546 A.D.) would go on to confirm this

32. *DV* §8; cf. *VD* §18.
33. Benedict XVI, *Principles of Catholic Theology*, 148.

canon for all the Christians of their age. It is important to note that in all these councils we observe the Magisterium authoritatively reaffirming sacred tradition in the face of contemporary challenges to the faith, not inventing new truths but guarding and transmitting what is already there for future generations. Moreover, one cannot overstate the truth that in Catholicism these magisterial promulgations of the canon are not merely a matter of human judgment but rather the exercise of a *charism* given by God. For as Bl. John Henry Newman demonstrated, if this charism to ascertain the canon had not been given to the Magisterium, Christians would never have had any way of knowing with certitude which books belonged in the Bible or not. Without the Magisterium of the Catholic Church, we would never have had the Bible in the first place.[34]

METHOD A AND THE INTERPRETATION OF SCRIPTURE

The final aspect of Method A exegesis we need to consider at this point concerns how those who follow the church can guarantee that any given biblical interpretation of theirs is accurate. It is one thing to say that the Magisterium has authoritatively defined the list of books which comprise the Bible, but does that really get today's reader anywhere if he does not know whether he is reading the sacred page correctly? As it turns out, the Bible not only does not contain its own table of contents, it does not interpret itself, either. Against the Protestant doctrine of scriptural "perspicuity," *Dei Verbum* relates that the Bible is understood correctly only within the interpretative tradition of the church and under the guidance of her Magisterium:

34. Newman states, "The most obvious answer, then, to the question, why we yield to the authority of the Church in the questions and developments of faith, is, that some authority there must be if there is a revelation given, and other authority there is none but she. A revelation is not given if there be no authority to decide what it is that is given.... The absolute need of a spiritual supremacy is at present the strongest of arguments in favour of the fact of its supply." John Henry Newman, *An Essay on the Development of Christian Doctrine* (Notre Dame, Ind.: University of Notre Dame Press, 1989), 88–89.

The task of authentically interpreting the word of God, whether written or handed on, has been entrusted exclusively to the living teaching office of the Church, whose authority is exercised in the name of Jesus Christ. This teaching office is not above the word of God, but serves it, teaching only what has been handed on, listening to it devoutly, guarding it scrupulously and explaining it faithfully in accord with a divine commission and with the help of the Holy Spirit, it draws from this one deposit of faith everything which it presents for belief as divinely revealed.[35]

The same Magisterium which guarded sacred tradition and defined the biblical canon in the early church today has the charism of searching the tradition in order to provide authoritative interpretations of the Bible when human efforts alone fail to clarify its meaning.

The Catechism contains a concise summary of Method A's interpretive principles as they have been exercised by the Magisterium and the faithful over the centuries. As the Catechism observes, those who wish to interpret scripture according to the mind of the church must follow three guidelines. First, interpretation of difficult passages must be done bearing in mind the rest of scripture and how these passages fit into the unified whole: "Scripture is a unity by reason of the unity of God's plan, of which Christ Jesus is the center and heart," the Catechism states.[36] When passages seem to contradict one another, the church assures believers that there is an answer to the difficulty if these passages are placed within the context of scripture as a unified work given to man by God for his salvation. Even the most difficult of passages take on light when they are viewed as participating in God's plan as it has developed throughout the history of revelation. In other words, when texts of scripture are approached from the perspective of God's gradual, providential education of mankind rather than as mere monadic moments in linear history, it is easier to understand why God might have permitted there to be various difficulties in Scripture.[37]

35. *DV* §10. Granted the importance of the Catholic magisterial tradition for biblical interpretation, it is worth noting that the church only rarely steps in and defines how a particular text must or must not be interpreted.

36. *CCC* §112.

37. Moreover, many of the same places in scripture that present difficulties on the literal level have providentially led the church to a deeper understanding of divine

Second, the Catechism indicates that a correct interpretation of scripture must be in harmony not only with other scripture but also with the entire living tradition of the church throughout history. It invokes the church's "heart" here as an image to convey the reality of sacred tradition passed on through the ages: "According to a saying of the Fathers," the Catechism reminds us, "Sacred Scripture is written principally in the Church's heart rather than in documents and records."[38] Ultimately, no human being can adequately understand scripture on his own. The church alone enjoys this prerogative because she is the subject whose heart bears the living memory of God's word throughout history.[39]

Third, the Catechism states that faithful Christian exegesis must look to the "analogy of faith," by which it means "the coherence of the truths of faith among themselves and within the whole plan of revelation."[40] This is extremely valuable because it tells the Method A exegete that if his own interpretation of a contentious biblical passage contradicts a dogma verified by the Magisterium, it is his own interpretation that is erroneous, not the dogma. To expound on a beautiful statement of Matthew Levering in this regard, the church's exegesis today is an ongoing participation in God's own act of educating mankind throughout history, and so if the Christian exegete is to faithfully execute this mission he must do so from within the heart of the church and in accordance with her dogmas.[41]

It is appropriate to conclude this exposition of the principles of Method A exegesis with a few words on the role the church's liturgy

---

realities because they have driven exegetes to search out scripture's various spiritual senses. Indeed, insofar as they bring the reader to an encounter with Christ, these senses may be the very *telos* of the literal sense, or at least illumine it. As Matthew Levering states, "Since historical realities are richer than a solely linear or atomistic understanding of time might suggest, the Church's theological and metaphysical 'reading into' biblical texts may largely be expected to *illumine* the realities described in Scripture rather than to obscure them." *Participatory Biblical Exegesis: A Theology of Biblical Interpretation* (Notre Dame, Ind.: University of Notre Dame Press, 2008), 5.

38. *CCC* §113.

39. For a thorough discussion of the church as the subject who bears God's word through history, see Congar, *The Meaning of Tradition*, 47–81.

40. *CCC* §114.

41. Cf. Levering, *Participatory Biblical Exegesis*, 15.

plays in guiding Method A's interpretation of scripture. The liturgy is one of the principal sources of sacred tradition and has always been a privileged means employed by the Magisterium in her approach to scripture. As the great Benedictine Abbot Prosper Guéranger wrote, "It is in the liturgy that the Spirit who inspired the Scriptures speaks again; the liturgy is tradition itself in the highest degree of power and solemnity."[42] Guéranger's words are but a modern expression of the ancient dictum *lex orandi, lex credendi*, which indicates that the church's law of prayer is her law of faith.[43] That is to say, if Christians want to know what the church should believe today about the nature of scripture and how to interpret it, we need to look at how she has *prayed* the scriptures over the centuries. While it is by not means sufficient on its own, following this rule assists the Method A exegete in his effort to confirm that even the toughest challenges raised as a result of discoveries in modern biblical scholarship do not contradict the tradition kept alive in the church's heart through constant prayer over the millennia. For even if there appear to be ambiguities or contradictions between the extant text of scripture and certain Christian doctrines, Method A exegetes enjoy the comfort of knowing that the meaning of the texts in question has been preserved in the church's heart, especially in her liturgy. This is but a corollary of Congar's thought in stating that not a single Catholic dogma is derived from scripture alone without being explained by sacred tradition (and vice versa).

The reality that Catholic belief does not depend exclusively on a given passage of scripture likewise goes hand in hand with biblical textual expert Bruce Metzger's observation that "no doctrine of the Christian faith depends solely upon a passage that is textually uncertain."[44] All of this is to say that while the truths of inspiration and inerrancy are inextricably bound up with the physical text of scripture, they are found above all in that scripture which resides in the church's heart. It is to this heart, pulsing through sacred tradi-

---

42. Guéranger's work is cited in Congar, *The Meaning of Tradition*, 134.

43. Cf. *CCC* §1124.

44. Bruce Metzger, *The New Testament: Its Background, Growth, and Content* (Nashville, Tenn.: Abingdon, 1991), 281.

tion and guarded by the Magisterium, that the Method A exegete seeks to conform himself and his understanding of scripture. Let us conclude this section with the words with which the Second Vatican Council articulates the relationship between scripture, tradition, and Magisterium:

It is clear, therefore, that sacred tradition, Sacred Scripture and the teaching authority of the Church, in accord with God's most wise design, are so linked and joined together that one cannot stand without the others, and that all together and each in its own way under the action of the one Holy Spirit contribute effectively to the salvation of souls.[45]

A POTENTIAL WEAKNESS OF METHOD A AND THE PRINCIPLES OF METHOD B'S RESPONSE

Despite all the strengths of Method A exegesis and its pivotal role in the life of the believer, at times those who employ this method have tended to emphasize the unity and inerrancy of scripture and dealt largely with its spiritual sense while neglecting its literal sense with the evidence of development and the apparent contradictions that can be observed through study.[46] For historical-critical scholars, this neglect of the literal remains a continual source of skepticism with regard to traditional exegesis, and as such constitutes a

---

45. *DV* §10.

46. For instance, in his *On First Principles* Origen employs a helpful image to describe Scared Scripture as having a "body" (historical sense) and "soul" (spiritual sense). However, at times in his exposition he dismisses the importance of the literal sense and goes so far as to say that it sometimes does not even exist. (4.12.) In contrast, St. Augustine tends to provide a much more balanced view. Yet although his *Exposition on the Psalms* is profound, its particular aim was not to show how the Psalms's Christological meaning presupposed and built upon their literal meaning in ancient Israel. *Exposition on the Psalms [Enarrationes in psalmos]*, translated by J. E. Tweed, vol. 8, *Nicene and Post-Nicene Fathers, First Series*, edited by Philip Schaff (Buffalo, N.Y.: Christian Literature Publishing Co., 1888). The commentary of St. Thomas Aquinas, on the other hand, draws more on the literal and spiritual senses in the Psalms and shows how they are united. It is for reasons such as this that Aquinas was chosen as the primary Method A representative in this study. Even though he died before he was able to complete his commentary on the Psalms, when compared to other exegesis of the patristic and medieval periods his stands out as a forerunner to the Method C exegesis called for by Benedict.

weakness on the part of many Method A exegetes. Pope Benedict's work stands on a solid middle ground between the excesses of certain Method A exegetes and the skepticism typical of Method B. He typically gives a positive but sober assessment of patristic spiritual exegesis, as we see in the case of the parables of the Good Samaritan and the Prodigal Son. Concerning the Good Samaritan, he writes:

> The Church Fathers understood the parable Christologically. That is an allegorical reading, one might say—an interpretation that bypasses the text. But when we consider that in all of the parables, each in a different way, the Lord really does want to invite us to faith in the kingdom of God, which he himself is, then a Christological interpretation is never a totally false reading. In some sense it reflects an inner potentiality in the text and can be a fruit growing out of it as from a seed.[47]

The pope proceeds to meditate on the parable's various features over a span of several pages. Of particular interest here is how he views the interpretation given by the church fathers of the man who was stripped and beaten, wounded and left half dead. He notes that the fathers interpreted this particular man's sufferings as an allegory of mankind's twofold alienation due to sin—which has "stripped" us of the grace we had received and "wounded" us in our nature. Benedict explains, "Now that is an instance of allegory, and it certainly goes far beyond the literal sense. For all that, though, it is an attempt to identify precisely the two kinds of injury that weigh down human history."[48] Notice the pope's language here. He states that the patristic interpretation "bypasses the text" and "certainly goes far beyond the literal sense." The language that follows seems to indicate a defect in the emphasis the fathers placed on the spiritual sense. "For all that, though," their exegesis is a worthy attempt to plumb the depths of the passages. Thus he can say that the Christological interpretation "is never a totally false reading." Why does the pope insert the adverb "totally" before the adjective "false"? It is not perfectly clear, but it would seem to be because he thinks there are not only strengths but also defects in the way the fathers deal with this parable.

47. Benedict XVI, *Jesus of Nazareth*, 199.
48. Ibid., 20.

Similar language can be found in Benedict's dealings with the Prodigal Son. Noting the difficulty involved in the effort to locate the figure of Jesus in this parable when it is read allegorically, he asks: "Where does Jesus Christ fit into all of this? Only the Father figures in the parable. Is there no Christology in it? Augustine tried to work Christology in where the text says that the Father embraced the son, explaining that 'the arm of the father is the Son.'" The pope comments, "This is a very evocative exposition, but it is still an 'allegory' that clearly goes beyond the text."[49] Once again, Benedict's assessment of patristic exegesis involves the observation that the fathers often go "beyond the text." In telling us that Augustine "tried" to work Christology into the parable, he implies that Augustine's interpretation is not entirely convincing. For Benedict, successful spiritual exegesis can only go beyond the text of scripture once it has gone *through* the text by dealing with its literal sense. This is not an easy task to achieve, for even the most brilliant fathers of the church themselves struggled with it.

If then a hallmark of Method A is that it views scripture from a spiritual perspective and is able to discern the voice of Christ within it, then a strength of Method B is that it attends to scripture's literal meaning and desires to hear the voice of scripture's human authors at work therein. Method B does not so much approach scripture as God's word but instead operates according to the principle that it ought to bracket out the question of faith and study these words as human words that reflect a past context, a definite cultural milieu with its own language and mindset. In the foreword to his book *Jesus of Nazareth*, Pope Benedict gives the parameters of historical-critical work: "It attempts to identify and to understand the past—as it was in itself—with the greatest possible precision, in order then to find out what the author could have said and intended to say in the context of the mentality and events of his time."[50] It employs all the scientific tools at the disposal of modern man, not limited to but including a broader knowledge of history, recent discoveries

49. Ibid., 207.
50. Ibid., xvi.

in archaeology and the various natural sciences, and an increased competence in Semitic languages, that helps to attain a clearer understanding of the original meaning the texts had in Israel.

The "critical" attitude is not necessarily critical in the way many people initially think. Concerning the attempt to employ historical-critical exegesis in his own search for the face of Jesus, Benedict writes:

Naturally this will require of us a readiness not only to form a "critical" assessment of the New Testament, but also to learn from it and to let ourselves be led by it: not to dismantle the texts according to our preconceived ideas, but to let our own ideas be purified and deepened by his word.[51]

According to Benedict, historical criticism does not of its own nature seek to dismantle or criticize the faith, but it does entail a willingness to be purified by asking questions—and entertaining corresponding answers—that faithful Christians of previous ages did not tend to raise. Some examples of such questions are: whether an explicit teaching of the resurrection of the body is found throughout the entirety of the Bible, whether the Old Testament presents a unified account of God's oneness, or whether the Bible is entirely accurate in its understanding of evil. A Method B approach to texts such as Psalm 30 discussed above would question St. Thomas's claim that the human author of this text originally intended it to be understood literally of Christ and his deliverance from death. In this way, whereas Method A sees literal bodily resurrection in passages such as this throughout the entire Bible, Method B sees authors often speaking of resurrection in an analogous sense, for example a man's being delivered from the moment of physical death as a kind of "resurrection" from the perilous pit of Sheol, or Israel's restoration to the promised land as a kind of "resurrection" from exile.

Moreover, given Method B's observation that the literal sense of scripture does not intend a doctrine of bodily resurrection in all the places many once thought it did, it is not a big step for those who make this observation to further claim that the same texts some-

---

51. Benedict XVI, *Jesus of Nazareth: Holy Week: From the Entrance into Jerusalem to the Resurrection*, (San Francisco: Ignatius Press, 2011), 120.

times appear to be erroneous when it comes to such matters as the afterlife—that writers like the psalmist were not the least bit interested in or even aware of the notion of bodily resurrection, and that whenever such a possibility was raised they actually tended to reject it. The way one deals with this claim is pivotal for a synthetic, Method C approach to scripture, because it is one thing to acknowledge that natural science does not fall within the scope of scripture's intended teaching, but it is an even greater challenge to account for the traditional Christian view of scripture when scripture appears to be teaching on a matter of faith, and teaching it incorrectly. Method B's attentiveness to the literal sense and its willingness to challenge traditional assumptions about scripture is precisely what raised this challenge, and the rest of this work will continue the search for an answer to precisely such problems.

METHOD B's WEAKNESSES

Of course, Method B's willingness to question traditional Christian assumptions about scripture is not always accompanied by a desire to build up the faith. It is well known among faithful Christians that many of those belonging to the historical-critical school have sought to undermine central tenets of the faith, especially when it comes to the figure of Jesus. As Benedict indicates, "Historically, this method was first applied at the time of the Enlightenment, with the aim of using history to correct dogma, setting up a purely human, historical Jesus against the Christ of faith."[52] The pope goes so far as to insinuate the presence of a demonic element in certain areas of historical-critical scholarship. Meditating on the exchange between the devil and Jesus narrated in Mt 4, he suggests, "The devil proves to be a Bible expert who can quote the Psalm exactly. The whole conversation of the second temptation takes the form of a dispute between two Bible scholars." The pope bases his comments on Vladimir Soloviev's short story "The Antichrist," a work we may surmise he finds important because he also refers to it in his Eras-

---

52. Benedict XVI, *Behold the Pierced One: An Approach to a Spiritual Christology*, translated by Graham Harrison (San Francisco: Ignatius Press, 1986), 43.

mus Lecture and his book *Eschatology*. In Soloviev's work, the figure of the Antichrist tries to seduce Christians by touting the honorary doctorate in theology he has been awarded by the University of Tübingen. Tübingen has long been known among biblical scholars as a mecca for historical-critical biblical research. Soloviev, then, is unabashedly connecting the hermeneutic of suspicion practiced at Tübingen with the work of the Antichrist, and ultimately the devil. Nevertheless, the pope nuances Soloviev's story:

This is not a rejection of scholarly biblical interpretation as such, but an eminently salutary warning against its possible aberrations. The fact is that scholarly exegesis can become a tool of the Antichrist. Soloviev is not the first person to tell us that; it is the deeper point of the temptation story itself. The alleged findings of scholarly exegesis have been used to put together the most dreadful books that destroy the figure of Jesus and dismantle the faith. The common practice today is to measure the Bible against the so-called modern worldview, whose fundamental dogma is that God cannot act in history.... And so the Bible no longer speaks of God, the living God; no, now *we* alone speak and decide what God can do and what we will and should do. And the Antichrist, with an air of scholarly excellence, tells us that any exegesis that reads the Bible from the perspective of faith in the living God, in order to listen to what God has to say, is fundamentalism; he wants to convince us that only his kind of exegesis, the supposedly purely scientific kind, in which God says nothing and has nothing to say, is able to keep abreast of the times. The theological dispute between Jesus and the devil is a dispute over the correct interpretation of Scripture.[53]

According to Benedict, the Antichrist wants to show that scripture's teaching is false and that its spiritual meaning is a mere human invention, a fundamentalist's abuse of the text.[54] He wants to have us

53. Benedict XVI, *Jesus of Nazareth*, 35–36.

54. Indeed, this was even the case at the very outset of the historical-critical movement. See Baruch Spinoza, *Theological-Political Treatise* (Cambridge: Cambridge University Press, 2007) and the analysis of Matthew Lamb and Matthew Levering in *Vatican II: Renewal within Tradition*, edited by Matthew Lamb and Matthew Levering (New York: Oxford University Press, 2008), 6: "Spinoza set forth the presuppositions of this denigration of revealed truth in his *Theologico-Political Treatise*. Like nature, the Bible can no longer be treated as a whole; it must be broken up into fragmented parts. These isolated texts must then be reinterpreted only by other texts. Because the wise attunement to the whole Bible was lost, Spinoza remarks that one must never raise the truth question, only the meaning question to be answered solely with reference to other fragmented texts. The development of doctrine within the Bible from Old to New Testament and within

believe that an "objective" reading of the biblical text is one done with the caveat that the spiritual and the material are incompatible, that God could never enter into human history and disclose himself. He has noted that in the present age these philosophical tenets of some biblical critics have grown to the stature of academic dogmas, to the point that criticizing them at all is considered tantamount to sacrilege.[55] Because of this bias, scholars and others committed to creedal Christianity have rightly been taken aback by many of the presuppositions of critical scholars.[56] In light of these circumstances, Benedict argues that if historical criticism is to play a role in the exegesis of believers today, there must take place a "criticism of criticism," as he described it in his Erasmus lecture.[57]

Benedict's critique helps us to see that, despite its capacity to challenge longstanding assumptions of exegetes who profess the Christian faith, Method B's fundamental strength turns out also to constitute its principal weakness: its willingness to ask radical questions of scripture and its ability to provide a scientific analysis of scripture often leads to excess of regard for its own competence and lack of regard for Christ.[58] To illustrate, in his treatment of Peter's

---

the ongoing mission of the Church is rendered impossible. Wisdom is replaced with arbitrary power." See also Matthew Lamb, *Eternity, Time, and the Life of Wisdom* (Naples, Fla.: Sapientia Press of Ave Maria University, 2007), ix–x.

55. Benedict XVI, "Biblical Interpretation in Crisis," 21. Cf. Francis Martin, "Joseph Ratzinger, Benedict XVI, on Biblical Interpretation: Two Leading Principles," *Nova et Vetera* 5 (2007): 285–314. Among the achievements of Martin in this article, he appropriates Benedict's criticism of reductionist modern cognitional theories.

56. By employing the term "creedal Christianity" one includes not only Catholics but all Christians who profess faith in the revelation of the triune God as expounded in the church's early creeds. The term "Chalcedonian Christianity" is also frequently used by scholars of various denominations to articulate their shared belief in the nature of God and his revelation in Jesus Christ. For more on the subject of scholars ruling out the possibility of God's self-disclosure in human history, see also Benedict's "Biblical Interpretation in Crisis" as well as the more recent *VD* §36, where he elucidates the simple rule: "In applying methods of historical analysis, no criteria should be adopted which would rule out in advance God's self-disclosure in human history."

57. "Biblical Interpretation in Crisis," 6. In *Light of the World* (San Francisco: Ignatius Press, 2010), 171, he also argues, "What is needed is not simply a break with the historical method, but a self-critique of the historical method; a self-critique of historical reason."

58. As is often the case, here I am indebted to a conversation with Gregory Vall for insights and distinctions of his that I have tried to appropriate in my own work.

confession "You are the Christ," the pope criticizes scholarship's excesses in no uncertain terms:

The attempt to arrive at a historical reconstruction of Peter's original words and then to attribute everything else to posterior developments, and possibly to post-Easter faith, is very much on the wrong track. Where is post-Easter faith supposed to have come from if Jesus laid no foundation for it before Easter? Scholarship overplays its hand with such reconstructions.[59]

While the pope certainly does not hesitate to engage and even tentatively accept certain historical-critical hypotheses, he shows that scholarship often "overplays its hand with such reconstructions" which are "very much on the wrong track." In the case of Peter's confession, he is countering theories which would have the printed text of Peter's confession in complete discontinuity with Jesus's original spoken words. To such proposals he replies: "Where is post-Easter faith supposed to have come from if Jesus laid no foundation for it before Easter?" Benedict makes a commonsense argument: if the words of Jesus and the words of the Gospels are in complete discontinuity, then why do the Gospels say what they do? From Benedict's commonsense point of view, the obvious answer is that the Gospels' portrait of Jesus are based on real, historical events in the life of Jesus which are presented theologically, to be sure, but by no means haphazardly or without due respect for the events themselves.

Aside from its excesses, there is a more fundamental problem often present in historical-critical exegesis. Since faith is a not a fundamental component of Method B exegesis, those who employ this method sometimes miss the ultimate end, the very *raison d'être* of scripture: the opportunity to encounter the living God who teaches man through his sacred word. As Benedict puts it, "Approaches to the sacred text that prescind from faith might suggest interesting elements on the level of textual structure and form, but would inevitably prove merely preliminary and structurally incomplete efforts."[60]

---

59. Benedict XVI, *Jesus of Nazareth*, 303. In his second volume of *Jesus of Nazareth* one also finds Benedict criticizing excessively self-confident historical-critical scholars: "Exegetical hypotheses ... all too often make exaggerated claims to certainty." *Jesus of Nazareth: Holy Week*, 105.

60. *VD* §29.

When exegetes thus fail to rise up to appreciate the divine teaching in Scripture and remain solely at the level of scripture as a collection of texts, it is impossible for them to see its inspired unity:

[The historical-critical] method is a fundamental dimension of exegesis, but it does not exhaust the interpretative task for someone who sees the biblical writings as a single corpus of Holy Scripture inspired by God.... The unity of all these writings as one "Bible" is something it can see only as an immediate historical datum.[61]

For the pope, what we call the Bible is not truly the Bible unless we see it "as a single corpus of Holy Scripture inspired by God." Method B exegesis can examine lines of development and the growth of traditions in Sacred Scripture, yet it cannot make the further step of seeing them as a unity. For Method A, on the other hand, the many books of scripture have a unity precisely insofar as they participate in the economy of salvation and manifest the divine pedagogy. Accordingly, to the extent that historical criticism disavows the possibility of an economy of salvation, it denies scripture its unifying principle. Thus, granted that Old Testament passages ought to be read with more attentiveness to their Israelite context, as Method B does well to observe, the pope demonstrates what a travesty it would be not to accept the Method A principles which enlighten and heal the defects in Method B and which alone enable scripture to be experienced as God's holy word.

BOTH APPROACHES ARE NECESSARY
FOR THE METHOD C PROJECT

In light of this "criticism of criticism" initiated by Benedict, Method B exegetes must be attentive if they are to ensure that their efforts do not neglect the role of faith and ultimately end up bankrupt. The pope counsels exegetes today to take the "further step" of acknowledging faith as a hermeneutic:

If it wishes to be theology, [exegesis] must take a further step. It must recognize that the faith of the Church is that form of "sympathia" without which

61. Benedict XVI, *Jesus of Nazareth*, xvi–xvii.

the Bible remains a *closed* book. It must come to acknowledge this faith as a hermeneutic, the space for understanding, which does not do dogmatic violence to the Bible, but precisely allows the solitary possibility for the Bible to be itself.[62]

Contrary to the tenets of those who approach Scripture with a hermeneutic of suspicion, Benedict understands that Method A's hermeneutic of faith is in reality the key to unlocking the true meaning of Scripture, without which it remains "a closed book."

Lest one assume that Benedict's proposal of an exegetical synthesis is solely a theoretical affair, it is important to emphasize that he has long been instantiating it in his work, especially in the two recent volumes of *Jesus of Nazareth*. In the foreword to the second volume, he speaks to the necessity of synthesizing the "historical hermeneutic" (Method B) and "faith hermeneutic" (Method A) and his own attempt to do so in his work on Jesus:

> If scholarly exegesis is not to exhaust itself in constantly new hypotheses, becoming theologically irrelevant, it must take a methodological step forward and once again see itself as a theological discipline, without abandoning its historical character. It must learn that the positivistic hermeneutic on which it has been based does not constitute the only valid and definitively evolved rational approach; rather, it constitutes a specific and historically conditioned form of rationality that is both open to correction and completion and in need of it. It must recognize that a properly developed faith-hermeneutic is appropriate to the text and can be combined with a historical hermeneutic, aware of its limits, so as to form a methodological whole. Naturally, this combination of two quite different types of hermeneutic is an art that needs to be constantly remastered.[63]

Here, Benedict warns that scholarly exegesis will become an endless, "theologically irrelevant" maze of hypotheses unless it takes a "methodological step forward." It must continue its patient attentiveness to the historical nature of scripture, but this must be at the service of theology. "A faith-hermeneutic" helps correct and complete the historical method. The two methods can be "combined … so as to form a methodological whole." However, he notes that "this combination of two quite different types of hermeneutic is an

---

62. Benedict XVI, "Biblical Interpretation in Crisis," 22–23; cf. *VD* §§51–52.
63. Benedict XVI, *Jesus of Nazareth: Holy Week*, xiv–xv.

art that needs to be constantly remastered." The church is therefore constantly working *toward* an adequate approach to scripture and learning the art of balancing two very different exegetical methods. Our efforts toward a synthesis will necessarily remain imperfect, but their goal is always the same: an encounter with the Lord. Writing as a theologian rather than in his capacity as the Roman Pontiff, he humbly confesses:

I would not presume to claim that this combination of the two hermeneutics is already fully accomplished in my book. But I hope to have taken a significant step in that direction. Fundamentally this is a matter of finally putting into practice the methodological principles formulated for exegesis by the Second Vatican Council (in *Dei Verbum* 12), a task that unfortunately has scarcely been attempted thus far.... In the combination of the two hermeneutics of which I spoke earlier, I have attempted to develop a way of observing and listening to the Jesus of the Gospels that can indeed lead to personal encounter and that, through collective listening with Jesus's disciples across the ages, can indeed attain sure knowledge of the real historical figure of Jesus.[64]

The pope concludes that the Method C synthesis he is searching for is ultimately a matter of "finally putting into practice the methodological principles formulated for exegesis by the Second Vatican Council." The council's teaching demands that exegetes have recourse to the strengths of both the faith hermeneutic ("Method A") and historical hermeneutic ("Method B") if they wish to plumb the depths of scripture. Each method on its own is insufficient for this endeavor and eventually leads to problems.[65]

Benedict certainly acknowledges the many problems prevalent in Method B exegesis, but he is very clear that the historical-critical approach may not be discarded any more than Method A may be. In fact, as he writes in *Jesus of Nazareth*, "The historical-critical method—specifically because of the intrinsic nature of theology and faith—is and remains an indispensable dimension of exegetical work. For it is of the essence of biblical faith to be about real histori-

64. Ibid., xv–xvii.
65. In point of fact, in *Verbum Domini* the pope goes so far as to claim that the two levels of exegesis "exist only in reciprocity." *VD* §35.

cal events."[66] As the Holy Father explains, God has really entered into human history in his revelation to Israel and with the coming of Christ, and for this reason historical-critical exegesis must be carried out in order that the historical dimension of scripture might be more greatly penetrated. Moreover, although Method B has the weakness of sometimes thinking it can arrive at a pure and perfect understanding of Sacred Scripture devoid of all reference to its role within the church, the implementation of this method nevertheless keeps one from the opposite extreme view of paying heed to ecclesiastical traditions while neglecting discoveries in the field of critical scholarship. Thus he says, "There should be no particular need to demonstrate that on the one hand it is useless to take refuge in an allegedly pure, literal understanding of the Bible. On the other hand, a merely positivistic and rigid ecclesiasticism would not do either."[67] In other words, one's adherence to the pronouncements of

66. Benedict XVI, *Jesus of Nazareth*, xv. He recently reiterated the same teaching in *VD* §32: "Before all else, we need to acknowledge the benefits that historical-critical exegesis and other recently-developed methods of textual analysis have brought to the life of the Church. For the Catholic understanding of sacred Scripture, attention to such methods is indispensable, linked as it is to the realism of the Incarnation." Benedict's words also corroborate what Pius XII wrote in *Divino afflante Spiritu*, the most recent encyclical devoted to the topic of biblical studies. Concerning the place of modern methods in biblical exegesis, he stated: "Hence the Catholic commentator, in order to comply with the present needs of biblical studies, in explaining the Sacred Scripture and in demonstrating and proving its immunity from all error, should also make a prudent use of this means, determine, that is, to what extent the manner of expression or the literary mode adopted by the sacred writer may lead to a correct and genuine interpretation; and let him be convinced that this part of his office cannot be neglected without serious detriment to Catholic exegesis.... Let those who cultivate biblical studies turn their attention with all due diligence towards this point and let them neglect none of those discoveries, whether in the domain of archaeology or in ancient history or literature, which serve to make better known the mentality of the ancient writers, as well as their manner and art of reasoning, narrating and writing." *VD* §§38, 40; cf. Pontifical Biblical Commission, *Sancta Mater Ecclesia* §4.

67. Benedict XVI, "Biblical Interpretation in Crisis," 6; cf. 118, where he states, "We cannot seek refuge in an ecclesiastical positivism." Cf. *VD* §44, which cites the Pontifical Biblical Commission's *The Interpretation of the Bible in the Church*: "The basic problem with fundamentalist interpretation is that, refusing to take into account the historical character of biblical revelation, it makes itself incapable of accepting the full truth of the incarnation itself. As regards relationships with God, fundamentalism seeks to escape any closeness of the divine and the human ... for this reason, it tends to treat the

the Magisterium in matters of biblical interpretation ought not to be done in a positivistic manner, that is to say in such a way that one closes the door to modern findings without considering the possibility that scripture's mysteries might be more deeply penetrated with their help. Likewise, this means that Catholics should be cautious in theorizing about the nature of biblical inspiration and inerrancy if they are familiar with these dogmas yet lack a firm grasp of the Bible's content. This situation has unfortunately led many Catholics to write off modern biblical scholarship without ever having honestly considered its claims and evidence.

Benedict is a great model for believers as he displays great confidence in historical criticism's ability to refine the Christian faith. This is evident in the way he deals with what otherwise might appear to be attacks on the faith. For example, he treats at length the discrepancies between the various Gospels' accounts of Jesus's Last Supper. He speaks in a way that might catch some Christians off guard, as in the following two examples:

The problem of dating Jesus's Last Supper arises from the contradiction on this point between the Synoptic Gospels, on the one hand, and Saint John's Gospel, on the other.[68]

Despite all academic arguments [that attempt to vindicate the Synoptic Gospels' chronology of the Last Supper], it seems questionable whether the trial before Pilate and the crucifixion would have been permissible and possible on such an important Jewish feast day [as the Passover].[69]

Many Christians may feel uncomfortable that Benedict acknowledges a "contradiction" in the Gospels' dating or that he says it seems "questionable" that the Last Supper took place on the Passover, as the church has accepted for centuries. The pope, however, is not afraid of these problems and indeed goes on to employ the relevant conclusions of historical criticism in his quest to grasp the mystery of the Last Supper. It is clear that by calling certain things "questionable"

---

biblical text as if it had been dictated word for word by the Spirit. It fails to recognize that the word of God has been formulated in language and expression conditioned by various periods."

68. Benedict XVI, *Jesus of Nazareth: Holy Week*, 106.
69. Ibid., 107.

or "contradictions," he remains firmly convinced that these contractions are only apparent—that they can be explained if only we work
through them instead of ignoring them. For Benedict, a healthy
"critical" or Method C attitude sees advances in historical criticism
and the other sciences as the work of providence which ultimately
assists us in the effort to better elucidate the church's teachings.[70]

Spelling out the interplay between patristic-medieval and historical-critical exegesis, Benedict writes that there are two exegetical
"operations" pertinent to the examination of any given text of scripture from a Method C perspective:

> Certainly texts must first of all be traced back to their historical origins and
> interpreted in their proper historical contexts to the extent possible. But the
> second exegetical operation is that they must also be examined in the light
> of the total movement of history and in the light of history's central event,
> our Lord Jesus Christ. Only the combination of both these methods will
> yield understanding of the Bible.[71]

70. After discussing the various advances in the field of biblical studies over the
fifty years prior to writing his encyclical letter on promoting biblical studies, Pius XII
suggests that these be viewed by Christians in light of providence: "All these advantages
which, not without a special design of Divine Providence, our age has acquired, are as
it were an invitation and inducement to interpreters of the Sacred Literature to make
diligent use of this light, so abundantly given, to penetrate more deeply, explain more
clearly and expound more lucidly the Divine Oracles." Pius XII, Promotion of Biblical
Studies [Divino afflante Spiritu], 1943 (hereafter *DAS*), §12. In this way, notwithstanding the abuses of many who participate in (and of those who initiated the movement
of) modern critical scholarship, there may be a special providence to the advent of
this discipline, since it has brought about progress precisely because of its willingness
to question traditional assumptions. A Method C hermeneutic aims to appropriate
the tools and questions of modern scholarship while purifying these from any anti-
metaphysical or anti-Christian bias (Gregory Vall, conversation with author).

71. Benedict's words are cited in Stallsworth, "The Story of an Encounter," 107. He
repeats this theme in various works. For example, in his *Feast of Faith: Approaches to a
Theology of the Liturgy* (San Francisco: Ignatius Press, 1986), 58, he states, "The whole
Old Testament is a movement of transition to Christ." In *Eschatology: Death and Eternal Life*, translated by Michael Waldstein (Washington, D.C.: The Catholic University
of America Press, 1988), he likewise examines how this second exegetical operation
of examining events in light of Christ played out in the nascent church: "The risen
Lord became the canon within the canon, the criterion in whose light tradition must
be read. In the illumination which he brought, the internal struggles of the Old Testament were read as a single movement towards the One who suffered, was crucified, and
rose again." (113.) As regards the topic of tracing texts back to their historical origins,

The first operation, examining the historical origins and contexts of biblical texts, is the prerogative of Method B. In a Method C hermeneutic that incorporates the good of both Method A and Method B, this comes first in the order of execution and provides ground for the subsequent operation of Method A spiritual exegesis.[72] It is important to know as much as possible about the realities signified by the words of a text (the literal sense) if one is to correctly grasp any signification these realities might themselves have (their spiritual sense). Meanwhile, just as grace perfects man by building on nature, so Method A's spiritual encounter with scripture perfects Method B's exegetical operation by placing the texts of scripture within the total movement of history and understanding them in light of Christ as history's central event.[73] Benedict makes this same point in so many words:

Pius XII penned these words: "What is the literal sense of a passage is not always as obvious in the speeches and writings of the ancient authors of the East, as it is in the works of our own time. For what they wished to express is not to be determined by the rules of grammar and philology alone, nor solely by the context; the interpreter must, as it were, go back wholly in spirit to those remote centuries of the East and with the aid of history, archaeology, ethnology, and other sciences, accurately determine what modes of writing, so to speak, the authors of that ancient period would be likely to use, and in fact did use." DAS §35.

72. In reality, of course, the ordinary Christian's canonical reading of scripture is not necessarily concerned with historical-critical questions and therefore comes "before" Method B academic treatment. However, I am trying here to describe the order that is necessary in order to ensure a warranted rather than arbitrary canonical reading, and this is achieved with the help of Method B.

73. Constitutive of this "perfection" wrought by Method A exegesis is the fact that it does not negate, but rather preserves, the text's original meaning ascertained through Method B. For a Method C exegete, the spiritual sense apprehended through praying biblical texts over the centuries makes the most sense when it is seen in continuity with the historical events that gave rise to it. It is in this vein that John Paul II wrote, "The truth of the biblical texts, and of the Gospels in particular, is certainly not restricted to the narration of simple historical events or the statement of neutral facts, as historicist positivism would claim. Beyond simple historical occurrence, the truth of the events which these texts relate lies rather in the meaning they have *in* and *for* the history of salvation. This truth is elaborated fully in the church's constant reading of these texts over the centuries, a reading which preserves intact their original meaning." *On the Relationship between Faith and Reason [Fides et ratio]*, 1998, §94. For John Paul II as for Benedict XVI, the historical and the spiritual are both vital dimensions of the word of God, and one could not do away with one or the other without detriment to Christian theology.

The inner nature of the [historical-critical] method points beyond itself and contains within itself an openness to complementary methods. In these words from the past, we can discern the question concerning their meaning for today; a voice greater than man's echoes in Scripture's human words; the individual writings [Schriften] of the Bible point somehow to the living process that shapes the one Scripture [Schrift].[74]

Method B exegesis may therefore come first in order of execution, but it is not first in an absolute sense. What is first absolutely is something the historical-critical method can only examine on a material level and thus point toward—the reality of scripture as God's word, and the end of scripture which is to encounter God teaching through his word (both of which are principles of Method A).[75] In other words, Method A gives the exegete the real reason for his investigation because it gives him God's word, whereas Method B by itself does not formally study scripture as God's word; it examines only its material components and therefore "does not transmit the Bible to today, into my present-day life."[76] Method B's investigation of the human dimension of scripture must therefore be conducted with the view of showing the inherent openness of scripture's words to a reality which transcends them and which they serve to make present. Its operation should serve the reader by making it easier for him to achieve what Method A seeks: an encounter with Christ, who is not a mere figure of the past but is present teaching the reader of scripture today.

Benedict has described this interplay between the operations of Method A and Method B in various other ways throughout his corpus of work. He often uses different terms to describe the two exegetical methods from different angles. He may speak of "Method

74. Benedict XVI, *Jesus of Nazareth*, xviii.

75. As Benedict will write with regard to his own historical-critical work in *Jesus of Nazareth*, "This book presupposes historical-critical exegesis and makes use of its findings, but it seeks to transcend this method and to arrive at a genuinely theological interpretation of the scriptural texts." *Jesus of Nazareth: Holy Week*, 295. For Benedict, historical criticism is not an end in itself but rather an aid to our encounter with Christ through "a genuinely theological interpretation of the scriptural texts."

76. Benedict XVI, *Truth and Tolerance: Christian Belief and World Religions*, translated by Henry Taylor (San Francisco: Ignatius Press, 2004), 133.

A" versus "Method B" at one moment and "historical hermeneutic" versus "faith hermeneutic" in another; he has also referred to "scholarly" and "scientific" exegesis in contradistinction to *lectio divina.* In an *Angelus* address delivered during the 2008 bishops' synod on God's word, he taught Christians how to encounter Christ in scripture in the following manner: "Scientific exegesis and *lectio divina* are therefore both necessary and complementary in order to seek, through the literal meaning, the spiritual meaning that God wants to communicate to us today."[77] This quote concisely encapsulates the goal of the pope's twofold exegetical approach. "Scientific exegesis" (Method B) ascertains the literal meaning of scripture, but it is when the Christian turns to the prayer of *lectio divina* (a feature of Method A's approach) that he discovers the biblical text has a spiritual meaning relevant to his own life. According to Benedict, this spiritual sense is arrived at "through" the literal.[78] In other words, Method A does not negate Method B but rather presupposes and builds upon it.

The upshot of Benedict's work is that, when employing the tools of Method B, the Method C exegete will be such only to the extent that his Method B operation (investigating the origins and the literal sense of scripture) remains faithful to the principles of Method A exegesis (e.g., sacred tradition, the Magisterium, inspiration, inerrancy, the spiritual sense, etc.).[79] In other words, even before he

77. Benedict XVI, *Angelus.* October 26, 2008.

78. It is significant that Benedict dedicated a section of his recent *Verbum Domini* not only to the theory behind *lectio divina* but also to teaching Christians how to practice it today. As is frequently the case, here we have Benedict not only laying out theoretical principles for Christians but also offering guidance for instantiating them in real life. Cf. *VD* §§86–87.

79. This schema seems to be consistent with the type of integration to which Francis Martin has recently alluded as being a necessary part of implementing the teachings of *Dei Verbum.* See his "Revelation and Its Transmission," in *Vatican II: Renewal within Tradition,* edited by Matthew W. Lamb and Matthew Levering (New York: Oxford University Press, 2008). Martin notes that although recent developments in the historical sciences have challenged the traditional Christian model for approaching scripture, little progress has been made since the council in terms of elucidating the truth of scripture's inspiration and dual authorship. He goes on to propose: "The solution lies in a retrieval of the ancient principles and their application to our understanding of the whole process of text production and text preparation as we now understand it. It

attempts to carry out Method A's operation of spiritual exegesis, the Method C exegete already begins his Method B operation in accordance with the rule of faith adhered to by Method A.

In this way, it really is possible for the Method C exegete to incorporate Method B into his work: he is able to set aside the accidental features or assumptions of particular exegetical "traditions" without abandoning the principles of sacred tradition as a source of revelation. For Pope Benedict, faith does not require that Christians espouse patristic-medieval assumptions to the extent of believing that Moses authored the entire Pentateuch, that the man Job was a historical person, that the book of Isaiah was the work of a single author, or that the Gospel of Matthew was the first of all the Gospels to be composed.[80] The Method C exegete can remain completely committed to the faith while asking questions and accepting answers never entertained by exegetes of previous ages, and he

---

will also involve a profound reassessment of our modern and postmodern understanding of cognition, history, and language." (67.) Without naming them as I do, in this brief statement Martin shows the importance of a "retrieval of the ancient principles" (provided by Method A) as well as "their application to our understanding of the whole process of text production and text preparation as we now understand it" (the work of Method B). Also in this volume of collected essays on the documents of Vatican II, *Vatican II: Renewal within Tradition*, Denis Farkasfalvy, OCist, presents a detailed study of *Dei Verbum* along with many insightful suggestions for projects that need to be undertaken in order to build upon the theology presented therein. Cf. "Inspiration and Interpretation," in ibid., 77–100.

80. Indeed, in this respect Pope Benedict's work often appears to endorse a divergent view not only from the fathers but also from the Pontifical Biblical Commission's decrees in the early twentieth century, for example those which required Catholics to hold Matthean priority and Mosaic authorship of the Pentateuch. For just a few indications of this, see his *Eschatology*, 37, 86; *God and the World*, 228–30; *Daughter Zion: Meditations on the Church's Marian Belief* (San Francisco: Ignatius Press, 1983), 44–54; *In the Beginning: A Catholic Understanding of the Story of Creation and the Fall*, translated by Boniface Ramsey (Grand Rapids, Mich.: Eerdmans, 1995), 10–11; *Jesus of Nazareth: Holy Week*, 106, 179; "Exegesis and the Magisterium of the Church," in *Opening Up the Scriptures: Joseph Ratzinger and the Foundations of Biblical Interpretation*, edited by José Granados, Carlos Granados, and Luis Sánchez-Navarro (Grand Rapids, Mich.: Eerdmans, 2008), 126–34; *Theological Highlights of Vatican II* (New York: Paulist Press, 1966), 11–21, 116; "On the Instruction Concerning the Ecclesial Vocation of the Theologian," in *The Nature and Mission of Theology: Approaches to Understanding Its Role in Light of the Present Controversy*, translated by Adrian Walker (San Franciso: Ignatius Press, 1995), 106.

can do this because his work stands in accord with the principles of the Christian faith—not the least of which is the belief that greater knowledge of the historical dimension of scripture leads to greater knowledge of Christ.

It is appropriate to conclude this chapter with some of Benedict's most recent comments in *Light of the World*. In this book-length interview, he once again reiterates the importance of historical-critical exegesis and the need to establish a synthesis between critical and faith-based approaches to scripture. Writing over twenty years after the Erasmus lecture in which he introduced his Method C proposal, the pope provides the following summary of its main principles:

The application of the historical method to the Bible as a historical text was a path that had to be taken. If we believe that Christ is real history, and not myth, then the testimony concerning him has to be historically accessible as well. In this sense, the historical method has also given us many gifts. It has brought us back closer to the text and its originality, it has shown us more precisely how it grew, and much more besides. The historical-critical method will always remain one dimension of interpretation. Vatican II made this clear. On the one hand, it presents the essential elements of the historical method as a necessary part of access to the Bible. At the same time, though, it adds that the Bible has to be read in the same Spirit in which it was written. It has to be read in its wholeness, in its unity. And that can be done only when we approach it as a book of the People of God progressively advancing toward Christ. What is needed is not simply a break with the historical method, but a self-critique of the historical method; a self-critique of historical reason that takes cognizance of its limits and recognizes the compatibility of a type of knowledge that derives from faith; *in short, we need a synthesis between an exegesis that operates with historical reason and an exegesis that is guided by faith* We have to bring the two things into a proper relationship to each other. That is also a requirement of the basic relationship between faith and reason.[81]

81. Benedict XVI, *Light of the World: The Pope, the Church, and the Signs of the Times* (San Francisco: Ignatius Press, 2011), 171–72 (emphasis added). See also Benedict's recent comments in *VD* §34: "The Synod Fathers rightly stated that the positive fruit yielded by the use of modern historical-critical research is undeniable. While today's academic exegesis, including that of Catholic scholars, is highly competent in the field of historical-critical methodology and its latest developments, it must be said that comparable attention needs to be paid to the theological dimension of the biblical texts, so that they can be more deeply understood in accordance with the three elements indicated by the Dogmatic Constitution *Dei Verbum*."

It is once again clear that for Benedict the historical-critical method plays a key role in exegesis. At the same time, he quotes Vatican II in explaining that scripture "has to be read in its wholeness, in its unity." The only way to achieve this is to read it as the story of "the People of God progressively advancing toward Christ." It would be difficult to find a better endorsement of the hermeneutic of the divine pedagogy than what Benedict has here. He likewise reiterates the call for a "synthesis between an exegesis that operates with historical reason and an exegesis that is guided by faith." For Benedict, the truth and unity of scripture cannot be reconciled in the face of modern challenges unless exegetes have recourse to the tools of both Method A and Method B exegesis and seek to illumine the divine pedagogy at work within scripture. If therefore one grapples with the greatest of problems within scripture in light of Benedict's plan for exegesis, it will lead Christians to a deeper encounter with the mystery of Christ in scripture as well as a better understanding of the nature of scripture itself.

CHAPTER 3

THE PROBLEM OF DEVELOPMENT

Having surveyed problematic themes within scripture in chapter 1 and elucidated Benedict's Method C exegesis proposal in chapter 2, we are now in a position to explore more precisely how a Method C approach to scripture might operate. In the next two chapters, we will demonstrate that the theology of St. Thomas Aquinas provides the proper basis on which to carry out Benedict's exegetical proposal.

The present chapter elucidates Aquinas's "theology of the history of revelation," in which he is able to show the unity of scripture (emphasized by Method A exegesis) while acknowledging the significant developments observable within its Old and New Testaments (emphasized by Method B exegesis). We will use Aquinas's thought in the effort to account for the first major difficulty raised by the historical-critical observations of the first chapter: the fact that not all portions of scripture explicitly teach the fullness of revealed truth Christians expect to find in the Bible. In what follows, we will see that, according to St. Thomas, the *substance* of the Judeo-Christian faith did not change throughout the course of salvation history even though there was a development or increase in the *number* of truths believed by the faithful as God gradually taught them about himself. Aquinas's framework illumines the phenomenon of development within scripture, thus making it possible to defend the inerrancy of early biblical texts which fail to explicitly display a clear conception of the divine oneness (Theme 1), an understanding of evil consonant with Christian doctrine (Theme 2), or hope for the resurrection of the dead (Theme 3). Later in the book we will return to these problematic biblical themes and apply Aquinas's thought to them, but in this chapter our task is simply to elucidate his theological principles.

THE "SUBSTANCE" OF FAITH

"Faith is the 'substance' of things hoped for; the proof of things not seen." Such is the translation of Hebrews 11:1 offered by Benedict XVI in his second encyclical, *Spe salvi*.[1] Benedict's translation squares precisely with the Latin translation of this text produced at the time of the early church and taken up by St. Thomas Aquinas. The term "substance" used above is a translation of the Latin *substantia* and the original Greek *hypostasis* (ὑπόστασις). Benedict indicates that this word choice is important because it emphasizes something about the nature of the faith that other translations fail to convey. Unlike translations which translate Heb 11:1 so as to define faith as the mere "assurance" of things hoped for (as the RSV has it) or a "standing firm" (*feststehen*) in what one hopes, *substantia* or "substance" implies that the Christian faith is an organism with a unique and enduring identity.[2] In his *Commentary on the Epistle to the Hebrews*, St. Thomas deals with precisely this issue of what it means for faith to be the "substance" of things for which Christians hope. His considerations in this commentary will be foundational for our own work of articulating how the "substance" of our faith remained one and the same throughout the course of divine revelation and throughout the scriptures.

The importance of correctly translating the term *hypostasis* as substance becomes apparent when we read St. Thomas's treatments of the virtue of faith that show up throughout his corpus, including

---

1. Benedict XVI, *Saved in Hope* [*Spe salvi*], 2007, §7.
2. "Now faith is the assurance of things hoped for, the conviction of things not seen" (RSV). The other rendition of the term *hypostasis* as "standing firm" in one's faith appears in the Einheitsübersetzung, the ecumenical translation of the Bible approved by the German Catholic bishops.

his *Commentary on the Epistle to the Hebrews* as well as the questions on prophecy and faith in *De veritate* and the *Summa Theologiae*. It is precisely the reality that our faith has a "substance" that allows Aquinas to develop his theology of the history of revelation, which is able to vindicate the unity of divine revelation (a key component of Method A exegesis) while recognizing its development over the course of time (acknowledged above all by Method B exegesis).[3] Specifically, Aquinas is able to argue that the "substance of the articles of faith," that is to say the essence of divinely revealed truth, did not change over time even though the people of Israel affirmed an increasing "number of the articles of faith" throughout salvation history. He writes:

As regards the substance of the articles of faith (*substantia articulorum fidei*), they have not received any increase as time went on: since whatever those who lived later have believed, was contained, albeit implicitly, in the faith of those Fathers who preceded them. But there was an increase in the number of articles (*numerus articulorum*) believed explicitly, since to those who lived in later times some were known explicitly which were not known explicitly by those who lived before them.[4]

This distinction made by St. Thomas will help us to see that the faithful of ancient Israel—and in turn their sacred writings—in some way possessed the Christian faith and affirmed its beliefs. This point is pivotal for the present study because righteous men who never met Christ in the flesh cooperated with God in authoring the Old Testa-

---

3. The term "theology of the history of divine revelation" seems most fitting here as we attempt to synthesize various writings of St. Thomas and show that he really does have a comprehensive theological account of the unity and development of divine revelation as attested by Sacred Scripture. This term was not used by St. Thomas himself, but my use of it was inspired by similar expressions of two great Thomistic theologians. Jean-Pierre Torrell explained that "Thomas had a clear consciousness of the temporal condition of faith and of prophecy—or in other words the history of revelation (*histoire de la revelation*) and of the Church." "Saint Thomas et l'histoire," 359 (my translation). Charles Journet also spoke of a "théologie de l'histoire du salut" (theology of salvation history). See his *L'Église du Verbe incarné*, Vol. 3: *Essai de théologie de l'histoire du salut* (Paris: Desclée De Brouwer, 1969). The reason I do not employ Journet's term is because I am focusing on Aquinas's theology of history from the standpoint of divine revelation rather than the salvation of those who receive salvation through it. I might just as easily have also called it "theology of revelation history."

4. Thomas Aquinas, *ST*, II-II, q.1, a.7.

ment. One can say that the Old Testament, and indeed the whole of scripture, conveys revealed truth precisely because its authors possessed the substance of the Christian faith—even if it was in an inchoate manner that fell short of belief in the Trinity, hope for the Resurrection, or a clear articulation of the nature of good and evil.

Before delving deeper into St. Thomas's treatment of faith, it is important to review some basic definitions of terms operative in his theology of the history of revelation. In particular, we must identify the meaning of the expressions "substance of the articles of faith" and "number of the articles of faith" introduced above, as well as the meaning of the term "article of faith" which concerns them both. According to Aquinas, the deposit of faith is made up of "articles" or subject matters.[5] These articles act like joints that connect the truths of the faith to one another.[6] Each one of them designates a fundamental revealed truth, from the Trinity to the Incarnation of Christ to the resurrection of the dead—in short all the truths we profess in the creed. These are the principles upon which the entirety of Christian theology rests.

---

5. Thomas Aquinas, *De veritate*, q.14, a.2. Translations from *De veritate* in the rest of this chapter are mine.

6. Thomas Aquinas, *ST*, II-II, q.1, a.6. The Latin word for joint is *articulus*, and Aquinas notes that in Greek it is *arthron* (from which we get words such as arthritis). The deposit of faith is also a unified body of knowledge to which a man can assent as a whole, according to its substance, as it were. John Henry Newman in his *An Essay in Aid of a Grammar of Assent* (Notre Dame, Ind.: University of Notre Dame Press, 1989), gives an apt description of this act of assent: "He who believes in the *depositum* of Revelation, believes in all the doctrines of the *depositum* ... whether he knows little or much, he has the intention of believing all that there is to believe whenever and as soon as it is brought home to him, if he believes in Revelation at all. All that he knows now as revealed, and all that he shall know, and all that there is to know, he embraces it all in his intention by one act of faith." (130.) Aquinas himself addresses this point in dealing with the problem of those who do not have explicit faith in Christ. These individuals may have implicit faith in him because they have assented to the substance of the faith as a whole and would be ready to assent to more articles if they become known to them: "As regards the primary points or articles of faith, man is bound to believe them, just as he is bound to have faith; but as to other points of faith, man is not bound to believe them explicitly, but only implicitly, or to be ready to believe them, in so far as he is prepared to believe whatever is contained in the Divine Scriptures. Then alone is he bound to believe such things explicitly, when it is clear to him that they are contained in the doctrine of faith." Thomas Aquinas, *ST*, II-II, q.2, a.5.

Having defined what Aquinas means by an article of faith, now
it is important to explain the meaning of the other expressions introduced above. To say that the number of the articles of faith increased is another way of stating Method B's observation that divine revelation developed over time, that the faithful of later stages
within the history of revelation were privileged to affirm a greater
number of beliefs or articles than the faithful of previous ages. To
say the substance of the articles of faith remained the same, meanwhile, is to affirm with Method A that the essential content of the
faith did not suffer change on account of its development over time.
The substance of the articles of faith denotes the essential content
of what God has revealed about himself and about his plan for the
redemption of mankind. For St. Thomas, any person who has the
virtue of faith possesses its entire substance even if he is not privy to
explicit knowledge of how the substance has grown to maturity in
history and cannot affirm all the articles of the creed.

An illustration will serve to elucidate the importance of this
distinction between the substance of the articles of faith and the
number of the articles of faith. Say a certain man who does not consciously accept Christ makes an act of faith in God and his providence, that God has ordered him to the end of beatitude and that he
will lead him there no matter what adversity afflicts him. Another
man similarly believes in God and his providence, but because of
God's teaching he is also privy to specific details regarding how
God's promise has been providentially fulfilled: that Jesus Christ
became man, that he died and rose to redeem man, and that the
man who believes in him will also rise from the dead on the last
day. Recalling that for St. Thomas the substance of the articles of
faith did not suffer an essential change even though the number of
the articles of faith increased over time, the first man in the example (who held a more general belief in divine providence and was
not aware of the truth of the Resurrection) possessed substantially
the same faith as the man who was privy to explicit knowledge of
Christ's death and Resurrection, which is the ultimate answer of divine providence to the problem of affliction and death. Although
the second man explicitly assented to more parts or articles of faith,

the first man also possessed the entire substance of the Christian faith because he demonstrated belief in God and his providence and would have readily assented to more articles of faith if only they had been revealed to him.

THE "ROSEBUD" OR "EMBRYO" OF FAITH

By itself what was said above does not suffice to explain precisely *how* a rudimentary faith can be substantially the same as explicit Christian faith. The answer lies in St. Thomas's exegesis of Heb 11:6. The verse reads: "Whoever would draw near to God must believe that he exists and that he rewards those who seek him." For St. Thomas, this verse already contains the whole "substance of the faith" that is mentioned in Heb 11:1:

All the articles are contained implicitly in certain primary matters of faith, [namely] God's existence and His providence over the salvation of man, according to Hebrews 11: "He that cometh to God, must believe that He is, and is a rewarder to them that seek Him." For the existence of God includes all that we believe to exist in God eternally, and in these our happiness consists; while belief in His providence includes all those things which God dispenses in time, for man's salvation, and which are the way to that happiness: and in this way, again, some of those articles which follow from these are contained in others: thus faith in the Redemption of mankind includes belief in the Incarnation of Christ, His Passion and so forth.[7]

For St. Thomas, all that is essential to the Christian faith (the Resurrection, the triune nature of God, the moral law, etc.) is rooted in the two primary "matters" (*credibilia*) of faith mentioned Heb 11:6, namely, God's existence and his providence. In his insightful reflection on this passage from St. Thomas, Charles Journet explains that the Trinity is already involved in the more fundamental revelation of God's existence and is contained therein as a rose in its bud. Like a rose that has yet to bloom, the doctrine of the Trinity is present within the doctrine of God's existence, but it is only over time that God makes it fully available to man. In the same way, even though people who lived before Christ could not see it, the revelation that

7. Ibid., II-II, q.1, a.7.

God cared for the salvation of men already implicitly involved the promise of his redemptive Incarnation and all the articles of faith bound up with it, including the resurrection of the body.[8] As Journet observes, these latter truths can only be known by an act of divine revelation, and yet they flower from the primary matters of faith which can be assented to on the basis of reason alone.

Journet employs another helpful analogy to convey how the various articles of faith developed out of the two primary matters or *credibilia* of God's existence and providence: "Christianity existed in embryo form before Christ.... Those who were saved before Christ were saved through him; they constituted, by anticipation, his Mystical Body, his Church. For, even then, grace was Christian."[9] Journet thus likens affirmation of the two *credibilia* to an embryo that contains the whole substance of Christian faith in a manner that has yet to fully develop. Like a rosebud, an embryo contains the whole substance of an entity that is growing and developing, but its mature state is something that humans can only see over the course of time. Journet is not the only theologian to employ this analogy in reference to the substance of the faith and its various modes of presence in believers. In *Spe Salvi* Benedict XVI offers a strikingly similar example to illustrate this principle in the life of Christians today. He likens the faith of Christians to an embryo that contains the whole substance of the faith in a manner that will be fully developed only in Heaven. He writes, "Through faith, in a tentative way, or as we might say 'in embryo'—and thus according to the 'substance'—there are already present in us the things that are hoped for: the whole,

8. Charles Journet, *What Is Dogma?* translated by Mark Pontifex, OSB (New York: Hawthorn Books, 1964), 38–39.

9. Charles Journet, *The Meaning of Grace*, translated by Geoffrey Chapman, Ltd. (New York: P. J. Kenedy and Sons, 1960), 38–39. Ultimately, only a robust understanding of time and eternity can adequately account for how Christ's grace reached back into the time before his coming. For a lucid discussion of time and eternity, see Matthew Lamb, *Eternity, Time, and the Life of Wisdom* (Naples, Fla.: Sapientia Press of Ave Maria University, 2007). Lamb states, "All of creation, including the totality of concrete durations with all of the events occurring in them, is present in the Divine Eternal Presence." (21–22.) In this way, the benefits of Christ's Passion can touch any individual at any time in human history, because the historical moment of Christ's Passion is eternally present in God and in God all human beings are present to it.

true life."[10] In other words, according to Benedict, Christians now enjoy the fullness of truth revealed by God, and yet the reality to which we assent will be fully manifest only in the beatific vision after the "embryo" of our faith has grown to maturity. Although Benedict's analogy is made in order to describe the passage from the state of Christian belief to the state of glory, and Journet's is made describing the passage from the state of the Old Law to the New Law, both illustrate the presence of development or flowering within the substance of the faith. Those who have faith but have not explicitly accepted Christ are fellow travelers with Christians. Christians are blessed to have received additional divine revelation. We possess substantially the same faith right now, and God willing we will possess substantially the same faith on the other side of the grave when that faith will at last fully bloom.

Notwithstanding the precision and beauty of the above accounts, it is not as if these men were the first to come up with analogies to illustrate the development of faith in terms of substance. Aquinas himself provides an analogy to illustrate the journey Christians make when rising from faith in God in this life to vision of him in Heaven.. This time belief in the primary matters of the faith is likened to grasping the principles of geometry and drawing conclusions based on them:

Whoever has the principles of a science, say geometry, has its substance. And if geometry were the essence of beatitude, whoever possessed the principles of geometry would, in some way, have the substance of beatitude. But our faith is such that we believe the blessed will see and enjoy God. Therefore, if we will to attain this, it is necessary that we believe the principles of that knowledge. And these [principles] are the articles of faith, which contain the entire summary of this knowledge.... In these words is shown the order of the act of faith to its end, for faith is ordered to things to be hoped for, as a beginning in which the whole is, as it were, contained essentially as conclusions are in principles.[11]

10. Benedict XVI, *Saved in Hope* [*Spe salvi*], 2007, §7.
11. Thomas Aquinas, *Super Epistolam B. Pauli ad Hebraeos lectura*, caput 11, lectio 1. Translations in this chapter from Aquinas's commentary are mine.

In conjunction with the images provided by Journet and Benedict, Aquinas helps clarify that an individual Christian, by virtue of his belief in the articles (here called "principles") of faith, already possesses the whole "substance" he hopes to see and enjoy in heaven. In order to possess the substance of the faith, the individual does not have to explicitly affirm every "conclusion," but only the "principles" of faith. Given Aquinas's understanding that believers of all times and places possess substantially the same faith, it stands to reason that believers of pre-Christian times who demonstrated sincere belief in the two *credibilia* of Heb 11:6 but were unaware of other Christian doctrines had faith in these truths as latent "conclusions" to be drawn from the "principles" of their faith.

ST. THOMAS ON THE DIVINE PEDAGOGY

The hermeneutic of divine pedagogy beautifully illumines this dynamic whereby "primary matters" of the faith develop and grow numerically throughout the course of revelation without changing the substance of the faith. To reiterate what was introduced in chapter 1, the divine pedagogy refers to God the Father's plan whereby he gradually prepared his chosen people to welcome the revelation that culminated in the coming of Jesus Christ. Without using this precise expression, St. Thomas has his own account of the divine pedagogy, and it shows up in many places throughout his corpus. For St. Thomas as for the fathers from whom he inherited this image, God is the teacher or master who little by little delivered to his disciple Israel the knowledge of the faith and the art of upright living.[12] In *De veritate*, St. Thomas develops his divine pedagogy hermeneu-

---

12. Among the various fathers who employed the image of a divine pedagogy, of particular note is Clement of Alexandria's *Paedagogus*, which provides a thorough treatment of how Christ teaches mankind in the moral life. Clement ends Book III of this work with an indication that he will go on to compose a (now non-extant) work called the *Didaskalos*. Another relevant work is Athanasius's *On the Incarnation of the Word* (Crestwood, N.Y.: St. Vladimir's Seminary Press, 2000), in which God is described as a good teacher who condescends to mankind and instructs them through simple means adequate to our bodily nature. (42–43.) See also Augustine's *On the Teacher* and *On Christian Doctrine*. Aquinas himself treats of the teacher in *De veritate*, q.11.

tic by comparing the education of the whole human race in divine things to the education of an individual. He states, "Just as there is a progress in the faith of an individual man over the course of time, so there is a progress in faith for the whole human race. This is why Gregory says that divine knowledge has increasingly grown over the course of time."[13] In the same way that an individual believer slowly appropriates the truths of the faith into his life, so, too, the people of God gradually appropriated divine knowledge over the course of time in which God taught them through revelation.

As Aquinas goes on to explain, God had to hand on the faith to men in piecemeal form, not because he is an inept teacher, but because this is the only way men can digest its content: "Man acquires a share of this learning, not indeed all at once, but little by little, according to the mode of his nature."[14] Israel, God's pupil, could not perfectly receive the divine teaching precisely because she received this teaching according to the mode of our weak human nature. It is for this reason that it took time for God's children to come to explicit knowledge of the full number of the articles of faith, even though they possessed the substance of the faith throughout the entire duration of the divine pedagogy. A perfect pedagogue who has perfect knowledge of himself and his salvific plan, God did not reveal to Israel more than she could handle at any given moment in history but rather proposed truths in such a way that his pupil would struggle with and internalize them in due time.

At the very foundation of Aquinas's theology lies his astute observation that scripture itself likens the state of Israel in the Old Testament to spiritual childhood before God the Father. At every stage of the divine pedagogy, God gave his children knowledge perfectly adapted to their need and their ability to receive it. In the *Summa* St. Thomas offers a concise yet robust account of this divine pedagogy:

The master, who has perfect knowledge of the art, does not deliver it all at once to his disciple from the very outset, for he would not be able to take it all in, but he condescends to the disciple's capacity and instructs him little

13. Thomas Aquinas, *De veritate*, q.14, a.11.
14. Thomas Aquinas, *ST*, II-II, q.2, a.3.

by little. It is in this way that men made progress in the knowledge of faith as time went on. Hence the Apostle (Galatians 3:24) compares the state of the Old Testament to childhood.[15]

For St. Thomas as for St. Paul whose theology he invokes, God's firstborn son Israel gradually made progress in knowledge of him in accordance with the divine teacher's most wise pedagogy. God condescended and taught man in accordance with the way he learns best, which is "little by little." In this way, as time went on and revelation progressed, the people's faith in God was able to grow ever more explicit as truths previously unfathomable to the unaided human intellect became accessible through God's teaching. Ultimately, through the life and ministry of Jesus Christ, man attained the perfection of knowledge with the explicit revelation of, among other things, the resurrection of the body, the triune nature of God, and a robust account of the nature of good and evil.

Aquinas explores this divine teaching method elsewhere in commenting on the same text just cited from St. Paul. He argues that God's teaching was perfectly suited to the needs and ability of the people of God at every stage of divine revelation, despite the fact that God did not attempt to convey the fullness of truth to them when he theoretically could have done so. In the words of St. Thomas:

Nothing prevents a thing being not perfect simply, and yet perfect in respect of time: thus a boy is said to be perfect, not simply, but with regard to the condition of time. So, too, precepts that are given to children are perfect in comparison with the condition of those to whom they are given, although they are not perfect simply. Hence the Apostle says (Gal. 3:24): "The Law was our pedagogue in Christ."[16]

Here the word "pedagogue" explicitly appears in personification of the law. God the divine pedagogue made instruments like the law "pedagogues" in their own right. For St. Thomas, this does not mean God was unable or unwilling to teach Israel himself; rather, it was precisely because of his knowledge of frail human nature that he used tangible and even transitory means like the law. Thus he is able to say that "nothing prevents a thing being not perfect simply,

15. Ibid., II-II, q.1, a.7 ad 2.
16. Ibid., I-II, q.98, a.2 ad 1.

and yet perfect in respect of time." In other words, the fact that God had to teach Israel little by little and use means like the law does not mean that it was the best teaching method in all conceivable circumstances, but given man's frail intellect and hard heart it was "perfect in respect of time," meaning that God adapted his teaching to the needs of his disciple Israel at every moment throughout the course of divine revelation.[17]

THE THREE AGES OF MAN

Aquinas is not content simply to state that the substance of the faith developed over time as God gradually led his children to more explicit knowledge of its various articles; he actually provides a working schema that shows how the divine pedagogy unfolded and the number of the articles of faith increased throughout salvation history. Not surprisingly, he achieves this once again in the context of a discussion of Heb 11:

Now our faith consists chiefly in two things: first, in the true knowledge of God, according to Hebrews 11:6, "He that cometh to God must believe that He is"; secondly, in the mystery of Christ's incarnation, according to John 14:1, "You believe in God, believe also in Me." Accordingly, if we speak of prophecy as directed to the Godhead as its end, it progressed according to three divisions of time, namely before the Law, under the Law, and under grace. For before the Law, Abraham and the other patriarchs were

17. In his work *La rivelazione e l'ispirazione della Sacra Scrittura* (Rome, Italy: Edizioni ADP, 1998), Giovanni Blandino, SJ, offers an illuminating analogy for how God accommodated himself to Israel's weaknesses as he gradually instructed the people in the realities of God's nature, the afterlife, and moral law. Like a missionary teaching a catechumen, God began with a pagan people who knew little about the divine nature or human destiny: "God worked through a gradual revelation: teaching Israel to believe in one God, then revealing man's destiny, the moral law, etc. He used the same method a missionary does: beginning by teaching some simple and important truths, then others. The catechumen at first has in mind a mix of exact and inexact ideas. Little by little as the teaching progresses, the exact ideas increase more and more, while inexact ideas gradually get eliminated." (9, my translation.) When speaking of the divine pedagogy in terms of Blandino's analogy, however, it is crucial to emphasize the inspired nature of scripture so as to clarify that scripture contains no formal assertions of error despite the fact that it witnesses to growth in Israel's knowledge and a gradual transformation of "inexact ideas."

prophetically taught things pertinent to faith in the Godhead. Hence they are called prophets.... Under the Law prophetic revelation of things pertinent to faith in the Godhead was made in a yet more excellent way than hitherto, because then not only certain special persons or families but the whole people had to be instructed in these matters ... because previously the patriarchs had been taught to believe in a general way in God, one and Almighty, while Moses was more fully instructed in the simplicity of the Divine essence, when it was said to him, "I am Who am." ... Afterwards in the time of grace the mystery of the Trinity was revealed by the Son of God Himself.[18]

According to St. Thomas, history can be divided into three principal epochs: the time before the law, the time under the law, and time under grace. These epochs are marked precisely according to the progress in knowledge of God made by mankind as a result of the divine pedagogy. Those before the law such as Abraham were prophetically taught things pertaining to God's nature. Under the law, however, God taught these things in a more excellent way, since the whole people was then able to receive them. Moreover, under the law knowledge of the Godhead was more explicit in that God revealed to Moses his name, "I am Who am." Finally, St. Thomas indicates that in the time of grace "the mystery of the Trinity was revealed by the Son of God Himself" thus bringing to culmination the history of divine revelation.

For this reason, St. Thomas can say that those who lived right before the coming of Christ received the mysteries of salvation "more fully" than did those who lived in previous epochs. Specifically, according to Aquinas, those who lived closer to the time of Christ were more fully instructed about his Incarnation: "As to the faith in Christ's Incarnation, it is evident that the nearer men were to Christ, whether before or after Him, the more fully, for the most part, were they instructed on this point, and after Him more fully

18. Thomas Aquinas, *ST*, II-II, q.174, a.6. As Jean-Pierre Torrell observes, Aquinas was well aware of previous schematizations of history besides this three-tiered one he received from Dionysius. He prefers this one, however, because it is based more directly upon scripture's presentation of salvation history. See Jean-Pierre Torrell, "Saint Thomas et l'histoire: état de la question et pistes de recherches," *Revue Thomiste* 105 (2005): 363–67.

than before."[19] Aquinas elsewhere buttresses this argument by calling upon the authority of St. Gregory: "Gregory says that 'the knowledge of the holy fathers increased as time went on ... and the nearer they were to Our Savior's coming, the more fully did they receive the mysteries of salvation.'"[20] The reason why men of later times needed to have more explicit knowledge of the mysteries of salvation, says St. Thomas, was so that they would be prepared to welcome Christ's coming. For if the people did not possess a deep need and hope for redemption but only thought of divine providence in a general way, none of them would have accepted the man who claimed to be their redeemer. They therefore not only needed the more general revelation of God's nature and providence that came before the law, they also needed the law and the prophets to teach them more specifically who God is and what he promised to accomplish for mankind through the coming of the Messiah.[21]

In his affirmation that the people of Israel received revelation from God in different degrees throughout history, St. Thomas went so far as to affirm that Moses saw the Lord face to face and therefore had full knowledge of the nature of God.[22] He likewise wrote that

19. Ibid., II-II, q.174, a.6.

20. Ibid., II-II, q.1, a.7. To illustrate how deeply rooted this thought is in Aquinas's thought, one may refer to his question on angelic knowledge where he makes a similar point: "Among the prophets also, the later ones knew what the former did not know." Ibid., I, q.57, a.5 ad 3.

21. According to St. Thomas, preparation for the coming of Christ was not the only reason people of later times needed fuller knowledge of divine things. They needed this revealed knowledge because their natural knowledge had been clouded by sin: "For as time went on sin gained a greater hold on man, so much so that it clouded man's reason, the consequence being that the precepts of the natural law were insufficient to make man live aright, and it became necessary to have a written code of fixed laws, and together with these certain sacraments of faith. For it was necessary, as time went on, that the knowledge of faith should be more and more unfolded, since, as Gregory says (Hom. vi in Ezech.): 'With the advance of time there was an advance in the knowledge of Divine things.'" Ibid., III, q.61, a.3 ad 2.

22. See Thomas Aquinas, ST, II-II, q.2, a.7. Here St. Thomas speaks of "learned" men before the time of Christ who knew of his Incarnation, Passion, and Resurrection. To illustrate further, see De veritate q.12, a.14 and ST, II-II, q.174, a.4, in which St. Thomas states that "Moses was greater than the other prophets. First, as regards the intellectual vision, since he saw God's very essence, even as Paul in his rapture did, according to Augustine (Gen. ad lit. xii, 27)." In this statement, Aquinas takes the words

David was privy to an explicit knowledge of Christ's Incarnation.[23] In fact, according to St. Thomas, there were many in Israel both before the law and under the law who were privy to explicit knowledge of the mystery of Christ. Contrasting the knowledge mankind had of Christ before the Fall versus after the Fall, Aquinas writes:

> But after sin, man believed explicitly in Christ, not only as to the Incarnation, but also as to the Passion and Resurrection, whereby the human race is delivered from sin and death: for they would not, else, have foreshadowed Christ's Passion by certain sacrifices both before and after the Law, the meaning of which sacrifices was known by the learned explicitly, while the simple folk, under the veil of those sacrifices, believed them to be ordained by God in reference to Christ's coming, and thus their knowledge was covered with a veil, so to speak.[24]

It is interesting to note that in Aquinas's view there were men before the time of Christ's coming in the flesh who knew *explicitly* of him and who expressed this knowledge through their sacrifices. Although most men, the "simple folk," did not know of Christ precisely in this way, the fact remains that for St. Thomas many Israelites were granted explicit knowledge of him before he came in the flesh. Given this view, it is not at all surprising that Aquinas says that they possessed the entire substance of the Christian faith.

Aquinas's stance vis-à-vis the faith of Israelites before and under the law becomes even less surprising when we examine what he

---

of Exodus quite literally and seems to imply that Moses had just as clear a vision of the Godhead as St. Paul in the New Testament era did. He even goes so far as to affirm that Moses's gift of prophecy was greater than that of John the Baptist: "And yet, even if none was greater than John the Baptist, it does not follow that none was greater than he as to his grade of prophecy, for since prophecy is not a gift of sanctifying grace, one who is less in merit can be greater in prophecy." Ibid., q.12, a.14 ad 5.

23. In *De veritate*, q.12, a.14 ad 1, St. Thomas notes that although Moses is the greatest of the prophets, those who came later (in particular, David) actually knew certain other mysteries more fully than Moses: "Yet the vision of Moses was more excellent as regards the knowledge of the Godhead; while David more fully knew and expressed the mysteries of Christ's incarnation." In *De veritate*, q.12, a.14 ad 1, Aquinas speaks in similar terms, all while still affirming the primacy of Moses as prophet: "Some later [prophets] received more explicit revelation about [the Incarnation] than Moses did, but they did not receive more explicit knowledge of the divinity, concerning which Moses was most fully taught."

24. Thomas Aquinas, *ST*, II-II, q.1, a.7.

writes concerning the gentiles who lived in those same epochs. According to St. Thomas, there were righteous gentiles before the advent of Christ who knew him and attained salvation through true, though *implicit*, belief. He states:

If, however, some were saved without receiving any revelation, they were not saved without faith in a Mediator, for, though they did not believe in Him explicitly, they did, nevertheless, have implicit faith through believing in Divine providence, since they believed that God would deliver mankind in whatever way was pleasing to Him, and according to the revelation of the Spirit to those who knew the truth.[25]

For Aquinas, if a man who lived without explicit knowledge of Christ attained salvation, it was on account of his affirmation of God's ability "to deliver mankind in whatever way was pleasing to Him," by virtue of which he assented to the whole substance of the faith. Unlike the "learned" of Israel, this man did not know specific details regarding the form that his redemption would ultimately come to take in Christ, and yet he could still possess the substance of the faith. Given that Aquinas thus entertains the possibility of salvation even for gentiles who were not privy to divine revelation, it is all the clearer that an Israelite's lack of explicit knowledge would not necessarily hinder him from possessing the substance of the Christian faith. Regardless, therefore, of whether or not one accepts Aquinas's assumption that learned men of pre-Christian times had *explicit* knowledge of Christ,

25. Ibid, II–II, q.2, a.7 ad 3. Cf. Thomas Aquinas, *Super Epistolam B. Pauli ad Hebraeos lectura*, caput 11, lectio 1. As regards the extent to which gentiles need to demonstrate explicit belief in God and his providence in order to be saved, Charles Journet takes a step beyond St. Thomas in suggesting there exists a situation in which an individual could possess the entire substance of the Christian faith and be saved even if he lacks conscious assent to God's existence and providence. This would take place in a preconceptual manner through the will. Sooner or later in life, every individual is compelled to choose for or against a rational human good. If a person chooses this good, "without yet even thinking explicitly either of God or of his final end … he is tending at once and directly, even though he is unaware of it, towards that good without which the good proper to man would not exist for a single instant, towards God, the final end of human life." *What Is Dogma?* [*Le dogme chemin de la foi*], translated by Mark Pontifex, OSB (New York: Hawthorn Books, 1964), 30. In Journet's theology, this person arrives at possession of the entire substance of the Christian faith through an act of the will rather than the intellect. He there encounters in an implicit manner the full mystery of the church. Cf. 35.

his theology of the history of revelation wonderfully illumines Old Testament texts that fall short of explicitly affirming the full range of Christian belief.[26] For, the fact that particular biblical authors fail to explicitly affirm the full number of articles of the Christian faith does not thereby entail that the substance of the Christian faith is not present within them and their writings. With Method A exegesis, we can therefore affirm that the word of God has a substantial unity, while with Method B we recognize that this unity is not that of a monolith but rather that of a living and progressively maturing organism.

DEVELOPMENT OF DOCTRINE WITHIN REVELATION AND WITHIN THE CHURCH

At this point we need to consider a possible misunderstanding of Aquinas's approach to the history of divine revelation: he states that the substance of the faith remained the same throughout the course of divine revelation, yet it is not as if the number of articles

---

26. Those who adhere to the Method B approach for the most part tend to reject the premise that individuals living before Christ had explicit knowledge of his mystery. Based on this modern insight (if it is correct), a Method C approach to the impasse might entail the argument that there were indeed many before Christ who had knowledge of him in an *implicit* rather than an *explicit* way. For, these particular thoughts of St. Thomas concerning the degree to which Old Testament personages had explicit knowledge of Christian mysteries do not form part of the body of revealed sacred tradition. A Method C exegete therefore does not have to hold that Moses literally saw the face of God or that David had conscious knowledge of Christ's Resurrection. There is indeed precedent in Aquinas's work for seeing implicit knowledge of Christ among those who lived before him, for we observed above that gentiles of any epoch could be saved due to their implicit faith in Christ. Cf. *ST*, I-II, q.106, a.1 ad 3; II-II, q.2, a.7 ad 3. The question here is whether the learned Israelites who lived under the Law were saved because of *explicit* faith in Christ (as Aquinas assumes), or because they had *implicit* faith in him (as a Method C exegete might say). I suspect Aquinas would still wish to distinguish the implicit faith of Israelites from the implicit faith of gentiles, and this certainly needs to be done; for, many gentiles only knew of the two primary *credibilia* of faith whereas Israelites were privy to knowledge of these as well as to what came to them through divine revelation. At the same time, it is interesting that Aquinas affirms there were times that gentiles received "revelations" directly from God: "Many of the gentiles received revelations of Christ, as is clear from their predictions. Thus we read (Jb 19:25): "I know that my Redeemer liveth." The Sibyl too foretold certain things about Christ, as Augustine states (*Contra Faust.* xiii, 15). *ST*, III, q.2, a.7 ad 3.

increased by a mere process of deduction. It can hardly be said that those who merely believed in God and assented to the reality of his providence could have arrived at knowledge of the entire Creed if only they thought hard enough about it. A cursory reading of St. Thomas's exposition might lend itself to such an interpretation. Upon closer inspection, however, one can see that the people of God's progress from implicit to explicit faith throughout the history of revelation involved more than mere thought, explanation, and deduction. Put simply, those who live in later epochs of salvation history have benefitted from additional divine revelation.

In this lies the difference between the scriptures' witness to development of doctrine within divine revelation (which has been the principal subject of our discussion) and the development of doctrine that has taken place through theology since the completion of divine revelation in the early church. There is indeed a real analogy between the development of doctrine within revelation and the development of doctrine within the church, as prominent theologians have noted.[27] Yet as Charles Journet points out, a man's passage from implicit to explicit knowledge of the faith differs according to whether it requires fresh revelations or occurs by "simple development," the type of development described masterfully by John Henry Newman.[28] For, on the one hand, the development within revelation

27. For example, in the volume *Explorations in Theology: The Word Made Flesh* (San Francisco: Ignatius Press, 1989), Hans Urs von Balthasar states, "There is an inner analogy between the progress of revelation and that of doctrine." (89–90.) Not only does Balthasar argue that the church's doctrine has maintained a single substantial form in its development over the centuries, in the work *A Theology of History* (San Francisco: Ignatius Press, 1994), he also describes divine revelation as a single form (*gestalt*) that progresses over time in a way clearly distinct from the way mankind's natural religious knowledge grows. Cf. 135–36. In his *In the Fullness of Faith: On the Centrality of the Distinctively Catholic* (San Francisco: Ignatius Press, 1988), Balthasar also speaks of Sacred Scripture having a "form": "This total picture," he says, "is held fast in a corpus of writings that outwardly seems strangely fortuitous; yet inwardly its parts are seen to be related to one another in inexhaustibly new ways. As a picture, a form, it is open." (95.)

28. Journet, *What Is Dogma?* 42. The Second Vatican Council likewise treats this kind of doctrinal development: "This tradition which comes from the Apostles develops in the Church with the help of the Holy Spirit. For there is a growth in the understanding of the realities and the words which have been handed down. This happens through the contemplation and study made by believers, who treasure these things in

we witness in the Bible was only possible due to fresh revelations and new teaching on the part of God. The faith became more "explicit" to the people of God not merely because their knowledge of the faith grew more conscious but also insofar as they received revelation of realities which previously had lain "implicit" within the realities they did know. Thus the Israelites could not have known about realities such as the Trinity, Incarnation, and Resurrection on their own; these had to be directly revealed by God himself.

On the other hand, development of doctrine within the church ("simple development") does not require, and indeed excludes, God's direct teaching of man through new revelation. The church's faith becomes more "explicit" insofar as we gradually apprehend, or become more conscious of, the revelation entrusted to us once and for all. Thus truths such as purgatory, papal infallibility, or Mary's Immaculate Conception are not taught explicitly in the Bible, but when we take into account sacred tradition—which Vatican II describes as commanding "the same sense of loyalty and reverence" as scripture itself—the church needed no additional revelation from God in order to teach such realities.[29] Those who are familiar with Newman's treatment of doctrinal development will recall that he ad-

---

their hearts (Lk 2:19, 51) through a penetrating understanding of the spiritual realities which they experience, and through the preaching of those who have received through episcopal succession the sure gift of truth. For as the centuries succeed one another, the Church constantly moves forward toward the fullness of divine truth until the words of God reach their complete fulfillment in her." DV §8.It is significant that Newman himself sees an analogy between development of doctrine within revelation and within the church. Addressing the notion of prophetic revelation in *An Essay on the Development of Christian Doctrine*, (Notre Dame, Ind.: University of Notre Dame Press, 1989), Newman states, "The prophetic Revelation is, in matter of fact ... a process of development: the earlier prophecies are pregnant texts out of which the succeeding announcements grow; they are types. It is not that first one truth is told, then another; but the whole truth or large portions of it are told at once, yet only in their rudiments, or in miniature, and they are expanded and finished in their parts, as the course of revelation proceeds." (64.) Newman has the correct intuition that there exists an underlying "idea" behind revelation itself which was clarified gradually over time as Israel grew in her ability to apprehend the Lord's teaching. Indeed right after the passage just cited he says, "The whole Bible, not its prophetical portions only, is written on the principle of development," and "It is certain that developments of Revelation proceeded all through the Old Dispensation down to the very end of our Lord's ministry." (65, 67–68.)

29. Second Vatican Council, *Dei Verbum, 1965*, §9.

amantly rejects the possibility that growth of dogma in the church is due to additional divine revelation over the centuries. Revelation ended at the death of the last apostle. No Christian has ever known more than the apostles knew, although their knowledge may be more explicit (in the sense of being more conscious) than that of the apostles. According to Newman, the church today "knows more" than the apostles only in the sense that she has had time to contemplate the implications of the deposit of faith in view of applying it to modern exigencies.[30] Despite the many developments that have occurred, the substance of the faith is the same now as it was two thousand years ago at the church's foundation.

In contrast to this doctrinal development within the church, Journet points out that the development of doctrine within revelation permitted, and even demanded, fresh revelations from God. For Journet grants that the substance of the faith is the same in believers regardless of whether they affirm only the primary matters of faith or any and all of the articles of the Christian Creed. However, he notes that while the article of the Trinity is in itself implicitly contained in the dogma of the existence of a supernatural God, and the articles that follow from Christ's redemptive Incarnation are implicitly contained in the dogma of a God who rewards man, Journet observes that these truths are not implicit in relation to man. In other words, whereas an apostle may have explicitly confessed fewer truths than Christians do today, all these truths would have resided in his consciousness in an implicit way. An early Christian who had never heard the word "Trinity" could have understood and assented to it once it was explained to him. In contrast, those who lived be-

---

30. Cf. John Henry Newman, "The Theory of Developments in Religious Doctrine," in *Fifteen Sermons Preached before the University of Oxford* (Notre Dame, Ind.: University of Notre Dame Press, 1998), 312–51; cf. John Henry Newman, *The Theological Papers of John Henry Newman on Biblical Inspiration and on Infallibility*, edited by J. Derek Holmes (Oxford: Clarendon Press, 1979): "The Church does not know more than the Apostles knew ... I wish to hold that there is nothing which the Church has defined or shall define but what an Apostle, if asked, would have been fully able to answer and would have answered, as the Church has answered, the one answering by inspiration, the other from its gift of infallibility." (157.) Cf. Ian Ker, foreword to Newman's *An Essay on the Development of Christian Doctrine*, xxiii–xxiv.

fore the fullness of revelation in Christ confessed fewer truths for a very different reason: they could not explicitly assent to the dogmas of the Christian Creed because these truths were in no way available to their intellects in the first place.

CONCLUSIONS REGARDING AQUINAS'S THEOLOGY OF THE HISTORY OF REVELATION

In this chapter, we have seen that Aquinas's theology provides a compelling framework within which to explain the presence of problematic biblical texts which fail to paint an accurate portrait of God's nature, the relationship between good and evil, or the afterlife. The authors of the Old Testament are no exception to the rule that no man ever came to full knowledge of the Christian faith apart from the revelation of Christ. Nevertheless, as we have seen through our examination of the writings of St. Thomas, all the articles of the Creed are implicitly contained in the fundamental reality of God's existence and providence, the primary *credibilia* of the faith to which blessed men of every epoch have assented. However, since revealed truths are not naturally knowable by man, God needed to give him fresh revelations throughout the course of history. This is what caused the people of God to affirm an increasing number of articles as salvation history progressed and in accordance with their ability to receive them. St. Thomas maintains that the substance of the faith did not suffer change over the course of revelation on account of this gradual maturation in Israel's explicit knowledge of the faith. For St. Thomas, all the articles of the Christian faith are in themselves contained implicitly in the dogma of a supernatural God who rewards man, and consequently anyone who affirms these truths by that very act demonstrates implicit knowledge of the Trinity, Incarnation, and all the articles of faith bound up with them.

What is the upshot of Aquinas's theology of the history of revelation, and how does it fit into the big picture of our present work? Aquinas's theology dispels the first objection raised in the first chapter by demonstrating that divine revelation has a unified substance (as Method A has long affirmed) despite the fact that vast developments occurred within it over history (which Method B has brought to light in recent times). His hermeneutic of divine pedagogy makes room for Method C exegetes who find less than compelling certain non-essential traditions which disregard the presence of development within scripture. It gives believers a rational basis for accept ing the inerrancy of biblical texts even when they say disconcerting things and refrain from explicitly teaching the fullness of the faith in such matters as the nature of God, the nature of good and evil, and the afterlife. That said, a Christian who admits the presence of development within scripture would still argue that scripture cannot *deny* the articles of faith or make affirmations that contradict other parts of scripture. The question we have to ask at this point is whether this expectation squares with the problematic biblical data presented in chapter 1. Thus we now turn to address the second objection raised in chapter 1 regarding the presence of apparent contradictions in scripture.

CHAPTER 4

THE PROBLEM OF APPARENT
CONTRADICTIONS

The preceding chapters have emphasized that the problems of development, diversity, and apparent contradictions in scripture can be reconciled only if we develop a robust theology of scripture based on a synthesis of the best of ancient and modern exegesis. To this end, chapter 3 proposed a Method C approach to the problem of scriptural development on the basis of St. Thomas's theology of the history of revelation. Aquinas demonstrates that divine revelation—and consequently scripture as its inspired witness—maintained a unity over the centuries (in accordance with Method A's principles) despite the fact that it greatly developed throughout this same time frame (as emphasized by the Method B approach). However, the apparent presence of blatant contradictions in scripture poses an even greater problem—in particular in times when later texts seem to constitute regressions rather than developments with respect to texts written earlier in the course of divine revelation. We therefore need to delve deeper yet into the thought of St. Thomas. This will involve turning from his theology of the *history* of revelation, which enables us to account for development and diversity in what God reveals, to his theology of the *act* of revelation. In this chapter, we will see that examining what takes place when God reveals truth to a prophet is key to making sense of biblical inspiration even in the face of apparent contradictions.

PROPHECY AND DIVINE REVELATION

In line with those who wrote before him on the topic, St. Thomas wrote that the act of divine revelation was best understood in relation to the Holy Spirit's gift of prophecy. If we are to tackle the problem of apparent contradictions in biblical revelation, we must therefore understand something about prophecy. It is important to observe that Aquinas's use of the term "prophet" is quite broad in comparison with today's standards. For example, though not usually counted among the prophets, for Aquinas all the authors of scripture (David, Job, the chronicler, the authors of the New Testament, etc.) were true prophets precisely because they received revelation from God. Seeing, therefore, that Aquinas views the authors of scripture as prophets, we stand to benefit greatly from an investigation of his treatment of prophecy insofar as it applies to the composition of Sacred Scripture.[1] The precision and depth of Aquinas's work in this area is all too unknown by Christians today, but we will see that it is crucial since it provides us a framework within which to assess the various kinds of truth claims—including the apparently false ones—made by the scriptures. With the help of Aquinas's theology we will be able to show that passages in which the sacred authors seemingly contradict either one another or what Christians know to be true today do not in fact contain errors. For from the perspective of Aquinas, the truth of scripture depends on what its authors intend to affirm or teach, and if a given passage appears to contain something contradictory then the exegete must seek within this passage an aim beyond that of definitively teaching an erroneous point of view.

Let us begin by exploring the term "prophecy" itself. For Aquinas, the object of prophecy is "something known by God and sur-

1. Prophecy is all the more relevant in this context because we have been treating scripture in light of its development, and Aquinas himself views prophecy as God's successive illumination and teaching of chosen men. Cf. Thomas Aquinas, *Super I Epistolam B. Pauli ad Corinthios lectura*, caput 14, lectio 2. "If [the divine light] ... is infused successively (*infunditur successive*), then it is prophecy, which the prophets did not have at once but successively and in piecemeal fashion (*non subito sed successive et per partes*), as their prophecies show" (my translation).

passing the faculty of man."[2] Man cannot attain prophetic knowledge by his own power; God must grant it to him from above in the form of a gratuitous grace, also known as a charism or gift. In Aquinas's view, prophecy is an "imperfect" form of divine revelation. Through the gift of prophecy, God enables men on their earthly sojourn to participate in the fullness of revelation which will occur only in the beatific vision.[3] Aquinas's treatise offers a much more robust view of prophecy than those who consider prophecy to be merely a matter of predicting future events. He writes, "Prophetic knowledge comes through a divine light, whereby it is possible to know *all things* both divine and human, both spiritual and corporeal; and consequently the prophetic revelation extends to them all."[4] In this way, a prophet may be granted knowledge of things which in themselves are unknowable to all men by nature, including the future contingent events typically associated with prophecy. However, according to Aquinas God can also grant prophetic revelation to teach a man something which is remote from the knowledge of all men but is in itself knowable. For example, Aquinas observes that the mystery of the Trinity is in itself knowable to man, but it cannot be known by natural reason. Finally, a prophet may be granted knowledge of things which are remote only from the knowledge of particular men. Such is the case when the secret thoughts of one man are manifested prophetically to another.[5] This broad understanding of prophecy will be helpful in our exploration of the scriptures since Method B exegetes will quickly point out that the Scriptures do not always contain information Christians typically associate with prophecy and divine revelation (the earthiness of the Song of Songs, the mun-

2. Thomas Aquinas, *ST*, II-II, q.174, a.1.

3. Ibid., II-II, q.171, a.4 ad 2. "Hence it is written (1 Corinthians 13:8) that 'prophecies shall be made void,' and that 'we prophesy in part,' i.e., imperfectly. The Divine revelation will be brought to its perfection in heaven; wherefore the same text continues (1 Corinthians 13:10): 'When that which is perfect is come, that which is in part shall be done away.'"

4. Ibid., II-II, q.171, a.3 (emphasis added).

5. At this point I would also refer the reader to Matthew Lamb's lucid analysis of prophecy in Thomas Aquinas, *Commentary on Saint Paul's Epistle to the Ephesians*, translated by Matthew Lamb (Albany, N.Y.: Magi Books, 1966), 254nn14–15.

dane histories in 1–2 Chronicles, and the problematic areas studied in this work are but a few examples of things one would typically not expect to see in a work which is considered to be inspired in its entirety). Indeed, Christians who tend to follow a Method A approach expect to see divine revelation in all the scriptures, yet Method B scholarship observes that the scriptures frequently appear as mundane works which at times even contradict the revelation contained in other parts of scripture.

TWO DIMENSIONS OF PROPHECY: INSPIRATION AND REVELATION

Before we can apply Aquinas's account of prophecy to the problem of apparent contradictions within scripture, it is necessary to explore his description of how God causes knowledge to come about in the inspired intellect of the prophet. From this point through much of what follows in this chapter, we will be drawing on the work of Aquinas's twentieth-century commentators Paul Synave and Pierre Benoit as they provide a thorough and insightful interpretation of Aquinas's theology of scripture. Their work is by no means definitive, yet it remains one of the most serious scholarly proposals in terms of attempting to articulate a theology of scripture in a way that is faithful to the Church's dogmatic principles (emphasized by Method A) yet unafraid to confront the most serious of challenges to these same teachings (a characteristic of Method B).[6] The work of St. Thomas as interpreted by Synave and Benoit is therefore by no means the final word regarding the nature of scripture, but it provides the Method C exegete with a viable framework within which he can confront apparent contradictions in God's word.

As St. Thomas explains and his commentators observe, there are two dimensions to prophecy. In the first, God gives an "inspiration" in which he elevates the prophet's mind so that he can then go on to

---

6. The fact that their proposal remains in need of correction and nuance has been well observed. See James Tunstead Burtchaell, *Catholic Theories of Biblical Inspiration since 1810: A Review and Critique*, 238–45; Peter Paul Zerafa, OP, "The Limits of Biblical Inerrancy," *Letter and Spirit* 6 (2010): 359–76.

perceive divine realities through "revelation," the second dimension of prophecy. The light of inspiration is precisely what makes revelation possible since man cannot apprehend objects which exceed the capacity of his unaided natural reason. In the only passage in which Aquinas expressly juxtaposes and distinguishes these terms, he comments:

> It is requisite to prophecy that the intention of the mind be raised to the perception of divine things; wherefore it is written (Ez 2:1): "Son of man, stand upon thy feet, and I will speak to thee." This raising of the intention is brought about by the motion of the Holy Ghost, wherefore the text goes on to say: 'And the Spirit entered into me … and He set me upon my feet.' After the mind's intention has been raised to heavenly things, it perceives the things of God; hence the text continues: "And I heard Him speaking to me." Accordingly *inspiration* is requisite for prophecy, as regards the raising of the mind, according to Job 32:8, "The inspiration of the Almighty giveth understanding": while *revelation* is necessary, as regards the very perception of Divine things, whereby prophecy is completed; by its means the veil of darkness and ignorance is removed, according to Job 12:22, "He discovereth great things out of darkness."[7]

This passage from Aquinas is clearly an attempt to develop a theology of inspiration, a biblically-based account that uses texts from the Bible itself in order to explain the phenomena of inspiration and revelation we witness in the Bible. Synave and Benoit elucidate the dynamic interplay of these different dimensions of prophecy as follows:

> Inspiration is the antecedent influence which raises the mind above its ordinary level and endows it with greater intellectual vigor; revelation results from it, and is found in the judgment which is formed by the mind thus elevated, and by which it perceives divine truths. Understood in this sense, inspiration always accompanies revelation and is a necessary prerequisite for it. The mind is unable to discover divine mysteries unless it has first been reinforced from above. There is no revelation without inspiration.[8]

7. Ibid., q.171, a.1 ad 4 (emphasis added).
8. Paul Synave and Pierre Benoit, *Prophecy and Inspiration: A Commentary on the Summa Theologica II-II, Questions 171–178* (New York: Desclee Co., 1961), 70–71. Cf. Pierre Benoit, *Aspects of Biblical Inspiration*, translated by J. Murphy-O'Connor, OP and S. K. Ashe, OP (Chicago: The Priory Press, 1965), 50. In this chapter, I will rely primarily upon the analysis in these two works. However, I would also refer the reader to

Inspiration refers to the "motion" of the Holy Spirit which comes upon the prophet from the outside and raises his human intellect in order to prepare it for the moment in which God will disclose a truth to him in a revelation.[9] Revelation, meanwhile, expresses the essence of prophecy: the discovery that results when a truth hitherto unknown is unveiled to the prophet whose mind has been elevated through the motion of the Holy Spirit.

While the above discussion makes it clear that the prophet can receive no revelation without the prior elevation that takes place through divine inspiration, Synave and Benoit go on to inquire whether there may ever be a case in which a man receives inspiration without revelation. This is a poignant question since we have witnessed that many portions of scripture plainly involve authors who write concerning realities which are knowable without supernatural revelation or which even seem to contradict divine revelation. Therefore if the Catholic Church is correct in teaching that all of scripture is inspired, it is worth examining this hypothesis to see if it might help elucidate Method A's doctrine of inspiration in the face of Method B's observation that passages often not only lack evidence of, but moreover positively seem to contradict, what is otherwise known by divine revelation. As Synave and Benoit state, the fundamental question at this juncture is how we are to explain the confluence of divine and human activity in the authorship of scripture.[10]

APPROACHING THE DIVINE AUTHORSHIP AND INSPIRATION OF SCRIPTURE "FROM ABOVE"

Exploring the hypothesis that scripture might at times entail instances where inspiration occurs without revelation, Paul Synave and Pierre Benoit observe that one of two avenues can be followed when one considers the divine authorship and inspiration of scrip-

---

a couple of pertinent articles by Pierre Benoit: "Note complémentaire sur l'inspiration," *Revue Biblique* 63 (1956): 416–22; "Révélation et Inspiration selon la Bible, chez Saint Thomas et dans les discussions modernes," *Revue Biblique* 70 (1963): 321–70.

9. Cf. Thomas Aquinas, *ST*, I–II, q.68, a.1

10. Synave and Benoit, *Prophecy and Inspiration*, 88.

ture. On the one hand, one can begin from below, letting his inquiry be driven by the human notion of authorship. From this perspective, one looks at what a human author is and from there proceeds to ask how God's authorship of scripture resembles that of a human author. On the other hand, one can begin his enquiry from above, with the first principle of faith in the divine authorship of scripture, and from there proceed to articulate how scripture's human authors cooperate with the Holy Spirit. Synave and Benoit indicate that if we approach inspiration in this second way, our account of scripture's divine authorship need not be confined to human notions of authorship. For although the authors of human books conceive all the ideas contained therein, this may not be the case when it comes to the divine authorship of scripture. Synave and Benoit state:

> It is certain that, among men, the author of a book must at least have conceived the ideas; this seems to be a minimum requirement…. But there is another possibility of which human psychology offers no instance, that of one mind causing another to think by communicating an interior light to it: it is this which the doctrine of inspiration teaches us to be the case with God, and which transforms the ordinary meaning of the word "author."[11]

In this brief comment, Synave and Benoit offer a reasonable Thomistic account of scripture's divine authorship, albeit one that differs from many common explanations that approach the matter on the basis of a human notion of authorship. They put forth the thesis that God can truly be the author (*auctor*) of scripture even if not every individual "idea" contained therein is his. This very simple thesis rests on St. Thomas's distinction between inspiration and revelation, and Synave and Benoit believe it allows one to avoid the conundrum of having God be the cause of scripture's imperfect ideas.

11. Ibid., 102. Pope Benedict also offers some thought-provoking insights on the topic of how our concept of purely human authorship must be transformed and transcended: "The extent of the Word's meaning cannot be reduced to the thoughts of a single author in a specific historical moment; it is not the property of a single author at all; rather, it lives in a history that is ever moving onward and, thus, has dimensions and depths of meaning in past and future that ultimately pass into the realm of the unforeseen. It is only at this point that we can begin to understand the nature of inspiration; we can see where God mysteriously enters into what is human and purely human authorship is transcended." Benedict XVI, *Pilgrim Fellowship of Faith: The Church as Communion*, translated by Henry Taylor (San Francisco: Ignatius Press, 2005), 32–33.

How, precisely, can God be called the author of scripture if not every idea contained therein is his? It is important at this point to draw on some authors who expound upon the subject at greater length. As John Henry Newman explains in his work *On the Inspiration of Scripture*, the Latin *auctor* used in the tradition to describe God's authorship does not primarily refer to "author" in the literary sense of the term most people associate with the term today:

"Auctor" is not identical with the English "Author." Allowing that there are instances to be found in classical Latin in which "auctores" may be translated "authors," instances in which it even seems to mean "writers," it more naturally means "authorities." Its proper sense is "originator," "inventor," "founder," "primary cause."[12]

Newman's point is similar to that of Congar when he writes, "An *auctor* is he who is responsible for something because he stands first and decisively at its origin."[13] In other words, God is wholly responsible for the Bible and he is its originator, but that does not necessarily mean every idea therein is his. Still, it is important to keep in mind that God is not merely the originator of scripture, as if he set the authorship of scripture into motion and then let human instruments put the Bible together on their own. On the contrary, just as God as author of the universe did not leave the universe once he created it, so God was intimately involved in the composition of Sacred Scripture even after he initially inspired each of its writers to write. Nevertheless, an important difference between God's authorship of the universe and his authorship of scripture is that scripture came about through the medium of free secondary causes, whereas secondary causes in nature are not all free as humans are. It is precisely this presence of freedom within the instrumental causes of scripture that accounts for the presence of human ideas that do not issue directly from the mind of God.

As Matthew Lamb points out in his notes on Aquinas's *Commen-*

---

12. *On the Inspiration of Scripture*, edited by J. Derek Holmes and Robert Murray (Washington, D.C.: Corpus Books, 1967), 10. See also Karl Rahner, *Inspiration in the Bible*, and Yves Congar, *Sainte Église: études et approches ecclésiologiques* (Paris: Éditions du Cerf, 1963), 187–88.

13. Congar, *Sainte Église*, 187 (translation mine).

tary on Saint Paul's Epistle to the Ephesians, if we are to properly understand the particular kind of instrumental authorship operative in scripture, it is necessary to recall that it is a special instance of God's "universal instrumentality." Lamb nuances the work of Synave and Benoit in warning that it is easy to fall into the trap of approaching the divine impulse of inspiration in an atomistic manner, that is to say without adequately accounting for the role that inspired works in their totality play within divine providence as a whole:

> For Benoit the whole Bible is inspired because the Almighty controlled every single writer and literary piece. St Thomas's concept of instrumentality, as Lonergan has demonstrated, affirms that God controls each event because he controls all. Applied to Scripture, this means that each and every part of it is authored by God because he *originated* ... the whole process of the Bible's formation.... The difference between the instrumentality operative in the composing of the Scriptures and the Universal Instrumentality discussed by Lonergan ... is that the Providence guiding the genesis of the Bible is an essential element in the special Providence concerned with salvation history.... Note the affinity this has with K. Rahner's thesis: God's willing of the Scriptures as a constitutive element in his willing of the Church.[14]

As Lamb explains, God is the author of scripture precisely insofar as he "originated ... the whole process of the Bible's formation." What makes the scriptures unique, then, if we assume that God originates other works besides the scriptures? According to Lamb, it is crucial to grasp that "the Providence guiding the genesis of the Bible is an essential element in the special Providence concerned with salvation history." In other words, God in his eternal providence inspired the scriptures in order that they could serve a unique role in salvation history and in the formation of the church. Lamb here references

14. Lamb, trans., Thomas Aquinas, *Commentary on ... Ephesians*, 259n22 (emphasis added). Lamb is contrasting his view here with the reflections of Synave and Benoit on the possibility of a text having multiple authors and redactors who "share" the charism of inspiration. See their *Prophecy and Inspiration*, 124. Cf. Bernard Lonergan, "St. Thomas' Theory of Operation" and "St. Thomas' Thought on *Gratia Operans*," *Theological Studies* 3 (1942): 375–401, 533–78, especially 391–95. For more on the complexities involved with attributing inspiration to multiple individual authors and redactors rather than looking at it from Lamb's point of view, see Kenton Sparks, *Sacred Word, Broken Word: Biblical Authority and the Dark Side of Scripture* (Grand Rapids, Mich.: Eerdmans, 2011), 92–99.

Karl Rahner, who eloquently summarized this dynamic in his work *Inspiration in the Bible*: "The inspiration of the Scriptures ... is but simply the causality of God in regard to the Church, inasmuch as it refers to the constitutive element of the Apostolic Church, which is the Bible."[15] The inspiration of scripture and the causality of the church are inseparable from one another. Inspiration is not an end in itself; the scriptures were inspired *for the church*.

Lamb also calls on the authority of Yves Congar to clarify this point. Affirming Rahner's thesis, Congar states, "Certain writings are inspired because they were integral to the living establishment of the Church not at any moment whatsoever in her history but in the moment of her birth and constitution."[16] This is an important statement because it helps believers answer the age-old challenge of explaining what makes certain books worthy to be part of the Bible when they are not necessarily any more enlightening or beautiful than other works of the same time period that did not make it into the canon. For Lamb, Rahner, and Congar, the simple answer is that the inspiration of these works lies precisely in the role they played in salvation history and in the constitution of the church. In his eternal wisdom, God willed them to fill a niche that no other sacred writings would fill. As such, they must be approached in their totality and in light of this role. If we may draw for a moment on the wisdom of Pope Benedict, we will perhaps better understand this approach. He recently wrote to members of the Pontifical Biblical Commission:

15. Karl Rahner, *Inspiration in the Bible*, translated by Charles H. Henkey (New York: Herder, 1964), 50–51. Pope Benedict speaks in similar terms with regard to the formation of the canon: "The establishment of the canon and the establishment of the early Church are one and the same process but viewed from different perspectives." Benedict XVI, *Principles of Catholic Theology: Building Stones for a Fundamental Theology* (San Francisco: Ignatius Press, 2009), 148.

16. Congar, *Sainte Église: études et approches ecclésiologiques* (Paris: Éditions du Cerf, 1963), 188–89 (translation mine). See also Thomas Aquinas, *Hic est liber*, 1 and note 284 above on the importance of correctly understanding what it means for God to be the "originator" of scripture. For a more recent discussion of divine providence and inspiration, see Denis Farkasfalvy, *Inspiration and Interpretation: A Theological Introduction to Sacred Scripture* (Washington, D.C.: The Catholic University of America Press, 2010), 217–19.

Lastly, I would only like to mention the fact that in a good hermeneutic it is not possible to apply mechanically the criterion of inspiration, or indeed of absolute truth by extrapolating a single sentence or expression. The plan in which it is possible to perceive Sacred Scripture as a Word of God is that of the unity of God, in a totality in which the individual elements are illuminated reciprocally and are opened to understanding.[17]

For Pope Benedict as for our other authors, the notion of unity is key to understanding the nature of scripture. The Bible has a unity and cannot be done justice if we "apply mechanically the criterion of inspiration ... by extrapolating a single sentence or expression." Likewise, the unity of the Bible itself has to be viewed within the context of that unity which is God's providential plan to prepare a people for himself and lead them into the fullness of truth.

Having elucidated the reality of scripture's unity and divine authorship in more detail, we are now in a position to return to the work of Synave and Benoit and the issue of how scripture's human authors receive the gift of inspiration from God. They point out that in granting human authors the interior light of inspiration, God in no way suppresses their freedom or furnishes them knowledge without making use of their own powers. On the contrary, Synave and Benoit suggest the distinctive feature of scriptural authorship is precisely that the Holy Spirit allows the human writer to work and discover his ideas just like any other man, though with the added assistance of a supernatural light. It is in this vein that Aquinas, following St. Jerome, contrasts Israel's official prophets who spoke directly in God's name (e.g., Isaiah, Jeremiah) with those whom here he calls the "hagiographers" (e.g., Job, David, Solomon) whose works appear in the Bible but do not typically report God's words for us in a direct manner:

Hence they [the official prophets in Israel] spoke as God's representatives (*ex persona Domini*), saying to the people: "Thus saith the Lord": but not so the authors of the "sacred writings," several of whom treated more frequently of things that can be known by human reason, not in God's name, but in their own, yet with the assistance of the divine light withal (*non*

17. Benedict XVI, Address to Participants in the Plenary Meeting of the Pontifical Biblical Commission (May 2, 2011).

quasi ex persona Dei, sed ex persona propria, cum adiutorio tamen divini luminis).[18]

According to Synave and Benoit, when Aquinas states that the authors of scripture speak "in their own" name, he does not mean to say that their authority is merely human, but rather that their ideas come about in a truly human way, that they did not receive a ready-made message dictated by God. Synave and Benoit tentatively propose that these are cases in which inspiration might occur without revelation. The authors are true authors, and their works are truly human works. The difference between these and non-inspired works, then, is not that they treat of things which surpass human reason, but that they are written in response to a special impulse of the Holy Spirit, who has enabled their human authors to pen everything God wanted written in them, and nothing more.

At this point it appears Synave and Benoit have made a reasonable case for the hypothesis that scripture contains instances where inspiration occurs in the absence of revelation. Before moving on to our next section, however, it is important to describe the correction to this hypothesis that Pierre Benoit made in his later work *Aspects of Biblical Inspiration.*[19] Here, Benoit decisively concludes that revelation and inspiration are inseparable in the authorship of scripture. For, although the sacred authors do not always receive supernatural

18. Thomas Aquinas, *ST*, II-II, q.174, a.2 ad 3. Aquinas speaks in strikingly similar terms about the nature of the hagiographers's writing in his inaugural sermon on the commendation and division of Sacred Scripture: "The third [part of the Old Testament] is contained in the [works of] the hagiographers, who were inspired by the Holy Spirit and spoke not on behalf of God but as it were on behalf of themselves (*Agiographis, qui spiritu sancto inspirati locuti sunt non tamen ex parte domini, sed quasi ex se ipsis*). Hence the hagiographers are called sacred writers or writers of sacred things, from *agios* meaning 'sacred,' and *graphia* meaning 'scripture.'" Thomas Aquinas, *Hic est liber*, 8 (translation mine).

19. Benoit discusses this in *Aspects of Biblical Inspiration*, 40. He notes that other prominent theologians also expressed this view in their treatises on inspiration. Cf. Augustin Bea, *De Scripturae Sacrae inspiratione* (Rome: Pontificio Instituto Biblico, 1935); Reginald Garigou-Lagrange, "L'inspiration et les exigences de la critique," *Revue Biblique* 5 (1896): 496–518; Jacques-M. Vosté, *De divina inspiratione et veritate Sacrae Scripturae* (Rome: Collegio Angelico, 1932); Thoma Maria Zigliara, *Propaedeutica ad sacram theologiam in usum scholarum, seu, Tractatus de ordine supernaturali* (Rome: S. C. de Propaganda Fide, 1903).

ideas from God, they deal with all natural material in light of God's plan, and thus their writing results in a "lesson of supernatural value, which is a secondary but nonetheless fully authentic mode of revelation."[20] According to Benoit, there thus exists a mode of revelation which is akin to, but distinct from, that of the prophet who has received supernatural ideas (what Christians typically think of as "revelations") from God. What distinguishes the two modes of revelation is whether or not the infusion of a supernatural idea is involved in the process. In this way, Benoit proposes a more accurate way of naming these modes than he previously employed. Rather than referring to one as "inspiration without revelation" and the other "inspiration with revelation," he adopts the terms "revelation in the broad sense" (referring to those parts of scripture which do not contain ideas specifically of the supernatural order) and "revelation in the strict sense" (as occurs when God grants a sacred author or another prophet the knowledge of a truth known only through supernatural means).[21] The precision of Benoit's distinction is precisely what is demanded in a Method C treatment of scripture. It takes seriously the challenges of Method B, yet it maintains Method A's steadfast conviction in the inspiration of scripture and seeks to refine the faith in light of Method B's findings.

SCRIPTURE'S INSTRUMENTAL AUTHORSHIP

Summarizing the importance of approaching scripture's divine authorship in light of the Thomistic distinction between inspiration and revelation, Synave and Benoit write:

---

20. Benoit, *Aspects of Biblical Inspiration*, 48. As Lamb explains in his notes on Thomas Aquinas, *Commentary on … Ephesians*, "Much of the Scriptures deal with otherwise naturally knowable subjects, such as Israel's history, but as Aquinas points out (*ST* I, q.1, a.7) they are related *in the light of* God's plans for salvation-history … Even the most 'natural' books of the Old Testament deal with their material in the light of Yahweh and his plans for his people." (256nn17, 21.)

21. Cf. ibid., 45. See also the work where Benoit himself discovered this distinction: Christian Pesch, *De inspiratione sacrae scripturae* (Friburgi Brisgoviae: Herder, 1906), 414.

Consequently we realize that the Bible takes on an entirely different aspect according as we see in it only "revelations" from God ["revelation in the strict sense"], or, on the contrary, recognize in it, more often than not, the product of simple "inspiration" ["revelation in the broad sense"]. In the first case there is danger of looking upon it as a catalog of absolute truths, in which each proposition comes directly from God through the passive, almost negligible channel of the human instrument. In the second case it appears more under the human aspect, which it really has, with the limitations, the lacunae, and even the defects which that implies, not only in the language, but even in the thoughts. Hence the Bible can resemble any other book, as a concrete study of it shows. At the same time it is also, in the true sense of the word, a divine book, different from any other. For it is in truth God who immediately originates the entire thought process of the interpreter whom he inspires. He is quite truly the Author of the Book, of the entire book, just as man too is its author, each in his own degree: God is the principal Author, and man his faithful instrument.[22]

This last reference to scripture's human author as God's "instrument" is central to St. Thomas's account. Aquinas envisions the concurrence of divine and human activity in scripture in terms of a "dual authorship." For St. Thomas, the same effect can at once be wholly the work of two efficient causes, one instrumental and one principal, one human and one divine.

Method C exegetes today have many good reasons for adopting Aquinas's framework of principal and instrumental scriptural authorship.[23] For instance, it is helpful to know that by its nature an

22. Synave and Benoit, *Prophecy and Inspiration*, 98–99. For a more detailed criticism of theological models that would seek a mere catalog of propositional truths from Scripture, see Avery Dulles, *Models of Revelation* (Maryknoll, N.Y.: Orbis Books, 1992).

23. Not the least of reasons why one might employ this terminology is because the Magisterium itself has done so. Pius XII wrote of the theologians of his day: "Catholic theologians, following the teaching of the Holy Fathers and especially of the Angelic and Common Doctor, have examined and explained the nature and effects of biblical inspiration more exactly and more fully than was wont to be done in previous ages. For having begun by expounding minutely the principle that the inspired writer, in composing the sacred book, is the living and reasonable instrument of the Holy Spirit, they rightly observe that, impelled by the divine motion, he so uses his faculties and powers, that from the book composed by him all may easily infer 'the special character of each one and, as it were, his personal traits.' Let the interpreter then, with all care and without neglecting any light derived from recent research, endeavor to determine the peculiar character and circumstances of the sacred writer, the age in which he lived, the sources written or oral to which he had recourse and the forms of expression he employed." *DAS* §33.

instrument is not the source of its own action and moreover does not act all the time. Aquinas shows that the instrument to whom God has granted the gift of prophecy cannot simply use his gift whenever he wishes. Considering the question of whether the gift of prophecy habitually abides in the intellect of the prophet, St. Thomas states: "The prophetic light is in the prophet's soul by way of a passion or transitory impression."[24] Unlike a habit or power, the prophetic light is transient, supplied only momentarily to the prophet and even then entirely at the discretion of the Holy Spirit. Thus, sacred authors as diverse as Moses, Solomon, and St. Paul all could have written many beautiful works which were not preserved in the Bible, but these would not have been inspired since prophecy is a gift God gives at specific times and for specific reasons. The prophet is dependent on God for the inception of this knowledge and for its entire duration. Prophecy for St. Thomas is truly a *gratia gratis data*, a grace freely given.

Another, more pivotal reason to describe man's role in the authorship of scripture in terms of instrumentality has to do with the effects God is able to produce in him through the gift of prophecy. The gift of prophecy enables man to attain knowledge he never could on his own power precisely because God is the principal agent and the true cause of the knowledge.[25] However, granted that the knowledge received by the prophet surpasses that which he could attain on his own, this does not mean he perfectly receives the prophetic gift from God since he is a frail human being with his own sins, prejudices, and darkened intellect. In the case of scripture's authorship, this boils down to the plain truth that the sacred writer does not receive the light of inspiration in such a way that he pierces the depths of what God is revealing to him. Aquinas will thus indicate that the sacred writer's knowledge ranks midway between that of faith and beatific vision. He is a prophet to the extent that he has some vision of God, yet unlike those in the beatific vision he still sees God from afar. In this way, it is only fitting that the scriptures themselves

---

24. *Lumen propheticum insit animae prophetae per modum cuiusdam passionis vel impressionis transeuntis.* Thomas Aquinas, *ST*, II–II, q.171, a.2; cf. *De veritate*, q.12, a.1.
25. Synave and Benoit, *Prophecy and Inspiration*, 77.

testify to the work of human authors who could see more than mere men can see and yet still not see perfectly.

Finally, apart from the inherent limitations of man's capacity as an instrument to receive and appropriate divine revelation, one must reckon with the fact that prophets sometimes exhibit a less than perfect use (*usus*) of the gift (*donum*) given them. Aquinas explains:

> The use of any prophecy is within the power of the prophet.... Hence, one could prevent himself from using prophecy; the proper disposition is a necessary requirement for the correct use of prophecy since the use of prophecy proceeds from the created power of the prophet. Therefore, a determinate disposition is also required.[26]

As we will see below, these insights of Aquinas have significant consequences when it comes to our effort to describe how it is possible for scripture to contain human imperfections (times when an author denies the afterlife, appears to accept the existence of multiple gods, or that the one true God can command evil) without also containing formal errors. For, although prophecy is a gift from God, it is a gift given to imperfect men who must make judgments on how to use the gift. In order to further articulate the import of this, it is necessary to turn to Aquinas's account of the act of judgment, the primary place in which divine inspiration works on the intellect of scripture's sacred writers.

THE ROLE OF THE AUTHOR'S JUDGMENT

Before stating anything further about the role of judgment in scripture's authors, it is necessary to point out that judgment itself is the second of two acts which take place in the intellect of the prophet whom God grants divine revelation. This becomes apparent when reading Aquinas:

> Two things have to be considered in connection with the knowledge possessed by the human mind, namely the acceptance or representation of things, and the judgment of the things represented.... Now the gift of

26. Thomas Aquinas, *De veritate*, q.12, a.4. Lamb, trans., *Thomas Aquinas, Commentary on ... Ephesians*, 258. Lamb provides references to many other places in Aquinas's corpus in which he distinguishes the prophetic *donum* and *usus*; cf. 258n20.

prophecy confers on the human mind something which surpasses the natural faculty in both these respects, namely as to the judgment which depends on the inflow of intellectual light, and as to the acceptance or representation of things, which is effected by means of certain species. Human teaching may be likened to prophetic revelation in the second of these respects, but not in the first. For a man represents certain things to his disciple by signs of speech, but he cannot enlighten him inwardly as God does. But it is the first of these two that holds the chief place in prophecy, since judgment is the complement of knowledge.[27]

According to Aquinas's cognitional theory, God imparts revelation to the prophet first by granting him a "representation of things." Like a human teacher who represents realities to his disciple by means of speech and images, God reveals supernatural truths to the prophet by presenting his intellect with some "species" (e.g., a dream, a vision, or a locution which ultimately furnishes the material for an idea). However, Aquinas explains that God is unlike a human teacher in that he not only provides his pupil with the material for an idea but can also enlighten a soul from within. Having presented the prophet's intellect with some species, he then grants the prophet a light that enables him to interpret reality from a God's-eye perspective. With the assistance of this light, the prophet reflects on whether or not his initial apprehension of the species corresponds to reality, whether it is truly of God. It is only in the judgment that follows this reflection that the prophet can be said to have apprehended revealed truth. As Aquinas makes clear, the fact that God grants a given prophet some species like a dream or vision does not yet mean that the prophet has knowledge, because in order to know he must judge that what he has apprehended is indeed of God. For Aquinas, it is in this act of judgment that prophetic knowledge finds its "complement" or completion (*completivum*).[28] As Synave and

27. Thomas Aquinas, *ST*, II-II, q.173, a.2. St. Thomas takes up a similar discussion of the role of judgment in prophecy in *De veritate*, q.12, a.7. For a contemporary evangelical approach to the role of judgment in speech acts that is distinct from but akin to that of the approach followed here, see Kevin Vanhoozer, *The Drama of Doctrine: A Canonical-Linguistic Approach to Christian Theology* (Louisville, Ky.: Westminster John Knox Press, 2005).

28. According to St. Thomas, the first act of apprehending a species does not yet result in truth, because the prophet must reflect and make sure he is not being deluded

Benoit describe, it yields "a penetration, a clarity, a certitude which man could not have achieved if left to his own resources."[29]

In order to confirm Aquinas's claims as to the importance of the act of judgment in relation to prophetic knowledge, it is instructive to observe that in Scripture God sometimes presents an individual with a species without giving him the ability to judge concerning it. Immediately following the passage cited above, in the same article Aquinas writes:

Wherefore if certain things are divinely represented to any man by means of imaginary likenesses, as happened to Pharaoh (Gn 41:1–7) and to Nabuchodonosor (Dn 4:1–2), or even by bodily likenesses, as happened to Balthasar (Dn 5:5), such a man is not to be considered a prophet, unless his mind be enlightened for the purpose of judgment; and such an apparition is something imperfect in the genus of prophecy.[30]

As Aquinas points out, Pharaoh, Nebuchadnezzar, and Balthasar all received certain species such as dreams from God, yet they were not given the ability to judge concerning the truth of what they received. He goes on to contrast these men with true prophets like Joseph, who exercised the prophetic charism by judging and explaining the meaning of those dreams which could not be interpreted by Pharaoh himself.

REVELATION IN THE BROAD SENSE AND THE CONDITIONING OF AN AUTHOR'S JUDGMENT

In the above example, God enabled a faithful man to make prophetic judgments concerning a revealed species even though he himself was not the one who received it; but we have also seen, above,

---

by this apprehension. In other words, he must not only know *what* a thing is but *that* it corresponds to reality. The saint writes, "Truth is defined by the conformity of intellect and thing; and hence to know this conformity is to know truth.... But the intellect can know its own conformity with the intelligible thing; yet it does not apprehend it by knowing of a thing 'what a thing is.' When, however, it judges that a thing corresponds to the form which it apprehends about that thing, then first it knows and expresses truth." *ST*, I, q.16, a.2.

29. Synave and Benoit, *Prophecy and Inspiration*, 97.
30. Thomas Aquinas, *ST*, II-II, q.173, a.2.

that there exist cases in which prophets receive the light to judge reality in a supernatural manner without the involvement of any revealed species at all ("revelation in the broad sense"). As Synave and Benoit suggest, this is precisely what occurs when an inspired scriptural author composes a text based on his own judgment, without any intention of teaching a truth of the revealed order. He may, for example, wish to teach a naturally knowable truth or convey a historical detail that he received through ordinary means of human communication (e.g., when the chronicler reports a deed of David).[31] He may likewise be inspired to pen words which represent more his own authoritative thoughts rather than ideas directly from God, as in the case when Paul writes, "Now concerning the unmarried, I have no command of the Lord, but I give my opinion as one who by the Lord's mercy is trustworthy."[32] As Synave and Benoit relate, an author can speak about many things but does not have to be making formal truth judgments about every single one of them. They elaborate:

Truth is the *adequatio rei et intellectus* [conformity of mind and thing]. It exists only in the judgment. And by "judgment" we obviously do not mean every proposition made up of subject, verb, and predicate, but the formal act by which the intellect (*intellectus*) affirms its conformity (*adequatio*) to the object of knowledge (*res*).... An author does not speak of everything in an absolute way; we must always inquire into his point of view. He tells the truth or he is mistaken only within the limits of the field of vision which he has established for himself and in which he forms his judgment. Furthermore, he does not always make an affirmation. He may assent either totally or in a restricted way to the objective truth contained in the proposition which he is enunciating. Sometimes his affirmation will be categorical; sometimes it will be made with reservations of one sort or another: he accepts it as probable, he thinks it likely, he considers it possible, a matter of conjecture, etc.... He cannot be denied the right to limit the extent of his own subjective conviction and to involve himself only to the extent he wishes. We must therefore respect the varying degrees of his assent, rather than take all his sentences as categorical affirmations.[33]

31. In *Aspects of Biblical Inspiration*, Benoit goes so far as to say that many times "the inspired person does nothing but judge and present under divine light merely natural truths. This case being, in point of fact, the most frequently met with in the Bible, it was important to link with prophecy in the strict sense." (38.)

32. 1 Cor 7:25.

33. Synave and Benoit, *Prophecy and Inspiration*, 134–35.

As we saw above, revealed truth lies in the act of judgment where-in a prophet's intellect correctly apprehends a supernatural reality shown to it by God. However, according to Synave and Benoit, not every statement in scripture constitutes such a judgment. Indeed, it seems clear that biblical authors conditioned their judgments, sometimes speaking about divine affairs without intending to make definitive judgments or to teach regarding them—even sometimes in matters of "faith and morals" such as the nature of God, the nature of good and evil, and the afterlife, all of which are examined in this book.

According to Matthew Lamb, this conditioning fits with the nature of Sacred Scripture as a testimony to the divine pedagogy by which God gradually revealed himself to his people. He explains:

> We tend to regard a truth as either clearly and explicitly revealed or not revealed at all. But for St. Thomas man's knowledge of the faith grows, [and] truths are revealed slowly over a period of time.... The Bible communicates this organic development of salvation-history to men up to its definitive apex in the revelation of the Word Incarnate himself. The whole of the Bible must be approached with faith; this does not mean that every sentence is a definable dogma.[34]

In this way, the authors of scripture understood and taught revealed truth with varying degrees of clarity depending on their place within the course of salvation history and the divine pedagogy. As Lamb indicates, it is not as if one can find a definable dogma in every sentence of scripture; indeed, scripture never claims this about itself. Pope Benedict himself has spoken to this point many times in the way he instantiates his exegetical principles, attempting to determine the "essential point" asserted in concrete biblical texts. Benedict demonstrates keen awareness that certain texts seem plainly to contradict the assertions of other texts:

> It is because faith is not set before us as a complete and finished system that the Bible contains contradictory texts, or at least ones that stand in tension to each other.[35]

---

34. Lamb, trans., Thomas Aquinas, *Commentary on ... Ephesians*, 256n17.

35. Benedict XVI, *God and the World: A Conversation with Peter Seewald* (San Francisco: Ignatius Press, 2002), 152; cf.: "The problem of dating Jesus's Last Supper

It follows straightaway that neither the criterion of inspiration nor that of infallibility can be applied mechanically. It is quite impossible to pick out one single sentence and say, right, you find this sentence in God's great book, so it must simply be true in itself.[36]

As Benedict well knows, the problem of admitting the presence of contradictory biblical texts lies in squaring it with the doctrine of inerrancy as it is articulated in *Dei Verbum*: "[E]verything asserted by the inspired authors or sacred writers must be held to be asserted by the Holy Spirit."[37]

When it comes to applying this concept to the works of scripture, one must therefore inquire into the field of vision that a particular author has established for himself and the point of view from which he treats the subject at hand. With this in mind, biblical scholar and abbot Denis Farkasfalvy goes so far as to affirm that biblical texts may be found "faulty" in certain regards so long as one recognizes that they do not aim to assert the imperfect or faulty statement in question:

---

arises from the contradiction on this point between the Synoptic Gospels, on the one hand, and Saint John's Gospel, on the other." Benedict XVI, *Jesus of Nazareth: Holy Week: From the Entrance into Jerusalem to the Resurrection* (San Francisco: Ignatius Press, 2011), 106.

36. Benedict XVI, *God and the World*, 153; cf. Benedict XVI, Address to Participants in the Plenary Meeting of the Pontifical Biblical Commission (May 2, 2011): "Lastly, I would only like to mention the fact that in a good hermeneutic it is not possible to apply mechanically the criterion of inspiration, or indeed of absolute truth by extrapolating a single sentence or expression. The plan in which it is possible to perceive Sacred Scripture as a Word of God is that of the unity of God, in a totality in which the individual elements are illuminated reciprocally and are opened to understanding."

37. Second Vatican Council, *Dei Verbum*, 11. The text continues: "... it follows that the books of Scripture must be acknowledged as teaching solidly, faithfully, and without error that truth which God wanted put into sacred writings for the sake of salvation." An illuminating example of Benedict's attempt to determine the assertions of biblical authors can be seen in his treatment of Christ's descent into hell. As the pontiff explains, "We can now define exactly what this word [hell] means: it denotes a loneliness that the word love can no longer penetrate.... This article [of the Creed] asserts that Christ strode through the gate of our final loneliness, that in his Passion he went down into the abyss of our abandonment. Where no voice can reach us any longer, there is he.... From this angle, I think, one can understand the images—which at first look so mythological—of the Fathers, who speak of fetching up the dead, of the opening of the gates." Benedict XVI, *Credo for Today: What Christians Believe* (San Francisco: Ignatius Press, 2009), 89–90.

Divine inspiration does not imply that each passage and sentence of the biblical text must be found free of error from every conceivable point of view. The grammarian, the scientist, the historian, and others may point out a particular passage which, when examined from some limited point of view by some specialized endeavor of human learning, can be found faulty. But such a realization does not prove that God's word asserts error. Rather, it only means that God's message is expressed, at one or another point of salvation history, with the imperfections characteristic of human existence. Nevertheless, in the way it serves both the human author's concretely defined purpose and its divine author's salvific purpose, every passage expresses the truth which it is supposed to express according to God's salvific will.[38]

Here, Farkasfalvy acknowledges that the scriptures are not inerrant "from every conceivable point of view." One might expand upon Farkasfalvy by employing the Thomistic form-matter distinction so as to clarify that any purported errors are in reality material imperfections rather than true, formal errors.[39] This is significant because the charism of inspiration still conveys "the human author's concretely defined purpose and its divine author's salvific purpose," in such a way that "every passage expresses the truth which it is supposed to express according to God's salvific will."[40]

38. Farkasfalvy, *Inspiration and Interpretation*, 232. Farkasfalvy's explanation has many resonances with the following of C. S. Lewis. Writing on the subject of the Psalms, Lewis observes: "The human qualities of the raw materials show through. Naiveté, error, contradiction, even (as in the cursing psalms) wickedness are not removed. The total result is not 'the word of God' in the sense that every passage, in itself, gives impeccable science or history. It carries the word of God; and we ... receive that word from it not by using it as an encyclopedia or an encyclical but by steeping ourselves in its tone or temper and so learning its overall message." C. S. Lewis, *Reflections on the Psalms* (London: Harvest Books, 1964), 111–12.

39. Though Thomas does not apply this hylomorphic distinction in the present context, one can see the principle in various places throughout his corpus: "Now, in a voluntary action, there is a twofold action, viz. the interior action of the will, and the external action: and each of these actions has its object. The end is properly the object of the interior act of the will: while the object of the external action, is that on which the action is brought to bear. Therefore just as the external action takes its species from the object on which it bears; so the interior act of the will takes its species from the end, as from its own proper object.... Consequently the species of a human act is considered formally with regard to the end, but materially with regard to the object of the external action." Thomas Aquinas, *ST*, I-II, q.18, a.6. The material or external dimension in question here lies in the words of the sacred author, while the formal dimension or end concerns what the author intends to assert for its own sake by means of said matter.

40. This distinction between "material imperfections" and "formal errors" is ab-

In order to draw out this distinction between material imperfections and formal errors, we need to consider Synave and Benoit in their argument to the effect that while certain authors personally may have held views that were mistaken to some degree, the charism of inspiration prevented these authors from teaching such views. They illustrate how it can be that these opinions of the sacred writers do not result in formal written errors:

[God] certainly cannot prevent [the sacred author] from using in one way or another these erroneous views and, consequently, from letting them show through in his text. For example, no one will deny that the biblical authors had now outmoded cosmological ideas in which they believed, and that they employed them in their writings because they were unable to think apart from contemporary categories. But they do not claim to be teaching them for their own sakes; they speak of them for a different purpose, e.g. to illustrate creation and divine providence.[41]

In this passage, Synave and Benoit propose an example from the creation account(s) of Genesis 1–2 in order to clarify how an inspired work can be free of error despite the fact that its author personally held erroneous views. A Method B analysis of Genesis's creation account clearly indicates that its author held, and allowed to be visible, in his work a view of the universe and its creation that does not square with modern science. However, while a Method C exegete may admit that the author of Genesis held problematic views, he is certain that Genesis was not intending to teach views which are in-

---

solutely crucial. I could equally have employed the term "material errors" instead of "material imperfections," but have not done so here in the effort to make it clear that statements which fail to correspond to reality but which are not *asserted* or *taught* for their own sake are not errors in the true sense of the term. The Catholic tradition lacks the distinction between material/formal errors in scripture, but it does make such a distinction elsewhere with respect to heresy, for example. A material heresy objectively fails to conform to Christian doctrine, but one is not a true or formal heretic unless he knowingly and willingly asserts a claim that contradicts orthodox Christian doctrine.

41. Synave and Benoit, *Prophecy and Inspiration,* 142. Regarding this topic, an authority no less than Leo XIII explains that professors of scripture must seek to ascertain the communicative intention of the sacred author with the awareness that what science demonstrates about the nature of the universe does not contradict the message of scripture. He states, "There can never, indeed, be any real discrepancy between the theologian and the physicist, as long as each confines himself within his own lines." *Providentissimus Deus* §18.

accurate with respect to what has since come to be known through natural science. In this, then, lies the difference between material imperfections and formal errors: a material imperfection may exist within a person's statement or may be held by a person, while a formal error is asserted or taught for its own sake. A formal error occurs when what an author asserts for its own sake does not conform to reality.[42]

Even in her Method A approach, the church has long taught that scripture does not treat of astronomy or the natural sciences for their own sake. It teaches man about God and addresses other realms in relation to their religious dimension, insofar as they are ordered to God. When it comes to Genesis, the author's interest lies not in the number of days it took for the world to be created or in the order in which the various animals came into being, but the place of man and woman within a universe wisely ordered by the one true God so that things are directed to and find their fulfillment in the sabbath. Synave and Benoit expand upon this notion by explaining that the authors of scripture were concerned more with the religious significance of science and history than science and history themselves:

42. One might object that Synave and Benoit here make an unwarranted presupposition in stating that scripture's authors could not affirm or teach erroneous views. However, beginning with the principle that the scriptures cannot assert or teach falsehoods is precisely what is required by the decision to approach scripture "from above," that is to say from the church's doctrine regarding the inerrancy of scripture. Still, critics could easily object that Catholics may appear to admit the presence of material imperfections in scripture, but then turn around and quickly dismiss all of them with the facile and disingenuous claim that anything problematic in scripture is not actually being asserted or taught for its own sake. While this logic may arouse skepticism, there is no way around it for a Method C exegete. Because Catholics acknowledge the harmony of faith and reason, if our reason (in the form of natural science, philosophy, biblical scholarship, etc.) indicates the presence of a material imperfection in scripture, then our first principle of faith in the inspiration and inerrancy of the scriptures *necessitates* that this material imperfection cannot be part of an assertion being made or taught for its own sake, as that would constitute a formal error and therefore disprove Catholic dogma. Lest one find himself overwhelmed at this point, it is important to keep in mind that, for Aquinas, Catholic teaching—including its doctrine on the inspiration of scripture—does not need to be proven by the Christian but rather *defended* against objections. Cf. *ST*, I, q.1, a.8.

It is quite clear that the inspired author, and behind him God, treats many subjects only for their religious interest. The sun and the moon speak to him of the wisdom and omnipotence of God; he is not interested in the scientific laws which govern their revolutions.... Scientific history, which seeks the minutest accuracy for its own sake, is one thing; quite different is history of a religious or apologetic tendency, which is intent on bringing out the important lessons from the dusty past and is concerned with events for this sole purpose. While it assuredly does not falsify the events, it does not worry about minute exactitude.[43]

By emphasizing the religious interest of scripture's authors, however, Synave and Benoit are not advocating the popular view that one should draw a divide between "religious" or "saving" truths (dealing directly with God and his providence) and "profane" truths (e.g. historical details). The former would be intended in scripture and the latter would be excluded entirely from its scope of teaching and therefore considered "non-inspired." According to Synave and Benoit, this view is falsified by the fact that scripture's authors sometimes clearly do intend to convey so-called profane truths (though one ought to remember that their presentation is always governed by a greater theological concern).[44] Thus, for a Method C exegete, even those areas of scripture in which one might be tempted to admit the

43. Synave and Benoit, *Prophecy and Inspiration*, 137. In the volume *The Intellectual Adventure of Ancient Man: An Essay on Speculative Thought in the Ancient Near East* (Chicago: University of Chicago Press, 1946), William Andrew Irwin sheds insight into the purpose of history for the ancient Israelite. Like Synave and Benoit, Irwin thinks that the authors of scripture at times personally held less than ideal views of the universe and of the history that has transpired within it. Irwin is not bothered by the presence of these views in scripture, but rather attributes them to the fact that the sacred authors often concerned themselves with the *meaning* of history rather than with a mere account of facts: "Some of the defects of the historian's method are traceable to the fact that his interest was not so much in recording events as in explaining them. And such a temper can mean only one thing. Hebrew history was primarily a philosophy of history." (322.) Here, Irwin speaks of the Hebrew historian's method as containing "defects," but there could certainly be discussion over whether it is defective *in se* or rather defective according to the standards set up for history in the modern world.

44. Various examples of Hebrew historiography being shaped by theological (and even political) concerns are presented in Kenton Sparks, *God's Word in Human Words: An Evangelical Appropriation of Critical Biblical Scholarship* (Grand Rapids, Mich.: Baker Academic, 2008), 73–132. For example, in chapter 1 we discussed how the chronicler's writing about David differs in important ways from what one observes in Samuel-

presence of formal errors must still be considered inspired and iner-rant since the Holy Spirit employs their "profane" elements for his own purpose. The task at hand, then, does not consist in adjudicat-ing which passages of scripture are religious and inerrant on the one hand, and which are profane and prone to error on the other hand; rather, the real goal here must be to discern what precisely consti-tutes the inerrant message scripture's authors are intending to teach us in each of their writings and as a whole.

When considering the entire gamut of Pope Benedict's corpus, one discovers a consistent attempt on the part of the pontiff to as-certain precisely this message. One such example can be seen in how he deals with the giving of the Ten Commandments on Mt. Sinai. Benedict insists that the narrative refers to a real event in history, but to the discomfort of the Christian, he observes that "whether there really were any stone tablets is another question."[45] Even if it were the case that one could disprove the existence of these physi-cal artifacts, for Benedict it would not change "the essential point" of the Sinai narrative, namely "that God, through the agency of his friend, really makes himself known in an authoritative way." This is the *substance* of the narrative, the author's principal concern in light of the entire context. Benedict is adamant that the Christian need not worry about whether the account conforms to contemporary Western standards of historiography. Many details Christians con-sider essential today are in truth accidental features of the text and as such must be understood within the context of the entire Bible. They were a part of the author's presentation as a whole but not his principal concern, and for this reason they cannot be deemed formal "errors." Indeed, it is doubtful that the compilers of the canon would have been unaware of the problems people raise today: it seems they deliberately left ambiguities in scripture so that later genera-tions could "struggle with God" as they had done and perhaps build

---

Kings. For another example of an evangelical Christian scholar who deals seriously with modern challenges in this area, see Peter Enns, *Inspiration and Incarnation,* (Grand Rapids, Mich.: Baker Academic, 2005)

45. Benedict XVI, *God and the World*, 166 (emphasis added). See also his attempt to ascertain the essential point passages concerning creation, 75–95.

on the tradition they were blessed to receive from their ancestors.

One finds the same *modus operandi* in Benedict's discussion of whether the events that unfolded on Sinai were myth or history. Here, he concretely applies the principle he elsewhere praised in Aquinas concerning his "open philosophy" that is capable of accounting for a God who enters history and speaks through human words. Benedict does not deny that the Sinai narrative is imbued with a certain mythological flare (thunder, lightning, clouds, trumpets, flames, quaking, God's hand writing on stone, etc.), but he affirms that it "refers to a *real event*, a real entering into history by God, to a real meeting between God and his people," and through them to a meeting with mankind. This, according to Benedict, is the "essence of the event."[46]

Benedict follows this line of reasoning for matters concerning the New Testament. At the very least, Pope Benedict suggests that in his day Jesus often employed existing images of the afterlife and Hades without intending to formally teach or assert their conformity to reality:

Jesus uses ideas that were current in the Judaism of his time. Hence we must not force our interpretation of this part of the text. Jesus adopts existing images, without formally incorporating them into his teaching about the next life. Nevertheless, he does unequivocally affirm the substance of the images.... But, as we saw earlier, this is not the principal message that the Lord wants to convey in this parable. Rather, as Jeremias has convincingly shown, the main point—which comes in the second part of the parable—is the rich man's request for a sign.[47]

What Benedict has in mind here are Jesus's apparent assumptions about Hades such as they manifest themselves in Luke 16. Benedict indicates that Jesus's pedagogy involved the use of ideas and images current in his day without "formally incorporating them" into his

46. Ibid., 165 (emphasis added).

47. Benedict XVI, *Jesus of Nazareth*, translated by Adrian J. Walker (New York: Doubleday, 2007), 215–16. On the question of the extent to which Jesus himself was limited in his theological vision as a first-century Jew, see Sparks, *Sacred Word, Broken Word*, 26–27; I. Howard Marshall, *Beyond the Bible: Moving from Scripture to Theology* (Grand Rapids, Mich.: Baker Academic, 2004), 66–69; Colin Gunton, *Christ and Creation* (Grand Rapids, Mich.: Eerdmans, 1992), 41.

teaching. While Jesus did "unequivocally affirm the substance of the images," the images themselves do not constitute "the principal message the Lord wants to convey in this parable." Agreeing with Joachim Jeremias, the pope proposes that the "main point" of this parable, when taken in light of the whole, concerns the rich man's request for a sign rather than the nature of the afterlife, which may or may not be accurately conveyed through the imagery employed by Jesus. Benedict's work here thus provides the Method C exegete with an example of how he is to go about his work of reconciling apparently contradictory texts with Catholic teaching on biblical inspiration and inerrancy. The pope does not go so far as to allow that Jesus himself held imperfect ideas about the afterlife, but his exegesis at least implies that an inspired author does not formally assert every last problematic thing that he says.

We may bolster the claims of Benedict and the other authors above by examining the issue of authorial affirmations or judgments from two more angles. In the first, we will consider suggestions made by James Burtchaell in his *Catholic Theories of Biblical Inspiration since 1810*. Like the authors drawn from above, Burtchaell recognizes the presence of material imperfections in the Bible. What he brings to the table is a theological meta-narrative that attempts to reconcile the Bible's imperfections in light of the divine pedagogy. Without using this precise patristic term, he conveys many of the ideas discussed already throughout the present volume. For example, he calls the Bible "the chief record of the faith's gestation, of those long years when Christianity was carried in the womb of Israel. It documents that time—never to be repeated—when God's revelation was slowly and painfully trying to assert itself amid the night of human disinterest."[48] This statement is particularly illuminating for our study because it speaks of the Christian faith having a "gestation" period in which it gradually developed inside the "womb" of Israel—an idea comparable to the conception of Benedict and Aquinas according to which the "substance of the faith" develops over

---

48. James Tunstead Burtchaell, *Catholic Theories of Biblical Inspiration since 1810: A Review and Critique* (London: Cambridge University Press, 1969), 301.

time like an embryo or a rose. Burtchaell also highlights the uniqueness of this process, a time "never to be repeated," as well as the fact that God's efforts were repeatedly met with disinterest and rejection on the part of his people.

Burtchaell extends his narrative in the effort to illumine the broader issue of how Christians are to reconcile the doctrine of biblical inerrancy with the Bible's many difficulties:

> Both by those who accept these claims [of inerrancy and infallibility] and by those who reject them, they have been imagined as some sort of flawless, eternal ownership of the truth, expressed in formulas that might from time to time need a little translating, but never need replacing. In this sense, there has probably never been an inerrant declaration uttered or book written, nor need we look forward to one. But if inerrancy involve wild, and sometimes even frightening movement, if it mean being pulled to the right and to the left, being tempted constantly to deviate, yet always managing somehow to regain the road, then it begins to sound rather like what the Church has been about.... In sum, the Church does find inerrancy in the Bible, if we can agree to take that term in its dynamic sense, and not a static one. Inerrancy must be the ability, not to avoid all mistakes, but to cope with them, remedy them, survive them, and eventually even profit from them. In a distinct selection of faith-leavings from a distinct epoch of faith-history, we have the archives of the process by which our ancestral faith began from nothing, involved itself in countless frustrating errors, but made its way, lurching and swerving, "reeling but erect," somehow though never losing the way, to climax in Christ.[49]

Burtchaell's key contribution here is to suggest that Catholics take the doctrine of inerrancy in a "dynamic" sense. He is criticizing what he takes to be the common, "static" approach wherein Christians isolate individual statements of scripture and expect to find perfect correspondence to reality in every single one of them without considering the context of the Bible as a whole and the divine pedagogy at work therein. He believes that this approach to scripture is not faithful to the scriptures themselves, nor is it "what the Church has been about" over the millennia.

According to Burtchaell, the insufficiency of a "static" approach that would focus exclusively on the Bible's formal truth claims is evi-

49. Ibid., 299, 303–4.

dent from an investigation of the Hebrew term אֱמֶת. Often translated into English as "truth," אֱמֶת occurs 126 times in the Old Testament and is accepted in a variety of definitions, including "reliability," "permanence," "faithfulness," and "truth." As the Hebrew language bears witness, ancient Israelites did not view truth simply as theoretical but also in *relational* terms. In other words, for the Israelite, God does not only teach what is true; he is also true (i.e. faithful) to his word:

> The Old Testament, speaking of God's truth, or *emeth*, intends not so much that his word is true, as that He is true to his word.... For the Old Testament, God's truth is primarily given through his faithfulness.... While the idea is never absent that God's words are true, this never has reference to the Scriptures, as if to imply that they contain no historical error.... This attitude confuses the truth of Scripture with faultless historical chronicle.[50]

Burtchaell's argument here is not perfect, nor does it need to be. It may not give adequate attention to scripture's propositional truth claims, but he is certainly on to something. For, to a certain extent, challenges to biblical inerrancy actually present something of a pseudo-problem if we understand inerrancy correctly. It is unlikely that many things we demand of scripture today in the Western world were concerns for those who wrote it. This is why it is crucial to discern the intention of the sacred authors and to demonstrate that their purpose was not always to teach propositional truths after the manner of a textbook.

Interestingly, Burtchaell sides with Method B scholars in his desire to seriously confront evidence that the Bible contains material imperfections, yet he also argues in favor of Method A's doctrine of inerrancy. This scholar's synthesis is precisely the sort of effort one would expect in a Method C exegete, because it does not fit neatly within traditional or modern categories. For Burtchaell, if one takes the biblical data seriously, he cannot claim that inerrancy entails the complete absence of individual statements that fail to accurately describe reality. Rather, if even some of the "wild" and "frightening" variations within scripture that Burtchaell observes are real, then in-

50. Ibid., 266–67; cf. *Theological Dictionary of the Old Testament* (hereafter *TDOT*) 1:310; cf. *Theological Dictionary of the New Testament* (hereafter *TDNT*) 1:232–37.

errancy must consist in the biblical authors' uncanny ability to "regain to road," that is to correct the Bible's various material imperfections over time through the charism of inspiration granted to them by God. Indeed, from a Thomistic perspective one might argue that this is to be expected, that the good of God's entire educational plan for mankind is not hindered by the presence of occasional "departures" on the part of the secondary instruments whom he chose to execute it.[51]

A final avenue of approaching the Bible's apparently erroneous truth claims dovetails with that of Burtchaell and builds on contemporary scholarly debates concerning the epistemology of religious belief. The suggestion run as follows: Given the premises their environment provided them, any sacred authors who penned materially imperfect statements often could not help but have inferred these conclusions from their respective premises. For example, we will see later that Ecclesiastes's denials of the afterlife were the only

51. While Burtchaell speaks of dynamic inerrancy entailing the ability of the Bible to gradually correct "countless frustrating errors," I have continued to employ the term "material imperfections" here. While not addressing this specific issue, Aquinas's response to an objection that "the will of God is not always fulfilled" is helpful here. He writes, "Corruption and defects in natural things are said to be contrary to some particular nature; yet they are in keeping with the plan of universal nature; inasmuch as the defect in one thing yields to the good of another, or even to the universal good.... Since God, then, provides universally for all being, it belongs to His providence to permit certain defects in particular effects, that the perfect good of the universe may not be hindered, for if all evil were prevented, much good would be absent from the universe." *ST*, I, q.22, a.2. Applying this principle to the "particular defects" in scripture, we might suggest that a great good would be absent if God had chosen a different means of revelation (e.g., wherein he prevented the sacred authors from writing with inaccurate understanding at times), namely, man's complete freedom to collaborate in the divine act of revelation as a secondary cause. Aquinas likewise explains, "The rule in forms is this: that although a thing may fall short of any particular form, it cannot fall short of the universal form.... Something may fall outside the order of any particular active cause, but not outside the order of the universal cause; under which all particular causes are included: and if any particular cause fails of its effect, this is because of the hindrance of some other particular cause, which is included in the order of the universal cause.... Hence that which seems to depart from the divine will in one order, returns into it in another order." *ST*, I, q.19, a.6. This is a statement Burtchaell would likely endorse wholeheartedly. For, while the sacred authors of scripture may "depart" from the fullness of truth at particular moments, God ensured that scripture would never stray unrecoverably from the path of legitimate development. Since the "universal cause" of God's divine authorship encompasses "all particular causes"—in this case the human authors of scripture—anything they write while inspired is ultimately that which God wanted written, and nothing more.

logical conclusion to be drawn from his accurate observation that the traditional Israelite theology of retribution dominant in his day did not square with his experience of justice in the real world. If we then grant that Ecclesiastes was correct in observing that God's justice does not manifest itself fully in this life (as his community at the time believed), combined with the fact that he had no knowledge of the justice that Christ renders believers after death, then it appears relentlessly honest that Ecclesiastes could not help but draw the logical conclusion that "the fate of the sons of men and the fate of beasts is the same." To borrow the language of philosopher Stephen Wykstra, in Ecclesiastes we are presented with evidence of an "environmental glitch" that causes the sacred author to draw a conclusion which is inconsistent with Christian doctrine. Wykstra carefully distinguishes the former sort of malfunction exhibited in Ecclesiastes from what some philosophers call an "error of rationality." If the Method C exegete is to make use of this distinction, we must deny the existence of any "error of rationality" within the Bible; for, such an error would entail a sacred author making an invalid inference and therefore a formal error since he drew a false conclusion while having full access to the revealed premise(s) necessary for arriving at the truth. In this way, for example, if a New Testament author who knew of Christ's Resurrection had denied the afterlife after the manner of Ecclesiastes, he would have committed a formal error or "error of rationality," whereas Ecclesiastes did not err in this manner since he was not privy to the premises of Christian revelation.[52]

As we have already seen to some extent and will examine more deeply in later chapters, the presence of environmental defects or "glitches" within the Bible does not violate the doctrine of inerrancy. For, as we saw above, truth or error results from an author's judgment, and the Catholic faith requires us to hold that the *substance* of what the sacred author wishes to affirm corresponds to reality. In point of fact, in cases such as Ecclesiastes we have a state of affairs in which a sacred author is not only epistemically warranted in his im-

52. See Stephen Wykstra, "Toward a Sensible Evidentialism: On the Notion of 'Needing Evidence,'" in William Rowe and William Wainright, *Readings in the Philosophy of Religion* (Fort Worth: Harcourt Brace Publishers, 1998), 481–91.

perfect conclusion but might even be *obligated* to it. To illustrate, let us consider an example unrelated to the Bible. Say you are attending a fundraiser and, without your knowledge, an accomplished actor is also in attendance, disguised as Donald Trump. If you have seen Trump on TV, you will be familiar with his appearance, voice, mannerisms, etc. If this actor is truly accomplished, you will quite likely conclude that he is Trump when in fact he is not. However, assuming you are given no reason to doubt Trump's identity at the moment he introduces himself to you, the principle of charity *requires* you to believe that he is who he claims to be, even though, absolutely speaking, you are mistaken. A similar dynamic seems to be at work in parts of the Bible that contain material imperfections. Wise men like Ecclesiastes did not always arrive explicitly at the fullness of Gospel truth, but they wrote precisely what God wanted them to write at their respective points within the divine pedagogy. As with you and your mistake with respect to Trump, Ecclesiastes and other sacred authors may have made mistakes, but since these were due to environmental factors that could not have been avoided at the time, they must not be considered true, formal errors.[53]

THE PRACTICAL JUDGMENT

As illuminating as the above suggestions may be, it is important to remember that they are precisely that: suggestions. They are important because the problems we face in this book are not limited to the scientific or historical sphere. Indeed, it is one thing to assert that a sacred writer had only limited interest in the minute details of astronomy, but it is another matter when one seeks to apply this reasoning to overtly religious matters. The nature of God, the nature of good and evil, and the afterlife are among the most clearly religious issues one can imagine, and we need a deeper explanation to account for apparent mistakes concerning them.

Up to this point in the chapter, we have observed that God may

53. For the Wykstra source and other insights of the previous two paragraphs, I am indebted to fruitful conversations with Jim Madden, my colleague in philosophy at Benedictine College.

grant his prophets the light to judge reality in a supernatural manner even if this judgment does not directly concern things knowable only through divine revelation. We have even raised the possibility that a sacred author may make a mistake in judgment if he could not have done otherwise given his environment. Now, however, we may trace the work of Synave and Benoit as they further propose that God sometimes grants a prophet the light to judge reality in a supernatural manner without primarily intending to teach a truth in the first place. Using characteristically Thomistic terms, Synave and Benoit suggest that inspiration may at times primarily enlighten a prophet's judgment not in the "speculative" order (influencing his intellect in view of teaching some truth) but rather in the "practical" order (influencing his will in view of achieving some good). They propose:

[Scriptural inspiration] influences the will and practical judgment of the writer as much as, and sometimes even more than, his intellect and speculative judgment. This is the first very important respect in which St. Thomas's doctrine on "prophecy" must be adapted if one wishes to extend it to "scriptural inspiration."[54]

Writing seven centuries after their predecessor and in response to new challenges to the doctrine of inspiration, Synave and Benoit realized it was important to expand upon Aquinas's work in order to elucidate prophecy's impact on both the speculative and practi-

54. Benedict XVI, *Jesus of Nazareth*, 62. Cf. Benoit, *Aspects of Biblical Inspiration*, 43. It is important to reiterate that this position of Synave and Benoit is not universally agreed upon, and remains in need of nuance. For example, in a recently republished essay, Peter Paul Zerafa, OP, argues, "Can we get around this difficulty [of problematic biblical texts] by supposing that in such cases the principal judgment applied by the writer is a practical one? Hardly ever.... [The Bible's] message remains the principal factor of the book, and brings with it the speculative judgment as his principal intellectual activity." Zerafa, "The Limits of Biblical Inerrancy," 372. Zerafa does accept many of the distinctions made by Synave and Benoit, but he argues that exegetes should focus their attention more on ascertaining the Bible's literary forms than on the type of judgment being made by biblical authors: "As a result of Benoit's imposing apparatus, one has to admit that the speculative judgment is not a universal characteristic of the Bible. We must not search for inspired truth in all that is said by the sacred writer, since some apparent judgments are incorporated in the Bible for practical reasons, and not as representing divine thought. This conclusion is sound, and it is exactly the duty of the exegetes to ascertain, by studying the literary forms, where the sacred writer expresses speculative judgments and to disclose their import." (371.)

cal judgments of scripture's sacred authors. After explaining the better known purpose of a speculative judgment, they offer a profound statement of the difference between a speculative judgment, which is made in view of teaching some truth, and a practical judgment, which is made with the view of achieving some good. Of course, an author will often write with the purpose of instructing his audience:

[B]ut he can also appeal to their affective side, working on their feelings and emotions. There are many objects which an author can have in view—to console, threaten, charm, relax, amuse, entertain, etc.—all of which are quite distinct from the search for pure truth; they may even hinder or supplant it.... It makes use of the speculative judgment as one element in the psychological complex which it wishes to deposit in the book, but not the only one, since the presentation of truth is not its only purpose. It limits the formal object of the speculative judgment or regulates its degree of affirmation and of presentation according to its assigned function in the plan of the work.... Not only does the practical judgment direct and moderate the expression of the speculative judgment; it can even do without it. This will be the case when the author says certain things merely for the sake of elegance, amusement, or relaxation, without attributing to these statements any importance in the intellectual or doctrinal order and without making any appraisal of their intrinsic truth. This will also be the case when he cites the remarks of another author without having himself thought them through or made them his own, but simply because he thinks it opportune to make them known.... It is enough to open the Bible to realize that the sacred writers, under the divine impulse, spoke with all the varying shades of meaning which men employ in their daily speech and that they had in view other objects besides doctrinal instruction.... Finally, we note more than once that even they are anxious to transmit to posterity the recollection of ways of acting or of thinking which they thought it useful to preserve, without intending to inculcate them or to teach them.... As a result, the practical judgment too receives its share of inspiration, and it does so in a higher or lower degree according to its relative importance in the actual thought processes of the inspired subject. To which of the two judgments will the first, principal impulse of inspiration be directed? This depends on God's intention, that is to say, on the mission he is entrusting to the one inspired.[55]

55. Synave and Benoit, *Prophecy and Inspiration*, 104–6. For a related but distinct recent treatment of the "practical judgment" of scripture's authors, see Sparks, *Sacred Word, Broken Word*, 99–101. Sparks does not use the term "practical judgment," but he does discuss the fact that the biblical authors had other intentions in addition to giving instruction. For example, "Empathy is another element in good reading. The point is not to recover an author's 'intention' but rather to enter into the human situation of the

Entire studies could be based upon what is said in this rich passage, but we should at least make the following observations.

To begin, Synave and Benoit point out that a sacred author may receive the prophetic gift in such a way that he writes primarily in order to achieve a practical end, for example the good of arousing his audience's affective side rather than instructing them regarding a particular truth. An author may seek to console, threaten, admonish, charm, relax, amuse, or simply entertain with a good story. The law codes in Leviticus, for example, were not simply drawn up for the purpose of teaching truths or elucidating the nature of good and evil but in order to govern the people and lead them toward God.[56] Similarly, the wise maxims in the wisdom literature (including the negative statements of Ecclesiastes) were often aimed at instructing the people in prudent conduct more than in speculative knowledge of God. The Psalms themselves were often composed for non-speculative ends, for example prayer, song, and liturgical worship (rather than for articulating the nature of God). Furthermore, Synave and Benoit state that authors sometimes intend "simply to hand on to posterity the memory of some customs or beliefs which he wants to save from oblivion, without, however, proposing them as models for imitation or as truths for belief." This end is shown most clearly through the fact that Scripture presents us with a broad and sweeping history of the chosen people which includes the good, the bad, and the ugly. When the sacred author recounts the misdeeds of David, for example, it is unlikely that he wants his audience simply to learn new truths or to imitate David's behavior. Far from it; he probably has the practical goal of getting his audience to learn from the failures of his ancestors and to appreciate the work of the divine pedagogy that had led the nation despite the successes and failures of its great men.[57] It would be easy to come up with dozens of similar examples which illustrate the role of practical judgment in the books of Sacred Scripture.

author and audience." (100.) This dynamic will unfold in later chapters as we discuss biblical works such as Job more concretely.

56. The "practical" nature of many of these statutes is likewise indicated by the fact that Jesus saw them as provisory.

57. The examples I offer above are based on the work in Benoit, *Aspects of Biblical Inspiration*, 104.

An examination of Aquinas's biblical commentaries suggests that he already acknowledged some of these practical ends in scripture. For example, in the prologue to his *Commentary on the Psalms* he states, "The mode or form in Sacred Scripture is found to be of many kinds."[58] He proceeds to enumerate these modes, many of which bear close resemblance to those discussed by Synave and Benoit. First, in the historical books one finds the "narrative" mode. Aquinas does not expound much upon what he has in mind here, but it seems consistent with the thought of Synave and Benoit to the effect that a writer may compose a narrative in order to pass on something rather than to propose it as a model for imitation or a truth for belief. Next, St. Thomas comes to the mode which is "admonishing, exhortative, and preceptive." He explains that this mode is found in the law, the prophets, and the books of Solomon. He goes on to elaborate on the "disputative" mode which is exemplified in Job. According to Aquinas, Job ought to be read as a dispute between man and God over the nature of divine providence rather a definitive teaching on the subject. As we will see later in this work, the afflictions and struggles of Job provide Christians with a theme for debate over the grave problem of the existence of moral and physical evil. Finally, Aquinas deals with the mode he calls "deprecative" or "laudative." The book of Psalms was composed by means of praise and prayer and for the purpose of prayer; it exists "in order that the soul might be joined to God." For Aquinas, a person does not just read the Psalms: he prays them in order to be united to God through this prayer.

In the various examples described above, Aquinas clearly has in mind something other than the mere intention by scripture's sacred authors to teach truths of the speculative order. He does not make use of the term "practical" in this particular context, but he seems to have viewed these various modes in terms of the practical order. However, we find evidence for this claim in Aquinas's commentary on 2 Tm 3:16, in which he writes that Sacred Scripture has a twofold purpose: "[Scripture] is profitable for knowing the truth and for directing action." He goes so far as to articulate this explicitly in terms

58. Thomas Aquinas, prologue to *In psalmos Davidis expositio* (translations of this work are mine).

of the practical and speculative: "For [Scripture] has a speculative as well as a practical dimension."[59] He does not explicitly refer to the latter aspect of scripture as an instance of prophecy, but once again his words appear consistent with such an interpretation. Whatever the case, the above analysis at least ought to show that Aquinas was well attuned to the fine details of scriptural authorship and not entrenched in a framework that would view scripture solely in terms of the speculative order. Far from it, as was observed above: Aquinas sees that the ultimate effect of scripture is that it "leads men to the perfect." And according to Aquinas, a man is perfect when he is "instructed, that is to say prepared for every good work."[60] To bring this discussion full circle, we may point out that, in the same way that Christian doctrine as a whole is both speculative and practical, for St. Thomas scripture "instructs" us with the view of teaching the truth as well as helping us achieve the good.[61]

CONCLUSION: THE SPECULATIVE AND PRACTICAL IN RELATION TO SCRIPTURE'S ULTIMATE PRACTICAL END

In concluding this chapter, we need to recall that whatever emphasis one may place on the role of practical judgment and the fact that scripture is not simply a vehicle for transmitting doctrinal propositions, scripture certainly does teach speculative truths. For

59. Thomas Aquinas, *Super II Epistolam B. Pauli ad Timotheum lectura*, caput 3, lectio 3 (translations from this commentary are mine). See also *ST*, II-II, q.173, a.2: "Intellectual light is divinely imprinted on the mind—sometimes for the purpose of 'judging' of things seen by others ... sometimes for the purpose of 'judging' according to Divine truth, of the things which a man apprehends in the ordinary course of nature— *sometimes for the purpose of discerning truthfully and efficaciously what is to be done.*"

60. Ibid.

61. See Thomas Aquinas, *ST*, I, q.1, a.4. "Sacred doctrine, being one, extends to things which belong to different philosophical sciences because it considers in each the same formal aspect, namely, so far as they can be known through divine revelation. Hence, although among the philosophical sciences one is speculative and another practical, nevertheless sacred doctrine includes both; as God, by one and the same science, knows both Himself and His works." Despite the fact that divine teaching is ordained primarily to the knowledge of God in which man's eternal bliss consists, God also teaches man in order that he might apply this knowledge in the moral life.

Synave and Benoit, it is important to have a balanced appreciation of the roles of speculative and practical judgment when approaching scripture, because there is no single hard and fast rule for telling when a particular type of judgment is being made:

It may be that the sacred writer categorically affirms a doctrinal truth which he has thought out by himself. In that event, his inspiration will include as complete an illumination of his knowledge as in the case of the prophet. It may happen, on the other hand, that he makes no affirmations, that he speaks or cites other authors' accounts without vouching for them as his own thought. In that case inspiration will affect only his practical judgment. Or finally—and this is the most frequent case—it may happen that he expresses a judgment of truth, but one which is conditioned in its formal object and in its degree of affirmation by the general demands of the end he has in view; in this case the light of inspiration will illuminate this judgment, not as an absolute, but to the exact extent to which the author conceives and expresses it.[62]

As Synave and Benoit write, it is most often the case that a given passage of scripture has been composed with an admixture of speculative and practical judgments on the part of its author. In this scenario, a truth claim is made by the sacred author, but he "conditions" this affirmation based on the more general end he has in view. This leads Synave and Benoit to conclude:

It is the practical judgment, as we have said, that ultimately controls all the possible formalities and limitations of the speculative judgment, and it is the practical judgment itself that comes primarily under the influence of inspiration. It is because God sets up a certain goal as the purpose of his interpreter's activity that he causes him to look at a given aspect of his subject, to make a stronger or weaker affirmation, to instruct to a greater or less degree—in short, that he causes him to choose a certain "literary type." *The first principle, then, should be to discern God's intentions through those of the author.*[63]

As we see here, an author's practical judgment is ultimately what governs the kind of speculative judgments he will make within his composition. Before the human author even begins his work, God the divine author already has an intention he wishes his instrument

62. Synave and Benoit, *Prophecy and Inspiration*, 108.
63. Ibid., 143 (emphasis added).

to carry out in his writing. The Holy Spirit enlightens the human's mind in order to direct him to particular realities and affirm them in accordance with the overarching purpose of the book. In this way, if Ecclesiastes writes with the overarching practical aim of getting his audience to think deeply and question a simplistic worldview, without necessarily arriving at a definitive answer to the problem of death, then his denials of life after death do not need to be taken as categorical truth claims that err with respect to what Christians know today. The same logic can be applied to biblical texts which apparently contradict Christian teaching on the nature of God and the nature of good and evil. For example, if God directed the psalmist to be more interested in his prayer than in the identity of "the gods" of which he speaks, it is not surprising that he sometimes employs concepts which fail to square precisely with Christian theology of the triune God. For this reason, Synave and Benoit tell us that the interpreter's primary task is to seek out God's intention as its shines through the intentions of scripture's human authors.

By this point in our endeavor, the reader is keenly aware that searching out a human author's intention is anything but a simple affair. Thankfully, even when the intention of scripture's human author is uncertain, Christians can know with certitude that the divine author has a clear end in mind for those who encounter his word. The Holy Spirit's ultimate "practical" aim for scripture is to convey not only truths but the Truth, inviting the reader to know not only propositions but to encounter the three persons of the Trinity.[64] Concerning this it is illuminating to read Benoit on the topic of truth according to the Semitic worldview. At the conclusion of his survey of prophecy scripture, he states:

64. See also ibid., 251–52, where Farkasfalvy proposes that theologians seek to rediscover scripture's "sacramental" character as part of the synthesis that will allow them to better account for its inspiration. At this point one might also do well to note that such an emphasis could help steer discussion of inspiration in the right direction by taking the emphasis off what Enlightenment rationalism would seek from scripture and placing the emphasis back on scripture's role in leading souls to an encounter with Jesus Christ. Many moderns read scripture as they would a scientific textbook—on the literal level alone, searching for propositions that will give them absolute certitude—but it does not seem that any of scripture's authors actually conceived of their work with such an end in view.

Revelation in the Bible is not the communication of abstract truths, but the concrete living manifestation of a personal Creator and Sanctifier who is the Truth of Life. Though visions and auditions are often associated with revelation, they are not demanded by its nature. Revelation can be conveyed by the immensely varied events of history in which God makes himself known to his people through inspired intermediaries.... Inspiration, then, is not merely a charism of knowledge (which, however, it normally implies), but an impulse which lifts up a man, and through him the whole Chosen People, into a vital encounter with God.[65]

As Synave and Benoit rightly observe, the believer's "vital encounter" with God is the ultimate practical aim of scripture's divine author. What this means with respect to problematic texts of scripture is that these sacred words, however challenging they may be, are aimed at leading "the whole Chosen People" more deeply into the mystery of the Word of God made flesh, Jesus Christ. This provides an excellent way for Christians today to see that all books of Sacred Scripture—not just the ones that neatly line up with Christian doctrine—are relevant both for their role in the salvation history of the past and in our lives today.

Above all else, the Method C exegete ought to emphasize this spiritual dimension of scripture and seek to elucidate it even when to all appearances the scriptures present us with nothing but confusion and contradictions. The spiritual side of scripture is pivotal for one final reason: at the end of the day: even if believer is able to account for all objections to the inspiration and inerrancy of scripture on the basis of Benedict's Method C proposal, this explanation itself does not necessarily yield an *encounter* with the word of God, which is scripture's ultimate reason for being. As we will see in the last part of this work, it turns out that the believer's spiritual encounter with scripture provides a final and definitive key for articulating a theology of scripture.

65. Benoit, *Aspects of Biblical Inspiration*, 87.

CHAPTER 5

METHOD C EXEGESIS, THE NATURE
OF GOD, AND THE NATURE OF
GOOD AND EVIL

In the previous chapter, we followed Aquinas and his commentators as they argued that problematic portions of scripture can be
understood only when the exegete takes into account the practical
ends that govern the composition of biblical texts. The sacred author is an instrument whom God chooses to convey his truth to the
world, but God often wanted works written for a reason other than
merely teaching clear-cut dogmas. The purpose of a work may lie
simply in prayer (e.g. the Psalms), while other times it may be to
propose a debate (e.g. Job), govern (e.g. Leviticus), or exhort (as is
often the case in Paul), just to name a few examples. However, the
highest practical end of every word in the Bible is to lead the chosen
people of both past and present to an encounter with the Word of
God incarnate, Jesus Christ. The insight of Synave and Benoit will
go a long way toward vindicating the inerrant nature of scripture in
the face of apparent contradictions, as their insight clarifies the fact
that even challenging texts which fail to perfectly convey the fullness
of revelation have played a vital role in the salvation history of the
past as well as in the lives of believers today. Still, it is not enough to
propose a framework that claims troublesome statements have their
place in the Bible; in these final chapters we have to instantiate the

proposal of previous chapters by applying it to challenging passages that relate to each of the themes introduced in chapter 1.

To summarize, our goal in this work has been to follow Pope Benedict in his call to synthesize the strengths of faithful and practical patristic-medieval exegesis (Method A) with the tools and findings of historical-critical exegesis (Method B). We began in chapter 1 by using Method B to lay bare the respective problems in our three themes of inquiry (God's nature, the nature of good and evil, and the afterlife). In chapter 2, we laid out Benedict's proposal in detail, elucidating the strengths and weaknesses in both the ancient and modern schools of exegesis. In chapters 3 and 4, we proposed Aquinas's theology as the ideal framework for instantiating Benedict's proposal. His theology of the history of revelation, based upon the hermeneutic of divine pedagogy, provides a sound defense of biblical inerrancy in light of its development throughout the course of salvation history. His theology of the act of revelation, meanwhile, is able to reconcile apparent contradictions as it elucidates the speculative and practical judgments of scripture's authors. Most importantly, it makes it possible to see that the ultimate practical end of all the scriptures—even the most challenging texts—is to lead believers to a vital encounter with the Word of God made flesh, Jesus Christ.

If we are to successfully apply Benedict's proposal in these final chapters, our first task must be to recall some of the problematic passages within each of the respective themes introduced through the Method B observations of chapter 1. Next, we will briefly consider insufficient and sometimes simplistic responses to these problems as they are commonly offered by the Method A approach when working in isolation from Method B. Our effort toward a Method C solution to these problems will then proceed on the basis of Aquinas's framework and the hermeneutic of divine pedagogy, examining the significance of problematic texts for both the past of salvation history and the lives of believers today. As regards the past, we will turn to Aquinas's theology of the history of revelation to elucidate how the chosen people gradually developed in their understanding of God's nature, the nature of good and evil, and the afterlife. We will likewise use Aquinas's theology of the act of revelation in order to search out the intentions of authors when they pen apparent contradictions to Christian doctrine, confident that these contradictions are precisely that: apparent. With respect to the significance of problematic texts for the present, we will go on to see that the pedagogy by which God gradually taught his chosen people as a whole throughout salvation history has an additional dimension: the divine author of scripture uses his word to teach individual members of the faithful still today.[1] Here we arrive at an investigation of the spiritual sense of the texts and consider the divine author's ultimate purpose in composing them.

It is vital that our hermeneutic emphasize this twofold character of the divine pedagogy, as it encapsulates the two components that go into Method C exegesis and provides a bridge between them. For on the one hand, even the most problematic of biblical texts have a definite literal sense. That is to say, their human authors had some pedagogical purpose in mind when they composed them for their original audience. Method B acknowledges this in an eminent way, and one who wants to do Method C exegesis must attend to it. Meanwhile, Method A tells us that these same texts signify something in addition to the meaning originallly intended by their human authors: namely, they signify realities in the lives of believers of all ages who meditate on these texts in order to gain the knowledge and strength they need to faithfully endure the strife that is human life, suffering, and death.

In his own turn, a Method C exegete, while acknowledging the literal sense, will seek out this spiritual sense and strive to show that it is not merely one among many possible readings of scripture but

1. This second dimension of the divine pedagogy is eloquently described by the Pontifical Council for Inter-Religious Dialogue, *Dialogue and Proclamation* (1991): "[The Church] takes her lead from divine pedagogy. This means learning from Jesus himself, and observing the times and seasons as prompted by the Spirit. Jesus only progressively revealed to his hearers the meaning of the Kingdom, God's plan of salvation realized in his own mystery. Only gradually, and with infinite care, did he unveil for them the implications of his message, his identity as the Son of God, the scandal of the Cross. Even his closest disciples, as the Gospels testify, reached full faith in their Master only through their Easter experience and the gift of the Spirit. *Those who wish to become disciples of Jesus today will pass through the same process of discovery and commitment.*" §69 (emphasis mine).

the end point for which God had been preparing the people through his pedagogy over the centuries.[2] By doing this, Method C exegesis does not deny the importance of the literal sense—upon which the spiritual is founded—but in light of the divine pedagogy it allows us to show how the literal sense opens up into spiritual senses that touch the lives of believers in every age. By attempting to facilitate a spiritual encounter with Christ teaching his people in the problematic or "dark" texts of scripture, our project will have completed the most significant and urgent task called for in the exegetical proposal of our Holy Father, Pope Benedict. With that said, let us begin our investigation of the nature of God and the nature of good and evil, reserving this entire chapter for the afterlife. Since biblical data and scholarship abound especially for this problem, we will develop it at greater length in order to offer a more detailed portrait of Method C exegesis.

METHOD C EXEGESIS
AND THE NATURE OF GOD

Review of the Problem from a
Method B Perspective

In his book *The God Delusion*, well-known atheist Richard Dawkins gives a scathing review of the Old Testament and its God:

The God of the Old Testament is arguably the most unpleasant character in all fiction: jealous and proud of it; a petty, unjust, unforgiving control-freak; a vindictive, bloodthirsty ethnic cleanser; a misogynistic, homophobic, racist, infanticidal, genocidal, filicidal, pestilential, megalomaniacal, sadomasochistic, capriciously malevolent bully.... It is unfair to attack such an easy target. The God Hypothesis should not stand or fall with its most unlovely instantiation, Yahweh, nor his insipidly opposite Christian face, "Gentle Jesus meek and mild."[3]

---

2. I have borrowed this terminology from Gregory Vall in his "Psalm 22: *Vox Christi* or Israelite Temple Liturgy?" *The Thomist* 66 (2002): 177. This article was seminal for my own thinking about the divine pedagogy and how to reconcile ancient and modern methods of biblical interpretation through it.

3. Richard Dawkins, *The God Delusion* (Boston: Houghton Mifflin, 2006), 31.

Dawkins's critique is thorough and definitive. Yahweh is "the most unpleasant character in all fiction" and the "most unlovely" example of a god, period. Jesus, meanwhile, is just as bad as Yahweh. However, he is evil because he represents Yahweh's "insipidly opposite face." Both are equally bad, though from Dawkins's point of view they are altogether different divinities. One would be hard-pressed to find harsher criticisms of God's nature than what we observe in Dawkins.

That said, it is interesting that most popular critics of the Judeo-Christian God focus on his moral (or immoral) attributes, apparently unaware of more subtle historical-critical observations that would seem to contradict orthodox doctrine on the nature of God. In particular, in chapter 1 we observed that Pope Benedict himself takes it as a clear given that there were times when the Israelites accepted the existence of multiple divine beings as a matter of course. Here we will recall just a few passages:

> God has taken his place in the divine council;
> in the midst of the gods he holds judgment (Ps 82:1)

> There is none like thee among the gods, O Lord,
> nor are there any works like thine (Ps 86:8).

When men began to multiply on the face of the ground, and daughters were born to them, the sons of God saw that the daughters of men were fair; and they took to wife such of them as they chose.... The Nephilim were on the earth in those days, and also afterward, when the sons of God came in to the daughters of men, and they bore children to them. These were the mighty men that were of old, the men of renown. (Gn 6:1–2, 4)

Then the Lord God said, "Behold, the man has become like one of us, knowing good and evil; and now, lest he put forth his hand and take also of the tree of life, and eat, and live for ever" (Gn 3:22).

Then the angel of God said to me in the dream, "Jacob," and I said, "Here I am!" And he said, "Lift up your eyes and see, all the goats that leap upon the flock are striped, spotted, and mottled; for I have seen all that Laban is doing to you. I am the God of Bethel, where you anointed a pillar and made a vow to me. Now arise, go forth from this land, and return to the land of your birth" (Gn 31:11–13).

And Joshua said to all the people, "Thus says the Lord, the God of Israel, Your fathers lived of old beyond the Euphrates, Terah, the father of Abraham and of Nahor; and they served other gods.... Now therefore fear the Lord, and serve him in sincerity and in faithfulness; put away the gods which your fathers served beyond the River, and in Egypt, and serve the Lord. And if you be unwilling to serve the Lord, choose this day whom you will serve, whether the gods your fathers served in the region beyond the River, or the gods of the Amorites in whose land you dwell; but as for me and my house, we will serve the Lord" (Jo 24:2,14-15).

In chapter 1, we also discussed problems concerning divine immutability, the attribute of God by which we understand his perfect nature cannot suffer change.

And the Lord repented of the evil which he thought to do to his people (Ex 32:14).

[The angel of the Lord] said, "Do not lay your hand on the lad or do anything to him; for now I know that you fear God, seeing you have not withheld your son, your only son, from me" (Gn 22:12).

The apparent contradiction here is that the Old Testament sometimes presents us with a God who changes his mind and learns new things, both of which are impossible according to our reason's grasp of the nature of God. This is merely a brief statement of a problem that runs deeply in scripture and therefore merits attention in our time.

Helpful but Insufficient Method A Responses

As the sampling of texts below shows, for centuries patristic-medieval exegesis has largely overlooked the elements of polytheism latent within the Old Testament. In light of the historical-critical evidence presented in chapter 1, however, it is no longer possible for the Christian to rely solely on even the best of traditional explanations like that found in St. Augustine.

In his *City of God*, Augustine tackles the issue of how divine immutability can be reconciled with statements which appear to indicate God changes his mind. He is very clear that God himself cannot "repent" or change that which he has foreknown he would do:

For though God is said to change His determinations (so that in a tropical [moral] sense the Holy Scripture says even that God repented), this is said with reference to man's expectation, or the order of natural causes, and not with reference to that which the Almighty had foreknown that He would do.[4]

Augustine's answer is brilliant. God cannot literally repent or change his mind. What changes over time is "man's expectation" with regard to God and "the order of natural causes." In other words, when we think we see a change in God's behavior, the change that has taken place really lies in us rather than in him. While this explanation is consonant with Christian doctrine today, we have to ask the same question we asked before in reference to patristic exegesis on the afterlife in scripture: does Augustine arrive at this conclusion *because* of the text of scripture or rather *despite* the intended meaning of its human author? For it is one thing to say that Augustine's account is true in light of what Christians know today, but whether it is true to the text of scripture is another question.

As for those places in scripture which appear to acknowledge the existence of many gods, the doctor of grace is very adamant that the "gods" of which scripture speaks are not divine beings. Rather, at times the term "gods" refers to the men who worship the one true God. As he writes on Psalm 82:1: "For it begins," he says, "*God stood in the synagogue of gods.* Far however be it from us to understand by these Gods the gods of the Gentiles, or idols, or any creature in heaven or earth except men."[5] In his work on Psalm 29, meanwhile, it is clear that for Augustine this is "a Psalm of the Mediator Himself, strong of hand, of the perfection of the Church in this world, where she wars in time against the devil." The "heavenly beings" described in this psalm are not members of a divine council in heaven but rather the sons of the church who have been begotten for Christ: "The Prophet speaks, *Bring unto the Lord, O you Sons of God, bring unto the Lord the young of rams.* Bring unto the Lord yourselves, whom the Apostles, the leaders of the flocks, have begotten by the Gospel."[6]

4. Augustine, *City of God* [*De civitate Dei*], translated by Marcus Dods, vol. 2, *Nicene and Post-Nicene Fathers, First Series,* edited by Philip Schaff (Buffalo, N.Y.: Christian Literature Publishing Co., 1888), 14.11.

5. Augustine, *Exposition on the Psalms* [*Enarrationes in psalmos*], translated by J. E. Tweed, vol. 8, *Nicene and Post-Nicene Fathers, First Series,* edited by Philip Schaff (Buffalo, N.Y.: Christian Literature Publishing Co., 1888), 82.

6. Ibid., 29. One might enquire why Augustine's citations of biblical texts differ so

Augustine's treatment of Psalm 136 explains the nature of these
"gods" at greater length:

*Give thanks to the God of gods, for His mercy endures for ever. Give thanks to
the Lord of lords, for His mercy endures for ever.* We may well enquire, Who
are these gods and lords, of whom He who is the true God is God and Lord?
And we find written in another Psalm, that even men are called gods. The
Lord even takes note of this testimony in the Gospel, saying, *Is it not written in your Law, I have said, You are gods.* It is not therefore because they
are all good, but because the word of God came to them, that they were
called gods.... But it is asked, If men are called gods to whom the word of
the Lord came, are the Angels to be called gods, when the greatest reward
which is promised to just and holy men is the being equal to Angels? In the
Scriptures I know not whether it can, at least easily, be found, that the Angels are openly called gods; but when it had been said of the Lord God, *He
is terrible, above all gods,* he adds, as by way of exposition why he says this,
for the gods of the heathen are devils, that we might understand what had
been expressed in the Hebrew, the gods of the Gentiles are idols, meaning
rather the devils which dwell in the idols.[7]

As he does in his commentary on Psalm 82 and on various other
psalms, Augustine here reiterates the idea that the "gods" of which
the psalmist speaks are none other than the holy men who worship the one true God. He then takes up the question of whether
the angels can be called gods. Interestingly, he refers to the original
Hebrew of Psalm 96 to help establish his point that the "gods" of
the Gentiles are not really divine beings but rather devils who dwell
in their man-made idols. This is a wonderful move from the standpoint of Method C exegesis. For, whereas in other places Augustine
seems to bypass the literal sense of the text in favor of a Christological interpretation, here he is willing to consider how the text in its
original language might shed light on its fullest meaning.

Nevertheless, despite the beauty and erudition of his efforts, Augustine on his own ultimately fails to fulfill today's requirements of
a Method C approach to scripture. Because he is not privy to knowl-

---

much from what we read in our English Bibles. This is explicable due to the fact he used
a Latin translation (and therefore interpretation) of the original Greek and Hebrew
text. Thus when Ps 29:1 in the RSV reads, "Ascribe to the Lord glory and strength," the
Vulgate has "bring unto the Lord the young of rams" (*adferte Domino filios arietum*).

7. Ibid., 136.

edge of the complexities involved with the authorship of the Psalms, Augustine unquestioningly applies what he knows from Psalm 96 to a problem that appears in Psalm 82. While it is a guiding principle of Catholic exegesis to read scripture in light of other parts of scripture, Method C exegesis must do this while respecting the context of each particular text, being careful not to read into it what we think we know based on other texts. Historical-critical scholarship helps keep Method C exegetes honest in this regard, for those who take Christianity's critics seriously constantly have to ask the question: is what we are saying at least plausible in the eyes of those who take seriously the literal sense of Scripture? The Method C exegete thus may not convince his critics of the Bible's truth, but at least they cannot accuse him of brushing aside its greatest difficulties.

Toward a Method C Response

A Method C approach to the problem of God's nature in scripture must begin with an appreciation of the magnitude of the task God had before him when he set out to prepare his people for the coming of Jesus Christ and the revelation of the Trinity. What many Christians do not realize is that the divine pedagogy of the Old Testament begins at square one with a people who worshiped many gods. The book of Joshua recounts Joshua telling the people of Israel, "Your fathers lived of old beyond the Euphrates, Terah, the father of Abraham and of Nahor; and they served other gods" (Jo 24:2). Throughout the Old Testament, we witness Yahweh's struggle to woo the hearts of his people away from false gods and back to himself.

The narrative portions make this abundantly clear as they describe Israel's idolatry in no uncertain terms: "And the people of Israel did what was evil in the sight of the Lord and served the Baals.... They forsook the Lord, and served the Baals and the Ashtaroth" (Jgs 2:11, 13). The admonitions of the prophets, meanwhile, are nothing less than scathing. As God reminds his people through the prophet Ezekiel, "You trusted in your beauty, and played the harlot because of your renown, and lavished your harlotries on any passer-by.... And you took your sons and your daughters, whom you had borne to me, and these you sacrificed to them to be devoured" (Ez 16:15,20). The prophet Elijah was so zealous to blot out Baal worship that he slew many of the prophets of Baal (cf. 1 Kgs 18). The vast evidence of this dynamic leads John Scullion to write:

God in popular Judean or Israelite religion is not necessarily the God of the definitive Hebrew Bible.... One can speak of two religions in Israel: (1) the official one, concerned with the one God and his law ... (2) the popular one, crass, ignorant, with emphasis on the periphery and with practices outside official control.[8]

Scullion goes on to pinpoint some of the places where the official and unofficial Israelite views of God show up in the Old Testament. The popular, unsanctioned theology appears in the books of Samuel and Kings (e.g., the necromancy of 1 Sam. 28 described in chapter 1) as well as in the behavior of Israelites which was condemned by the prophets and prohibited in Deuteronomic literature. In this literature it becomes clear that "those who followed strictly the first commandment (Ex 20:2–5; Dt 5:6–10) and the *Shema* (Dt 6:4–9) were few."[9] Given the prevalence of heterodox views among the chosen people, it ought not to come as a complete surprise that sometimes even the inspired authors of scripture themselves appear to hold ideas about God which are incompatible with monotheism in the sense Christians intend it today. Indeed, the many books of the Old Testament exhibit great diversity with respect to the question of God's identity. How, then, is the Method C exegete to explain that these deviations are not formal errors?

Although the Old Testament fails to paint an utterly unified portrait of God, one may observe a definite trajectory of growth in the chosen people's knowledge of the one true God over the course of divine revelation. Scullion aptly refers to this phenomenon as the Bible's "monotheizing" tendency:

The Hebrew Bible and its final expression of one God is the end result of a struggle for God that has been long and complicated. "The Bible probably should not be thought of as a monotheistic book but as monotheizing literature. There is no serious treatise in it arguing monotheism philosophi-

8. *ABD*, vol. 2, 1042.
9. Ibid.

cally. But every bit of it monotheizes—more or less well." This process of monotheizing came to an official end with the editing and crystallization in writing of the struggle for the one God.... The religious history of Israel is the story of constant falling away from the one God.... There are many stages in the process that lead to the monotheism of Deutero-Isaiah. The journey was not along a straight path.[10]

The Bible's "monotheizing" process indicates its efforts to gradually establish and vindicate monotheism. It did not take the form of a philosophical treatise but was rather a process of trial and error carried out "more or less well," depending on the time period and biblical author one reads. The Old Testament was composed over a span of some eight hundred years, with many high and low points along the path that led to what many consider its culmination when God speaks through the prophet Isaiah: "I am the first and I am the last; besides me there is no god" (Is 44:6), and "I am the Lord, and there is no other.... They have no knowledge who carry about their wooden idols, and keep on praying to a god that cannot save" (Is 45:18,20). Scullion points out that this section of Isaiah, along with Chronicles and Daniel, contains the Old Testament's clearest declaration of God's oneness and uniqueness, that is to say "monotheism in the strict sense."[11]

The low points of the Old Testament's monotheizing efforts are many and evident, as demonstrated in chapter 1. At this juncture, therefore, we may turn our attention specifically to the high points in the process and propose a way to account for their coexistence in the canon with texts that seem to contradict orthodox Christian doctrine. Our first task will be to address the nature of the "divine council" described in chapter 1. There we saw that "such allusions to a plurality of divine beings, occurring especially in the Psalms

10. Ibid. The citation within this citation is from James Sanders, *Canon and Community: A Guide to Canonical Criticism* (Philadelphia: Fortress Press, 1984), 51. The "Deutero-Isaiah" spoken of here refers to the second of three portions of the book of Isaiah (chapters 40–55) that have been distinguished by historical-critical exegesis.

11. Ibid. However, it is by no means the only Old Testament passage that endorses a strict monotheistic view. The psalmist, for example, plainly states with regard to the gentiles, "Their idols are silver and gold, the work of men's hands. They have mouths, but do not speak; eyes, but do not see" (Ps 115:4–5).

and related poetic literature, represent a *stage* when Israel's Yahwism found room for a pantheon in many ways similar to Canannite models."[12] For a Method C hermeneutic that approaches divine revelation in terms of the divine pedagogy, the operative word here is "stage." Israel's belief in the existence of a divine council comprised of "sons of God" was not the nation's definitive view but rather one major stage or step in the process of monotheizing that eventually prepared her to welcome the coming of Jesus Christ as the incarnation of the one true God.

How did the divine pedagogy eventually lead Israel out of her early, polytheistic worldview? First, it is important to remember that all along "these beings are clearly *subordinate* to Yahweh, forming his heavenly court or divine council."[13] In other words, the Bible never presents us with polytheism in the strict sense of the term but rather a form of henotheism, a system that acknowledged the existence of many gods while refusing to worship any of them but one. Thus, when we encounter statements to the effect that "there is none like thee among the gods, O Lord" (Ps 86:8), we are really dealing with a variation of henotheism, or at least a remnant of it. When the psalmist makes the proclamation, "Ascribe to the Lord, O heavenly beings, ascribe to the Lord glory and strength" (Ps 29:1), he is not simply equating Yahweh with the gods of the nations; he is demonstrating that all these gods are subordinate to the God of Israel.

Over time, Israel's fundamental belief in Yahweh's superiority over "sons of the gods" led to the recognition that these beings were not gods at all. As Brendan Byrne informs us, "Eventually the 'sons of the gods' were fused with the concept of angels, a *development* already to be seen in Dn 3:25 and reflected, for the most part, in the LXX."[14] Again, the key word here is "development." Dn 3:25 represents a later stage in the divine pedagogy, a theological development with respect to Israel's understanding of who God is. Daniel recounts the astonishment of King Nebuchadnezzar when, after casting the three Israelite boys into the fiery furnace, there myste-

12. *ABD*, vol. 6, 156 (emphasis added).
13. Ibid (emphasis added).
14. Ibid.

riously appears a fourth being which he apparently takes to be an angel: "But I see four men loose, walking in the midst of the fire, and they are not hurt; and the appearance of the fourth is like a son of the gods."

While this passage from Daniel does not explicitly equate the "sons of the gods" with angels, in other places the Septuagint makes their identity indisputable. Translated only a couple of centuries before the coming of Christ, the LXX represents the culmination of the divine pedagogy insofar as it not only translates but also interprets the original Hebrew text of the Old Testament based on its more mature knowledge of divine realities. For instance, the LXX version of Job repeatedly changes the Hebrew expression "sons of the gods" (בְּנֵי הָאֱלֹהִים) to "the angels of God" (οἱ ἄγγελοι τοῦ θεοῦ) Thus, when our RSV translation of Jb 1:6 (basing itself on the Hebrew) reads, "Now there was a day when the sons of God came to present themselves before the Lord," the LXX actually reads, "Now there was a day when the angels of God came to present themselves before the Lord" (cf. Jb 2:1; 38:7). The LXX of Psalm 96:5 likewise makes a significant change to its Hebrew original. In order to make the true identity of "the gods of the peoples" perfectly clear, it demonstrates that they are not merely "idols"; rather, according to the LXX, "all the gods of the peoples are demons (δαιμόνια)." Emendations of this sort abound in the LXX, but these two are among the most helpful in terms of demonstrating the way Israel's more mature thought articulated the nature of those beings they once described as "the gods" or "sons of the gods."[15]

To round out our treatment of high points in the Old Testament's portrait of the divine nature, we need to examine some other aspects of God's identity and how they pointed towards the New Testament's revelation of the Trinity. The first of these concerns God's father-

---

15. See also Gn 6:2, in which the LXX rescriptor substituted "angels" for "sons" of God. The LXX also emends the Hebrew of Dt 32:8 from "sons of Israel" to read "angels of God." The LXX of Dt 32:43 adds the statement "let all the angels of God worship [God]." It is interesting to note that the LXX is not alone in its emendations. For example, the Targum (early translation of the Bible from Hebrew into Aramaic) also substitutes "angels" for "sons of God."

hood. Our overview of Israel's gradually developing monotheism would remain far from complete if we did not make it clear that the cultivation of man's relationship with God the Father was the end to which the rest of the Bible's monotheizing process was ordered. The Old Testament contains several statements of God's fatherhood, but perhaps the clearest of these forms the Old Testament's *Pater Noster*, found in Is 63:7–64:11.[16] Here, the prophet prays:

> For thou art our Father,
> though Abraham does not know us
> and Israel does not acknowledge us;
> thou, O Lord, art our Father,
> our Redeemer from of old is thy name (Is 64:8).

> Yet, O Lord, thou art our Father;
> we are the clay, and thou art our potter;
> we are all the work of thy hand (Is 63:16).

It is worth observing that this prayer is found in Trito-Isaiah, which Method B exegesis pinpoints as the last of three parts of the book of Isaiah, composed during the Babylonian exile or shortly thereafter. It provides a nice complement to the clear monotheistic affirmations of Deutero-Isaiah we saw above, for here the prophet's goal is not merely to denounce the gods of the nations as idols. Rather, now we see that the purpose of denouncing the idols was to clear the path for something overwhelmingly positive: Israel's relationship with God the Father and the union of all Israelites with one another in him. In another statement of staunch monotheism, the prophet Malachi will take the reality of God's fatherhood as a basis for exhorting the people of God to union with one another: "Have we not all one father? Has not one God created us? Why then are we faithless to one another, profaning the covenant of our fathers?" (Mal 2:10)

16. Other Old Testament statements of God's fatherhood not described in detail here include: "Thus says the Lord, Israel is my first-born son, and I say to you, 'Let my son go that he may serve me'" (Ex 4:22–23); "You are the sons of the Lord your God; you shall not cut yourselves or make any baldness on your foreheads for the dead" (Dt 14:1); "Do you thus requite the Lord, you foolish and senseless people? Is not he your father, who created you, who made you and established you?" (Dt 32:6); "When Israel was a child, I loved him, and out of Egypt I called my son" (Hos 11:1).

The other aspect of God's nature that comes into full view at the height of divine revelation in the Old Testament is his spousal relationship with Israel. Several passages from the prophets portray God as the jealous husband who seeks to woo back his unfaithful lover, Israel.[17] As God proclaims through the mouth of the prophet Hosea:

> And I will punish her for the feast days of the Baals
> when she burned incense to them
> and decked herself with her ring and jewelry,
> and went after her lovers,
> and forgot me, says the Lord.
> Therefore, behold, I will allure her,
> and bring her into the wilderness,
> and speak tenderly to her …

And in that day, says the Lord, you will call me, "My husband," and no longer will you call me, "My Baal" …

I will betroth you to me in faithfulness; and you shall know the Lord (Hos 1:13–14, 16, 20)

The apex of Old Testament doctrine on the nature of God thus reveals that he is not only Israel's father but also her bridegroom. As we discovered in the case of God's fatherhood, so once again we find that Trito-Isaiah provides us with perhaps the loftiest of all depictions of God's spousal nature in the Old Testament. The prophet tells his people:

> You shall be a crown of beauty in the hand of the Lord,
> and a royal diadem in the hand of your God.
> You shall no more be termed Forsaken,
> and your land shall no more be termed Desolate;
> but you shall be called My delight is in her,
> and your land Married;
> for the Lord delights in you,
> and your land shall be married.
> For as a young man marries a virgin,
> so shall your [Builder] marry you,

17. Especially noteworthy are the denunciations of Jer 2–3 and Ez 16. The Song of Songs is also an invaluable witness to the beauty of Israel's spousal relationship with God. Although it is a secular love poem that never once mentions the word "God," it has always been read by Method A exegetes—as it still is today—as an allegory of Yahweh's love relationship with his people.

> and as the bridegroom rejoices over the bride,
> so shall your God rejoice over you (Is 62:3–5).[18]

Isaiah reveals that God's love for his people is so great that it can be described as nothing less than spousal. As a groom rejoices in his bride, so Yahweh rejoices in us. We are his people, his virgin spouse, and he is our bridegroom and builder who yearns to unite himself to us despite our sinfulness and constant rejections of his love. Trito-Isaiah's lofty theology of God's spousal nature thus splendidly anticipates the New Testament's revelation of Christ, who revealed himself as the bridegroom of the church (cf. Mt 9:15; 25:1ff; Rv 19:7; Eph 5:21–33; etc.).

To be sure, the Old Testament's mature view of God as father and bridegroom does not amount to a trinitarian theology. Trito-Isaiah does not distinguish multiple persons in God, yet we can see it points in that direction, especially when taking other relevant aspects of Old Testament thought into account. For example, the Old Testament hints at the presence of a mysterious plurality within the unity of God's nature when it speaks of the divine "Spirit" (רוּחַ) and "Word" (דְּבַר). The Old Testament mentions the "Spirit of God" sixteen times, while the related expressions "Spirit of Yahweh" and "Spirit of the Almighty" show up twenty-eight times and two times, respectively. The "Word of God" makes 400 appearances in the same body of literature, in addition to the "Word of Yahweh," which is mentioned 240 times. Despite all this evidence, Method B exegesis is quite clear that the sacred authors of the Old Testament did not consciously have in mind the second and third persons of the Trinity when they employed this vocabulary.

On the other hand, Old Testament wisdom literature—partic-

---

18. "Builder" is in brackets here because of an emendation suggested by historical-critical scholarship. Following the best available Masoretic Text (hereafter MT) manuscript evidence, the RSV actually reads "sons" here, whereas I have followed other translations such as the New American Bible (hereafter NAB) in using the word "Builder." This emendation is explicitly suggested by the editors of the *Biblia Hebraica Stuttgartensia*, (hereafter *BHS*) in the critical apparatus (technical footnotes) because "sons" does not seem to fit the context of the passage. The MT word בָּנָיִךְ ("your sons") is possibly the result of a scribal error which lost the original, very similar word meaning "your Builder."

ularly its figure of Lady Wisdom—seems to have exerted a strong influence on the chosen people as God prepared them to accept Christ's revelation of a plurality within the divine unity. The book of Proverbs personified wisdom as Yahweh's companion who cooperated with him in his act of creation.

> The Lord created me at the beginning of his work,
> the first of his acts of old.
> Ages ago I was set up,
> at the first, before the beginning of the earth.
> When there were no depths I was brought forth,
> when there were no springs abounding with water ...
> When he established the heavens, I was there ...
> then I was beside him, like a master workman;
> and I was daily his delight,
> rejoicing before him always (Prv 8:22–24,27,30).

The figure of wisdom described here is not equivalent to the Word (Λόγος) of God whom the Gospel of John describes as being with him from all eternity and cooperating in the creation of the universe (cf. Jn 1). For, setting aside additional complicating factors, Proverbs and its feminine "wisdom" (Σοφία) explicitly contrast with the New Testament and its masculine Λόγος. The book of Wisdom itself describes it in this way:

> For she is a breath of the power of God,
> and a pure emanation of the glory of the Almighty;
> therefore nothing defiled gains entrance into her.
> For she is a reflection of eternal light,
> a spotless mirror of the working of God,
> and an image of his goodness.
> Though she is but one, she can do all things,
> and while remaining in herself, she renews all things;
> in every generation she passes into holy souls
> and makes them friends of God, and prophets (Ws 7:25–27).

Here, we discover that wisdom is a "pure emanation" of God, a "reflection of eternal light," a "spotless mirror of the working of God," and "an image of his goodness." It would be hard to find better words within scripture itself to depict the presence of a plurality within the Godhead, yet the author of Wisdom does not posit his theology according to standard Christian categories.

Before wrapping up our look into the high points of Old Testament teaching on the nature of God, it is appropriate to revisit a final issue originally introduced in chapter 1. There we noted the confusion some Old Testament authors apparently made between Yahweh and his angel, the מַלְאַךְ יְהֹוָה. However, it turns out that this equivocation might have constituted more of a strength than a defect in the biblical text. Writing on Hagar's mysterious encounter with "the angel of the Lord" in Gn 16:7–13, Carol Newsome proposes:

> The explanation that seems most likely is that the interchange between Yahweh and [the angel of the Lord] in various texts is the expression of a tension or paradox. Yahweh's authority and presence in these encounters is to be affirmed, but yet it is not possible for human beings to have an unmediated encounter with God. Hagar is correct—she has seen God. But the narrator is also correct that the one who appeared to her was [an angel of the Lord]. The unresolved ambiguity in the narrative allows the reader to experience the paradox.[19]

As Newsome explains, some authors of the Old Testament had such a strong sense of God's transcendence that they insisted his encounters with humans had to take place through an intermediary, his "angel." Granted, authors of the Old Testament at times seem confused as to who precisely this angel is. According to the above explanation, however, the angel's mysterious presence in the text actually constituted a step in the right direction in terms of Israel's growing understanding of who God really is. In this life, we encounter God through a mediating presence; he cannot literally be seen "face to face" in this vale of tears, as some earlier Old Testament texts had indicated (e.g. Ex 33:11). Eventually, Israelite theology would go on to sharply distinguish Yahweh from his angelic mediators, but it is providential that parts of the Old Testament exhibit the paradox of a God who mediates himself to man, a God who is undeniably one and yet contains hints of plurality within his unity. Borrowing the words of Pope Benedict, we may therefore conclude that "although in the Old Testament, especially in its early books, there is certainly no kind of revelation of the Trinity, nevertheless in this process

there is latent an experience that points toward the Christian concept of the triune God."[20]

Pope Benedict refers to the revelation of God's nature in the Old
Testament as a "process." The word choice here is important because
it conveys the idea that the people of Israel did not arrive at the full
ness of revelation overnight but rather over the course of many centuries of preparation through the divine pedagogy. Benedict also
states that the Old Testament people of God had a "latent" experience that "points towards" the Trinity. This phrasing too is helpful
since it corroborates Aquinas's claim that the faith of God's people
in the Old Testament and New Testament is of the same *substance*
even though people who lived in later ages were privileged to affirm
more *articles* of faith in God in comparison with those who experienced the Trinity in a more "latent" manner. With all this said,
we may not claim to have proven this thesis beyond the shadow of
a doubt, nor may we affirm that the trajectory of Israel's growing
belief in God was an entirely linear process. We have simply pointed
to elements that indicate God had a unified plan by which he led his
people from early low points of polytheism to high points in which
they proclaimed a staunch monotheism that culminated in the revelation of the Trinity. In his Regensburg Address, Pope Benedict
spoke concerning this process:

Within the Old Testament, the process which started at the burning bush
came to new maturity at the time of the exile, when the God of Israel, an
Israel now deprived of its land and worship, was proclaimed as the God
of heaven and earth and described in a simple formula which echoes the
words uttered at the burning bush: "I am." This new understanding of God
is accompanied by a kind of enlightenment, which finds stark expression in
the mockery of gods who are merely the work of human hands.[21]

It is significant that the pontiff speaks of Israel's knowledge of God
in terms of a process that exhibited development over the centuries.
It was only at the time of the exile that Israel finally understood that

20. Benedict XVI, *Introduction to Christianity* (San Francisco: Ignatius Press,
2004), 125.
21. Benedict XVI, "Faith, Reason and the University: Memories and Reflections"
(September 12, 2006).

Yahweh was not merely their God but rather the *only* God, the other "gods" being merely human creations.

It is important to consider the following account from Robert Martin-Achard in this connection, as he dwells at greater length on the process described by Benedict:

Several assertions, implicitly contained in the ancient beliefs, were rendered explicit and defined with precision through resistance to the claims of rival faiths; little by little, the God of Israel took possession of the whole world. Thus it is that at the beginning, Yahweh appears as the Lord of a semi-nomadic clan, he is the "jealous God," semi-nomadic and haughty as the Bedouin, master of a rocky stronghold somewhere in the wilderness; but after Israel has taken possession of Canaan and the crisis brought on by the competition of the agricultural cults with Yahweh occurs, He is then manifested as the true master of the soil of Palestine, the God who alone provides water and rain and bread and wine, he upon whom Israel depends day by day in the land that has been given to it; thus Yahweh appropriates to himself prerogatives that belonged to Baal, but without becoming identified with any form of vital force. Still later, through the contact with the mighty Assyrian and Babylonian empires whose tutelary god is Marduk, Yahweh, when his people is dispersed among the nations, is revealed no longer as a divinity whose power is confined within the frontiers of Palestine, but as the absolute sovereign of the earth whose will determines the lot of Egypt and Assyria as well as that of Israel, as the creator of the universe who holds all things in the hollow of his hand.... At the very moment when Iran is proclaiming the destruction of the world and its total renewal, Yahweh makes himself known as he who is going to put an end to the power of death and utterly shatter the power of Sheol. He will raise the departed from the dust, he will awaken his faithful from the sleep of death, he will break open the gate of hell. Thus the Old Testament ends with the proclamation of Yahweh's victory over the last enemy; the revelation of the God of Israel begins in the wilderness, goes on to the conquest of nature, continues by taking possession of the universe itself, and ends in the annihilation of the forces of Chaos.[22]

One would be hard-pressed to find a more fitting description of God's gradual self-disclosure to his people than this. Martin-Achard

22. Robert Martin-Achard, *From Death to Life: A Study of the Development of the Doctrine of the Resurrection in the Old Testament*, translated by John Penney Smith (London: Oliver and Boyd, 1960), 194–95. For more on the topic of foreign influence on Israel's doctrine of the afterlife, see also Robert Martin-Achard, "Resurrection (OT)," *ABD*, vol. 5, 680–84.

illustrates several stages of growth in the Old Testament's doctrine on God's nature. In the beginning, the Israelites only knew of God as the Lord of their semi-nomadic clan but did not deny the existence of other divinities. Thus Moses and Aaron told Pharaoh, "The God of the Hebrews has met with us; let us go, we pray, a three days' journey into the wilderness, and sacrifice to the Lord our God, lest he fall upon us with pestilence or with the sword" (Ex 5:2–3). This was the "jealous" God who confused the nations at Babel (Gn 11:7) and who would change his mind or "repent" of doing evil (cf. Ex 32:14; 1 Sm 15:35; Am 7:2–3, etc.).

Later, after Israel had taken possession of Canaan, Yahweh began to acquire the prerogatives of Baal and be worshiped as the highest of the gods, as we have seen above. Still later, through her contact with Babylon and Assyria, Israel began to realize that their God was "absolute sovereign of the earth," the one true God who holds all things together and who will ultimately vindicate his people by putting an end to death itself. At this point, at last, Israel knew that there was no god besides Yahweh, and that the gods of the nations were mere idols (cf. Is 44:6; 45:18, 20). Even still, it is fascinating that the faithful Israelites who compiled the canon of scripture did not efface earlier statements that might appear problematic to later Israelites. We find traces of Israel's earliest traditions scattered throughout the Old Testament, especially in the Pentateuch. These remnants range from the apparent jealously of the divine council which caused Adam and Eve to be exiled from Eden (cf. Gn 3:22), to the ire of the council at the Tower of Babel (Gn 11:7), to the mythological Nephilim who came to earth to take human wives (cf. Gn 6:1–4), and even to the deliberations of the divine council at man's creation (Gn 1:26).

Notwithstanding Martin-Achard's illuminating narrative, if we wish to fully vindicate the presence of seemingly contradictory texts within the biblical canon, it is necessary to make some suggestions regarding the intention of the authors who penned them. For, even if we are able to make a plausible case for the presence of a divine pedagogy that gradually led the chosen people toward the fullness of revealed truth, the Method C exegete still has to reckon with those passages which appear to blatantly contradict Christian doctrine. Based on Aquinas's theology of the act of revelation, our response to these challenges must be simple and clear. Catholic dogma teaches that everything asserted by the human authors of scripture is also asserted by the Holy Spirit who cannot err.[23] Therefore, any statements in scripture that contain material imperfections must not have been asserted as such. When looked at in light of their entire context, they thus do not constitute true, formal errors since they are not the principal affirmations of the sacred writers and are not taught for their own sake.

Accordingly, when the psalmist proclaims that "there is none like thee among the gods, O Lord" (86:8), his purpose is not primarily to make a judgment about the nature of God but rather the practical end of praising and beseeching Yahweh. Similarly, when the book of Job states that "the sons of God came to present themselves before the Lord, and Satan also came among them" (1:6-7), its author may well be thinking of the "sons of God" as divine beings; there may well be an "environmental glitch" that causes him to hold imperfect ideas. However, if we look at such texts in light of the entire Bible, then it can be more clearly seen that their author's principal aim is not to speculate about the nature of the divine council. Rather, it could be suggested that the goal lies more in the effort to narrate Job's faithful struggle in the midst all the suffering Satan caused him and to propose Job as a model of endurance.

In like manner, if the book of Genesis uses mythological language (e.g., "Let us … ") in its account of the creation of man and the Tower of Babel, Catholic theological principles demand that we look at the entirety of scripture and its development in order to see that the author is not asserting the reality of polytheism for its own sake in his text. As C. S. Lewis rightly points out, the Bible had to depict the living God in terms that we would call anthropomorphic today—not because God literally thunders, pleads, changes his mind, or hates individuals, but because these attributions are the only way humans have of transmitting the sense of the *living* God

23. *DV* §11.

that evaporates when we speak of him in merely abstract terms.[24] Looked upon within the broader context of the Bible and its purposes, one can see that these types of images serve a practical end as they convey the sense of a God who engages in the affairs of man's daily life. They were not set forth as definitive metaphysical assertions about the nature of God and ought not to be taken as such. These are but a few examples of how the Method C exegete can apply Aquinas's theology of the act of revelation to biblical texts that seem to contradict orthodox Christian doctrine on the nature of God.

Finally, Method C exegesis completes its work by discerning the ultimate aim of biblical texts, that is to say their divine author's purpose in composing them. This requires us to ask the question: what do all these challenging biblical texts concerning the nature of God have to do with our lives today? At this point it becomes clear how indispensable patristic-medieval exegesis is to the Method C project. Although it has its weaknesses and excesses, spiritual exegesis

---

24. C. S. Lewis, *Miracles, a Preliminary Study* (New York: Macmillan, 1978), 146. In his various works, Lewis returns frequently to the phenomenon of myth in the Bible. His thoughts are directly relevant to our present study as they evince in their own way a clear articulation of the divine pedagogy. Reading the Old Testament, he says, "is like watching something come gradually into focus.... The earliest stratum of the Old Testament contains many truths in a form which I take to be legendary, or even mythical—hanging in the clouds, but gradually the truth condenses, becomes more and more historical ... 'God became Man' should involve, from the point of view of human knowledge, the statement 'Myth became Fact.'" *The Weight of Glory, and Other Addresses* (New York: Macmillan, 1980), 129. His emphasis on the gradual nature of divine revelation appears elsewhere in even greater detail: "Just as, on the factual side, a long preparation culminates in God's becoming incarnate as Man, so, on the documentary side, the truth first appears in mythical form and then by a long process of condensing or focusing finally becomes incarnate as History. This involves the belief that Myth in general is not merely misunderstood history (as Euhemerus thought) nor diabolical illusion (as some of the Fathers thought) nor priestly lying (as the philosophers of the Enlightenment thought) but, at its best, a real though unfocused gleam of divine truth falling on human imagination. The Hebrews, like other people, had mythology: but as they were the chosen people so their mythology was the chosen mythology—the mythology chosen by God to be the vehicle of the earliest sacred truths, the first step in that process which ends in the New Testament where truth has become completely historical." Lewis, *Miracles*, 218. For a splendid treatment of myth, see also G. K. Chesterton's *The Everlasting Man*, which can be found, among other places, in *The Collected Works of G. K. Chesterton* (San Francisco: Ignatius Press, 1986).

enables believers of all ages to encounter the living God through the text of scripture. For example, when reading in the first commandment to "have no other gods before me," believers who embrace the Method C approach thus immediately see in their own lives the danger of created realities or "gods" that threaten to enthrone themselves on our hearts in place of the one true God who alone deserves our worship. Like the translators of the LXX, we furthermore recognize that the things humans place before God are not always innocuous. Often times the idols we worship are placed before us by the devil.

This spiritual meaning of the scriptures is applicable to the life of every person who encounters them, regardless of one's age, race, gender, or circumstances. As such, it constitutes the scriptures' ultimate reason for being and the point at which revelation is able to take root in the human heart. However, Benedict's exegetical proposal is very clear in its insistence that we cannot jump to this spiritual level without engaging the literal first. If we respect the human authors who originally composed the Bible, our spiritual exegesis must flow from their work rather than simply bypassing it as insignificant. This is not to say that scripture's human authors were aware of the depths their words would have in light of divine providence. It simply means that the literal sense of scripture—which is the object of historical-critical exegesis in a privileged way—is a vital aid for Christians in their quest to arrive at an encounter with the living God in scripture. For Pope Benedict, we cannot have one without the other. Admittedly, in our application of the historical-critical method to problems concerning the Bible's portrait of God, we have not tried to resolve every last problem any more than we attempted to unveil the entire host of problems bound up with this theme. What we have done here represents only the beginning of an approach that would fully account for the many issues that challenge the Bible's inerrancy and inspiration.

METHOD C EXEGESIS AND
THE NATURE OF GOOD AND EVIL

Review of the Problem from a
Method B Perspective

Thus far we have addressed challenges to the Bible's teaching on the nature of God, but the issue of evil occupies the first place on the laundry list of criticisms leveled at the Bible in popular literature today. Many of these criticisms have a long pedigree. For instance, already in the nineteenth century Friedrich Nietzsche famously called attention to the Bible's dealings with good and evil in his *On the Genealogy of Morals*. In this work, the renowned nihilist boasted that the priestly people who authored sacred scripture were the greatest, most vengeful "haters" in world history. Such attacks continue to be popular today, appearing in books like Christopher Hitchens's *New York Times* bestseller, *God Is Not Great*. As part of his case for atheism, Hitchens presents his readers with everything from "demented pronouncements" in scripture to more serious "atrocities" committed by God and the people of God. Concerning Numbers 31:17–18, a passage similar to many of the texts discussed in chapter 1, he remarks that it is "certainly not the worst of the genocidal statements that occur in the Old Testament."[25] Hitchens is to a certain extent correct on this point. While this passage describes Moses telling the Israelites to "kill every male among the little ones, and kill every woman who has known man by lying with him," it could have been worse since it falls short of commanding the slaughter of young girls in addition to all the males and adult women. Even so, the passage is dark enough to make Hitchens utterly deny any claim that it is the Word of God.

Hitchens also condemns Exodus 32:27, where the sons of Levi follow the command of Moses to slay three thousand of their sinful brethren. He comments:

[This is] a small number compared to the Egyptian infants already massacred by god in order for things to have proceeded even this far, but it helps

---

25. Christopher Hitchens, *God Is Not Great* (New York: Twelve, 2007), 106.

to make the case for "antitheism." By this I mean the view that we ought to be glad that none of the religious myths has any truth to it, or in it. The Bible may, indeed does, contain a warrant for trafficking in humans, for ethnic cleansing, for slavery, for bride-price, and for indiscriminate massacre, but we are not bound by any of it because it was put together by crude, uncultured human mammals.[26]

In the first sentence, Hitchens is clearly referring to God's smiting of all first-born Egyptian males at the time of the Exodus (Ex 12:29). In comparison with this vengeful act, he argues, the slaughter of three thousand men looks insignificant. Hitchens states the implications of his evidence very plainly: it helps make the case for "antitheism." For Hitchens, the Bible is a myth, pure and simple, and we would come to the same conclusion no matter where we looked within the supposed word of God: "One could go through the Old Testament book by book, here pausing to notice a lapidary phrase ... and there a fine verse, but always encountering the same difficulties.[27]

Another fascinating criticism to this effect comes from what one might consider a surprising source given that we have just been dealing with apologetics of the New Atheism. One month after Benedict's Regensburg address in which the pontiff challenged Islam on the point that "violence is incompatible with the nature of God," some 100 influential Muslim leaders countered the pope with an open letter that included this argument:

Moreover, it is noteworthy that Manuel II Paleologus says that "violence" goes against God's nature, since Christ himself used violence against the money-changers in the temple, and said "Do not think that I came to bring peace on the earth; I did not come to bring peace, but a sword" (Matthew 10:34–36). When God drowned Pharaoh, was He going against His own Nature?[28]

At Regensburg, Benedict observed that Christianity made itself vulnerable to such criticisms when Duns Scotus broke from Augustine and Aquinas by maintaining a position that "might even lead to the image of a capricious God, who is not even bound to truth and goodness."[29]

26. Ibid., 101–2.   27. Ibid., 107.
28. www.sis.gov.eg/PDF/En/Arts&Culture/072607000000000010001.pdf
29. www.vatican.va.

But did the danger of fashioning for ourselves a capricious God really arise with late-medieval voluntarism? Are the Muslims not correct in their assertion that the Bible itself often depicts a bloodthirsty God who not only allows evil but even commands and rewards it?[30]

What immediately follows is a brief review of the biblical evidence to this effect as initially presented in chapter 1. Some of this data has been employed by popular authors like Hitchens, while other passages come up only in more erudite historical-critical scholarship:

[Yahweh] blotted out every living thing that was upon the face of the ground, man and animals and creeping things and birds of the air; they were blotted out from the earth. Only Noah was left, and those that were with him in the ark (Gn 7:23).

At midnight the Lord smote all the first-born in the land of Egypt, from the first-born of Pharaoh who sat on his throne to the first-born of the captive who was in the dungeon, and all the first-born of the cattle (Ex 12:29).

Moreover I swore to them in the wilderness that I would scatter them among the nations and disperse them through the countries, because they had not executed my ordinances, but had rejected my statutes and profaned my sabbaths, and their eyes were set on their fathers' idols. Moreover I gave them statutes that were not good and ordinances by which they could not have life; and I defiled them through their very gifts in making them offer by fire all their first-born, that I might horrify them; I did it that they might know that I am the Lord (Ez 20:23–26).

But in the cities of these peoples that the Lord your God gives you for an inheritance, you shall save alive nothing that breathes, but you shall utterly destroy them, the Hittites and the Amorites, the Canaanites and the Per'izzites, the Hivites and the Jeb'usites, as the Lord your God has commanded" (Dt 20:16–17)

And the Lord our God gave him over to us; and we defeated him and his sons and all his people. And we captured all his cities at that time and utterly destroyed every city, men, women, and children; we left none remaining" (Dt 2:33–34; cf. 3:6; Jo 6:21).

30. The gravity of this claim cannot be seen if we limit ourselves to addressing individual "dark" texts as they come to our attention from time to time. It is fully recognizable by following the inspiration of Newman in his *Grammar of Assent* and taking account of the "cumulation of probabilities" that points to a real problem in this area. It is for this reason that scholars ultimately need to continue the present work by dwelling at length on problems like the ones treated here.

> Samaria shall bear her guilt,
> because she has rebelled against her God;
> they shall fall by the sword,
> their little ones shall be dashed in pieces,
> and their pregnant women ripped open (Hos 13:16).

> O daughter of Babylon, you devastator!
> Happy shall he be who requites you
> with what you have done to us!
> Happy shall he be who takes your little ones
> and dashes them against the rock! (Ps 137:8–9)

Now the Spirit of the Lord departed from Saul, and an evil spirit from the Lord tormented him (1 Sm 16:14; cf. 18:10; 19:9).

For it was the Lord's doing to harden their hearts that they should come against Israel in battle, in order that they should be utterly destroyed, and should receive no mercy but be exterminated, as the Lord commanded Moses (Jo 11:20).

In some of these passages, God himself is the cause of apparently evil actions. In other places, he commands his people to commit what appear to be atrocities. How is the Christian to respond?

Helpful but Insufficient Method A Responses

In the section above we recalled a handful of the many challenges to the Bible one may raise based on the way it accounts for evil. While many traditional responses to these problems are quite beautiful and insightful, unfortunately they have often skirted the deeper issues which Method B shows to be at stake here. We will begin with Origen's thoughts on the "dashing" of babies in Psalm 137:

And in this way also the just give up to destruction all their enemies, which are their vices, so that they do not spare even the children, that is, the early beginnings and promptings of evil. In this sense also we understand the language of Psalm 137.... For, "the little ones of Babylon" (which signifies confusion) are those troublesome sinful thoughts that arise in the soul, and one who subdues them by striking, as it were, their heads against the firm and solid strength of reason and truth, is the person who "dashes the little ones against the stones"; and he is therefore truly blessed.[31]

---

31. Origen, *Against Celsus* [*Contra Celsum*], translated by Frederick Crombie, vol. 4, *The Ante-Nicene Fathers: Translations of the Writings of the Fathers down to* A.D. *325,*

For Origen, there is no question as to the psalm's meaning: the "little ones" who are to be slain are not human children but rather "the early beginnings and promptings of evil." He justifies the psalmist's words by appealing to the etymology of the word Babylon, which is related to the word "confusion." According to Origen, these nascent vices are called "the little ones of Babylon" because they arise in the form of troubling thoughts that confuse one's soul. The moral of the psalm is that we should put an end to our evil behavior at its outset—when it is still in its infancy, so to speak—lest it eventually develop into an unbreakable vice. True as this wisdom may be, we once again have to ask the question: does Origen's exegesis respect the text of Psalm 137 itself? Was the psalmist really thinking about crushing his vices when he composed this psalm, or was he rather thinking about vengefully crushing the heads of Babylonian children? From a historical-critical perspective, the latter explanation is patently the correct one.

Origen's treatment of the book of Joshua likewise follows the familiar lines of patristic-medieval thought. He exonerates Joshua's genocidal attacks because they prefigure the sacraments: "But meanwhile [Joshua] destroyed the enemies, not teaching cruelty through this, as the heretics think, but representing the future sacraments in these affairs."[32] Method A exegesis assumes that the Bible cannot condone cruelty since it is the word of God. Therefore, it rightly assumes that the true teaching of barbarous passages like those in Joshua must lie elsewhere. In the case of Psalm 137, it was to point out our need for eradicating vices; in the case of Joshua 10, it is a prefiguring of Christ's sacraments. In either case, the demands of historical-critical scholarship, and therefore Method C exegesis as well, are not met. In Origen we do not have a serious engagement with the literal sense of these texts or an appreciation for the gravity of the events recorded therein.

---

edited by Rev. Alexander Roberts and James Donaldson (Grand Rapids, Mich.: Eerdmans, 1989), 7.22.

32. Origen, *Homilies on Joshua* 11.6, in *Fathers of the Church: A New Translation* (Washington, D.C.: The Catholic University of America Press, 1947), 105:119. Cf. Jos 10:22ff.

Augustine, meanwhile, takes a different approach to these "dark" passages of the Bible. Even if his response is not satisfactory to many modern exegetes, he does attend to the literal sense of these texts as he writes:

One should not at all think it a horrible cruelty that Joshua did not leave anyone alive in those cities that fell to him, for God himself had ordered this. However, whoever for this reason thinks that God himself must be cruel ... judges as perversely about the works of God as he does about the sins of human beings. Such people do not know what each person ought to suffer.[33]

Augustine openly acknowledges both that Joshua obliterated the peoples he conquered and that God himself had commanded his action. According to Augustine, however, those who would blame God for this miss the point about "what each person ought to suffer."

Later authors like Aquinas will make Augustine's point even more clearly: man has merited death through original sin, and God therefore incurs no blame whenever he commands the slaughter of seemingly innocent people. Concerning God's commanding Abraham to slaughter his son Isaac, he explains:

All men alike, both guilty and innocent, die the death of nature: which death of nature is inflicted by the power of God on account of original sin, according to 1 Samuel 2:6: "The Lord killeth and maketh alive." Consequently, by the command of God, death can be inflicted on any man, guilty or innocent, without any injustice whatever.[34]

Immediately following this statement, Aquinas excuses a few more actions which many modern believers would find contrary to the nature of God. For instance, he justifies Hosea's marriage to a harlot by arguing that a man may have sex with any woman if God commands it: "In like manner adultery is intercourse with another's wife; who is allotted to him by the law emanating from God. Consequently intercourse with any woman, by the command of God, is

33. Augustine, *Questions on Joshua*, 16. Translation taken from vol. 4 of the *Ancient Christian Commentary on Scripture: Old Testament* (Downers Grove, Ill.: InterVarsity Press, 2005), 67. Cf. Jos 11:14.

34. St. Thomas Aquinas, *ST*, I–II, q. 94, a. 5 ad 2; cf. I–II, q. 100, a. 8; II-II, q. 154, a. 2 ad 2. Aquinas's approach to the subject in *De malo* is very similar; see q. 3, a.1, ad 17; q. 15, a. 1 ad 8.

neither adultery nor fornication." Such behavior is neither adultery nor fornication since the woman ultimately belongs to God who has willingly given her to the man in question. He likewise applies this logic to the actions of the Jews in plundering the Egyptians, narrated in Exodus 12: "The same applies to theft, which is the taking of another's property. For whatever is taken by the command of God, to Whom all things belong, is not taken against the will of its owner, whereas it is in this that theft consists."

From these passages, it is clear that Augustine and Aquinas share a strong sense of God's majesty and man's sinfulness. They are likewise willing to acknowledge what really happened according to the literal sense of some of scripture's most challenging texts. However, believers often cannot help but feel unconvinced by their explanations. Would God ever command a person today to steal, to kill, or to have sex with any woman? If not, why would he have commanded it before and had it recorded in the scriptures? Might we need to draw a distinction between what God actively wills and what he allows to happen? Is it possible the scriptures sometimes record for us what the people of God *thought* God wanted them to do rather than what he *actually* has willed? If so, then how can the scriptures be inerrant if they misrepresent the mind of God?

Toward a Method C Response

Tracing doctrinal development within the Bible's portrait of good and evil is difficult because problematic statements abound in the Old Testament canon, from the Pentateuch, to many of the prophets, to the Wisdom literature particularly the Psalms. Notwithstanding this hurdle, in this section we can still make important suggestions for how to apply Benedict's proposal to the problem of good and evil in specific biblical texts. A great place to start is by once again considering emendations of the Old Testament that shed insight into the trajectory of the divine pedagogy in ancient Israel. In chapter 1 we discussed biblical texts that portray the figure of the celestial "accuser" or הַשָּׂטָן. We noted that this figure makes few appearances in the Old Testament, and even when he does his role and identity is not always the same as it is in the New Testament. Indeed, the *Satan* of the Old

Testament is typically not inimical to God and sometimes appears to be acting on God's own behalf. However, historical-critical scholarship shows that, by the time of the post-exilic author of 1–2 Chronicles, *Satan* (שָׂטָן) began to serve as the proper name for an antagonistic celestial being who works against God and causes men to do evil.

Perhaps the clearest illustration of this development can be found in 1 Chronicles 21:1, which pinpoints Satan as the cause of David's sinful act of numbering Israel: "Satan stood up against Israel, and incited David to number Israel." It is of the utmost importance to realize that this is the only place in the Old Testament where שָׂטָן is mentioned without the definite article "the" (הַ). *Satan* is therefore not merely a title for the prosecuting attorney of the heavenly court, according to this text, but rather a unique celestial being who attempts to lead man down the path of evil. The picture painted here much more resembles that which Christians typically have in their minds when pondering the role of Satan. He "incites" us to evil and is therefore, along with our own free will, the cause of our evil actions.

In this passage we observe a marked development in comparison with the event's parallel narration in 2 Samuel 24:1, which states: "Again the anger of the Lord was kindled against Israel, and he incited David against them, saying, 'Go, number Israel and Judah.'" The difference between the two texts is clear. Whereas 1 Samuel indicates Yahweh was the cause of David's evil action, the later work 1 Chronicles tells us that the cause was *Satan*. Although we mentioned in chapter 1 that Method B scholars tend to see the chronicler's adaptation as a piece of political propaganda, now that we are approaching the text from the standpoint of a Method C hermeneutic we may glimpse a different, more sublime dynamic at work here. While it is perfectly possible that the driving force behind the chronicler's adaptation was to make David look good, the fact that he attributed the instigation of the evil deed to Satan suggests that he and his audience were already beginning to suspect that Yahweh was not the direct cause of man's evil actions.[35]

---

35. See also the discussion of this text and the Targum's connecting it with Job in Scott Hahn, *The Kingdom of God as Liturgical Empire: A Theological Commentary on 1–2 Chronicles* (Grand Rapids, Mich.: Baker Academic, 2012), 87–88.

If this explanation is correct, it helps demonstrate the presence of a substantial unity in the Bible's developing grasp of the nature of good and evil, for both earlier and later texts shared in common a clear understanding that Yahweh was in charge of the entire cosmic order. Earlier authors were aware that Yahweh's omnipotence meant that he was ultimately, in some mysterious way, the "cause" of man's evil deeds, since they knew that man depends on God for everything from food to shelter to success to God's upholding him in existence from moment to moment. However, they explain this reality in a way that many Christians today would find unacceptable. It seems that they spoke in such terms because they were operating on the (incorrect) premise that God was the direct cause of both good and evil.[36] For example, if Saul was possessed by a demon, they concluded, it must have been at Yahweh's command: "Now the Spirit of the Lord departed from Saul, and an evil spirit from the Lord tormented him" (1 Sm 16:14; cf. 18:10; 19:9).[37] If the earth was flooded and everything on it killed, it must have been because Yahweh was angry at man's sinfulness: "[Yahweh] blotted out every living thing that was upon the face of the ground, man and animals and creeping things and birds of the air" (Gn 7:23). If Israel suffered because she failed to live up to God's commands, perhaps even this was directly willed by God for the nation's greater good. The prophet Ezekiel thus reports God's words: "I gave them statutes that were not good and ordinances by which they could not have life; and I defiled them through their very gifts in making them offer by fire all their first-born, that I might horrify them; I did it that they might know that I am the Lord (Ez 20:25–26). According to Ezekiel's report, God made his people kill their own children in order that they might be

36. For a helpful discussion of this point, see Kenton Sparks, *Sacred Word, Broken Word: Biblical Authority and the Dark Side of Scripture*, (Grand Rapids, Mich: Eerdmans, 2011), 70–71, 105–6; John Collins, "The Zeal of Phineas: The Bible and the Legitimation of Violence," *Journal of Biblical Literature* 122 (2003): 3–21.

37. See also the book of Judges, which narrates that "God sent an evil spirit between Abim'elech and the men of Shechem; and the men of Shechem dealt treacherously with Abim'elech" (Jgs 9:23). 1 Kings and 2 Chronicles also indicate through the prophet Micaiah that "the Lord has put a lying spirit in the mouth of all these your prophets; the Lord has spoken evil concerning you" (1 Kgs 22:19–22; cf. 2 Chr 18:21ff).

horrified and eventually repent—a good end on the part of God, but can we justify the means Ezekiel says he used to achieve it?

The Bible's sacred authors applied this same line of reasoning in the case of genocidal wars that they victoriously fought for the sake of Yahweh. If it seemed clear that God wanted a certain battle won, and the tactics employed therein were successful, then God must have sanctioned or even directly willed these tactics: "And the Lord our God gave him over to us; and we defeated him and his sons and all his people. And we captured all his cities at that time and utterly destroyed every city, men, women, and children; we left none remaining" (Dt 2:33–34; cf. 3:6; 7:1–2; 20:16–17; Jo 6:21).[38] This type of case is particularly interesting when we consider what happens in the Old Testament when Israel's kings fail to execute Yahweh's brutal command to exterminate their enemies. Ultimately, the Bible's sacred authors observed that it led to national disaster. For instance, at a pivotal point in the Old Testament narrative, King Saul "took Agag the king of the Amal'ekites alive, and utterly destroyed all the people with the edge of the sword. But Saul and the people spared Agag, and the best of the sheep and of the oxen and of the fatlings, and the lambs, and all that was good, and would not utterly destroy them (1 Sm 15:8–9). However, since Saul failed to carry out "the ban" to its utmost extent, Yahweh actually removes him from office: "I repent that I have made Saul king; for he has turned back from following me, and has not performed my commandments" (1 Sm 15:11).

The case of Pharaoh's "hardened" heart likewise represents a splendid example of how ancient Israel's assumptions about God's causality colored the way they viewed good and evil. If Pharaoh's heart was hardened, it must have been at least in part because Yahweh desired it to be so: "And the Lord said to Moses, "When you go back to Egypt, see that you do before Pharaoh all the miracles which

38. Though one might wish to express the following statement differently, it is quite helpful to consider: "We are right, I think, to notice that the biblical author's casual attitude toward genocide caused him to put words in God's mouth that were warped by human limitations.... The author knows that God is holy and just, that humanity stands in rebellion against him and by right faces justice, that an all-out effort is needed to eradicate evil from a fallen world, that God himself will ultimately secure this victory." Sparks, *Sacred Word, Broken Word*, 112.

I have put in your power; but I will harden his heart, so that he will not let the people go" (Ex 4:21; cf. 9:12; 10:1, 20, 27; 11:10; 14:8, etc.). The example of Pharaoh is uniquely instructive because in it we witness firsthand the author(s) of Exodus struggling with the issue of how God's causality relates to Pharaoh's evil actions. Although the majority of the time Exodus narrates that "the Lord hardened Pharaoh's heart" (Ex 9:12) or even reports God's words, "I will harden his heart," as we saw above, in other places it states that "Pharaoh hardened his [own] heart" (Ex 8:32), or simply that "Pharaoh's heart was hardened" (Ex 7:13).

What reasons can the Method C exegete offer for this discrepancy? First, most Method B scholars concur that the Pentateuch as we have it today is the product of many different authors writing over many centuries. If this is the case, then one might argue that the differences in Exodus's approach to Pharaoh are due to the influence of these different authors. In addition, a Method C approach would acknowledge that, no matter how many authors had a hand in composing and transmitting Exodus, the final redactors who gave shape to the book would have been well aware of the discrepancies in the text and could have eliminated them if they so desired. Implementing the principles we outlined in chapter 4, we might therefore conclude that the authors and compilers of the biblical canon were not attempting to teach definitively on the causality of God with respect to evil, and that this is the reason that Exodus offers ambiguous and even seemingly contradictory explanations for Pharaoh's behavior. These faithful Israelites were intent on discerning the truth about God, and precisely because of this they did not wish to overstep their intellectual boundaries. It seems that they deliberately left ambiguities in scripture so that later generations could "struggle with God" as they had done and perhaps build on the tradition they were blessed to receive from their ancestors.

What all the authors we have just surveyed have in common is that they were apparently not privy to the distinction made by later thinkers between God's active will and his permissive will. This distinction is the key to reconciling God's attribute of omnipotence with his attribute of *omnibenevolence*, the reality that he is all good and therefore cannot directly cause evil. According to this distinction, God directly causes some things to happen (active will), while other things he indirectly causes or allows to happen (permissive will). It turns out that, as later biblical authors discovered through divine inspiration, the all-good and all-powerful God *allows* evil, but does not directly cause it. This is where Satan eventually comes into play. In Chronicles as in the New Testament, God allows Satan to exercise his free will in tempting humans.

With the end of the Old Testament era and the advent of the New, we find other significant developments in the chosen people's understanding of good and evil that are related the free will of Satan and of man. Written around the time of Jesus, the book of Wisdom is clear that "God did not make death, and he does not delight in the death of the living. For he created all things that they might exist" (Ws 1:13–14). While this passage fails to prove beyond the shadow of a doubt that God cannot directly will the death of humans, it certainly points in that direction. The next chapter of Wisdom clarifies Satan's role with respect to the presence of death in the world: "God created man for incorruption, and made him in the image of his own eternity, but through the devil's envy death entered the world, and those who belong to his party experience it (Ws 2:23–24). Of course, the devil is not wholly to blame for death entering the world any more than he was to blame for David's sin described above. At the end of the day, although Satan's causality is a factor in man's sinning, it is not the *entire* cause. As St. Paul tells us, "Sin came into the world through one man and death through sin, and so death spread to all men because all men sinned" (Rom. 5:12). Because of biblical revelation, we know that the blame for the problems of the human race rests just as much on Adam as it does on Satan, and not on God at all.[39]

---

39. For a more thorough understanding of how the Jewish people continued to penetrate the mystery of evil in the centuries leading up to Christ's coming, it is also instructive to read how the presence of evil in scripture was reinterpreted in non-canonical Jewish religious works from the second Temple period. For example, the book of Jubilees rewrites Genesis 1 to Exodus 14 and blames "the prince Mastema" (a demon) for some strange actions that had been attributed to Yahweh in the Pentateuch. For ex-

What, then, are we to make of the phenomenon of evil in the Bible in light of Aquinas's principles? First, we must once again affirm that God had a unified plan by which he led his people from their early beliefs to the fullness of truth concerning the nature of good and evil, from the belief that God himself was the direct cause of evil to the recognition of Satan's pivotal role in inciting men to perform wicked deeds. In light of St. Thomas's framework and given the trajectory of development in this area, the Method C exegete will acknowledge that the faith of God's people in their earliest days was of the same *substance* as it would be at its full flowering in the New Testament era. In other words, sacred authors who penned incriminating statements shared a common faith with those who would come later and purify their understanding of good and evil.

In this way, simply because sacred authors of earlier periods lacked the fullness of divine revelation does not mean that their writings contained error. They knew that their all-powerful Father was Lord of the entire universe, but they were not privy to additional revelation of distinctions that would help later inspired authors to articulate the relationship of good and evil more profoundly. Just because the Old Testament does not teach us to turn the other cheek (Mt. 5:39) or to return a blessing for an insult (1 Pt 3:9) does not mean it is corrupt. Even though Jesus apparently contradicts the Old Testament when he teaches his disciples to disregard the "eye for an eye" morality of the Old Law, the truth is that Jesus himself understood that he was fulfilling the essence of the law and elevating its standards for those who would partake in the New Covenant. Like Jesus, St. Paul understood himself within the tradition of the Judaism of his time and shared that same faith. He himself did not hesitate to appropriate the language of Exodus that many find problematic today: "So then [God] has mercy upon whomever he wills, and he hardens the heart of whomever he wills" (Rom 9:18; cf. 11:8–8). The Method C exegete might even point out that the

_____

ample, in Jubilees Mastema has a hand in God's commanding Abraham to sacrifice Isaac (Jubilees 17:15–18:13; cf. Gn 22:1–2), and he rather than God seeks to slay Moses (Jubliees 48:1–3; cf. Ex 4:24).

thought of Paul, while playing a key role in the New Testament, it-self needed to be elucidated by the church after divine revelation ended with the death of the last apostle. Paul did not distinguish God's active will from his passive will, but like the Bible's other sa-cred authors, he gave later Christians the ability to do just that.

Nevertheless, the problem we have just discussed, of under-standing God's active or passive will, is the lesser of two problems when it comes to the Bible's understanding of good and evil. The Christian must confront an array of texts that not only exhibit devel-opment but moreover seem to contradict Christian teaching in an overt manner. Once again, however, the Method C answer is simple: since Catholic dogma teaches that everything asserted by the hu-man authors of scripture is also asserted by the Holy Spirit who can-not err, it is necessary to hold that any statements in scripture which contain material imperfections do not thereby constitute formal er-rors. Because the Method C exegete has the dogmatic principles of the Catholic faith as his guide, he knows that any imperfect percep-tion of reality on the part of the sacred author is not being taught for its own sake. It may be the result of an "environmental glitch" that causes him to draw an invalid conclusion about some aspect of the faith or another. For example, if the environment of the authors discussed above assumed that Yahweh's omnipotence meant that he directly caused evil, then these authors would be epistemically justi-fied in concluding that Yahweh did what we today would recognize as evil. This does not mean that their imperfect statements conform to reality. It simply offers one avenue by which to explain that scrip-ture does not contain error in the sense that Catholic magisterial teaching understands it.

Ultimately, the exegete's key task is to analyze God's word for the purpose of elucidating its message according to both the liter-al and spiritual senses, as Pope Benedict's own discussions of the scandal of evil in scripture wonderfully illustrate. In particular, *God and the World* contains a number of examples that are germane to our present question concerning the nature of good and evil. In one instance, interviewer Peter Seewald challenges Benedict with the Levites' slaughter of three thousand men at the command of God uttered through Moses's mouth: "So, basically, the story of the Ten Commandments began with an enormous violation of commandment number five: Thou shalt not kill. Moses really ought to have known better."[40] Benedict's first move in response is a characteristically honest acceptance of his interlocutor's observation, namely that this account "does sound terribly bloodthirsty." His next is an instantiation of one of the principles he professed to hold in common with Aquinas, namely to observe that if the episode is to make sense, "we have to look forward, toward Christ," that is, to see scripture as a whole. Third, rather than simply saying what the passage *cannot* mean, he offers a suggestion for what God in his pedagogy intended it to mean: "What happens expresses the truth that anyone who turns from God not only departs from the Covenant but from the sphere of life; they ruin their own life and, in doing so, enter into the realm of death."[41]

In another instance, Pope Benedict instantiates his principles as he responds to challenging passages that describe God as jealous, wrathful, and violent in his punishments:

The wrath of God *is a way of saying* that I have been living in a way that is contrary to the love that is God. Anyone who begins to live and grow away from God, who lives away from what is good, is turning his life toward wrath.... When God inflicts punishment, this is not punishment in the sense that God has, as it were, drawn up a system of fines and penalties and is wanting to pin one on you. "The punishment of God" is in fact an expression for having missed the right road and then experiencing the consequences that follow from taking the wrong track and wandering away from the right way of living.[42]

Without employing the same vocabulary as he did above, Benedict does not shy away from raising the tough question here: Is God actually wrathful, as the text states? This need not be admitted if one understands that, while Old Testament authors may have held that the "wrath" of the all-powerful God was the direct cause of all evil,

40. Benedict XVI, *God and the World: A Conversation with Peter Seewald* (San Francisco: Ignatius Press, 2002), 167.

41. Ibid., 168.

42. Ibid., 104.

the main point they taught when speaking this way was that turning away from God's love brings about disastrous consequences for man. In other words, in the sacred author's mind the mechanism by which man gets punished for turning against God was subordinate to his teaching about the reality of the punishment itself.[43]

The necessity and appropriateness of Benedict's method is quite clear in cases such as Psalm 137, the problematic text which appeared in the opening paragraph of this book. When the author of Psalm 137 declares blessed those who would dash Babylonian infants against the rock, Catholic teaching seems to necessitate that this outburst not be the main point of the text according to its literal sense. What was the principal affirmation of Psalm 137, then? In any given biblical text, a human author might wish to make multiple points. In this case, there seem to be two related purposes of the psalm taken in light of the whole. On the one hand, in his catechesis on this text Pope Benedict explains, "We have before us a national hymn of sorrow, marked by a curt nostalgia for what had been lost."[44] The Israelites who went into Babylonian captivity "sat down and wept," "hung up" their lyres, and were "required" by their captors to sing songs. On the other hand, the psalm reads as a prayer of hope in God's covenant faithfulness: "If I forget you, O Jerusalem, let my right hand wither!" (Ps 137:5) In the words of Benedict, "This heartfelt invocation to the Lord to free his faithful from slavery in Babylon also expresses clearly the sentiments of hope and expectation of salvation."[45] In any event, the last two lines of the psalm which seek vengeance for the destruction of Jerusalem are very problematic, but they are subordinate to these other ends of the text.

As for the spiritual sense of "dark" passages like Psalm 137, the Method C exegete must constantly return to the question of what relevance they have for our lives today. While it may be difficult to find a fitting spiritual interpretation of every passage that is problematic with respect to good and evil, many are profoundly illumi-

43. Paul Synave and Pierre Benoit, *Prophecy and Inspiration: A Commentary on the Summa Theologica II–II, Questions 171–178* (New York: Desclée Co., 1961), 142.
44. Benedict XVI, General Audience, 30 November 2005.
45. Ibid.

nating. To be sure, the Method C exegete may not simply pass over the literal sense in favor of the spiritual, as we have seen above.[46] However, what Christian would not find wisdom for life in the patristic-medieval approach to texts such as Psalm 137? Regardless of the accuracy of the above attempt to determine the text's literal sense, who would not agree with Origen's spiritual exegesis that exhorts us to blot out nascent sins in our lives before they grow up and develop into unbreakable vices? This is precisely the sort of exegesis that makes a difference in our lives, and our Holy Father earnestly desires that Christians will avail themselves of it.

46. Indeed, it is tempting at times to bypass the literal sense of such texts altogether, as in the case of certain psalms (53, 83, and 109) which have been eliminated in the Catholic Church's current *Liturgy of the Hours* prayed by clergy and the faithful across the world. The words which advocate the slaughter of children in Ps 137 have likewise been omitted from the liturgy. For more on this subject, see William Holliday, *The Psalms through Three Thousand Years: Prayerbook of a Cloud of Witnesses* (Minneapolis, Minn.: Fortress Press, 1993), 304–5.

CHAPTER 6

METHOD C EXEGESIS AND
THE AFTERLIFE

Whereas the Method C treatment of our first two themes was fairly concise and to the point, I have devoted an entire chapter to treating the theme of the afterlife in order to paint a thorough and concrete portrait of Method C exegesis. The reason why the afterlife was chosen for this task is because of the disproportionately vast amount of biblical evidence we have of ancient Israel's developing understanding of the afterlife, as well as a correspondingly disproportionate abundance of scholarly ink spilled on the subject—not the least important of which is found in the work of Pope Benedict himself.

REVIEW OF THE PROBLEM FROM A
METHOD B PERSPECTIVE

As we saw in chapter 1, Method B scholarship demonstrates that the Bible's portrait of the afterlife is quite diverse at points. Biblical doctrine on the afterlife developed significantly over the course of divine revelation, from Israel's early view of Sheol to her later hope for bodily resurrection. In his magisterial work on the Bible's portrait of the afterlife entitled *The Resurrection of the Son of God*, N. T. Wright observes that the belief in resurrection makes few appearances within the Old Testament, and even then mostly in texts that came late in the development of the canon.[1] Pope Benedict further adds that "the doctrine of the resurrection had not been generally accepted in intertestamental Judaism."[2] Certain Old Testament writers like Ecclesiastes went so far as to deny altogether the reality of life after death for man:

> For Sheol cannot thank thee,
> death cannot praise thee;
> those who go down to the pit cannot hope
> for thy faithfulness (Is 38:18).

> I am a man who has no strength,
> like one forsaken among the dead,
> like the slain that lie in the grave,
> like those whom thou dost remember no more,
> for they are cut off from thy hand. (Ps 88:4–5)

> As the cloud fades and vanishes,
> so he who goes down to Sheol does not come up (Jb 7:9).

> As waters fail from a lake,
> and a river wastes away and dries up,
> so man lies down and rises not again (Jb 14:11).

> From the dead, as from one who does not exist,
> thanksgiving has ceased;
> he who is alive and well sings the Lord's praises ...
> For all things cannot be in men,
> since a son of man is not immortal (Sir 17:28,30).

1. N. T. Wright, *The Resurrection of the Son of God* (Minneapolis, Minn.: Fortress Press, 2003), 85. For further reading regarding the dearth of evidence for a postmortem hope of beatitude among the Israelites, one might consult the article by Richard Friedman and Shawna Bolansky Overton entitled "Death and Afterlife: the Biblical Silence," in *Judaism in Late Antiquity*, edited by Alan J. Avery-Peck and Jacob Neusner (Boston: Brill Academic Publishers, 2000), 35–59. It is interesting to note that some of the most important of these statements (e.g., Ws 3; 2 Macc. 7 and 12) are found in books only in the Catholic canon of scripture. The presence of the doctrine of resurrection in these texts provides important testimony to the fact that God continued to teach Israel and prepare the nation to receive the Paschal mystery up to the very time of Christ's coming.

2. Benedict XVI, *Eschatology: Death and Eternal Life,* translated by Michael Waldstein (Washington, D.C.: The Catholic University of America Press, 1988), 112.

For the fate of the sons of men and the fate of beasts is the same; as one dies, so dies the other. They all have the same breath, and man has no advantage over the beasts; for all is vanity. All go to one place; all are from the dust, and all turn to dust again (Eccl 3:19–20).

For the living know that they will die, but the dead know nothing, and they have no more reward; but the memory of them is lost.... Whatever your hand finds to do, do it with your might; for there is no work or thought or knowledge or wisdom in Sheol, to which you are going (Eccl 9:5,10).

Recalling the spectrum of evidence presented in chapter 1, these are just a few passages in which the problem of biblical doctrine on the afterlife comes sharply into focus.

Why is Method B's emphasis on these observations so important? In one way or another, Christians today will inevitably have to confront historical criticism's challenges regarding biblical doctrine on the afterlife. Many popular thinkers reject Christianity's hope for bodily resurrection precisely on the basis of historical criticism's ability to highlight apparent contradictions in the way the Old and New Testaments handle the issue of the afterlife. For instance, well-known scholar Bart Ehrman argues forcefully that even the New Testament is not utterly uniform in its depiction of eschatological reality, including the very foundation of Christian hope: Jesus's Resurrection. "Nowhere are the differences among the Gospels more clear," he writes, "than in the accounts of Jesus' resurrection.... There are scads of differences among the four accounts, and some of these differences are discrepancies that cannot be readily (or ever) reconciled."[3] Based on the number of problems in the accounts of Jesus's death and Resurrection, Episcopal Bishop John Shelby Spong similarly asserts, "This means, of course, that we are relegating that tradition of the empty tomb, the visit of the women, the burial by Joseph, and the mention of Nicodemus to the realm of legend. Contemporary scholarship points in exactly that direction."[4] In contrast with Pope Benedict, Ehrman and Spong assert that some discrepancies in the Bible simply cannot be reconciled, and that we must therefore relegate much of it to the realm of legend. In his number

3. Bart Ehrman, *Jesus, Interrupted* (New York: Harper, 2009), 47.
4. John Shelby Spong, *Resurrection: Myth or Reality?* (New York: Harper, 1994), 226.

one *New York Times* bestseller *God Is Not Great*, Christopher Hitchens will go so far as to claim concerning Jesus's Resurrection:

Having no reliable or consistent witnesses, in anything like the time period needed to certify such an extraordinary claim, we are finally entitled to say that we have a right, if not an obligation, to respect ourselves enough to disbelieve the whole thing. That is, unless or until some superior evidence is presented, which it has not been. And exceptional claims demand exceptional evidence.[5]

For Hitchens, the evidence proffered by modern scholarship is so great that educated people today "have a right, if not an obligation" to reject the entire Christian claim. With critics like Hitchens among the most read authors in America today, Christians must take their challengers seriously.

HELPFUL BUT INSUFFICIENT METHOD A RESPONSES

At this point we will review a few representative Method A attempts to deal with problematic statements regarding the afterlife in scripture. Patristic-medieval exegesis is often powerful and enlightening, but many modern Christians find it wanting in terms of accounting for the deeper problems raised by historical-critical scholarship. For example, in commenting on Psalm 6, St. John Chrysostom plainly rejects the suggestion that a deceased person ceases to exist:

[When the psalmist says] "for in death there is no one to remember you," [he is] not implying that our existence lasts only as far as the present life perish the thought! After all, he is aware of the doctrine of resurrection. Rather, it is that after our departure from here there would be no time for repentance.[6]

Chrysostom is well aware of the apparent implications of Psalm 6. They are the same implications chapter 1 teased out in demonstrating the hopelessness of Sheol from the early Israelite perspective. However, according to this father of the church, the psalmist

5. Christopher Hitchens, *God Is Not Great* (New York: Twelve, 2007), 143.

6. St. John Chrysostom, *Commentary on the Psalms*, vol. 1, translated by Robert Charles Hill (Brookline, Mass.: Holy Cross Orthodox Press, 1998), 6.4.

is "aware of the doctrine of resurrection." Given this assumption, Chrysostom is sure that the passage cannot mean that one ceases to exist after death, but rather that one has no opportunity to repent after death. While what he says is true in terms of what Christians know today, we have to ask whether his explanation is true to the text—in other words, whether he arrives at a conclusion consonant with Christianity *because* of the text or rather *despite* its intended meaning. From a Method B perspective, the answer is clearly negative: the psalmist plainly denied the reality of an afterlife and demonstrated no awareness of the doctrine of resurrection, arguing against Chrysostom's assumption. While his conclusion might ultimately be correct, he did not arrive at it through a correct interpretation of the biblical text.[7]

St. Jerome's commentary on Ecclesiastes is similar to Chrysostom's treatment of Psalm 6 in that it seems to bypass the original meaning of the text. Responding to Ecclesiastes's claim that man has no advantage over the beasts and that both return to the dust as their final resting place, he writes, "Except that our belief in Christ raises us up to heaven and promises eternity to our souls, the physical conditions of life are the same for us as for the brutes.... Man and beast alike are dissolved into dust and ashes."[8] According to St. Jerome, belief in Christ is ultimately the only thing that differentiates man from the subhuman universe. If we lack a relationship with Christ, then indeed our fate as humans is no better than that of brute animals. However, notice how St. Jerome arrives here at a conclusion consonant with Christian doctrine almost in spite of what the text of Ecclesiastes says. Method B exegesis is quick to observe that Ecclesiastes makes no mention of Christ and gives readers no reason to believe its author had foreknowledge of him. This begs the question of whether Jerome's conclusion, while ultimately correct, really does justice to the words of Ecclesiastes. In short, it fails to

7. Although we will not deal here with the problems involved with this specific passage, it is worth noting that Chrysostom's exegesis is not unlike that of St. Peter himself as recorded in the Acts 2:22–36. We will return to this point below.

8. St. Jerome, *Letter 108*, translated by W. H. Fremantle, G. Lewis and W. G. Martley, vol. 6, *Nicene and Post-Nicene Fathers, Second Series*, edited by Philip Schaff (Buffalo, N.Y.: Christian Literature Publishing Co., 1893), 28.

confront the literal sense of the text because it has preconceived notions of what the text "must" mean.

Let us consider one final example of an insufficient Method A approach to problematic biblical texts touching on the afterlife. Commenting on the bleak outcries of Psalm 88, St. Cyril of Jerusalem explains:

[The psalmist] said not, I became a man without help; but, *as it were a man without help*. For indeed He was crucified not from weakness, but willingly and His Death was not from involuntary weakness. *I was counted with them that go down into the pit. And what is the token? You have put away Mine acquaintance far from Me* (for the disciples have fled). *Will You show wonders to the dead?* Then a little while afterwards: *And unto You have I cried, O Lord; and in the morning shall my prayer come before You.* Do you see how they show the exact point of the Hour, and of the Passion and of the Resurrection?[9]

Once again, this is a beautiful piece of patristic exegesis, and its insight into the mystery of Christ is profound. However, St. Cyril ignores the actual situation the psalmist is lamenting and instead begins with a parsing of the text (emphasizing that the psalmist is not actually but only "as it were" a man without help) which is highly questionable. With this he attempts to demonstrate that the psalm is speaking of Christ, who was only "without help" insofar as he willed to be so. He is convinced that the psalmist's words "show the exact point of the Hour, and of the Passion and of the Resurrection." As in the other two examples above, however, he arrives at conclusions which affirm Christian doctrine yet bypass the literal sense of the text. While St. Cyril has a more or less accurate grasp of Psalm 88's spiritual sense, our pope's exegetical proposal demands a more robust hermeneutic that arrives at the spiritual truth of a passage not in spite of but rather *through* an examination of its literal sense.

9. St. Cyril of Jerusalem, *Catechetical Lectures*, translated by Edwin Hamilton Gifford, vol. 7, *Nicene and Post-Nicene Fathers, Second Series*, edited by Philip Schaff (Buffalo, N.Y.: Christian Literature Publishing Co., 1894), 14.8.

TOWARD A METHOD C RESPONSE

In the sections above we have reviewed Method B's observations with regard to problematic areas in scripture's account of the afterlife, and we have examined Method A responses that fail to address Method B's concerns in a convincing way. At this point, then, it is indispensable for us to apply the principles of Method C exegesis to the problem of the afterlife in scripture. First, we will elucidate the trajectory by which Israel gradually developed her understanding of the afterlife as a result of the divine pedagogy, proposing that earlier biblical texts which fail to affirm the fullness of revelation are not erroneous on that account. Based on Aquinas's theology of the history of revelation, we will argue that they simply constitute a phase in which the same "substance of the faith" present throughout the duration of divine revelation had yet to fully bloom. We will likewise employ Aquinas's theology of the act of revelation in order to search out the intentions of the biblical authors and show that they did not make formal truth claims that contradict Christian doctrine on the afterlife. Finally, having proposed solutions to the various problems in the Bible's presentation of the afterlife, we will search out the divine author's purpose in composing these texts in order to ascertain what their spiritual sense has to teach Christians today (the second dimension of the divine pedagogy).

The Afterlife and Aquinas's Theology of the
History of Revelation: Why Are There "Dark" Areas in
the Bible's Portrait of the Afterlife?

Our Method C response to the issue of the biblical doctrine on the afterlife must begin with an honest encounter with the many "dark" passages introduced in chapter 1 and reviewed above. In particular, one who studies other ancient Near Eastern religious systems such as the Egyptian and Canaanite will inevitably ask: why did Israel continue to accept the gloomy view of Sheol for so long when her neighbors whom she knew well—and who were bereft of divine revelation—enjoyed the hope for a blessed afterlife? The thoughts of John McKenzie represent a healthy contribution of Method B exegesis to this question; they explain a challenging phenomenon in the honest yet constructive manner needed in Method C exegesis. According to McKenzie, it was Israel's awareness of the drastic difference between hers and neighboring nations' worldviews that ironically delayed her arrival at hope for a blessed immortality. For example, concerning Egypt he writes:

The Egyptian idea of the afterlife, exhibited in the well-preserved tombs of Egypt and in Egyptian literature, conceives of survival after death as a two-dimensional continuation of earthly human existence and not as a new and genuinely different state.... The Egyptian idea is incompatible with basic Israelite beliefs about Yahweh and about humanity. The Egyptian afterlife is not a world dominated by the personal divine presence and will, but is really a thoroughly secularized world.... Perhaps Israel's failure to reach an idea of survival after death was partly due to revulsion for Egypt's unmitigated secularism.[10]

As McKenzie explains, Egypt's view of life after death was not one of an eschatological new life in a new world but rather a kind of continuation of earthly life only by new means. Unlike in Israel, where all life was imbued with the personal divine presence and God constantly commanded his people to act in a way befitting his dignity

10. John L. McKenzie, "Aspects of Old Testament Thought," in *The New Jerome Biblical Commentary,* edited by Raymond Edward Brown, Joseph A. Fitzmyer, and Roland Edmund Murphy (Englewood Cliffs, N.J.: Prentice-Hall, 1990), 78:168. Hereafter NJBC. The same logic is applicable with regard to Israel's rejection of Canaanite views of the afterlife. Far from being a source of Israel's belief in the resurrection, the religion of Canaan actually seems to have *prevented* Israelites from coming to such a belief during the time they spent there. The people certainly would have been familiar with Canaanite resurrection myths, but they knew that these were fundamentally incompatible with worship of Yahweh. As Robert Martin-Achard thus argues, the doctrine of resurrection could not have been revealed to Israel by God until it was forever freed from its ties with nature-mysticism. Robert Martin-Achard, *From Death to Life: A Study of the Development of the Doctrine of the Resurrection in the Old Testament,* translated by John Penney Smith (London: Oliver and Boyd, 1960), 204. Indeed, based on a comment by Gerhard von Rad he states, "It was one of the glories of the Chosen People that it refused [to adopt a doctrine of resurrection] at that particular moment in its history." (203.) Wright adds, "This [Israel's conviction that Yahweh was sovereign over creation] indeed may help to explain why Jewish thinkers came to a belief in resurrection only very late, when the main opponent to traditional belief was not a local vegetation-cult, but the power of Babylon and, later, Syria." *The Resurrection of the Son of God,* 126–27. It is this same faith in the absolute sovereignty of Yahweh that prevented Israel from the attainment of hope in a blessed immortality during their time spent in Canaan as well as in Egypt.

as a child of Yahweh, entrance into the Egyptian afterlife was not contingent on one's moral character, and the afterlife itself was not theocentric. Because of this, N. T. Wright similarly concludes that Egypt's idea of the afterlife would have been seen by ancient Israel as more of a denial than an affirmation of the hope for nation, family, and land to flourish.[11] When seen in this light, the Method C exegete may surmise that Israel's arrival at hope for immortality was delayed because part of the nation's task early on in the divine pedagogy was to sort out her own worldview from that of her neighbors. Sometimes these worldviews differed from hers in few respects, yet these particular differences (e.g., whether the one true invisible God played a large role or not in human affairs) were fundamental. It was crucial that Israel not adopt a facile, prefabricated view of the afterlife that would have individuals continue to exist forever but in a way that was meaningless, and that neglected life's most important dimension: man's relation with one true God. Accordingly, even if the nation of Egypt had great concern for the reality of life after death long before Israel exhibited such an interest, this does not make Egypt's way any better.

Overtly committed to building up the faith through his exegesis, C. S. Lewis approaches the issue from an angle that complements the proposals described immediately above. Though a man of letters rather than a biblical scholar by trade, Lewis offers profound insights into the subject at hand. According to him, Egypt's problem was not only that its view of the afterlife was devoid of the personal divine but that its very concern for the afterlife hindered Egyptians' relationship with God in the present life:

To some it may seem astonishing that God, having revealed so much of himself to that people, should not have taught them [about the afterlife]. It does not now astonish me. For one thing there were nations close to the Jews whose religion was overwhelmingly concerned with the afterlife. In reading about ancient Egypt one gets the impression of a culture in which the main business of life was the attempt to secure the well-being of the dead. It looks as if God did not want the chosen people to follow that example.[12]

11. Wright, *The Resurrection of the Son of God*, 122.
12. C. S. Lewis, *Reflections on the Psalms* (London: Harvest Books, 1964), 39.

Lewis adds that it may even have been dangerous for God to teach Israel to hope for eternal life at too early a stage in history:

It may have been absolutely necessary that this revelation should not begin with any hint of future Beatitude or Perdition. These are not the right point to begin at. An effective belief in them, coming too soon, may even render almost impossible the development of (so to call it) the appetite for God; personal hopes and fears, too obviously exciting, have got in first. Later, when, after centuries of spiritual training, men have learned to desire and adore God, to pant after him, "as pants the hart," it is another matter.[13]

As Lewis understood, Yahweh did not want Israel's belief in the afterlife to be naïve or facile but wholeheartedly centered on himself as the God who would not forsake his promise to bless his people even in this life. As part of his pedagogy, Yahweh instructed those who worshiped him to look for his faithfulness in the here and now. Once they succeeded in taking this step of faith and become sufficiently clear on what his promises meant for the *present* life, they would be better prepared to make the much greater step of hoping for life beyond the grave. The people of Israel were to wait on God to give them a deeper explanation for what occurs on the other side of this vale of tears.

The above discussion has focused on the negatives of Israel's gloomy Sheol view and her refusal to accept foreign concepts of the afterlife. What did the people of Israel positively affirm throughout the period in which they denied the afterlife? It is easy to miss that Israel's original position (absence of hope for life beyond death) had this in common with her final position (hope for eternal resurrected life): an overwhelmingly positive affirmation of the goodness and vital importance of the created order. However, the majority of pre-exilic Old Testament writers did not face the question of the afterlife head-on because for the most part their central concern was to make certain of the promise of God for the family's possession of the Promised Land. As Brian Schmidt states, "Prior to the exile, the ancient Israelites, like many of their Ancient Near Eastern neighbors, placed primary, if not sole, emphasis on the perpetuation of

13. Ibid., 40–41.

the memory of the family dead and on making the best of life on this side of the grave."[14] Almost everywhere in the Old Testament one can find the people of Israel loving life, meeting it with optimism, and seeing it as a gift from God. Unlike the adherents of some ancient Near Eastern religions, the faithful Israelite did not long to forsake the world and lose his carnal and personal self through a rapture or premature death.[15] He yearned to find himself alive in the land, worshiping Yahweh and basking in his steadfast love. For the Israelite, a happy life was one that abounded in offspring, possessions, and length of days. To die in peace at an old age was ideal. If an Israelite met this kind of death, he peacefully accepted it as a natural fact because, although dead, he would continue to live on in the land through his offspring.

To men of today, this stance on the afterlife may appear extraordinarily odd, but it was possible in Israel's culture because their fundamental worldview differed markedly from the individualistic one prevalent in contemporary Western society. Martin-Achard describes Israel's view of the human person and his place in the community of Israel:

For the Hebrews, there is nothing extraordinary in the thought that a human being continues to exist in his children; man is not an individual unrelated to his immediate or remote temporal and spatial environment. On the contrary, the Israelite forms an integral part of his family past and present, one body with his ancestors and descendents.... The future and the past of the whole people are present in the destiny of every member of Israel.[16]

Thus for the faithful Israelite the story of Abraham, Moses, David, and all the faithful men and women of Israel was his own story. If he saw nation, land, and offspring flourishing, he could go to the grave in

14. Brian Schmidt, "Memory as Immortality: Countering the Dreaded 'Death after Death' in Ancient Israelite Society," in *Judaism in Late Antiquity*, 99.

15. Martin-Achard, *From Death to Life*, 3–4, 18; cf. Gn 15:15; Jb 42:17. As Martin-Achard notes, there are some exceptions, notably Ecclesiastes. As for Job's imprecations against life (Jb 3:3) or Jeremiah's maledictions (Jer 20:14), these come off sounding more like blasphemy than reiterations of the typical Israelite view of death. For more on the ancient Israelite view of death, see Kent Harold Richards, "Death (OT)," *ABD*, vol. 2, 108–10; Benedict XVI, *Eschatology*, 80.

16. Martin-Achard, *From Death to Life*, 24.

peace, knowing that his descendents in the corporate person of Israel would continue to live his story just as he lived the story of his own forefathers.[17] In this way, it may never have occurred to many just men of ancient Israel that they ought to have hoped for a blessed afterlife peculiarly their own, for the life of their descendants *was* their life, and this life would be eternal. As Sirach 37:25 states, "The life of a man is numbered by days, but the days of Israel are without number."

Approaching the issue from yet another angle, Pope Benedict likewise offers a keen insight into the deeply positive side of Israel's early refusal to hope for the afterlife In view of explaining why Israel had a "this-worldly" view of the afterlife, he compares the pedagogy by which Israel learned of the afterlife to the pedagogy by which she learned of the oneness of God:

> A number of Old Testament texts show clearly how popular piety in Israel lovingly sought communication with the dead in just the way found in the pagan religions of the ancient Near East.... The official religion of Israel, as expressed in the Law, the prophets, and the historical books of the Hebrew Bible, did not accept these beliefs and practices. It no more denied all existence to Sheol than, at first, it denied the existence of other gods than Yahweh. But it chose not to deal with this area. It classified everything to do with the dead as "impure," that is, as disqualifying one for a share in Yahweh's *cultus*.... The refusal to admit the legitimacy of a cult of the ancestors—still, of course, widely practiced in that society—was the real reason for the naturalizing of death.... A certain demythologizing of death was needful before Israel could bring out the special way in which Yahweh was himself Life for the dead.[18]

According to Benedict, before Israel could learn to hope in the resurrection, death had to be naturalized and demythologized from elements bound up with popular ancestor worship (e.g., the necromancy of 1 Sm 28 discussed in chapter 1). Thus the Lord did not initially teach Israel the fullness of truth regarding the afterlife because Israel first had to pass through a stage in the divine pedagogy where her immature beliefs about the afterlife were completely eradicated. This occurred through the purity laws and prohibitions that eventually made clear the impossibility of worshiping or consulting the dead.

17. Wright, *The Resurrection of the Son of God*, 99–100.
18. Benedict XVI, *Eschatology*, 83–84.

Wrapping up his presentation on Israel's early view of the after-life, Benedict observes that the reason for Israel's view of Sheol was twofold. On the one hand, the "this-worldliness" of Old Testament faith was due in part to Israel's understanding of the divine nature and the incompatibility of the popular cult of the dead with belief in an eternal communion of man with God. On the other hand, the pope notes that the reason for Israel's view is that it "simply illus-trates a stage of awareness found in all cultures at a certain point in their development. As yet, Israel's faith in Yahweh had not un-folded in all its inner consistency."[19] Israel was not unique in her view of Sheol, but this is not problematic from Benedict's point of view because God gradually led Israel from this to a more mature understanding of the afterlife. As he explains, there was an inter-nal contradiction in Israel's early belief insofar as they believed God was omnipotent and yet unable to keep individuals alive after death. Benedict rightly points out that this state of affairs was inherently unstable, leading eventually to the crisis whereby Israel was forced to either abandon faith in Yahweh altogether or to admit the unlim-ited scope of his power—including his power to raise the dead and keep them in definitive communion with himself. Israel's belief in eternal life thus emerges out of a completely natural view of Sheol and is driven by her convictions about the nature of God, as he had already revealed himself to his people.

Once Israel had been purified from delusory notions of the world to come and was established in a healthy relationship with the goods of this world, she was ready for the next crucial step of the divine pedagogy: the people needed to be taught by God that their aspirations for prosperity, deliverance, and national unifica-tion would never fully be attained in this world, in the physical land of Israel. Endless tragedies of sickness, exile, and persecution para-doxically impelled the people to realize that their hope would be realized only on the other side of the grave.[20] Articulating this with

19. Ibid., 82.
20. Martin-Achard, *From Death to Life*, 161. In fact, according to Pope Benedict in his *Truth and Tolerance: Christian Belief and World Religions*, translated by Henry Taylor (San Francisco: Ignatius Press, 2004), the very fact that the Israelite religion flourished

respect to the martyrdom literature of Daniel, Maccabees, and Wisdom, Pope Benedict relates, "In the path followed by the men who wrote the Old Testament, it was suffering, endured and spiritually borne, which became that hermeneutical vantage point where real and unreal could be distinguished, and communion with God came to light as the locus of true life."[21] As we will observe below, when individual Israelites saw themselves suffering the same fate as their nation, they learned to hope for their own personal restoration to life after death and, eventually, to hope for resurrected life. Martin-Achard summarizes this learning process as it unfolded in ancient Israel:

Little by little, under the pressure of the tragic events that the people of Yahweh experienced (the disappearance of the northern kingdom in the eighth century, the fall of Jerusalem and the end of the Judean state in the sixth century; the exile and the difficult and precarious reconstitution of a Jewish community around Jerusalem under the Persians), the condition of the individual in the midst of a national and religious community came to assume the preponderant place, and, from this time forward, questions were asked about the fate of the faithful one and in particular of the ultimate future state reserved for him or her. The problem became especially acute during the crises that the Jewish people lived through under the declining Persian empire and during the time of Antiochus Epiphanes.... The Yahwistic cause seemed a lost one, and the martyrs to have died in vain; the prophecy of the resurrection of the dead then allowed people to address the challenge brought on by the circumstances they endured. With the resurrection doctrine, the last word remained with the God of Israel.[22]

---

in the face of persecution and exile testifies that it is of God. He writes, "In the normal way of things, a God who loses his land, who leaves his people defeated and is unable to protect his sanctuary, is a God who has been overthrown. He has no more say in things. He vanishes from history. When Israel went into exile, quite astonishingly, the opposite happened.... The faith of Israel at last took on its true form and stature.... He could allow his people to be defeated so as to awaken it thereby from its false religious dream." (148.) Although in this specific instance Benedict is discussing Israel's growth in understanding the nature of God, his reasoning is also consistent with a description of Israel's growth in understanding human destiny. Israel was required to go into exile before she could be awoken from the delusory hope for fulfillment in this world.

21. Benedict XVI, *Eschatology*, 91.
22. Robert Martin-Achard, "Resurrection (OT)," *ABD*, vol. 5, 683–84.

It is vital to emphasize that this ironic process by which Israel arrived at hope for the resurrection through the non-fulfillment of her worldly hopes was not a mere human invention but rather a result of divine pedagogy. There is indeed a fine but crucial difference between viewing non-fulfillment as the vehicle for prompting Israel to meditate deeply and discover the truth that God was teaching them versus viewing non-fulfillment as the cause of a doctrine invented by man out of desperation. As one may observe from the quote above, Israel's arrival at belief in a blessed immortality involved a kind of deduction process that was truly human, and yet faith indicates that the truth of the resurrection is not a mere product of human reasoning.[23] The truth is available to man only with the additional help of the divine light, but this does not change the fact that Israel had to employ reason (and patient love through suffering) to arrive at it.

The apparent non-fulfillment of Yahweh's promises to Israel drove the nation to a deeper penetration of what his promise had meant all along. It represented a sort of climax in the divine pedagogy in which the nation transcended her previous aspirations and attained a clearer glimpse of the true nature of divine providence and of human destiny.[24] The logical conclusion that Israel drew from the non-

23. Far from seeing Israel's developing belief in the afterlife as a mere human response to unfulfilled desires, Benedict XVI believes that a man's hope for a definitive post-mortem reckoning, a Last Judgment, presents the strongest of arguments in favor of human immortality. He writes that "faith in the Last Judgment is first and foremost hope—the need for which was made abundantly clear in the upheavals of recent centuries. I am convinced that the question of justice constitutes the essential argument, or in any case the strongest argument, in favour of faith in eternal life. The purely individual need for a fulfillment that is denied to us in this life, for an everlasting love that we await, is certainly an important motive for believing that man was made for eternity; but only in connection with the impossibility that the injustice of history should be the final word does the necessity for Christ's return and for new life become fully convincing." *Spe salvi* §43. Although here Benedict is speaking about the faith of Christians, this same reasoning applies to the people of Israel, who ever persevered through injustice and arrived at a hope for immortality before the coming of Christ.

24. In *The Origins of History* (New York: Basic Books, 1981), Herbert Butterfield and Adam Watson describe the effect of non-fulfillment on Israel's beliefs: "In the higher regions of ancient Hebrew thought—particularly the kind of thought which arises out of the non fulfillment of the Promise—there emerges an idea which brings the notion of promise to a kind of climax where the concept of Promise is in itself in a way transcended." (89.) Likewise, C. S. Lewis gives his own account of how Israel's material

fulfillment of her earthly aspirations, based upon their belief that God in his providence would ultimately deliver the people in his own way, was that this deliverance would take place *beyond* the grave. In what follows, we will explore how the above summary of Martin-Achard plays out in scripture itself, tracing the trajectory of Israel's developing belief in the afterlife throughout the Old Testament from its beginning stages to its full flowering, from the absence of hope for a blessed existence after death as seen in chapter 1 to a profound hope for bodily resurrection.[25] We will see that Israel's high regard for bodily existence in the Promised Land and for a return to it from exile was a central factor in establishing the hope that individual Israelites would return from the exile of death to live again in their own bodies. Indeed, we will observe that this second hope was a kind of reaffirmation or outgrowth of the first hope. In both cases, deliverance was envisioned as taking the form of a resurrection, on either the national or individual level as the case may have it. In his educational plan the Lord worked on both of these levels in order to teach his children the fullness of truth: the same pedagogy by which he led the *nation* of Israel to hope for deliverance or resurrection was used to lead *individuals* within the nation to hope that their own bodies would undergo a resurrection. The endeavor at hand calls for an examination of specific biblical texts that deal with these two aspects of Israel's belief in the resurrection and their relation to one another in the growth of doctrine on the afterlife.

---

losses contributed to her growth in understanding divine realities: "Century after century, by blows which seem to us merciless, by defeat, deportation, and massacre, it was hammered into the Jews that earthly prosperity is not in fact the certain, or even the probable, reward of seeing God." Lewis, *Reflections on the Psalms*, 43.

25. Although this is not to say that Israel's doctrine developed in a strictly linear fashion over the course of divine revelation, we will see that there was indeed an intelligible trajectory whereby the nation's hope gradually emerged from her initial belief that an individual would not live beyond death. St. Thomas himself recognizes that the mere passage of time does not imply progress on the part of mankind's knowledge of God. In the case of the sciences, time can be a "cause of forgetfulness." *Sententia libri Ethicorum*, Lib. I, lect. 11. Cf. Jean-Pierre Torrell, "Saint Thomas et l'histoire: état de la question et pistes de recherches," *Revue Thomiste* 105 (2005): 377–79. There is no reason why the same would not apply to Israel's growth, and therefore one must bear in mind that there may have been individuals living in later times who in a sense had less knowledge and less hope for a blessed afterlife.

Hosea 6 and 13

The first text in this investigation contains the most ancient biblical material in terms of divine revelation that explicitly concerns the doctrine of resurrection. The book of Hosea, which reports oracles originally delivered in third quarter of the eighth century B.C., is considered to have been behind the formation of later Israelite thought on the afterlife, including Isaiah 26.[26] The MT of 6:2 reads, "He [the Lord] will revive us after two days; on the third day he will cause us to rise (יְקִמֵנוּ) in order that we may live in his presence."[27] Robert Martin-Achard argues that Canaanite religion had an influence on this text:

Curiously enough, the numbers given by Hosea ["After two days ... on the third day"] are to be found in other documents relating to the agricultural cults practiced in the countries round about Palestine, which were fairly similar to those that must have led Hosea's contemporaries [i.e., the ones speaking the words recorded in Hosea 6:2] astray.[28]

As Martin-Achard explains, the cults of Adonis (Phoenicia), Tammuz (Babylon), Osiris (Egypt), Attis (Rome), Inanna (Sumer), Melqart (Tyre), and Baal (at Ras Shamra) all contain rituals in which they habitually bewail the death of a god. In these religions, the young god is thought to be periodically overcome by the powers of death coinciding with the time when the moon (which is often associated with fertility in cultic settings) vanishes for three days in its monthly cycle. Time and again the god makes a descent to the underworld and then rises back to life, usually within a matter of two or three days. According to Martin-Achard, many in Israel absorbed this myth of the dying and rising God from their neighbors whether they were conscious of it or not, and this influence shows up in the Book of Hosea. As a result of this interaction with Canaan, the people of

---

26. Phillip S. Johnston, *Shades of Sheol: Death and Afterlife in the Old Testament* (Downers Grove, Ill.: Intervarsity Press, 2002), 221; Martin-Achard, *From Death to Life*, 74; Wright, *The Resurrection of the Son of God*, 118; C. L. Seow, "Hosea, Book of," *ABD*, vol. 3, 291.

27. Translation mine.

28. Martin-Achard, *From Death to Life*, 82.

Israel began to appropriate its idiom, and this eventually translated into the aspiration for a metaphorical resurrection—the revivification of the nation of Israel and her restoration to the land.

However, as Martin-Achard shows, this is certainly not to say that the prophet Hosea himself espoused a view of resurrection that was influenced by the religion of Canaan or that his writings erred on the matter. Within the larger context of Hosea 5–6, one can see that 6:2 does not contain Hosea's own thought: it is the report of a petition made by the people to Yahweh in the hopes that he would deliver them from impending disaster at the hands of the Assyrian army.[29] And, as Wright points out, there is a certain irony that "in its original context it almost certainly was intended as a description of a prayer that the prophet regarded as inadequate. It indicated the people's failure to repent at a deep level, a simplistic hope that maybe Yahweh could be bought off."[30] Accordingly, the prophet Hosea by no means intends to espouse a doctrine of resurrection like that held in Canaan but on the contrary shows that Israel's alleged repentance from idolatry has left Yahweh skeptical. In response to Israel's prayer, in 6:4 he tells them "Your love is like a morning cloud, like the dew that goes early away." Yahweh's rejection of this prayer and the lament that follows are due not simply to its lack of fervor but to the deeper malaise of Baal worship that plagued Israel in that period. According to Wright, Yahweh's anger at this point results from the fact that his children have imported rituals and language of resurrection from a depraved culture and that this has impeded their conversion to himself. In this way, the language of Hosea 6:2 may point to some Israelites having an early aspiration for some sort of national restoration or resurrection, but in Hosea's eyes it was a false hope founded on the false beliefs of Canaanite fertility cults. So strong was this rejection on the part of Hosea and others that the

29. Ibid., 76–77. Although the RSV translates the first two verbs of Hosea 6:2 in the indicative ("he will revive us, he will raise us up"), an equally valid translation would have these verbs as part of a volitive-volitive sequence that fits Martin-Achard's understanding of it as a prayer: "After two days let him [may he] revive us; on the third day let him [may he] raise us up, that we may live before him."

30. Wright, *The Resurrection of the Son of God*, 118; cf. Martin-Achard, *From Death to Life*, 78.

nation did not entertain the idea of a literal bodily resurrection until several centuries afterwards, when they were freed from the yoke of Baal worship and its degenerate notion of a resurrection tied to sexual immorality and worship of the forces of nature.

Nevertheless, when Israel was finally prepared to receive the fullness of divine revelation regarding the resurrection, Hosea's words would play an important role in the development of her tradition, as we will see below in discussing Isaiah and Daniel. For although the view presented in Hosea 6 was repudiated by the prophet at the time it was composed, the language he introduced would later reappear and the concept of resurrection would be purged of impurities. By the time of Christ's coming, it had already long been interpreted in light of a blessed hope for the life to come. As Wright concludes, "No second-Temple reader would have doubted that this [Hosea 6:2] referred to bodily resurrection."[31] Discussing this passage in reference to Christ's resurrection, Pope Benedict nevertheless cautions Christians against seeing in Hosea's text an explicit prophecy of Jesus's Resurrection on the third day. Agreeing with Wright that the text represents above all a "penitential prayer," he writes:

The thesis that the third day may possibly have been derived from Hosea 6:1–2 cannot be sustained.... The text is a penitential prayer on the part of sinful Israel. There is no mention of resurrection from the dead, properly speaking. The text is not quoted in the New Testament or at any point during the second century.... It could become an anticipatory pointer toward resurrection on the third day only once the event that took place on the Sunday after the Lord's crucifixion had given this day a special meaning.[32]

31. Wright, *The Resurrection of the Son of God*, 148.
32. Benedict XVI, *Jesus of Nazareth: Holy Week: From the Entrance into Jerusalem to the Resurrection* (San Francisco: Ignatius Press, 2011), 258. In another passage, Benedict offers an illuminating explanation of the process by which New Testament Christians re-read Old Testament texts and found Christ in them: "The process of coming to Resurrection faith is analogous to what we saw in the case of the Cross. Nobody had thought of a crucified Messiah. Now the 'fact' was there, and it was necessary, on the basis of that fact, to take a fresh look at Scripture.... Admittedly, this new reading of Scripture could begin only after the Resurrection, because it was only through the Resurrection that Jesus was accredited as the one sent by God. Now people had to search Scripture for both Cross and Resurrection, so as to understand them in a new way and thereby come to believe in Jesus as the Son of God." (245.) Benedict's words likewise help us to make sense of Old Testament texts cited by the New Testament authors as

For Pope Benedict, Hosea 6 is an important Old Testament pointer to faith in the resurrection, but ultimately it could be seen fully as a pointer to *Christ's* resurrection only once Christ had risen from the dead. It was this "fact" of Jesus's Resurrection that prompted the early church to see in this text not merely a foreshadowing of resurrection in general, but a pointer to Christ's resurrection on the third day.

Before moving on to the next book, it is important to mention Hosea 13 alongside Hosea 6:2. Hosea 5–6 and 13–14 contain parallel imagery, which leads scholars to conclude that the two exhibit a similar interest in life after death.[33] For example, the Revised Standard Version (RSV), translating the Masoretic Text (MT) of Hosea 13:14, reads: "Shall I ransom them from the power of Sheol? Shall I redeem them from Death?" It is actually far from clear that the Hebrew of Hosea 13 exhibits hope for life after death. For, as was observed in the case of Hosea 6:2, it may not be the case that Hosea 13 was dealing with individual or bodily resurrection in the first place. Nevertheless, it is worth noting that the LXX—which was produced centuries after the original Hebrew version of the text—can be read as attempting to resolve any ambiguity with regard to the question of resurrection, a rather unlikely move if the translators thought the passage was dealing with a metaphorical resurrection.[34] As Wright

---

prophecies when it is clear that the human authors of the Old Testament texts in question displayed no interest in predicting future events. His exploration into this dynamic between fact and scripture, event and word, reflects the concern articulated in his 1988 lecture to "reexamine the relationship between event and word." In this second volume of *Jesus of Nazareth*, he takes up this same language to describe the dynamic at work here: "It was not the words of Scripture that prompted the narration of facts; rather, it was the facts themselves, at first unintelligible, that paved the way towards a fresh understanding of Scripture. This discovery of the harmony between word and event … is constitutive of the Christian faith." (203.)

33. Wright, *The Resurrection of the Son of God*, 118, 148.

34. Even if the possibility of life after death is being denied in the Hebrew version of this passage, it nevertheless played a critical role in Israel's resurrection tradition. In Wright's view, "The original Hebrew text is almost certainly denying that Yahweh will redeem Israel from Sheol and Death. However, the LXX and other ancient versions, and also the New Testament [1 Cor 15], take the passage in a positive sense, and there is no reason why the author of Isaiah 26:19 should not have read it thus as well. The evidence that he did so is cumulative but overwhelming: no fewer than eight features of text and context can be paralleled." Wright, *The Resurrection of the Son of God*, 118. Hosea 13:14

notes, whereas the Hebrew text of Hosea 13:14 is a question that expects the answer "No," the LXX reads as an indicative statement: "From the hand of Hades I will ransom (ῥύσομαι) them and from death I will redeem (λυτρώσομαι) them."[35] It is therefore consistent to read the LXX of Hosea 13:14 as proclaiming the victory of Yahweh over death. Still, it ought to be noted that the notion of resurrection operative here is one of the national rather than individual order. Hosea is still an early Old Testament work, and the imagery and ideas latent within it form the basis of more explicit developments to come. As in the case of both Hosea 6 and 13, by the third century B.C. when the LXX came on the scene, new meanings began to be seen in texts previously unclear as to their stance on the resurrection, as well as in texts that originally appeared to deny it.[36]

Ezekiel 37

Like the account of resurrection found in Hosea 6 and 13, Ezekiel 37 depicts a national or metaphorical resurrection, in this case the return of the Judean exiles from Babylon to the Promised Land. Ezekiel was active as a prophet between the years 593 B.C. and 571 B.C.[37] As the prophet himself records in the opening verses of his book, he lived as an exile and did his preaching in Babylonia, "the land of the Chaldeans." Wright observes that Ezekiel 37 is perhaps the most famous of all resurrection passages in the Old Testament, and it is

---

may not have originally been written with an eye to the resurrection, although it certainly was interpreted that way even centuries before Christ's coming.

35. Translation mine. Cf. ibid., 148. Although the Hebrew of this verse lacks an interrogative הֲ, this does appear to take the form of a question that again expects the answer "No." What the MT does contain is אֱהִי, an odd form that appears to be the result of a scribal error, the jumbling of three consonants. The RSV translation of the third and fourth questions (the "where" questions) is based on a slight emendation of the MT in light of the LXX, which, as noted in the BHS, translates אֱהִי with the word ποῦ ("where?"). So the RSV emended translation reads: "Shall I ransom them from the power of Sheol? Shall I redeem them from Death? O Death, where are your plagues? O Sheol, where is your destruction? Compassion is hid from my eyes."

36. Wright, *The Resurrection of the Son of God*, 147; cf. Melvin Peters, "Septuagint," *ABD, vol.* 5, 1094. Peters points to several papyri from the early second century to the first century that stand as primary witnesses to this date for the LXX translation.

37. Lawrence Boadt, "Ezekiel, Book of," *ABD,* vol. 2, 711.

also the "most obviously allegorical or metaphorical."[38] He explains that the overall aim of the prophecy in Ezekiel 37 was to point to a renewal of Israel's national life in which Yahweh would restore the Davidic monarchy, the nation would be reconstituted in peace, and a new temple would be built. The entire chapter is significant, but the following verses provide a concise demonstration of the point at hand:

Therefore prophesy, and say to them, Thus says the Lord God: Behold, I will open your graves, and raise you from your graves, O my people; and I will bring you home into the land of Israel. And you shall know that I am the Lord, when I open your graves, and raise you from your graves, O my people. And I will put my Spirit within you, and you shall live, and I will place you in your own land; then you shall know that I, the Lord, have spoken, and I have done it, says the Lord.... Then say to them, Thus says the Lord God: Behold, I will take the people of Israel from the nations among which they have gone, and will gather them from all sides, and bring them to their own land; and I will make them one nation in the land, upon the mountains of Israel; and one king shall be king over them all; and they shall be no longer two nations, and no longer divided into two kingdoms.... I will make a covenant of peace with them; it shall be an everlasting covenant with them; and I will bless them and multiply them, and will set my sanctuary in the midst of them for evermore.[39]

In this passage, God addresses his people through the prophet, promising to raise them from their graves and restore them to their "own land." The resurrection is intimately connected with Israel's return "home into the land of Israel." There the people will be constituted again as "one nation in the land ... and one king shall be king over them all." The Lord will put his Spirit in them, make with them "a new covenant," and once again set up his sanctuary in the midst of them.

As Wright comments, this and the few chapters preceding it make it sufficiently clear that the author's purpose was to provide a highly charged and vivid metaphor of the way in which unclean Israel was to be cleansed, exiled Israel to be restored to her land, and scattered Israel to be regathered through the establishment of a new

38. Wright, *The Resurrection of the Son of God*, 119.
39. Ez 37:12–14, 21–22, 26.

covenant and a new creation.[40] Although the text could certainly be taken in reference to a literal resurrection event in the distant future, it is generally agreed that this resurrection was thought to take place soon after the prophecy and so to be of a national or metaphorical nature.[41] Based on the metaphorical meaning of this passage, however, some think they have proof that the Old Testament as a whole understood resurrection only allegorically and never literally—that the nation of Israel remained focused solely on this world and had no interest in the reunification of body and soul after death. As Wright will show, however, the idea of national resurrection present in Ezekiel and Hosea does not conflict with the doctrine of the resurrection of an individual body but rather contributed providentially to the development of the resurrection doctrine in later texts of the Old Testament.

According to Wright, it cannot be proven that Ezekiel either influenced or was influenced by writers such as Hosea, Daniel, or Isaiah, and yet he notes that some of the parallels between them are remarkable.[42] Whatever the relationship between Ezekiel, Isaiah, and Daniel may have been in their composition; any initial allegorical character of Ezekiel 37 did not stop faithful Israelites from seeing it as a prediction of a literal resurrection of the body in the same way that they saw this type of prophecy in Hosea, Isaiah, and Daniel. It is therefore appropriate to turn to these other passages to show that the view of resurrection as the restoration of Israel to her land was not peculiar to Ezekiel but rather constituted a common thread in Israel's thought that was inherently open to the further development

40. Wright, *The Resurrection of the Son of God*, 120.

41. Nevertheless, it is interesting to note the pregnant pause after God's question: "Son of man, can these bones live?" (37:3) Ezekiel does not reply, "Of course not!" but rather "O Lord God, thou knowest." As Jeremy Holmes pointed out, this refusal to deny the possibility of bodily resurrection may represent a small step towards admitting its existence, despite the metaphorical meaning revealed to the prophet in this passage (Jeremy Holmes, conversation with author).

42. See also the discussion of possible relationships between Daniel, Isaiah, Ezekiel, and Hosea in Jon Day, "The Development of Belief in Life after Death in Ancient Israel," in *After the Exile*, edited by J. Barton and D. J. Reimer (Macon, GA: Mercer University Press, 1996), 242–48.

of the second view of resurrection as the reunification of man's body and soul.

Isaiah 24–27 (*The Isaiah Apocalypse*)

The "Isaiah Apocalypse" likewise contains a crucial contribution to the Old Testament's doctrine on the afterlife and represents a kind of transitional stage in which the text appears open to both metaphorical and literal interpretations. Dating of this text has been widely debated among historical-critical scholars, but it is likely representative of a sixth century B.C. proto-apocalyptic genre.[43] Like Hosea and Ezekiel, Isaiah 24–27 deals with resurrection in the context of a return from exile. Isaiah 25:6–8, however, may well be one of the strongest and clearest affirmations of the hope for a blessed afterlife in the Old Testament:

On this mountain the Lord of hosts will make for all peoples a feast of fat things, a feast of wine on the lees, of fat things full of marrow, of wine on the lees well refined. And he will destroy on this mountain the covering that is cast over all peoples, the veil that is spread over all nations. He will swallow up death for ever, and the Lord God will wipe away tears from all faces, and the reproach of his people he will take away from all the earth; for the Lord has spoken.

This passage has clear eschatological overtones. According to Wright, "The image of the eschatological banquet draws together the divine promise to the individual, to Israel, and to creation itself."[44] For Isaiah, God is not merely going to restore Israel from exile; he will destroy the covering that is cast "over *all* peoples," the veil that is spread "over *all* nations." The Lord "will swallow up death forever." He will wipe away tears from "*all* faces."

Turning to Isaiah 26, the prophet predicts that a great song will be sung in the land of Judah when death is swallowed up forever. The unfaithful dead who worshiped other lords are mere shades and will not survive their own deaths, but Yahweh's dead will live and rise.[45] Although 25:6–8 appeared to speak overtly of bodily resur-

---

43. William R. Millar, "Isaiah 24–27 (Little Apocalypse)," *ABD*, vol. 3, 489.
44. Wright, *The Resurrection of the Son of God*, 117.
45. Is 26:14, 19. Cf. Johnston, *Shades of Sheol*, 225.

rection, it is not obvious whether the view of resurrection conveyed by the original Hebrew of 26:19 was literal, allegorical, or both.[46] The RSV reads, "Thy dead shall live, their bodies shall rise. O dwellers in the dust, awake and sing for joy! For thy dew is a dew of light, and on the land of the shades thou wilt let it fall." The first part is clear enough: "Thy dead shall live." What comes next, however, appears somewhat jumbled in the original Hebrew. It requires a textual emendation of the next Hebrew phrase order to arrive at the RSV translation "their bodies shall rise."[47] Following this is the admonition to the dwellers of the dust to "awake and sing," which is not problematic from the standpoint of assessing that these bodies are both masculine plural imperative forms.

Although it is somewhat unclear whether the MT of Isaiah 26:19 expresses hope in bodily resurrection in the same way as it appears in 25:6–8, the LXX translation of the verse seems to espouse this hope just as it did in the case of Hosea above: "The dead shall rise and those who are in the tombs shall be raised, and those who are in the earth shall rejoice. For thy dew heals them, but the land of the ungodly shall perish."[48] Here, the LXX employs both synonyms for resurrection that appear in the Greek of Hosea 6:2 and Daniel 12:2 and has them in the plural form (ἀναστήσονται and ἐγερθήσονται). It furthermore adds words to make clear that this is a literal resurrection that will take place for those who lie "in the tombs" (ἐν τοῖς μνημείοις). In the eyes of its LXX translator, whatever Isaiah 26:19 may have to do with the restoration of the nation of Israel as a whole, it apparently intends to convey a doctrine of personal bodily resurrection.

Of course, the later translation from the LXX does not much help to clarify the question of whether the Hebrew prophet himself

46. N. T. Wright does well to point out this ambiguity in *The New Testament and the People of God* (Minneapolis, Minn.: Fortress Press, 1992), 322.

47. Based on evidence from the Syriac translation of this text, the critical apparatus of the BHS notes that scholars have proposed the emendation employed by the RSV. Otherwise, the noun נְבֵלָתִי would not agree with the verb that follows it. Without the emendation, one would probably have to translate it adverbially with the result "together with my dead body they will rise."

48. Translation mine.

had both national restoration of Israel and individual resurrection in mind in this particular passage, but support for the view can be found in other sources. One particularly impressive witness to this interpretation is St. Thomas Aquinas's *Literal Commentary on Isaiah.* Although we have been focusing primarily on what Method B exegesis has to contribute to understanding Old Testament doctrine on the afterlife, Aquinas's understanding of Isaiah 26:19 is valuable (and quite frankly surprising to see coming from a medieval exegete) because here modern insights into the two dimensions of resurrection under discussion are vindicated by a doctor of the thirteenth century who already perceived this dynamic. Commenting on Isaiah 26:19, St. Thomas writes that the text refers to "the promise of the people's restoration by means of the resurrection, whether this be a corporeal [resurrection] on the last day or [resurrection] from the misery of captivity" (*promissio restitutionis populi per resurrectionem, sive corporalem in die novissimo, sive a miseria captivitatis*).[49] According to Aquinas, Isaiah is concerned with both the captivity of death and the misery of Babylonian captivity, an expression that occurs repeatedly throughout the commentary. For present purposes what stands out even more in Aquinas's brief treatment of Isaiah 26:19 is that he not only refers to two types of resurrection, but immediately after he does so he cites Daniel 12 along with Hosea 6 and Ezekiel 37, the other two passages discussed above in which a metaphorical resurrection is presented.

To be sure, it does not follow of necessity from Aquinas's connecting these passages that the Hebrew prophet himself had in mind two types of resurrection or that he thought of these passages in connection with one another. It is in fact possible that the prophet was concerned strictly with one form of resurrection. Nevertheless, significant weight ought to be given to Aquinas's argument simply given the fact that patristic and medieval exegetes did not typically pay such careful attention to the ancient Israelite context of Old Testament texts. If anything, one might expect a Method A exegete to

49. Thomas Aquinas, *Expositio super Isaiam ad litteram*, caput 26 (translation mine).

skip directly to a text's spiritual sense if there is any doubt as to the text's historical referent. It is therefore remarkable that the ecclesiastical tradition represented by St. Thomas understood Isaiah to be describing the metaphorical resurrection of Israel as well as the literal resurrection of human beings at the end of time. All this goes to show that the notions of national and individual resurrection were intimately tied to one another in the minds of ancient Israelites, and that this interpretation of their writings was maintained even in the Christian tradition at a time when, if anything, one might have expected to see less attention paid to the significance of Israel's return from exile.

Isaiah 40–55

Continuing our exploration of Isaiah and its presentation of a twofold resurrection, it is now appropriate to examine how it may have influenced the development of doctrine on the afterlife in later writings, particularly Daniel. According to Wright, "The main source for Daniel's ideas and images in 12:2–3 is undoubtedly Isaiah."[50] It is for this reason that we have discussed Isaiah's account of the resurrection before addressing the later, lucid depiction of individual resurrection in Daniel. Still, in order to grasp Daniel's account of the resurrection of individuals, another aspect of Isaiah must first be examined: the role of the servant (עֶבֶד) who suffers for the sins of many and is vindicated by God in his righteousness. As we will see, what happens to this servant is a sign that Israel's belief in national resurrection also began to be extended to individuals, in this case an individual representative of the nation. The particular use of עֶבֶד which is of present concern appears 32 times throughout the portions of the book of Isaiah which were composed during the sixth century and which are conventionally referred to as Deutero-Isaiah (chs. 40–55) and Trito-Isaiah (chs. 56–66).[51]

Sometimes עֶבֶד occurs in the singular (beginning at 41:18) and

---

50. Wright, *The Resurrection of the Son of God*, 121.

51. The term also appears in Proto-Isaiah (chs. 1–39) but with a different use. For the dating of these portions of the book of Isaiah, see Richard J. Clifford, "Second Isaiah," *ABD*, vol. 3, 491.

sometimes in the plural (beginning at 54:17). The first time it appears it clearly refers to the people of Israel as a collective, a corporate person chosen by God to be a light to the world: "But you, Israel, my servant, Jacob, whom I have chosen."[52] Not long afterward, however, the prophet uses עֶבֶד to single out an individual Israelite who has the spirit of God and who will be God's representative to the nations: "Behold my servant, whom I uphold, my chosen, in whom my soul delights; I have put my Spirit upon him, he will bring forth justice to the nations. He will not cry or lift up his voice, or make it heard in the street."[53] Such references to the servant as an individual and as a collective alternate with one another in the chapters that follow. At times it is clear that the servant is Israel: "'You are my witnesses,' says the Lord, 'and my servant whom I have chosen, that you may know and believe me and understand that I am He.'"[54] Other times it is hard to think of the עֶבֶד as anything else but an individual human being:

> Behold, my servant shall prosper,
> he shall be exalted and lifted up,
> and shall be very high.
> As many were astonished at him—
> his appearance was so marred, beyond human semblance,
> and his form beyond that of the sons of men.[55]

Here the servant appears as a righteous man who is stricken with blows to the point of hardly being recognizable as a human being. He dies and is buried, and in recompense for his hardship, the servant will be "exalted and lifted up" and "shall see the fruit of the travail of his soul and be satisfied."[56] Given this and other uses of the term עֶבֶד, readers are often left dumbfounded at what to make of the servant. The servant seems to be an individual Israelite who suffers on behalf of the people in order to justify them, yet at the same time he is obviously a corporate personality, the nation of Israel itself. Is there any relation between these two meanings?

52. Is 41:18.   53. Is 42:1–2.
54. Is 43:10.   55. Is 52:13–14.
56. Is 53:7–9; 52:13; 53:11.

Daniel 12

Isaiah's highly nuanced account of the עֶבֶד demands patient attentiveness on the part of the reader, but if one can come to terms with the prophet's language he will possess the key to understanding the servant's role not only in Isaiah but also in authors that were influenced by it, including Daniel. Now at last, we may turn to the text of Daniel and elucidate the place of this book which ties together so much that can be found in Hosea, Ezekiel, and Isaiah.[57] Dating much later than the previous books studied thus far (the Hebrew-Aramaic version probably reaching its final form around 164 B.C.), the section of Daniel pertinent to the present study was composed during another time of crisis: the great persecution of the Jews by Antiochus Epiphanes.[58] The first few verses of Dn 12 are particularly

---

57. Describing the centrality of Daniel in the tradition of doctrine on the resurrection, Wright writes, "The text which became central for much later Jewish thought on this subject is Daniel 12:2–3. Though it is almost certainly the latest of the relevant passages [since Wright is a Protestant, in this section he is discussing only passages in the Protestant canon, meaning Maccabees and Wisdom are excluded from the present discussion], there are three good reasons for starting with it. First, it is the clearest: virtually all scholars agree that it does indeed speak of bodily resurrection, and mean this in a concrete sense. Second, it draws on several of the other, probably older, relevant texts, showing us one way in which they were being read in the second century B.C. Third, conversely, it seems to have acted as a lens through which the earlier material was seen by subsequent writers. To read Daniel 12 is thus to stand on the bridge between the Bible and the Judaism of Jesus's day, looking both backward and forward, and watching the passage of ideas that went to and fro between them. Cf. Wright, *The Resurrection of the Son of God*, 108. For more on the relationship between Daniel and the various texts studied thus far, as well as a broad treatment of many of the elements discussed above see Day, "The Development of Belief in Life after Death in Ancient Israel," 231–56, and Benedict XVI, *Eschatology*, 90.

58. John J. Collins, "Daniel, Book of," *ABD*, vol. 2, 30. On the topic of Daniel's dating, one must consider the relationship of its historical and fictive settings. Although the book is presented as taking place in Babylon, scholars are in agreement that his words were written and intended to refer to a persecution like that of Babylon but taking place centuries later under Antiochus Epiphanes. As Wright states, "The fictive setting is of course Babylon, and the historical setting is that of the 'continuing exile' of 9:24, under various pagan rulers climaxing in the Syria of Antiochus." Wright, *The Resurrection of the Son of God*, 115. Wright also comments, "The immediate context of the passage is martyrdom: the martyrdom which occurred during the crisis of the 160s (see 1 and 2 Maccabees), and, in particular, the martyrdom of faithful Israelites under the

relevant to the study of the Old Testament's doctrine on the resurrection:

At that time shall arise Michael, the great prince who has charge of your people. And there shall be a time of trouble, such as never has been since there was a nation till that time; but at that time your people shall be delivered, every one whose name shall be found written in the book. And many of those who sleep in the dust of the earth shall awake, some to everlasting life, and some to shame and everlasting contempt. And those who are wise shall shine like the brightness of the firmament; and those who turn many to righteousness, like the stars for ever and ever.[59]

According to N. T. Wright, historical criticism's attention to the Hebrew of this passage reveals its connection with the book of Isaiah. The מַשְׂכִּלִים ("wise") of Daniel 12:3 seem to be a plural version of the servant of Isaiah 52–53, who "prospers" or "deals wisely." Moreover, Daniel says that the wise ones will "turn many to righteousness," just as the servant in Isaiah 53:11 will "make many to be accounted righteous."[60] For Wright, this linguistic similarity is no coincidence, because the entire theme of Daniel—those who remain faithful to Yahweh despite torture and death and who are subsequently vindicated—fits squarely with the scenario in which Isaiah 40–55 reaches its great climax. From this Wright concludes that Deutero-Isaiah's servant figure who "deals wisely" was in the first place an individual who personified the nation of Israel but who has been repluralized now in the form of Daniel's "wise ones" who will awake to shine like the stars in eternity.[61]

---

persecution of Antiochus Epiphanes. Daniel 11:31 speaks of Antiochus's desecration of the Jerusalem Temple, and his setting up of the "abomination of desolation" mentioned already in 9:27. Verses 32–35 of chapter 11 describe what happens next, as some Judaeans compromise with the pagan invader and others stand firm and suffer for it, some of them being killed. Verses 36–45 then describe the final boasting and sudden fall of Antiochus, the earlier verses (36–39) staying close to what we know as actual events, and the later ones (40–45) diverging at the point, we assume, where the writer's own time is to be located. But what matters is that at the time of Antiochus's "fall, a time of unprecedented anguish for Israel (12:1), the angelic prince Michael will arise to fight on their behalf and deliver them. This is the context for the prediction of resurrection." (113.)

59. Dn 12:1–3.

60. Day also picks up on this in "The Development of Belief in Life after Death in Ancient Israel," 242–43.

61. Wright, *The Resurrection of the Son of God*, 115.

As Wright's work suggests, this passage of Daniel is precisely that point in the divine pedagogy where the belief that Israel's God would restore the nation from exile fully breaks through into the belief that he will restore the nation's righteous representative, and ultimately all the righteous of the nation, after death.[62] The process of suffering and death is a reality that both the nation of Israel as a whole and each one of her members must endure; and, since God is faithful there awaits a reward for everyone who undergoes this struggle. Initially, it was the suffering servant alone who would be vindicated by God, but as time went on and all Israelites saw themselves living the life of the servant through suffering, persecution, and martyrdom, they learned to hope that God would vindicate them in the same way he did Isaiah's servant of old. They had suffered and died for the sake of righteousness, and they knew they would receive a reward for their faithfulness, because they knew Yahweh would be faithful to his promise and providentially restore the people from exile. Wright offers a succinct summary of the passage toward hope in the resurrection that was brought about because of Israel's faith in Yahweh:

Yahweh's answer to his people's exile would be, metaphorically, life from the dead (Is 26, Ez 37). Yahweh's answer to his people's martyrdom would be, literally, life from the dead (Dn 12). This was a bold step, indeed, but it was the last step in a comprehensible line of thought going back to the earliest roots of Israelite belief.[63]

In this way, Israel's earlier national hope develops in a perfectly comprehensible and yet initially surprising direction: what began as a metaphor (e.g., Hosea and Ezekiel's depiction of the nation of Israel undergoing a kind of restoration or resurrection from their suffer-

---

62. In fact, John J. Collins observes in his article "The Afterlife in Apocalyptic Literature," in *Judaism in Late Antiquity*, edited by Alan J. Avery-Peck and Jacob Neusner (Boston: Brill Academic Publishers, 2000), "This is the only passage in the Hebrew Bible that clearly predicts the resurrection of individuals." (126.) Writing for a non-Catholic audience, Collins makes no reference in this article to the individual resurrection in 2 Maccabees, which will be discussed below. Nevertheless, his analysis is significant in showing how late and unique was the development of the doctrine of individual resurrection in Israel.

63. Ibid., 127.

ing and exile, and Isaiah's use of the servant as a corporate person chosen by God to bring light to the nations) is used by God in his divine pedagogy to prepare the people to receive the doctrine that he would do for righteous human beings what it was always hoped he would do for the nation as a whole. According to Daniel, it is not that all the righteous individuals of Israel will rise again metaphorically in a return to the Promised Land, but they will instead rise literally in the Promised Land of a renewed created order.[64] In this way, one can see that Israel's hope for resurrection in its literal and metaphorical dimensions was substantially the same hope, based on the singular faithfulness of her God. The hope was not static but developed throughout the centuries in the same direction in which it began, only this development extended infinitely farther than any of the people could have imagined before God revealed it to them. Unaided by divine revelation, it is most improbable that the people would ever have dreamed of the literal resurrection of their bodies as the form that national restoration would take—that not only temporal exile would end but that there would come an end to the deepest exile of all, death.

Although it took a long time for the people of Israel to learn the ultimate nature of the afterlife from God, once they received this revelation it laid a deep hold on their consciousness and became ever clearer to them as revelation continued to progress. In order to make this clear, it is appropriate to turn to doctrine on the afterlife as found in the deuterocanonical literature of the Old Testament.

---

64. As Wright does well to observe, this new created order envisioned by Daniel still did not necessarily imply the precise New Testament view of the resurrected state of heaven: "The Jews who believed in resurrection did so as part of a larger belief in the renewal of the whole created order. Resurrection would be, in one and the same moment, the reaffirmation of the covenant and the reaffirmation of creation. Israel would be restored within a restored cosmos: the world would see, at last, who had all along been the true people of the creator God.... *There is virtually no evidence that Jews were expecting the end of the space-time universe....* What, then, did they believe was going to happen? They believed that *the present world order* was going to come to an end." *The New Testament and the People of God*, 332–33. In the New Testament, meanwhile, resurrection appears as a state to be lived in heaven, outside of this space-time universe. The risen Christ has ascended and now reigns in his kingdom where there is a "new heaven and a new earth" (Rv 21:1).

This body of literature is history's most significant witness to the sharpening of the doctrine of resurrection in Israel before the time of Christ. Not only does it provide a bridge between Daniel and the New Testament, it actually demonstrates that God taught the doctrine presented throughout the books of Hosea, Isaiah, Ezekiel, and Daniel to Israel even more clearly in the years immediately before the coming of Christ.

2 Maccabees

Although as an Anglican N. T. Wright does not accept the canonicity of 2 Maccabees, according to him this second-century work "provides far and away the clearest picture of the promise of resurrection anywhere in the period [of second-Temple Judaism]."[65] 2 Maccabees begins where Daniel left off, with the promise of new bodily life at some future date for those who had died as martyrs for their faith in Yahweh under the persecution of Antiochus Epiphanes. Whereas in Daniel the persecution is cloaked with imagery evoking the suffering of Israel in Babylon, here this Syrian tyrant is clearly in control and is attempting to force loyal Jews to give up their God-given laws and comply with his imperial dictates, particularly the command that they conform to his rule by eating pork, an unclean food.

2 Maccabees 7 presents the story of the mother and her seven sons whom she encourages to abstain from consuming this food even though the penalty for doing so would be death. In what follows, one can see that the promise of resurrection described in Daniel has fully flowered and is impelling the faith of the Maccabean martyrs. As the second brother is having the skin and hair of his head ripped off by his persecutor, he speaks to him: "You accursed wretch, you dismiss us from this present life, but the King of the universe will raise us up to an everlasting renewal of life, because

65. Ibid., 150. For more on the presentation of the resurrection in 2 Maccabees and in many extra-biblical documents composed closely before and after the turn of the millennium, see George Nickelsburg, "Judgment, Life-after-death, and Resurrection in the Apocrypha and the Non-Apocalyptic Pseudepigrapha," in *Judaism in Late Antiquity*, edited by Alan J. Avery-Peck and Jacob Neusner (Boston: Brill Academic Publishers, 2000), 141–62. As Nickelsburg is writing from a non-Catholic perspective, in this article he includes 2 Maccabees under the category of apocryphal literature.

we have died for his laws."[66] Here, the Greek is undeniable: the King of the universe will raise up the young men because they have died for loyalty to his laws. The other brothers speak in similar terms. The third brother's words convey the understanding that God will restore the full bodily integrity of the human being who righteously loses any of his members for God's sake. Putting out his tongue and hands to be chopped off by his enemies, he speaks nobly, "I got these [his tongue and hands] from Heaven, and because of his laws I disdain them, and from him I hope to get them back again."[67] The next brother continues in the same vein: not only does he confirm that God will raise him and his brothers up again on account of their faithfulness, he also denies that his unrighteous persecutors will attain to the resurrection, or at least to the resurrection of life: "One cannot but choose to die at the hands of men and to cherish the hope that God gives of being raised again by him. But for you there will be no resurrection to life!"[68] Eventually, all seven brothers and their mother are killed in the same spirit of trust in God's promise for vindication through the resurrection of their bodies. For these faithful Israelites of the second century, resurrection is not merely a national affair; it touches their very being, and it alone manifests the justice of a God who will reward his servants by giving them back everything they offer him, even their own bodies.

This teaching on the resurrection, particularly evident in the exhortations of the mother to her sons, furthermore manifests Israel's belief in the goodness of God's creation which was a vital component that impelled them to hope for redemption.[69] The Maccabean martyrs who hope in the resurrection share this in common with their ancestors who were not privy to such a hope: they esteem man as the handiwork of God. The martyrs of 2 Maccabees, however, have taken another step, for it is noteworthy that this passage contains both of scripture's most explicit references to the doctrine of *creatio ex nihilo* and to the doctrine of bodily resurrection. For

66. 2 Mc 7:9. See also the discussion of these passages in Wright, *The New Testament and the People of God*, 323–24.

67. 2 Mc 7:11.   68. 2 Mc 7:14.

69. Cf. 2 Mc 7:22–23, 28.

in the Maccabean period, Israel's affirmation of creation's goodness translates into the belief that it would be unfitting for him who out of his great mercy created man out of nothing to let those who love him fade into nonexistence. The body was created by God to live, and live it shall if a man proves to be a faithful steward of this awesome gift.

One more passage from 2 Maccabees impressively witnesses to Israel's faith in the resurrection in the years preceding Christ's coming. Much more could be said about the passage that follows, but for the purpose of this study it is significant because it speaks of faith in the resurrection almost in passing—as a given and as a basis for other Jewish beliefs, such as the belief that they could pray for the dead and that those prayers could affect the salvation of the deceased. In 2 Maccabees 12, Judas and his comrades discover that those who died in battle against Gorgias's troops had been wearing sacred tokens of the idols of Jamnia under their tunics, and it was for this reason that they had been killed. Judas's response is twofold: first, he praises God, the righteous judge, for bringing this to light; second, he takes up a collection for a sin offering and prays that the sin might be blotted out so that the deceased might be able to join the rest of the righteous in the resurrection on the last day:

He also took up a collection, man by man, to the amount of two thousand drachmas of silver, and sent it to Jerusalem to provide for a sin offering. In doing this he acted very well and honorably, taking account of the resurrection. For if he were not expecting that those who had fallen would rise again, it would have been superfluous and foolish to pray for the dead. But if he was looking to the splendid reward that is laid up for those who fall asleep in godliness, it was a holy and pious thought. Therefore he made atonement for the dead, that they might be delivered from their sin.[70]

These men had gone to their graves in sin, but Judas and his companions had faith that the mercy of God could still bring about their salvation. The resurrection was to take place some time in the future, but from the point of view of 2 Maccabees the secret idolaters resided in an intermediate state between life and the resurrection.

70. 2 Mc 12:43-45.

There was hope that these could live eternally in the resurrection if forgiven their sin through the intercession of their comrades.

For present purposes, however, this begs the question regarding the temporary state of the deceased individuals described in 2 Maccabees. By this point in time, Israel had come to learn that Sheol would not swallow its dead for all eternity, yet the question remained as to what would happen to the dead in the meantime before their resurrection. The author of 2 Maccabees does not demonstrate any awareness of a life between death and the resurrection, but the later book of Wisdom clearly does. Wright repeatedly refers to this state as "life after death," and he distinguishes it from resurrected life or what he calls "life after life after death." In the discussion of Wisdom that follows, this distinction will be elucidated and Israel's mature view of the afterlife will be made more evident.

Wisdom: Life after Life after Death

Although the book of Wisdom often perplexes readers in its presentation of the afterlife, it actually can help clarify the distinction made above by Wright. A deuterocanonical book written in Greek within a few decades of the coming of Christ, the book of Wisdom is recognized for clearly teaching the immortality of the soul, but scholars often assume that on account of this teaching it cannot simultaneously teach the resurrection of the body.[71] As Wright strives to demonstrate, however, the author of the book of Wisdom does not simply believe in the immortality of the soul; he also holds to the Jewish notion of resurrection, and his writing corroborates 2 Maccabees in describing the existence of an intermediate state coming after death and before the resurrection of the body on the Last Day. At the beginning of his discussion, Wright cites the famous passage from Wisdom 3:

> But the souls of the righteous are in the hand of God,
> and no torment will ever touch them.
> In the eyes of the foolish they seemed to have died,

71. For the dating of this book, see Wright, *The Resurrection of the Son of God*, 163, nn. 137, 139.

and their departure was thought to be an affliction,
and their going from us to be their destruction;
but they are at peace.
For though in the sight of men they were punished,
their hope is full of immortality.
Having been disciplined a little, they will receive great good,
because God tested them and found them worthy of himself;
like gold in the furnace he tried them,
and like a sacrificial burnt offering he accepted them.
In the time of their visitation they will shine forth,
and will run like sparks through the stubble.
They will govern nations and rule over peoples,
and the Lord will reign over them for ever.
Those who trust in him will understand truth,
and the faithful will abide with him in love,
because grace and mercy are upon his elect,
and he watches over his holy ones.
But the ungodly will be punished as their reasoning deserves,
who disregarded the righteous man and rebelled
against the Lord.[72]

According to Wright, the most serious misreadings of Wisdom have occurred precisely in regard to this passage. It is often claimed that verses 1–4 (ending with "... full of immortality") and 7–10 (beginning with "In their time ...") represent parallel descriptions of the afterlife, namely two depictions of a disembodied state of immortality typically found in Greek writings. Against this, Wright takes pains to demonstrate the thoroughly Jewish nature of Wisdom, that the passage at hand lies within a narrative of how divine judgment will vindicate the suffering righteous of Israel in the face of persecution by the ungodly.[73]

That the book was written in a Jewish context is important for Wright because it means that one ought to see in it a notion of the resurrection held by the Jewish community at the time of the coming of Christ. Against the claims of scholars who impute a com-

72. Ws 3:1–10. Although Wright does not use the RSV translation in his treatment of Wisdom, I have continued to use it here as I have throughout this work.
73. Cf. Wright, *The Resurrection of the Son of God*, 165–67. See also Wright's discussion of Wisdom 3 in his *The New Testament and the People of God*, 329–30, and Pope Benedict's comments along the same lines in *Eschatology*, 91.

pletely Greek worldview to the book and this passage in particular,
Wright finds that it espouses a view in which there are two states
of existence after death for the righteous, one before their bodies
rise on the last day, and the state of bodily resurrection itself. In this
vein, Wright comments, "It should be clear that verses 7–10 are describing a *further* event which *follows upon* the state described in
verses 1–4. The passage is not simply a second, parallel description,
a reinterpretation. After all, the 'souls' in verse 4 still have a '*hope
full of immortality*.'"[74] For Wright, it would be meaningless to say
of deceased souls that their "hope is full of immortality" if they have
already reached their final state of existence.

Still, one who gives a mere surface reading to the text might
claim that the souls of the righteous being in God's hand simply
means that they are loved and protected by God in the present
life. If one more carefully observes the context of 3:1–10, however,
it becomes clear that the righteous have already suffered and died,
and that "the time when the souls are the righteous are 'in God's
hand' is simply the temporary period of rest during which they are
looked after, like Daniel going to his 'rest' or the souls under the
altar in Revelation, until the time when they, like him, rise for their
reward."[75] Indeed, as verses 2–3 state, these souls have already made
their "departure" (ἔξοδος) from the community. In the eyes of the
foolish they "seemed to have died," but they are now "at peace." And
although the souls are at peace in the afterlife, they nevertheless
await a day of "visitation" that will vindicate their hope for immortality. The author's use of this powerful word visitation (ἐπισκοπῆς)
leads Wright to his conclusion:

"The time of their visitation" clearly refers to an event still in the future. Within the book, "visitation" is a regular word for a day of judgment on which the
Creator will condemn the wicked and vindicate the righteous.... In the present context, the point is that verse 7 cannot be *reinterpreting* the events of
verses 1–4 from another point of view. It must be adding a new point: that,
after a time of rest, something new will happen to the righteous.[76]

74. Wright, *The Resurrection of the Son of God*, 167–68.
75. Wright, *The Resurrection of the Son of God*, 174; cf. Ws 2:12–20; 4:7.
76. Ibid., 169.

In this way, Wisdom and 2 Maccabees bring the Old Testament revelation on the afterlife to its climax. The souls of the righteous who have suffered for their faith in the one true God will indeed live forever, but they must first pass through an intermediate state in hope for the day of their visitation and resurrection.[77] In this state, the souls of Israel's righteous will need to be further purified and prepared so that they may attain to the fullness of life God took centuries to teach them to hope for: the reunification of body and soul that will enable them to enjoy the direct vision of God in the eternal Promised Land.[78]

To sum up the first part of this chapter, our effort has attempted to show forth the intelligibility of God's gradual revelation of himself, to make it plausible to see the divine hand at work in Israel's gradually developing hope for life after death. We have used the best of Method B exegesis to argue that what became the doctrine of the resurrection in Daniel, 2 Maccabees, Wisdom, and, ultimately, the New Testament, was not a mere change or deviation but rather an outgrowth of the most ancient of God's teachings regarding his own goodness, the goodness of his creation, and his plan to providentially restore this creation in a way known to himself alone. What God has done throughout the course of history as witnessed in these texts is to gradually reveal to his children the fullest possibilities that lay latent within their hopes. God cares for this material world and man's life within it, but his promise for restoration ultimately reaches far beyond what could be offered to man in this world.

What is the upshot of all this as regards the doctrines of scriptural inspiration and inerrancy? In light of Method C exegesis,

77. Cf. Ibid., 132–34, where Wright presents what he considers to be evidence from the Acts of the Apostles for Pharisaic belief in an intermediate state between death and the resurrection.

78. This passage of the book of Wisdom is pertinent for the Catholic Church's eventual doctrine of purgatory. As discussed above, Israel's understanding of the afterlife in its interim stage between a person's death and the Last Day developed over the centuries preceding the coming of Christ. Here in 2 Maccabees and Wisdom 3 it is evident that the dead were thought to have some form of life in the time before the day of resurrection, but it would be centuries before what constituted the form of life after death before the resurrection would be defined by the church in light of the revelation of Jesus Christ.

scripture can and must still be considered inerrant even though in certain areas it does not explicitly teach the fullness of revealed truth vis-à-vis the afterlife Applying terminology from Aquinas's theology of the history of revelation, we may say that such passages simply represent a phase of the divine pedagogy in which the same "substance of the faith" present throughout the duration of divine revelation had yet fully to bloom. In other words, those who lived in later ages and were privileged to affirm more *articles* of faith in God nevertheless possessed the same *substance* of the faith as those who lived earlier in the course of divine revelation. Christians are privileged to have explicit knowledge of the full range of revealed truth, but what we now enjoy was prepared for over the course of millennia by a God who lovingly and patiently taught us.

The Afterlife and Aquinas's Theology of the Act of Revelation

Having proposed a way to account for the fact that certain parts of Scripture do not explicitly teach the fullness of truth professed by Christians today, the other difficulty our Method C exegesis must now address is the fact that there are also *apparent contradictions* in the things that Scripture intends to teach—in particular the fact that there are some points in the Old Testament in which the sacred authors seem to positively deny that there is such a thing as life after death. Here we will search out the intentions of the biblical authors and show that they did not make formal truth claims that contradict Christian doctrine on the triune God. We will likewise seek the divine author's purpose in composing these texts in order to ascertain what their spiritual sense has to teach Christians today.

The Role of the Spiritual Sense

In chapter 4, we followed the argument of Aquinas's commentators Paul Synave and Pierre Benoit as they suggested that the various texts of scripture must be assessed not only in light of the truths of the speculative order contained therein but also taking into consideration their various practical ends. The sacred author is an instrument whom God chooses to convey his truth to the world, but God often wanted some things written for a reason other than teaching clear-cut dogmas. Thus, we considered the example of the creation account in Genesis, which according to Synave and Benoit was not written to teach science but rather to effect other ends such as illustrating divine providence, bringing man to appreciate creation, and enabling man to better understand his role within it. We further saw that the purpose of scripture is not limited to the meaning originally intended by its human author, for all the books of scripture are primarily the work of a divine author whose providence outstrips any conscious authorial intention on the part of man. In this way, scripture could have spoken in various ways to individuals in ancient Israel, and it can be just as relevant for believers today as it was over two millennia ago.

We will begin with a summary statement of Synave and Benoit which provides the basis for understanding how scripture may be relevant for believers today. While acknowledging that the inspired human author of scripture consciously decides to compose his work with an admixture of practical and speculative ends in view, Synave and Benoit recognize that the ultimate practical judgment concerning Scripture's purpose comes not from any human but from its divine author:

We realize how much an individual author, no matter how strong the illumination given him, is outstripped by the providential finality of the Sacred Book. Beyond what he has consciously included in his text, the text itself will always contain seeds of further development, refrains and resonances which are beyond his power of clear perception; but they have been put into the text with his concurrence, if not his knowledge, by the Sovereign Author of the whole Book. This is the whole richness of the secondary senses which are a continuation of the primary sense known by the author. For this whole residue of which he is not conscious, he is clearly an instrument in the strict sense of the word.[79]

Through the "secondary" or spiritual senses of scripture (described in more detail back in chapter 2), the divine author teaches believers truths that may never have been fathomed by the human au-

---

79. Paul Synave and Pierre Benoit, *Prophecy and Inspiration: a Commentary on the Summa Theologica II–II, Questions 171–178* (New York: Desclée Co., 1961), 118.

thors who penned the words containing them. In terms of the divine pedagogy, these human authors served, Synave and Benoit say, as instruments "in the strict sense of the word." Their task first and foremost was to be receptive to the gift of inspiration, and based on this faithful response God used their writings as a vehicle to teach his people and to lead them to contemplate spiritual truths ever more profoundly throughout the ages. These spiritual senses are "a continuation of the primary sense known by the author." In what follows, we will attempt to show that the way in which God continues to use texts from the Bible as a means of spiritual encounter with Christians is something far surpassing their original authors' expectations and yet truly in accord with them.[80]

Two Aspects of the Divine Pedagogy and the Struggles of Ecclesiastes, Job, and the Psalmist

The texts dealt with in this section come from Ecclesiastes, Job, and the Psalms. Our analysis of them will be twofold. On the one hand, their claims will be assessed in light of the framework provided by Synave and Benoit. If Synave and Benoit are correct, then although their view of the afterlife is sometimes quite bleak, these men were enlightened with the gift of inspiration to compose their text in such a way that a practical goal (e.g., showcasing the vanity

---

80. If I emphasize that the true spiritual sense of the Old Testament must be in accord or continuity with its literal meaning, it is because this element of continuity is a helpful criterion for distinguishing true and healthy interpretations from unfounded allegorizations that are not in harmony with the Christian tradition. For further discussion of the relationship between the literal and spiritual sense, see Sandra M. Schneiders, "Faith, Hermeneutics, and the Literal Sense of Scripture," *Theological Studies* 39 (1978): 719–36. See also the lucid introduction to biblical theology by Dominique Barthélemy entitled *God and His Image: An Outline of Biblical Theology*, translated by Dom Aldhelm Dean, OSB (San Francisco: Ignatius Press, 2007). Barthélemy tries to show that the Old Testament is not merely an archive or artifact but a living document which grew over the centuries and which still speaks to believers today. He argues that the spiritual senses of the Old Testament grew in accordance with its original intention precisely because it was the subject of a continual tradition of meditation in the believing community: "This revered Scripture remained deeply engraved in the minds of the people—not like a dead letter or forgotten archives, but as the object of continual meditation, which ensured that understanding would grow in the direction of its original orientation." (xxii–xxiii.)

of existence apart from hope in a redeemer) predominated over any imperfect concepts they might have had concerning the nature of the afterlife. While not the definitive word on the matter, this insight from Synave and Benoit goes a long way toward vindicating the inerrant nature of the Bible in the face of apparently contradictory statements on the question of the afterlife, because it offers an account of how particularly challenging texts might have fit within the divine pedagogy in ancient Israel. On the other hand, even if one accepts that a particular author's bleak statements were not made as definitive speculative judgments about the nature of the afterlife, it is reasonable to expect that all of God's word in scripture, even the most ordinary of passages, at least teaches something or provides some sort of occasion for today's reader to encounter the living Word of God. It will be of the utmost importance to examine how these challenging books may teach Christians today and help them enter into the mystery of Israel's (and ultimately Christ's) own suffering, death, and resurrection.

In this section, we continue to operate with the understanding that it was precisely in the greatest moments of strife, when Israel had to trust in God most, that he began to reveal the deepest of truths to them. As suggested above, it was through endurance of suffering and persecutions that the nation of Israel was opened to receive the fullness of divine teaching on the afterlife. Now, we shall discover that the process of struggle and growth in the lives of individual believers like Ecclesiastes, Job, and the psalmist represents a kind of microcosm of the strife Israel underwent as a nation on its path to receiving the fullness of divine revelation. God taught the nation to ponder the meaning of his promises by means of their exile, pain, and persecution, but each individual Israelite lived and meditated deeply upon these sufferings in his own life as well. In fact, it was this desert of spiritual aridity, sickness, and pain that prompted faithful Israelites to meditate deeply on what the divine promise meant for their personal destiny—eventually coming to understand that their final deliverance would not be brought about in this life but in the Promised Land beyond the grave. As we indicated above, a helpful way of stating this dynamic is that the pedagogy by which God gradually taught the chosen people as a whole is also observable in how God has taught individual members of the faithful throughout history. In order to make the twofold aspect of the divine pedagogy clear, it is now appropriate to turn once again to the scriptures to witness how God taught individual Israelites through the process of struggle and questioning over the problem of death.

Ecclesiastes

Among the three books focused upon in this section, Ecclesiastes presents the bleakest overall picture of human destiny. Seeing as it is dated to sometime in the third century B.C. by many Method B scholars today, the book with its stark outlook is particularly poignant for study of what is supposed to be a forward-looking development in Israel's belief.[81] However, it is not as if the late dating of the book is the only difficulty it presents for work on the inerrancy of biblical doctrine on the afterlife. Also to be reckoned with is the fact that Ecclesiastes was authored by a faithful Israelite (in fact, the patristic-medieval tradition held that the preacher in Ecclesiastes was Solomon himself). Even before modern scholarship was able to identify the style of the Hebrew in Ecclesiastes and conclude its dating with the help of linguistic tools, exegetes throughout the centuries have had to deal with passages like Eccleasiastes 3:19–20, which were known to come from a man of faith and yet which portrayed such desperation in the face of death.[82] As pointed out above, the problem

81. James Crenshaw, "Ecclesiastes, book of," *ABD*, vol. 2, 275; Addison G. Wright, "Ecclesiastes," *NJBC* 31:2. cf. Crenshaw, "Ecclesiastes, book of," *ABD*, vol. 2, 274. For more on death and the afterlife in the book of Ecclesiastes and in other wisdom literature, see Roland Murphy, "Death and Afterlife in the Wisdom Literature," in *Judaism in Late Antiquity,* edited by Alan J. Avery-Peck and Jacob Neusner (Boston: Brill Academic Publishers, 2000), 102–15.

82. "For the fate of the sons of men and the fate of beasts is the same; as one dies, so dies the other. They all have the same breath, and man has no advantage over the beasts; for all is vanity. All go to one place; all are from the dust, and all turn to dust again" (Eccl 3:19–20). It is worth noting that renowned biblical scholar Barthélemy suggests that the word "vanity" (הֶבֶל) used here and throughout Ecclesiastes would be better translated as "breath." For Ecclesiastes and for the Israelites he represents, the vanity of human life consisted in the observation that it was like a fleeting breath that condenses momentarily upon meeting cold air and then vanishes, absorbed back into it

raised by passages like these is that Ecclesiastes seems to contradict the truth about God and his providence. For faith tells Christians that man differs from the beasts, and that after death there is a reward for righteousness in this life, yet Ecclesiastes's words manifestly deny these truths.[83]

One attempt to counter this problem, employed frequently by Method A exegetes, has been to aver that problematic portions of Ecclesiastes were not written by Solomon but rather by an Epicurean philosopher who was simply unaware of revealed truth about the afterlife. However, this explanation itself raises numerous other questions and, most importantly, does not clearly fit the text itself. In lieu of this option, the problem of Ecclesiastes may be confronted in a way that accords more with the author's own claims by attending to the commentary on the book by St. Bonaventure. St. Bonaventure's solution is appropriate to call upon here because it tends toward what one would expect from a modern Method C exegete. For as one might expect from a Method B exegete, St. Bonaventure takes seriously the disconcerting claims of the text of Ecclesiastes, yet as a faithful Method A exegete he values its claims concerning the importance of faith and obedience to God. Like other patristic and medieval exegetes, this saint held that the work was authored by a faithful Israelite, namely Solomon. Unlike many Method A exegetes and in agreement with a more Method B approach, however, St. Bonaventure also held that some challenging statements issuing from Ecclesiastes's mouth expressed the author's own view and conveyed the literal sense he intended in composing his text.

St. Bonaventure does in fact raise the possibility that the bleak statement "there is no work or thought or knowledge or wisdom in Sheol, to which you are going" was written from the standpoint of an

---

as quickly as it first appeared. Hence, Barthélemy proposes the following translation of Eccl 1:2: "Breath of breaths, the most fugitive of breath, all is nothing but breath!" *God and His Image*, 221.

83. This difference between man and beast is not part of only the Christian heritage. It is clearly stated in the Old Testament itself and indeed in close proximity to portions of it which would seem to contradict this very teaching. For example, in Job 35:11 Elihu speaks of "God my Maker, who gives songs in the night, who teaches us more than the beasts of the earth and makes us wiser than the birds of the air."

Epicurean (*in persona Epicuri*).[84] However, in contrast with many exegetes of the Christian tradition, St. Bonaventure does not allege that
troubling passages in Ecclesiastes were being stated as a kind of foil
to indicate the position of what things look like from the perspective
of an Epicurean who does not have faith in God. St. Bonaventure
prefers to accept Ecclesiastes 9:10 from the point of view of Solomon,
showing the conclusion a man would draw if the premises were true
that one cannot know whether what he does is pleasing to God and
whether virtue ultimately will have any reward.[85] As for Ecclesiastes's
dark claim "the dead know nothing, and they have no more reward;
but the memory of them is lost," St. Bonaventure notes that its literal
sense is that the dead neither know the things of this world, nor remain in the memory of those in the world, nor have any affection for
things of the world. Knowledge presupposes life, but St. Bonaventure
observes that the dead have neither life, nor motion, nor sense.[86]

   This interpretation of St. Bonaventure is consistent with the medieval understanding of the underworld, a view which retained elements of the traditional Sheol imagery discussed earlier in this work.
According to this view, before the coming of Christ everyone who
died—the good and the wicked alike—went down into Sheol (*inf-
eros*). It is interesting that St. Bonaventure ties this into Job 10:20–22,
where Job speaks the words: "Are not the days of my life few? Let me
alone, that I may find a little comfort before I go whence I shall not
return, to the land of gloom and deep darkness, the land of gloom
and chaos, where light is as darkness." St. Bonaventure explains, "Sinners go there, and everyone [went there] before the advent of Christ,
as regards the outer part (*limbum*).[87] St. Bonaventure does not think

84. Eccl 9:10.
85. Bonaventure, *Expositio in Ecclesiasten*, in *Opera omnia; Sixti V., pontificis maximi jussu diligentissime emendata*, edited by Adolpho Carolo Peltier (Paris: Ludovicus
Vivès, 1864), 9:657. For a more thorough presentation of Bonaventure's commentary,
see Jeremy Holmes, "Biblical Scholarship New and Old: Learning from the Past," *Nova
et Vetera* 1 (2003). I am indebted to Jeremy Holmes for first drawing my attention to
this work of Bonaventure, and whatever good can be found in my presentation of it is
thanks to the more thorough and precise exposition given in his article.
86. Eccl 9:5; Bonaventure, *Expositio in Ecclesiasten*, 9:655–57.
87. Ibid., 9:656 (translation mine).

of this statement as a kind of spiritual exegesis or an extrapolation of the text of Ecclesiastes. For him, this is simply the literal sense, that is to say what the author had in mind when he wrote his book.

After citing the passage above, it is important to observe that in the medieval view of St. Bonaventure, the realm of the dead was not indifferent as to the status of those who dwelt therein, for it was thought to have several levels or layers. The lot reserved for the damned was believed to lie in the darkest, deepest, innermost realm of Sheol. However, there was also believed to be a place where the righteous dead went while they awaited the coming of Christ's redemption, and this was said to be the outer part or border (the *limbus* referred to above) of the underworld.[88] Although the Christian tradition held that there was hope that souls in this realm could eventually be freed by Christ at his coming, as one can see from works such as Dante's *Divine Comedy* their existence was not considered to be a particularly happy one. Jeremy Holmes states in light of St. Bonaventure's commentary, "Truth be told, there was not much to be said for being dead before Christ came. The ancient idea of the underworld as a shadowy realm of gibbering half-men may well be the way things were."[89] If St. Bonaventure's reading of Ecclesiastes is accurate, this was in fact the way things were before Christ, and it is precisely this that Ecclesiastes was intending to convey to his original audience.

If Bonaventure is correct that the dead of pre-Christian times had to wait to enter into God's presence, it helps show how Ecclesiastes's words are without error—and indeed teach a positive doctrine on the afterlife even on the literal level—even though they actually deny the possibility that the dead in Sheol had a blessed

---

88. As the Catechism states: "Scripture calls the abode of the dead, to which the dead Christ went down, 'hell'—*Sheol* in Hebrew or *Hades* in Greek—because those who are there are deprived of the vision of God. Such is the case for all the dead, whether evil or righteous, while they await the Redeemer: which does not mean that their lot is identical, as Jesus shows through the parable of the poor man Lazarus who was received into 'Abraham's bosom.' 'It is precisely these holy souls, who awaited their Savior in Abraham's bosom, whom Christ the Lord delivered when he descended into hell.' Jesus did not descend into hell to deliver the damned, nor to destroy the hell of damnation, but to free the just who had gone before him." *CCC* §633.

89. Holmes, "Biblical Scholarship New and Old," 319.

existence during the time before Christ's coming. For, from the perspective of the first aspect of the divine pedagogy (Ecclesiastes's role in ancient Israel), one may see the literal sense of Ecclesiastes's message as a necessary step in preparing Israel for the fullness of revelation, because it drove home the harsh truth that there is no justice or hope for man apart from Jesus Christ. As far as Ecclesiastes could tell, there would be no redemption for man after death, and all was indeed vanity. Given this, Ecclesiastes probably ought not to be blamed too harshly for his seemingly rash assertions.

Another reason one might view Ecclesiastes's argument positively is because it is likely it was mounted against the theology of retribution prevalent in his day. According to this view of retribution, exemplified in the book of Proverbs, the just would receive a reward for their righteousness in the present life, whereas the life of the wicked would be one of suffering and toil. As Ecclesiastes did well to observe, this notion of divine justice was at times unrealistic and demanded a strong response. The *NJBC* therefore explains, "Qoheleth's quarrel is with any theology that ignores experience and thereby tends to become unreal. Thus he attacks the simplistic statements of the traditional theology of retribution because they do not square with experience."[90] Ecclesiastes's negativity thus appears to the reader as hopelessness, but in fact it was a work of realism, and a work that helped prepare Israel for a positive answer from Christ. As Pope Benedict explains, it required a realistic jolt the like of which only Ecclesiastes (and Job) could provide in order to shatter the traditional theology of retribution and make it possible for Israel to realize that the answer to injustice ultimately reveals itself not on this earth but in the life to come: "In their different ways, Ecclesiastes and Job express and canonize the collapse of the ancient assumptions.... Job and Ecclesiastes, then, document a crisis. With their aid, one can feel the force of that mighty jolt which brought the traditional didactic and practical wisdom to its knees."[91] The pope has recently elaborated further on this dynamic:

90. Addison G. Wright, "Ecclesiastes," *NJBC* 31:6.
91. Benedict XVI, *Eschatology*, 86. See also his discussion of the shortcomings of

The early wisdom of Israel had operated on the premise that God rewards the righteous and punishes the sinner, so that misfortune matches sin and happiness matches righteousness. This wisdom had been thrown into crisis at least since the time of the Exile. It was not just that the people of Israel as a whole suffered more than the surrounding peoples who led them into exile and oppression—in private life, too, it was becoming increasingly apparent that cynicism pays and that the righteous man is doomed to suffer in this world. In the Psalms and the later Wisdom Literature we witness the struggle to come to grips with this contradiction; we see a new effort to become "wise"—to understand life rightly, to find and understand anew the God who seems unjust or altogether absent.[92]

For Pope Benedict, the works of late biblical Wisdom literature may not convey the fullness of truth one may wish for in investigating the nature of divine providence, but they represent an important stage in the divine pedagogy that prepared Israel to receive this fullness. In them, we catch a vivid glimpse of Israel's perpetual "struggle" with God.

Nevertheless, the Method C exegete will not be completely satisfied with Bonaventure's exegesis even though he incorporates elements typically associated with both Method A exegesis (e.g., his

---

this theology as expounded by Job's friends in *The God of Jesus Christ: Meditations on the Triune God* (San Francisco: Ignatius Press, 2008), 49–55. As Jeremy Holmes has observed, the fact that Ecclesiastes was concerned with jolting the simplistic popular notion of justice prevalent in his day may at the same time have made it impossible for him to introduce any solution to the problem of death lest it annul the effect of the aforementioned arguments. Holmes has suggested another possible reason for Ecclesiastes's apparently contradictory stance on the afterlife: perhaps he did not necessarily disagree with the writer of Proverbs but rather desired his work to function as a kind of proverb in dialectic with the notion of justice portrayed in the book of Proverbs. The wisdom writers characteristically set apparently contradictory sayings alongside one another in the form of proverbs so that their readers would discover truths more profoundly than they might through more didactic means. Ecclesiastes may therefore have viewed his own work (which itself contains many such proverbs) as a complement to the book of Proverbs which provided another piece to the puzzle that was discovering the nature of divine providence. In this way, Ecclesiastes would pen blatant contractions not because he was a post-modern comfortable with contradiction or because in reality he represented a group of editors with sharply divergent views, but because he was a typical Israelite faithful to God and seeking the truth of things (comments based on a communication of Jeremy Holmes with the author).

92. Benedict XVI, *Jesus of Nazareth,* translated by Adrian J. Walker (New York: Doubleday, 2007), 212–13.

hermeneutic of faith) and Method B exegesis (his admission of Ecclesiastes's dark claims). In other words, one may rightly argue that it is not enough for scripture to have a literal sense that states what is the case in a given time period (e.g., that divine justice would not be meted out on this earth, and that before Christ the dead resided as shades in the *limbus patrum*), but that scripture ought to teach the truth absolutely, namely that in light of Christ there is indeed hope for the dead, that the fate of man and beasts *really is* different in the end. For the Method C exegete, it is unfulfilling to say that Ecclesiastes had a pedagogical purpose for people of a given time period but has no truth to teach today. The Method C answer to the present objection thus requires further exploration of the second aspect of divine pedagogy: Ecclesiastes's role for believers today, its spiritual sense.

To begin, the book of Ecclesiastes is important for today's believer because he can look at it, as he can look at the whole Old Testament, and recognize that Israel's faith journey described therein itself has a signification insofar as it sheds profound insight into every man's walk with God. Every person who embarks on the journey of faith in the living God participates in the mystery of Israel's own journey. He must undergo the same process of questioning, struggle, and trust that Ecclesiastes, and indeed the entire nation of Israel, endured. Just as Ecclesiastes and the whole nation of Israel learned to believe in God from God himself, so every believer must learn from God. One who recognizes this second aspect of the divine pedagogy in Ecclesiastes may find strength to guide him in his life's journey because in witnessing that men of faith like himself struggle with the reality of death, he comes to see that he is not alone in his struggle. In his treatment of Ecclesiastes in the *NJBC*, a work comprised almost exclusively of Method B scholarship, Addison Wright makes an insightful comment that one might expect from a Method A exegete:

Clearly, countless thousands of devout people travel in the dark as did Ecclesiastes, and they can find dignity in the believing community because Ecclesiastes was deemed worthy to have a place among the biblical writings. Surely the book needs to be complemented by the other voices of Scripture, but its voice is of considerable importance.[93]

93. Addison G. Wright, "Ecclesiastes," *NJBC* 31:8.

Ecclesiastes may thus paint a bleak picture of man's struggle with his destiny, but at least its reader may find comfort in the knowledge that other faithful individuals before him have endured similar tests. Ecclesiastes teaches this person that it is part of human nature, even a human nature endowed with the gift of faith, to grapple with fear, doubt, and even despair in the face of death. This is not to say that an individual ought to give in to these temptations, but Ecclesiastes is realistic in showing that they are real even in the lives of the most faithful of people.

Another pedagogical aspect of Ecclesiastes is related to the previous explanation, as well as to the explanation of St. Bonaventure explored above: just as Ecclesiastes pointed to the vanity of existence for those who lived without Christ before his coming, so the believer of today can read Ecclesiastes and perceive what becomes of a human existence entrenched entirely in the cares of this world, without any conscious relationship with Christ. This point is put well by Peter Kreeft in a manner the ordinary lay believer can appreciate. As Kreeft explains, Ecclesiastes teaches the Christian the first thing he must recognize when embarking on his journey of faith:

Let me put the point in a single word. It is a word I guarantee will shock and offend you, though it comes from St. Paul. Paul used this to describe his life without Christ.... Before Christ put him into the post-Ecclesiastes relationship with God, what was his life? Shit. "Dung."

... Compared with the all-excelling knowledge of God in Christ Jesus, all of the greatest things in this world, according to Paul, are *skubala*—shit. Dung. Job's dung heap. *That* is the message of Ecclesiastes for a Christian.[94]

For Kreeft and his faith-based approach, the meaningfulness of Sacred Scripture hinges upon the lesson that Ecclesiastes teaches us, for it is only when one sees himself in the situation of Ecclesiastes that he appreciates why the coming of Christ was necessary in the first place. Ecclesiastes was philosophizing about the meaning of life from a merely human standpoint, without the assistance of revelation or grace, and the answer he came up with was that there

94. Peter Kreeft, *Three Philosophies of Life* (San Francisco: Ignatius Press, 1989), 27–28.

is none: life is vanity. Nowhere in scripture is this basic fact taught more clearly than in the book of Ecclesiastes. Kreeft does well to argue that the person who cannot learn Ecclesiastes's lesson will feel no need for Christ, and therefore will not embark on a quest for him. As in the case of Ecclesiastes himself, the person who faces death without hope in Christ finds it intolerable, insurmountable, devastating, the end of everything.

According to Kreeft, the fact that Ecclesiastes (whom tradition has long considered to be Solomon, the wisest of all philosophers) is unable to come up with a satisfying answer to life's most fundamental question was ironically the precise reason the book was included in the canon of scripture in the first place. He explains:

> Whatever rabbis first decided to include Ecclesiastes in the canon of Sacred Scripture were both wise and courageous—wise because we appreciate a thing only by contrast, and Ecclesiastes is the contrast, the alternative, to the rest of the Bible, the question to which the rest of the Bible is the answer. There is nothing more meaningless than an answer without its question. This is why we need Ecclesiastes.[95]

A university professor, Kreeft goes on to explain that when he teaches Sacred Scripture as a whole, he begins with Ecclesiastes because it frames the problem to which the rest of scripture is the answer. He admits it does not teach a positive doctrine on the afterlife, since its revelatory purpose is precisely the opposite of giving a definitive response to man's deepest question. It is thus that Kreeft adds to the explanation provided above:

> [Ecclesiastes] is inspired monologue. God in his providence has arranged for this one book of mere rational philosophy to be included in the canon of Scripture because this too is divine revelation. It is divine revelation precisely in being the absence of divine revelation. It is like the silhouette of the rest of the Bible. It is what Fulton Sheen calls "black grace" instead of "white grace," revelation by darkness rather than by light. In this book God reveals to us exactly what life is when God does not reveal to us what life is. Ecclesiastes frames the Bible as death frames life.[96]

95. Ibid., 19.
96. Ibid., 23. On the theme of darkness and divine silence, it is instructive to read Michael Rea, "Divine Hiddenness, Divine Silence," in Louis Pojman and Michael C.

Kreeft's explanation is strikingly consistent with the global mindset of the Old Testament. It was a unique strength of the people of Israel that they would perceive as sacred a work whose teaching does not provide a final answer to the problem of death but which instead frames the problem. The fact that Ecclesiastes is in the biblical canon testifies at once to the persistence and the humility of the faithful Israelite, who would incessantly search with his whole heart for an answer to the problem of death and yet admit in the end that only God knew what this answer was and how it would come about in time. The sort of faithful abandonment to God one sees in Ecclesiastes is precisely what the community of Israel that accepted the authority of this book recognized as necessary in the days before Christ's coming, and this same abandonment is required of Christians today even though they now know God's answer to the problem of death. Although the circumstances have changed and knowledge has increased, the faith of Israel witnessed to in Ecclesiastes—including the struggles that accompany it—remains the same today.

Finally, although it may be argued that Ecclesiastes's concern remained rooted in matters pertaining to this life, it is important to bear in mind the conclusion drawn at the conclusion of Ecclesiastes, which Method B scholarship indicates was composed by a later epilogist.[97] In giving final shape to the book, he strove to emphasize

Rea, *Philosophy of Religion: An Anthology* (Boston, Mass.: Wadsworth/Cengage Learning, 2012), 266–75.

97. Cf. Crenshaw, "Ecclesiastes, book of," *ABD*, vol. 2, 272. Crenshaw explains, "The additional verses in 12:9–14 derive from one epilogist, or more probably two. To this point in analysis a virtual consensus exists in scholarly discussion." In light of Method B's analysis of the history of biblical texts, a great discussion could be had on whether or how inspiration extended not only to individual authors but to communities and redactors, as well. Some authors would see the presence of redactors as a corruption of the original text rather than an inspired and providential development of it. For example, according to Jon Day, the redaction of Ecclesiastes was done merely to cover up its difficulties and make it appear more orthodox. See Day, "The Development of Belief in Life after Death in Ancient Israel," 252–53. On the other hand, a hermeneutic of faith would seem to demand the recognition that there were inspired redactors to the books of scripture. For a brief statement of how this might be explained, note the work of Synave and Benoit: "We therefore admit that the charism of inspiration may have been shared by a large number of individuals, but in different degrees. As in the case of the human faculties, the distribution of the divine influence must here be conceived in an analogical and

that the protagonist remained concerned with trustful obedience to God throughout his struggles. His inspired words testify to the faith of Ecclesiastes and to a vital message this book has for those who find themselves unsure of their destiny and of how God will work to accomplish it. Ultimately what is important is to "fear God, and keep his commandments; for this is the whole duty of man. For God will bring every deed into judgment, with every secret thing, whether good or evil."[98]

Job

The book of Job narrates a prolonged process of existential struggle and an investigation of divine providence akin to what one encounters in Ecclesiastes. Unlike Ecclesiastes, Job's protagonist is eventually led to hope in Yahweh's promise of eternal life, but like Ecclesiastes the literal sense of Job contains outright denials of the possibility that man could live forever in God's presence. Job seems to hold the traditional view of Sheol as the destiny of good and evil men alike, a land of hopelessness, gloom, and shadows.[99] Of course, in other places one sees a Job seemingly confident in divine vindication, as in this famous passage of the Christian tradition: "For I know that my Redeemer lives, and at last he will stand upon the earth; and after my skin has been thus destroyed, then from my flesh I shall see God, whom I shall see on my side, and my eyes shall behold, and not another. My heart faints within me!"[100] As one progresses through

---

proportional way. The share which each one receives of this influence will depend on the extent to which he collaborates in the composition of the sacred books. This can occur in the most varied ways, beginning with the known prophet who consciously receives divine revelations and personally writes them down, and extending to the anonymous editor who makes only some slight alteration in the sacred text without even being aware that God is inspiring him to do so." *Prophecy and Inspiration*, 124.

98. Eccl 12:13-14.

99. See the assessment of Job's gloomy view of the afterlife in Day, "The Development of Belief in Life after Death in Ancient Israel," 252.

100. Jb 19:25-27. Nevertheless, it must be acknowledged that this passage itself presents textual, grammatical, and exegetical difficulties and has been variously interpreted. For an analysis of these problems, see Edouard Dhorme, *A Commentary on the Book of Job*, translated by Harold Knight (Nashville, Tenn.: Thomas Nelson Publishers, 1984), 282–86; cf. Day, "The Development of Belief in Life after Death in Ancient

the narrative of Job, we witness a sort of vacillation between hope-fulness and hopelessness, and this makes it difficult to pinpoint one precise view of the afterlife being taught in the book of Job.

As in the case of Ecclesiastes, however, the purpose of Job's re-marks about the afterlife becomes clearer when viewed in light of the divine pedagogy. For as to the first aspect of the divine peda-gogy (the role of Job in its early Israelite context), it is not neces-sary to suppose that the original intent of the book of Job was to present a complete picture of the nature of the afterlife. To state it briefly, as with Ecclesiastes the purpose of this work may not have been to teach definitively on the nature of death and the afterlife but rather to teach other important truths and frame important ques-tions that would assist Israel in preparing to receive the fullness of revelation. This may help to explain why the community of Israel allowed statements to remain in the text which, taken on the literal level and outside the context of the work's broader purpose, would present grave problems. There may also have been practical aspects that drove Israel to read and meditate upon the text over the cen-turies. In James 5:11, for example, the man Job is referred to as an example of long-suffering patience.

One may find support for the above proposal by turning to the prologue to Aquinas's *Literal Commentary on Job*. Although written by a Method A exegete, this work is known for its keen attention to the literal sense of Job.[101] Aquinas explains that Job was composed not for the purpose of teaching the nature of the afterlife but for dis-coursing about and vindicating another, more fundamental truth: the reality of divine providence. In Job, the topic under discussion is that "of the varied and grave afflictions of a certain man perfect in every virtue called Job." As Aquinas observes, the fact "that a just

---

Israel," 251–52; and Benedict XVI, *Eschatology*, 85. With regard to the subject of escha-tological hope in Job, Benedict observes, "There may be a glimmer of hope here for an abiding life to come, but the textual tradition is too uncertain to allow any worthwhile judgment about the form such hopes might have taken."

101. At the end of his prologue, Aquinas himself states that his purpose is to ex-pound the literal sense of Job. See Jean-Pierre Torrell, *Saint Thomas Aquinas, vol. 1, The Person and His Work,* translated by Robert Royal (Washington, D.C.: The Catholic University of America Press, 2005), 57–59

man [such as Job] is afflicted without cause seems to totally undermine the foundation of providence." Being such an extreme example of the difficulties bound up with belief in divine providence in
human affairs, the case of Job is "therefore proposed as a kind of
theme for the question intended [for discussion]" St. Thomas even
goes so far as to say that "the whole intention (*tota intentio*) [of Job]
is directed to this: to show through probable arguments that human
affairs are governed by divine providence."[102] If Aquinas is correct
in claiming this, then it sheds light on the nature of the book of Job
and its original place in the Bible. Like Ecclesiastes, Job raises life's
most poignant questions. It does not necessarily give a definitive response with respect to the afterlife, but it assisted the nation of Israel
in her quest to do so as it taught them to acknowledge God's providence over all creaturely affairs.

Turning now to the significance of Job in relation to the second
aspect of the divine pedagogy (the role of Job in the canon today),
this same discussion of divine providence remains pertinent. Like
Ecclesiastes, Job shows what a struggle with the problems of suffering and death might look like not only in the character Job but in
the life of *any* man of faith.[103] Today's reader of Job enters into the
mystery of human suffering just as Job himself did, recognizing the
presence of apparently unmerited evil in his life and asking how this
can be if there exists a good God. Like Job and with the help of Job,
every man needs to confront the reality that good things happen to
wicked people and evil things befall virtuous people. Any man who
is to faithfully endure life's most excruciating hardships must with
Job pass through successive stages of growth in his life, from his first
conversion to his final and total transformation into the likeness of
God.[104]

102. Thomas Aquinas, prologue to *Expositio super Iob ad litteram*. Translations of
this work provided here are mine.

103. I use the word "character" in referring to Job as part of the narrative, but one
may debate whether Job was originally intended as character in a parable or a historical individual. In the same prologue under discussion, Aquinas asks this question and
concludes based on references to other parts of scripture that Job was indeed a historical character.

104. This aspect of the purpose of Job, along with a broader discussion of the book

If the Christian exegete approaches Job in light of this process of conversion and existential struggle, then he does not have to run to 19:25–7 in order to salvage the book as a part of the inspired canon, because the book of Job was not meant to teach whatever issues from Job's mouth as a sort of categorical statement concerning the nature of the afterlife. Like other works in the Old Testament, the book of Job contains a faithful protagonist whose virtues are to be modeled and whose words are generally to be heeded; yet it is not the case that one must approach every one of the character Job's words as if they could stand on their own as a dogmatic affirmation. This is not to say that God could never speak through Job or through any personage whose words are recorded in a biblical book, but rather that the message of Job must be found by looking at the work as a literary whole, how the character Job's words fit into this whole, and how this whole itself fits into the whole of Sacred Scripture.

As Kreeft explains in his matter-of-fact, accessible style, the role of Job in the canon of scripture is not necessarily meant to provide clear-cut answers so much as to help ordinary believers encounter God, who is the answerer to life's most poignant questions. Every book in scripture is meant to bring its reader to this encounter, but Job does so in a unique way: "Job is mystery. A mystery satisfies something in us, but not our reason. The rationalist in us is repelled by Job, just as Job's three rationalist friends were repelled by Job. But something deeper in us is deeply satisfied by Job, and is nourished."[105] According to Kreeft, Job nourishes the soul not because it gives it any definitive answer but because it puts the reader into prayerful dialogue with God. In Job's struggle with the nature of divine justice and providence a man recognizes his own struggle. God did not eliminate Job's struggles overnight or give him quick answers to his questions, and God does not do this for believers today either. As Pope Benedict puts it, "God's answer to Job explains nothing; rather ... it reminds us of our limitations. It admonishes

in general, can be found in Torrell, *Saint Thomas Aquinas, vol. 1, The Person and His Work*, 57–59, 120–22.

105. Kreeft, *Three Philosophies of Life*, 61.

us to trust the mystery of God in its incomprehensibility."[106] As a good teacher, God arranges for men to discover the truth in their own time and in a spirit of prayerful trust. They may have to endure a trial of purgatorial proportions in order to find the truth, but once they have found it they own it.

Thus far we have dealt with Job from the perspective of both Method A and Method B exegesis. However, a Method C account ought to incorporate all the resources of its respective hermeneutical methods, and in the case of Job this means a deeper examination of the book's structure and composition from a Method B perspective. In particular, a redactional history of Job can help show the book's purpose from the perspective of the Israelite community that composed it, prayed over it, and continued to interpret it throughout the centuries. As one observes the various additions and clarifications within the book of Job made throughout Israel's history, this helps to clarify what Israel gleaned from the text and how the text itself opened Israel into deeper understandings of God and his providence.

In short, the book of Job consists in a poetic dialogue and a prose prologue and epilogue.[107] Method B scholarship indicates that the book of Job most likely originated as an oral folktale sometime before the Babylonian exile and that its poetic portion was composed sometime thereafter, around 500 B.C.[108] The narrative frame was probably grafted on some fifty years later, and the Hebrew version of the book reached its final form with inclusion of the Elihu speeches (Job 32–37) sometime around 400 B.C. Particularly, the addition of the prologue and epilogue is significant because they provide evidence that the community of Israel that received and transmitted the book of Job did not endorse the character Job's denials of hope as if they were categorical statements regarding the nature of the af-

106. Benedict XVI, *Introduction to Christianity* (San Francisco: Ignatius Press, 2004), 26.

107. Jb 3:1–42:6, 1:1–2:13, and 42:7–17, respectively.

108. This presentation of Job's redactional history is not the fruit of my own labor but rather of communications with Gregory Vall. See also James L. Crenshaw, "Job, Book of," *ABD*, vol. 3, 863–64.

terlife. Rather, with the help of the book's prose frame, the reader is enabled to enjoy a perspective that characters in the story cannot: all that happens to Job is part of God's plan, even though Job himself cannot see it clearly. Through it the inspired redactor shows that the source of Job's suffering was not God but Satan, and that in the end God actually vindicates Job, who dies an old man blessed more in his latter days than he was before his trials.[109] Moreover, the Elihu speeches, written in a later Hebrew and inserted between Job's final plea and Yahweh's speeches, are significant because they vindicate God's punishing of Job as merciful chastisement. Elihu was angry at Job and his three friends because none of them had found this answer to the problem of Job's sufferings.[110] The redactor of this speech wanted to make known that an answer to Job's problems did indeed lie hidden within the depths of divine providence, but none of these men had found it.

Regarding the later LXX translation of Job, it is illuminating to see that, once again, additions were deliberately made in places in order to convey Israel's developed understanding of the afterlife. For example, it seems that the LXX translator attempted to show that the meaning of Job 14:14 included truth about the resurrection. The RSV, reflecting the MT of Job 14:14, reads: "If a man die, shall he live again? All the days of my service I would wait, till my release should come." Given the presence of the Hebrew interrogative marker, one can readily see that this is a question that clearly expects the answer "No."[111] When one turns to the LXX, however, it reads: "If a man dies, he will live having completed the days of his life. I will wait until I am born again."[112] In the LXX, Job 14:14 no longer contains a rhetorical question (the Greek here omitted the interrogative particle הֲ that was in the Hebrew) that seems to deny hope in the afterlife. Rather, here it is a declarative sentence that clearly supports a view of the afterlife: if a man dies, he "will live" (ζήσεται).

---

109. Jb 1–2; 42:12–17.

110. Jb 32:2–3.

111. If the author had expected the answer "Yes," he would most likely have used the Hebrew form הֲלֹא (meaning something like "won't he?") rather than הֲ.

112. Translation mine.

Finally, the LXX appends yet another section to the conclusion of Job in order to make clear what ought to be gleaned from the story of Job's trials. In the MT, Job 42:17 concludes the book: "And Job died, an old man, and full of days." The LXX, however, adds several verses, including this one which immediately follows upon the final verse of the Hebrew: "It is written that he will rise again (ἀναστήσεσθαι) with those whom the Lord raises up."[113] In the eyes of the book's final redactor, Job is a tale of suffering, death, and *resurrection*—a tale of existential struggle that ends with a clear answer from God. Since the community of Israel, and in turn the church, has read Job in this way, it presents a possible account of how the book contains inerrant doctrine. For what might not have been affirmed about the afterlife in the words of the character Job was indeed affirmed by the LXX redactor of the story, as well as by the community that continued to read Job as a testament of faith in Yahweh and in his providence.

Thus the truth of Job does not simply lie in any one character's words but must rather be viewed in the context of the book as a whole and in its history. It is a tale of suffering and of questioning but also, and ultimately as one can see in the final form of the work, a tale of trust and of hope. In contrast with Ecclesiastes, at least in the LXX the final form of Job explicitly affirms a hopeful final end for man, yet both Job and Ecclesiastes display the conviction that God is in control no matter what happens, and that no man can measure his wisdom. The community of Israel itself likewise was convinced of God's providential care for them throughout their times of trial, as demonstrated by the fact that earlier texts like Job were read in such a positive light. Especially given the Greek-speaking culture in which the LXX originated, one might have expected this translation to have flattened out references to the resurrection into something more Platonic, as was the case in the transition from the Greek of 2 Maccabees to 4 Maccabees.[114] On the contrary, what actually happened was that in the centuries immedi-

---

113. Translation mine.
114. Wright, *The Resurrection of the Son of God*, 150.

ately preceding Christ's coming, hope for the resurrection became all the more firm in Israel despite all earthly obstacles to this hope. Although this insight stems from a Method B analysis, in the context of the present work of Method C exegesis one ought to observe that it too lends itself to interpretation on another level: Christians often experience that their hope becomes vivid precisely through their encounter with earthly obstacles.

Psalms

We will conclude our treatment of the afterlife with a look into the book of Psalms because of its prominence in the church's tradition of prayer, liturgy, and the history of biblical interpretation. The Psalms offer a living record of what Israel believed, because texts such as the Psalms—which were an important part of the official liturgy of the Jewish Temple—reflect how Israel prayed. Here we operate with the understanding that if the church's law of prayer is the law of her belief, the same ought to hold true for the Old Testament people of God. The texts contained in the book of Psalms are far too vast and diverse to say that they intend a single definitive belief regarding the nature of the afterlife, but like the previous two works Psalms itself displays a twofold divine pedagogy that can help one gain a better sense of how to address difficulties vis-à-vis their account of the afterlife.[115]

In particular, we will turn to St. Thomas in order to ascertain the various senses Israel intended when praying the Psalms. This will hopefully serve to illustrate Israel's broader understanding of human destiny, as well as to point out how believers today might face life's ultimate questions. As St. Thomas said, the book of Psalms "has the general [material] of theology as a whole" and that it "contains the whole of Scripture (*continet totam Scripturam*)."[116] The Psalms

---

115. This diversity of views can be clearly observed through a brief reading of John Goldingay, "Death and Afterlife in the Psalms," in *Judaism in Late Antiquity*, edited by Alan J. Avery-Peck and Jacob Neusner (Boston: Brill Academic Publishers, 2000), 61–85.

116. Thomas Aquinas, prologue to *In psalmos Davidis expositio*. Again, translations of this work provided in the present chapter are mine.

contain a kind of synopsis of salvation history put to prayer and song. The book includes prayers for every situation in life, including songs of royal enthronement, historical remembrance, lamentation, repentance, wisdom, praise, and thanksgiving for deliverance.

When it comes to discussing doctrine on the afterlife in scripture, this last type of psalm is of unique importance. The people of Israel had a rich understanding of the reality of deliverance, and this is evident most of all in the way they prayed for it in the Psalms. Even a cursory reading of these texts shows them to be replete with references to deliverance from such forces as "death," "enemies," "the pit," and "Sheol." However, reading the Psalms literally, with an eye to physical reality alone, does not reveal the deeper meaning of deliverance the nation of Israel, and later the church, found therein. Drawing on these texts, St. Thomas distinguishes three sorts of deliverance that he thinks the reader of scripture ought to consider: deliverance from the moment of physical death (which is often the literal sense), deliverance from sin, and deliverance from the everlasting death of hell through the resurrection of the body (these last two senses are often spiritual senses in Psalms). Attending to these various meanings of deliverance in the exegesis of St. Thomas, we find that the psalmist composed texts open to being appreciated by believers of every age for meanings that surpassed any conscious intention on the part of their author.

It is now appropriate to turn to St. Thomas's commentary itself to see how his account of passages dealing with the afterlife in the book of Psalms can be illuminating for a theology of Sacred Scripture and for the reader of scripture. Aquinas was only able to comment on the first fifty-five Psalms before he died, but of those psalms several are highly pertinent to the study of Israel's view on the afterlife. In what immediately follows, we will consider Aquinas's exegesis of Psalms 6, 18, and 30 and make our own observations regarding Psalms 88 and 16.

St. Thomas's commentary on Psalm 6 offers a fine example of how his exegesis illumines passages that exhibit troubling perspectives on the afterlife. The verses of the psalm in question read:

> Turn, O Lord, save my life;
> deliver me for the sake of thy steadfast love.
> For in death there is no remembrance of thee;
> in Sheol who can give thee praise?[117]

A reading of the literal sense of this passage raises important questions regarding Israel's overall understanding of the afterlife in the book of Psalms. First, what is Sheol ?[118] Since the author does not speak of heaven or hell, does he mean that all the dead go to Sheol and remain there forever? Do those who die really lose the capacity to remember God? Is it true that no one who dies and goes to Sheol can praise God there? What precisely is the psalmist asking for when he beseeches God to save his life? Does he have hope in this life alone? As one might expect from a Method B exegete rather than from a Method A exegete, St. Thomas first attends to some of these issues surrounding the text's literal sense before approaching its spiritual sense, because according to him the spiritual sense is based upon the literal and presupposes it.[119]

He begins by noting that the words "save my life" have an immediate referent in the psalmist's act of praying for deliverance from his human enemies: "He shows that there is an imminent danger, and this is first of all a danger of the present, that is to say natural death."[120] This affirmation of St. Thomas regarding the text's immediate referent or literal sense stands in line with the initial analysis of many modern exegetes on the topic of deliverance in the Psalms—although some such scholars believe that on account of the psalmist's imperfect understanding of the afterlife he composed his text *exclusively* with concern for the danger of physical death and for preserving his earthly life.[121] According to many who read this

---

117. Ps 6:4–5.

118. In this section, I will continue to transliterate as "Sheol" the Hebrew term used by the psalmist and translated by St. Thomas in his commentary with the Latin *infernus*.

119. Thomas Aquinas, *ST*, I, q.1, a.10. The literal sense, whereby words signify things, is defined by St. Thomas as that which is intended by an author. The spiritual sense is that signification whereby things signified by words themselves have a signification. A human author may or may not be aware of the spiritual sense of his words in any given instance, but to be sure the divine author of scripture intends this sense.

120. Thomas Aquinas, *In psalmos Davidis expositio*, super Psalmo 6.

121. For instance, certain statements of Hans-Joachim Kraus in his *Theology of the*

passage today, when the psalmist says "in death there is no remembrance of thee," it means that the dead pass out of existence, and that the psalmist is beseeching the Lord to uphold him in being.

St. Thomas, on the other hand, does not even entertain the possibility that deliverance from Sheol exclusively denotes the psalmist's own deliverance from the moment of natural death and the preservation of his earthly life. Rather, for him this deliverance also has a spiritual meaning that applies not only to the psalmist himself but to every believer who prays the psalm. While it is important that the evident literal reading of scripture be attended to first in the operations of exegesis, as Method B exegetes do well to point out, nevertheless it would be irresponsible for one aspiring to do Method C exegesis to close off the possibility of a spiritual reading such as that given by St. Thomas in what follows his initial observation:

And second [the psalmist] shows an eternal death from which there is no return. Hence is said: "For in death," that is after death, "there is no remembrance of thee." Namely, no one ponders your steadfast love after death who was not mindful of it during his life.... This is a second danger, because there is a permanence to Sheol, and within Sheol there is no confession.... So it says: "In Sheol, who can give thee praise?" And, "In death," that is within the depth of sins, "there is no remembrance of thee."[122]

Psalms, translated by Keith R. Crim (Minneapolis, Minn.: Augsburg, 1986), exhibit strong opposition to admitting that the Psalms could be referring to deliverance on multiple levels: "Yahweh's saving actions take place in the midst of a life that is surrounded by death and faces the constant threat of being swept away into the depths. Therefore the songs of thanksgiving that testify to 'deliverance from death' are placed in the mouth of all those who have experienced God's saving intervention and the rescue of their life from the power of sudden, unwholesome death. These realistic contexts cannot and must not he modified or swept aside in favor of 'New Testament perspectives.'" (168.) The commentary of Hans-Joachim Kraus on Psalm 16 found in Psalms 1–59: A Commentary (Minneapolis, Minn.: Augsburg, 1988), likewise stands out in this regard: "Psalm 16 does not deal with resurrection, or even immortality, but with the rescue from an acute mortal danger." Kraus does, however, admit that Israel's prayer is ordered towards belief in the afterlife: "Basically, the problem of death is not solved in the Old Testament, and yet it is clear in which direction the assertions of trust point: man is destined for life. He learns to know Yahweh's liberating power which knows no limits." (1:240.)

122. Thomas Aquinas, In psalmos Davidis expositio, super Psalmo 6. Of course, debate could be had over whether this is truly a spiritual sense (intended by God but not by the human author) or merely an extension of the psalm's literal sense (in which case

In this piece of exegesis, St. Thomas clearly goes beyond what he previously said in reference to the literal sense of danger from sudden physical death. Man's residence in Sheol is now seen in terms of his being imprisoned in a state of sin. What Aquinas sees in this passage is that not just the psalmist but every man in a state of sin, remembering only himself and refusing to praise God, cuts himself off from God and thus in a real way causes his own spiritual death. Moreover, St. Thomas shows that this state of spiritual death has the potential to become a permanent death of both body and soul, since no one who persists in ignoring God in this life will be rewarded with eternal life, which consists precisely in the act of knowing God.[123] Again, it probably cannot be proven whether or not the psalmist himself was consciously considering this connection of sin and hell to physical death when he composed the psalm. This may be a spiritual sense in the very strict meaning of the term, that is to say an instance in which the reality the author intentionally signified (physical death) itself had a signification which he did not consciously intend (the death of sin or the permanent death of hell).[124] Whatever the case may be, this is a sense which believers of

---

the human author would have been consciously intending to speak not only of physical death but also of sin and hell. Based on what he says here, it appears that St. Thomas thought the psalmist consciously intended to connect sin, hell, and physical death. If I am correct in this assessment, it means St. Thomas would have considered all these meanings as literal. While accepting and valuing these meanings, a Method C exegete might wish instead to argue that they are spiritual senses (i.e., perhaps the psalmist did not intend to speak about sin and death, and these are spiritual meanings that grow out of the text that refers only to physical death on the literal level).

123. Cf. Ps 73, where the fate of sinners is contrasted with that of those who are close to Yahweh. The psalmist is confident he will be received into glory (73:24), whereas those who stray will be destroyed: "For lo, those who are far from thee shall perish; thou dost put an end to those who are false to thee" (Ps 73:27).

124. For more insight into this understanding of the spiritual sense, see especially Aquinas's discussion of the four senses of Scripture in *Quodlibet* VII. In q.6, a.3, he asks whether the spiritual sense can be found in writings other than Sacred Scripture and concludes that it cannot. Even a human writer (e.g., the poet) may intend that his words signify a reality that in turn signifies something else. However, St. Thomas observes that in Sacred Scripture, whose author is the Holy Spirit (*Scriptura, cuius spiritus sanctus est auctor*), realities are signified which never entered the consciousness of its human author, who is an instrument (*homo vero instrumentum*). See also Jean-Pierre Torrell, "Le savoir théologique chez saint Thomas," *Revue thomiste* 96 (1996), 392–96.

every age can apprehend and pray in their own lives. The Christian reading this psalm ought to take it as a warning to avoid falling into the "depth of sins," for in sin there is no remembrance of God, and he who does not care to be mindful of God in this life will not have eternal life: "No one ponders your steadfast love after death who was not mindful of it during his life."

Finally, it is significant that the author's principal focus in this psalm appears to remain on Yahweh. He begins the psalm with supplication, "O Lord, rebuke me not in thy anger," and he concludes with a kind of recognition or thanksgiving, "The Lord has heard the sound of my weeping. The Lord has heard my supplication; the Lord accepts my prayer."[125] Although the forces of death are threatening to cut the psalmist off from Yahweh, he knows that he is coming to his rescue. He might not be sure how Yahweh is going to solve such a dire problem as death, and, as in other cases above, he might really be of the opinion that the dead who reside in Sheol can no longer "remember" God. However, bearing in mind the work of the previous chapter on the role of speculative and practical judgments in scripture's authorship, one ought not to conclude based on this psalmist's prayer that he is intending to make a categorical affirmation that the dead will be eternally cut off from God in Sheol and that there is no possibility for a person to return from the dead. As we observed a moment ago, his eyes remain focused on God, and his attitude is much more that of a desperate but nonetheless trustful pleading and questioning, an attempt to find an answer rather than to give one: "O Lord, how long? … In Sheol who can give thee praise?"[126] The psalmist is exhausted and distraught, but he focuses on God's providence and remains confident that the Lord has heard his prayer for deliverance, even if it has not yet been revealed to him how this deliverance ultimately will be enacted. Accordingly, one may well argue that even as this sacred author remains in a state of questioning regarding the nature of the afterlife, his text has value for readers of every age precisely because it asks life's most challenging questions.

125. Ps 6:1, 8–9.
126. Ps 6:3, 5.

Moreover, as Aquinas has shown, the psalmist has composed texts that are open to profound truths about the nature of sin and death, truths not inconsistent with belief in the resurrection, which Christ would one day reveal as the ultimate answer to his prayer.

The next text pertinent to St. Thomas's discussion of passages dealing with the afterlife in the Psalms is Psalm 18. Right at the beginning, the psalm itself states that it was composed with the intention of describing deliverance not from eternal death but from a human enemy. The heading of the psalm itself thus indicates its literal sense: "A Psalm of David the servant of the Lord, who addressed the words of this song to the Lord on the day when the Lord delivered him from the hand of all his enemies, and from the hand of Saul."[127] This historical dimension or *vox Israelitica* of the psalm is the first thing Aquinas addresses in his commentary on it. He states that "this psalm is found word for word in 2 Kings 22. And it is history, because in 1 Kings 19 one reads how Saul sought to kill him; and that, again after Saul had died (2 Kings 2), Abner and his son were against him."[128] Despite the fact that this psalm clearly has the history of David's life as its primary referent, Aquinas has no problem also hearing the *vox Christi* in it: "And since Christ is signified by David, all these things can be referred to Christ, either according to the head, or according to the body, namely the Church, for it has been liberated from Saul, that is, from death."[129] In the remainder of his commentary on this psalm, St. Thomas focuses on this spiritual

127. This event is embedded within the story of David in 2 Sm 22:2–51. It is interesting to note that the two texts coincide verbatim in their discussion of deliverance from Sheol (Ps 18:5; 2 Sm 22:6). Although the MT vowel pointing of Ps 18 describes David's deliverance from the hand of Saul, the consonants forming the word Saul in the Hebrew title could just as well be vocalized so as to state that David was delivered not from Saul but from Sheol. This is stated simply to raise the possibility that those who read this text may have heard either or both of these meanings in it. Deliverance from human enemies was deliverance from Sheol. In this regard, it might also be helpful to note that the psalm embedded in 2 Sm 22 serves alongside the canticle of 1 Sm 2 as a bookend to the narrative of 1–2 Samuel, and that these passages contain similar themes and imagery, e.g., the horn, deliverance from Sheol, God's anointed, etc.

128. Thomas Aquinas, *In psalmos Davidis expositio*, super Psalmo 17. Note that the numbering of St. Thomas's commentary differs from the standard numbering of Psalms in the RSV.

129. Ibid.

meaning of death and takes advantage of the psalm's linguistic similarity to other psalms (i.e., the references to " Sheol" and "death")
in order to illumine for the reader the various "deaths" described
therein. The verses of Psalm 18 particularly pertinent to his exposition on death read as follows:

> I call upon the Lord, who is worthy to be praised,
> and I am saved from my enemies.
> The cords of death encompassed me,
> the torrents of perdition assailed me;
> the cords of Sheol entangled me,
> the snares of death confronted me …
> He delivered me from my strong enemy,
> and from those who hated me.[130]

Aquinas's commentary on this passage is noteworthy first of all for
its acknowledgement that death is not merely a physical phenomenon but is instigated by the activity of wicked forces, both human
and angelic. Not neglecting the Method B dimension of exegesis,
St. Thomas does recognize that the "strong enemy" spoken of by
David is first of all Saul, who had sought David's life, yet he does not
stop at the literal level of interpretation. Examining the language of
Psalm 18 and its connection with other psalms dealing with the various meanings of death, he also looks at the "enemy" of Psalm 18:17
according to its spiritual sense. He writes, "The powerful ones, in
a mystical sense, are carnal sins.… The hateful ones are demons."
Thus not only does David stand in danger of being killed by his human enemies, but demons constitute an even greater threat to his
life, or the life of any man, as they induce him first to die spiritually and ultimately to die physically and suffer eternal death in hell.
Once again, this insight which comes through spiritual exegesis of
the psalm may or may not have been intended by the psalm's human
author, but the church has indeed long read it as being intended by
its divine author. For spiritual exegesis shows that the psalm teaches
timeless truth on the nature of sin, death, and hell, even if the literal sense falls short of explicitly affirming all the articles of the faith
bound up the mystery of sin and death.

130. Ps 18:3–5, 17.

In this same section of commentary on Psalm 18, St. Thomas's exegesis brings out the inner ordering of the three deaths of sin, physical death, and hell and makes it clear that each of them inevitably involves the others, as well. He states:

Note that these three are thus ordered to one another: iniquity, death, and Sheol (*iniquitas, mors, et Infernus*). For from iniquity a man is led to death, and through death he is led down to Sheol: just as the first is the road to the second, so the second is the road to the third.[131]

For Aquinas, an iniquitous or sinful life (the first death, the literal sense) is already a participation in eternal damnation (the third and final death, the spiritual sense). Physical death is a mere cataract in the torrent that leads a man from the death of sin to eternal death in the pit of hell. Accordingly, the three deaths are not opposed to each other but rather mutually imply one another. It is for this reason that St. Thomas can have such confidence in his spiritual exegesis of the passage: of course the psalmist was praying about deliverance from sin and deliverance from hell, for he prayed for deliverance from physical death, which is a reality not at all separable from sin and hell.[132] Even though the obvious literal sense of the psalm describes David's deliverance from death at the hands of Saul, this does not prevent the same text from shedding light on the wider meaning of mankind's deliverance from death, including deliverance from the deaths of sin and of ell. As in other cases, here it is precisely this spiritual sense that gives the psalm such an important place within the lives of believers today. One might even argue that this psalm finds its *telos* precisely in that prayer by which God's people has learned to listen to the divine voice revealing the truth of spiritual deliverance through it.

131. Thomas Aquinas, *In psalmos Davidis expositio*, super Psalmo 17.

132. Indeed, in his work *Eschatology* Pope Benedict shows that ancient Israel understood well the interconnectedness of these three "deaths." He writes, "From this realization [that death is not just to be accepted as an event of the natural order], and above all in her life of prayer, Israel developed a phenomenology of sickness and death wherein these things were interpreted as spiritual phenomena. In this way Israel discovered their deepest spiritual ground and content, wrestled with Yahweh as to their import, and so brought human suffering before God and with God to a new pitch of intensity." (81.) Benedict goes on to observe that "sickness, death, and Sheol remain phenomenologically identical." (86.)

St. Thomas's commentary on deliverance in Psalm 30 likewise includes references to deliverance from death in both a physical and spiritual sense. His thoughts on the following verse are of particular significance: "O Lord, thou hast brought up my soul from Sheol, restored me to life from among those gone down to the Pit." Aquinas writes concerning this: "[The psalmist] indicates how he was freed. First, from interior evils. Second, from exterior ones: *O Lord, thou hast brought up my soul.*" Multiple forms of deliverance are observed here by St. Thomas. He begins by discussing interior evil. "Interior evil is infirmity, either bodily or spiritual." According to St. Thomas, the literal meaning of this text must again refer to David. David was infirm in both body and spirit, while Christ did not have spiritual but only bodily infirmity on account of his passibility. Thus, David needed to be delivered from interior evil of the spirit, but Christ did not.

Next, St. Thomas treats of exterior evils as they are depicted in this psalm: "Next, [the psalmist] says that he has been freed from exterior evils: *O Lord, thou hast brought up my soul.* And first, from imminent ones. Second, from those from which he has been preserved: *restored me to life from among those gone down to the Pit.*" At this point, Aquinas makes an interesting move, a move typical of Method A exegesis. Now, he sees that the "literal" sense of deliverance from evil applies not to David but to Christ:

This cannot be literally understood of David, because he was not dug up from Sheol when he composed this Psalm. It can be understood of him metaphorically, as if he was freed from a mortal danger. But it is literally understood of Christ, whose soul was drawn out of Sheol by God.[133]

St. Thomas's observation is fascinating, as it runs utterly counter to the standard approach of most Method B thinkers when it comes to the perspective or voice of the psalmist. St. Thomas realized that the human author's reference to Sheol (the literal sense, in the way Aquinas uses the term) was in this case an intentional metaphor.[134] The

133. Thomas Aquinas, *In psalmos Davidis expositio*, super Psalmo 29.
134. A similar phenomenon occurs in Ezekiel:37, in which the human author describes the restoration of the people of Israel under the metaphor of dry bones regaining their skin and returning to life. The prophet may not have had any intention of describing the individual resurrection in which Christians believe today, and yet the

psalmist did not literally intend to say that he had been dug up from his grave, nor did he pretend to have a final answer to the problem of the grave. Rather than reading this as an intentional metaphor, however, St. Thomas emphasizes the providential fact that some-one has "literally" been brought up from the pit: Christ.[135] When a Christian prays this psalm, he therefore enters into something greater than the psalmist's trials, sufferings, and joys. He recalls that these very words likely could have been found in Jesus's own mouth in his days on earth, and he acknowledges that Jesus's deliverance from the pit of death was not the least important way in which he recapitulated the life of the psalmist and the entire mystery of Israel.

---

literal sense of his text opened the way toward this spiritual signification that came to be understood later. In both this case and in the case of Psalm 30, the literal sense of the text (what the human author originally intended) is actually attained by reading the text metaphorically rather than in the way most today are accustomed to call "liter-ally." In this way, it seems necessary to distinguish two uses of the word "literal." One is what one ordinarily associates with the word literal, i.e., not metaphorical; the other is spoken of by St. Thomas, i.e., that which is intended by a human author and which may indeed be metaphorical. When discussing the use of metaphors and parables in *ST*, I, q.1, a.10 ad 3, Aquinas shows that the literal sense does not lie in the figure painted by an author (e.g., God having an arm, the dry bones in Ezekiel, deliverance from Sheol in Psalm 30), but in that which is figured (e.g., God's power, national restoration, deliver-ance from the moment of physical death). Meanwhile, the spiritual sense (what the human author may not have intended although it was intended by God) may at times be opened up by reading a text "literally," that is to say not metaphorically as the human author originally intended it to be read. In this way, it may be that the human author of Psalm 30 intended to speak of deliverance from physical death under the metaphor of Sheol, and yet his very words were also intended by God to speak "literally" of Christ's resurrection.

135. Note that here once again St. Thomas refers to the death of sin in relation to physical death and eternal death. Christ was brought up from the pit of eternal death precisely because he was first "brought up" from the pit of sin. Christ merited to be raised from the dead because he was faithful to the Father and never sinned against him. Aquinas comments, "*In the pit*, that is, in sin; for [Christ] was immune from sin." It is interesting to note that Kraus also sees a connection between deliverance from physical death and deliverance from elements of this world that diminish a man's life: "In our way of thinking, we would conclude that the one speaking in Ps 30:3 has not really died. But he did really die! For the reality of death struck deep into his life, in the concrete diminution of life that he experienced. Thus 'deliverance from death' is rescue from the power of anything that interferes with one's life in an unwholesome and de-structive way." Kraus, *Theology of the Psalms*, 166. Kraus does not mention sin by name, but if there ever was something that fit the bill of a destroyer of life, sin would be it.

For the Christian, Christ's living of this psalm brought it to the *telos* he had for it when he inspired it as the pre-incarnate Word.

Finally, the believer who engages a psalm like this in prayer can see that it not only applies to the psalmist or to Christ but also to his own life. As with the psalms discussed previously, here also every man finds himself on a journey where he must ask of the Lord the questions the psalmist asks: "What profit is there in my death, if I go down to the Pit? Will the dust praise thee? Will it tell of thy faithfulness?"[136] And with the grace of God, at the end of a believer's life, he may hope to join the psalmist in an exclamation of thanksgiving for the answer to his lifelong prayer for deliverance: "Thou hast turned for me my mourning into dancing; thou hast loosed my sackcloth and girded me with gladness, that my soul may praise thee and not be silent. O Lord my God, I will give thanks to thee for ever.[137]

St. Thomas died before having the opportunity to comment on Psalm 88. However, we will address it as our last text precisely because it is among the bleakest and most challenging of all writings in the canon of scripture, and therefore demands at least a moment of consideration. Like Ecclesiastes, Job, and the previous psalms, Psalm 88 offers the example of a faithful man who struggles with the problem of death without being privy to knowledge of God's answer to the problem. It appears as the prayer of a sick man nearing the end of his life and wondering what will become of him after his death. The psalmist's soul is "full of troubles" as his life draws near to Sheol. He moans:

> I am reckoned among those who go down to the Pit;
> I am a man who has no strength,
> like one forsaken among the dead,
> like the slain that lie in the grave,
> like those whom thou dost remember no more,
> for they are cut off from [God's] hand.

He has sunken into the nether regions of the pit of destruction, and the waves of chaos pass over him. He is the object of God's wrath

136. Ps 30:9.
137. Ps 30:11–12.

and his friends' scorn. For him it appears that there is no hope for life after death. Again he asks questions which expect a negative reply:

> Dost thou work wonders for the dead?
> Do the shades rise up to praise thee?
> Is thy steadfast love declared in the grave,
> or thy faithfulness in Abaddon?

As in the case of other authors discussed above, as far as the psalmist can tell man will not live to see another day after he passes from this earth, and yet once again this grim prognosis does not stop him from pouring out his soul to God and trusting in his deliverance. As the psalm begins, the psalmist cries to God by day and by night, and after his series of questions he immediately turns back to the Lord: "But I, O Lord, cry to thee; in the morning my prayer comes before thee."[138] Despite this prayer, at the end of this psalm the Lord still has not given the psalmist a definitive answer to his pleading, and he feels nothing but a sense of shunning.

In line with the trajectory of enquiry throughout this chapter, at this point one might well ask: how can such a text as Psalm 88 be inerrant when its author seems to blatantly contradict Christian doctrine by claiming without exception that he who dies is cut off from God's hand and utterly forgotten by him? In response, it first it ought to be remembered that Psalm 88 would have had a pedagogical purpose within its original context in Israel. Once again, the psalmist's purpose may have been more practical than speculative in nature. Psalm 88 does not have the tone of a writing meant to teach definitely on the nature of the afterlife. Rather, it appears as a spontaneous prayer, an attempt of the author to confront the uncertainties of death face to face, honestly and openly, in prayerful union with his Lord. It may well be that the author of Psalm 88 did not come up with an answer to the problem of death, but for a Method C exegete this in no way threatens the integrity of scripture. The fact that Israelites like the psalmist did not accept an easy answer to the problem of death but rather posed the most difficult of questions

138. Ps 88:4–5, 1–2, 10–11, 13.

to God about it is a testimony to their faith in his providence. The community in which this psalm originated was certainly concerned with finding an answer to the problem of death, but they were patient enough to pray about it, struggle over it, and plead with God to give it. The pleading of Psalm 88 is just one way it may have served ancient Israel in leading the nation toward the fullness of revelation in Christ. This is by no means a complete and exhaustive explanation, but it gives an idea of how one may approach the problem of accounting for the original intention of Psalm 88.

When it comes to the place of the Psalms with respect to the second aspect of the divine pedagogy (its role in the church today), the Christian instinct is to pray Psalm 88 Christologically. As observed earlier, any believer can relate to the trials endured by Ecclesiastes, Job, and the psalmist in their search for an answer to the problem of death. Indeed, these works all show how a faithful person may pray to God and grapple with the workings of divine providence. Psalm 88, however, strikes a special chord in the Christian consciousness precisely because it so easily lends itself to being heard as the *vox Christi*, the voice of Christ. As its recitation in Friday *Compline* of the church's Liturgy of the Hours suggests, Psalm 88 is not the prayer of just any faithful Israelite. Like other texts in the Psalter, this psalm is read as the prayer of the suffering Christ, who went to the tomb shunned by his companions and afflicted without any sign of vindication from God. By praying this psalm in union with the church in her liturgy, the faithful thus enter into the mystery of Christ's suffering and death and make his prayer their own. Psalm 88 therefore may not give an answer to the problem of death, yet its place in the divine pedagogy remains indispensable. For it exhorts the faithful man to cry to God in the midst of life's most harrowing moments, confident that despite all sensible evidence to the contrary his cry for final deliverance will be heard, just as Christ's was heard.

As we conclude our treatment of the afterlife as presented in the Psalms, we may greatly benefit from a consideration of Pope Benedict's own grappling with the prophetic nature of these sacred texts. In his second volume of *Jesus of Nazareth*, he takes up the question of what Christians are to make of how the Lukan author of Acts uses

Psalm 16. Here, we read that St. Peter applied the text of Psalm 16 to Christ, proclaiming boldly:

For David says concerning [Christ].... "For thou wilt not abandon my soul to Hades, nor let thy Holy One see corruption. Thou hast made known to me the ways of life; thou wilt make me full of gladness with thy presence." Brethren, I may say to you confidently of the patriarch David that he both died and was buried, and his tomb is with us to this day. Being therefore a prophet, and knowing that God had sworn with an oath to him that he would set one of his descendants upon his throne, he foresaw and spoke of the resurrection of the Christ, that he was not abandoned to Hades, nor did his flesh see corruption. This Jesus God raised up, and of that we all are witnesses.[139]

Method B exegetes would question the New Testament's interpretation here on at least two points. First, is it correct to assume that David composed this psalm? This challenge is important since historical-critical scholars often date psalms to centuries after the turn of the first millennium B.C. when David lived. Second, and more important, did the psalmist himself actually *foresee* the resurrection of Christ, as Acts describes Peter claiming, or is this a misleading spiritual interpretation that bypasses the original intended meaning of Psalm 16? Pope Benedict treats briefly of this question:

In the Hebrew version ["You do not give me up to Sheol, or let your godly one see the Pit ..."] the psalmist speaks in the certainty that God will protect him, even in the threatening situation in which he evidently finds himself, that God will shield him from death and that he may dwell securely: he will not see the grave. The version Peter quotes ["For you will not abandon my soul to Hades, nor let your Holy One see corruption ..."] is different: here the psalmist is confident that he will not remain in the underworld, that he will not see corruption.[140]

---

139. Acts 2:25, 27, 30–32.

140. Benedict XVI, *Jesus of Nazareth: Holy Week: From the Entrance into Jerusalem to the Resurrection*, 255. While the pope speaks of "'The version Peter quotes," it is worth observing that most scholars presume that this speech (and others like it) was composed by the Lukan author of acts and placed in the mouth of an apostle as a way to effectively summarize his message. In his book, Benedict acknowledges this but chooses not to pursue it: "We need not go into the question here of whether this address really goes back to Peter, and, if not, who else may have redacted it.... Whatever the answer may be, we are dealing here with a primitive form of Resurrection proclamation." (256.) He hints that the same applies to speeches described as issuing from Jesus's mouth. Speak-

Although the pope does not directly raise the issue of the New Testament possibly erring in its exegesis of the Old Testament, he recognizes the difficulty posed by this exegetical approach and therefore spends some time explaining the differences between the Hebrew and Greek versions of Psalm 16. As Benedict observes, it turns out that the version of the Old Testament used by the early Church in general was the LXX. In that version, the verbs οὐκ ἐγκαταλείψεις ("You will not abandon") and οὐδὲ δώσεις ("Nor will you allow") of Psalm 16:10 occur in the future tense and describe the restoration from physical death *after* his natural death occurs: "Here the psalmist is confident that he will not remain in the underworld, that he will not see corruption." The original Hebrew of Psalm 16, on the other hand, has rescue from physical death in its sights, reflecting the psalmist's hope that God would shield him from dying in the first place.

Which version is correct, then? For Benedict, the answer seems to be that both have their merits and that both are necessary for Method C exegesis. For, on the one hand, it would be disingenuous to ignore the reality that Psalm 16 referred to a historical event according to its original, literal sense. On the other hand, in light of Christ's resurrection Christians know that the psalm has a deeper, spiritual meaning which is arguably more significant and which cannot be ignored. As to the question of whether Acts is accurate in

---

ing of "all the problems that arise" from a redactional history of Jesus's eschatological discourse, he writes, "[T]he very fact that Jesus' words are intended here as continuations of tradition rather than literal descriptions of things to come meant that the redactors of the material could take these continuations a stage further, in the light of their particular situations and their audience's capacity to understand, while taking care to remain true to the essential content of Jesus' message." *Jesus of Nazareth: Holy Week: From the Entrance into Jerusalem to the Resurrection* (San Francisco: Ignatius Press, 2011), 27. Shortly thereafter he adds, "The extent to which particular details of the eschatological discourse are attributable to Jesus himself we need not consider here. That he foretold the demise of the Temple—its theological demise, that is, from the standpoint of salvation history, is beyond doubt." (34–35.) Although he does not delve into the particular details of what parts of Jesus's discourse issued verbatim from Jesus's mouth, the fact that the pontiff raises the question is what is significant. It reveals that his methodology is marked by a willingness to countenance the best insights of modern criticism even if it means Christians have to rethink certain assumptions about the nature of scripture.

relating that David composed this psalm or that the psalmist himself actually foresaw the resurrection of Christ, we may make a couple suggestions for a Method C approach to this passage based on the principles articulated in earlier chapters. The issue at stake here is whether the author of Acts intended to teach for its own sake that David foretold the resurrection of Christ in this psalm. If the Method C exegete accepts the principles of Synave and Benoit outlined in chapter 4 and takes to heart how Pope Benedict approaches Jesus's own use of imperfect eschatological imagery, he need not contend that the author of Acts was *asserting* David's authorship of the psalm or his explicit awareness of Christ's resurrection. An inspired author may employ images or speak of certain things within the broader context of his work without categorically affirming their conformity to reality or teaching them for their own sake.

Assuming this is the case, we then must ask by way of conclusion: What, then, was the principal affirmation of Peter's speech in Acts 2, if not to claim that David foretold the resurrection of Christ? The answer to questions such as these has been a major task of this book, and it is precisely the task that Method C exegetes must take up as they seek to apply Benedict's exegetical principles to scripture's most challenging texts. In this case, one helpful avenue of approaching the issue is to ponder how the author of Acts himself might explain his words today in light of what Peter's successors have taught about the nature of scripture. Perhaps he would concur with the present Roman Pontiff in his claim that certain Christological interpretations of the Old Testament could only be made after Christ actually came and rose from the dead: "Admittedly, this new reading of Scripture could begin only after the Resurrection.... Now people had to search Scripture for both Cross and Resurrection, so as to understand them in a new way and thereby come to believe in Jesus as the Son of God."[141] Following this approach, the fundamental message of Acts within its broader context would not be altered even if it turned out that David lacked explicit knowledge of Christ's resurrection or that he was operating based on the conventions of

141. Ibid., 245.

his day. For, given the fullness of truth that has come to us in light of Christ's resurrection, Christians know that Psalm 16 itself speaks of Christ whether David himself knew this or not.[142] For today's Christian, however, it does not come easily to admit the possibility that David may not have known his words pointed toward Christ as Luke indicates, that David himself may not have written the psalm in question as Luke assumes, or that even Peter may not have spoken the precise words recorded in Luke. This recognition is one of the keys to understanding Pope Benedict's exegetical principles and the way he instantiates them throughout his corpus. The Holy Father stands as a shining example of a believer who knows that the evangelization of modern man requires us to seriously engage the challenges of contemporary scholarship with the conviction that this need not be detrimental to belief but rather a necessary condition for maintaining the integrity of our Christian faith.

142. The same principles applied to the case of the Lukan author's exegesis in Acts 2 may also be applied to the interesting words of Jesus in Lk 20:37–42, where he cites Ex 3:6 as a proof of the resurrection ("But that the dead are raised, even Moses showed ..."). The Method C exegete must be able to answer the challenge of whether Moses himself intended to "show" the doctrine of bodily resurrection, and, if not, how Jesus' exegesis may be justified.

METHOD C EXEGESIS
IN THE CHURCH

Just as our endeavor to tackle the "dark" passages of scripture began under the guidance of the church's teaching on the nature of scripture, so we will conclude by underlining the vital role that the church ought to play in the life of a Method C exegete. Having applied Benedict's proposal to the themes of the nature of God, the nature of good and evil, and the afterlife, I hope one finishes this work better able to see the reasonableness of Catholic magisterial teaching on the inspiration and inerrancy of scripture, and to have confidence that apparently erroneous passages in scripture can be accounted for through a faithful application of Pope Benedict's principles for Method C exegesis. On the other hand, what one ought not to take from this study is some golden rule for determining the sense of every sentence of scripture. Not even the most lucid theology of scripture, much less the present one, provides the believer with the answer to every possible difficulty he may encounter in the revealed word of God. Although I am convinced readers will greatly benefit from approaching scripture in light of Benedict's Method C proposal, ultimately even a faithful application of the pope's principles can never guarantee the accuracy of a particular individual's reading of scripture.

As Pope Benedict lucidly explains, the exegete's most helpful ally in this regard is the community of the church herself:

A communal reading of Scripture is extremely important, because the living subject in the sacred Scriptures is the People of God, it is the Church.... Scripture does not belong to the past, because its subject, the People of God inspired by God himself, is always the same, and therefore the word is always alive in the living subject. As such, it is important to read and experience sacred Scripture in communion with the Church, that is, with all the great witnesses to this word, beginning with the earliest Fathers up to the saints of our own day, up to the present-day magisterium.[1]

Since the church is the living subject of the scriptures, the exegete who wishes to penetrate their mysteries may do so only to the extent that he is in communion with the people of God. For Benedict, the church is "the primary setting for scriptural interpretation."[2] The church's saints, moreover, are the true interpreters of scripture since "the meaning of a given passage of the Bible becomes most intelligible in those human beings who have been totally transfixed by it and have lived it out."[3] The church gives to exegetes today the saints as models for how they are to go about their work. The saints have truly encountered God in scripture because they have done theology on their knees, and today's exegete must do likewise.

As a community of interpretation, the church provides us with other indispensable aids which mediate fuller understanding of scripture, above all a context to acquire and practice the virtues.[4] By participating in the work of exegesis as a member of the Christian community, the interpreter of scripture becomes more attuned to the wisdom of the church's discernment in matters of faith and

1. *VD* §86.

2. *VD* §29.

3. Benedict XVI, *Jesus of Nazareth*, translated by Adrian J. Walker (New York: Doubleday, 2007), 78; cf. *VD* §48; John Paul II, *On the Relationship between Faith and Reason* [*Fides et ratio*], 1998 §101.

4. For an insightful discussion of this point, see Matthew Levering, *Participatory Biblical Exegesis: a Theology of Biblical Interpretation* (Notre Dame, Ind.: University of Notre Dame Press, 2008), 87. This point has been emphasized by theologians, but here I will briefly mention the words of John Paul II who wrote on this in the context of discussing philosophy's need to recover its relationship with theology. The pope stated, "In theology, philosophy will find not the thinking of a single person which, however rich and profound, still entails the limited perspective of an individual, but the wealth of a communal reflection. For by its very nature, theology is sustained in the search for truth by its ecclesial context."

thereby accustoms himself to prudence in his own life as an exegete. The virtue of prudence enables the reader to make the soundest judgment possible regarding difficult biblical texts, all the while realizing that the reliability of this very judgment is conditioned by his own presuppositions and shortcomings.

The exegete who breathes the life of the church also engages in the practice of charity. As St. Augustine indicated, this virtue builds up the love of God and neighbor within the bond of ecclesial communion, and thus constitutes the very end of Sacred Scripture.[5] As a result of his engagement with Sacred Scripture, Christ reorders man's loves and transforms his capacity to perceive the truth of scripture itself.[6] Saints throughout history have been unanimous in their teaching that Christians will be unable to plumb the depths of scripture unless they are united to Christ through the theological virtue of charity, precisely because the most profound meaning of scripture is Christ himself. As Pope Benedict puts it, there can be no theology without conversion: "In biblical language, in order to know Christ, it is necessary to follow him."[7] Even the most erudite exegete possessing the most up-to-date Method B techniques cannot on his own power elicit an encounter with Jesus Christ's teaching in scripture, for this will be given to him only in prayerful union with Christ.[8]

5. As stated by St. Augustine in *On Christian Teaching*, translated by James Shaw, *Nicene and Post-Nicene Fathers, First Series*, vol. 2, edited by Philip Schaff (Buffalo, N.Y.: Christian Literature Publishing Co., 1888), "We should clearly understand that the fulfillment and the end of the Law, and of all Holy Scripture, is the love of an object which is to be enjoyed, and the love of an object which can enjoy that other in fellowship with ourselves." (39.) Cf. Levering's comments on St. Augustine and his description of charity's role in exegesis in *Participatory Biblical Exegesis*, 88.

6. It is helpful to recall the words of St. Athanasius on this topic. Although many theologians have stated this in similar terms, some of the closing words of St. Athanasius's *On the Incarnation of the Word* are particularly concise and to the point: "But for the searching and right understanding of the Scriptures there is need of a good life and a pure soul, and for Christian virtue to guide the mind to grasp, so far as human nature can, the truth concerning God the Word." Athanasius, *On the Incarnation of the Word*, 96. See also Augustine, *On Christian Teaching*, 12.

7. Benedict XVI, *On the Way to Jesus Christ*, translated by Michael Miller (San Francisco: Ignatius Press, 2005), 67; cf. Benedict's *The Nature and Mission of Theology: Approaches to Understanding Its Role in the Light of Present Controversy*, translated by Adrian Walker (San Francisco: Ignatius Press, 1995), 57.

8. Note the concluding words of St. Augustine's discussion of scriptural interpreta-

Furthermore, the individual who has cultivated the virtue of charity within the bosom of the church will have been formed in such a way so as to recognize that he often must depend on an authority higher than himself in order to identify the meaning of scripture. It might sound ironic, but this exegete recognizes that he sometimes has to accept the meaning of God's word through faith and humble obedience to the church. Indeed, according to Pope Benedict, "The essential characteristic of a great theologian is the humility to remain with the Church, to accept his own and others' weaknesses."[9]

By placing his trust in the church, the exegete does not thereby abandon reason or neglect to employ all the modern exegetical tools at his disposal. As Benedict has shown, it is crucial for the Method C exegete first to determine the literal meaning of scripture through the operation of Method B exegesis, since Method A's spiritual meaning of scripture depends upon the literal and builds upon it. However, Benedict also makes it clear that the Method C exegete must carry out his initial operation in accordance with the premises of Method A outlined back in the introduction to this work: that scripture is God's word, that it is inerrant, and that Christ has entrusted this revelation to his church to guard and interpret it.

These truths of the faith are the first principles of authentic Christian biblical exegesis, based on divine revelation itself and handed on in the church for two thousand years. Not to accept them is to sever oneself from one half—and certainly the most important half—of the Method C project. Because they are first principles, we

---

tion in Book III of his *On Christian Teaching*: "Students of these venerable documents ought to be counseled not only to make themselves acquainted with the forms of expression ordinarily used in Scripture, to observe them carefully, and to remember them accurately, but also, what is especially and before all things necessary, to pray that they may understand them." Augustine, *On Christian Teaching*, 100.

9. Benedict XVI, General Audience (May 30, 2007). He later added that "intellectual humility is the primary rule for one who searches to penetrate the supernatural realities beginning from the Sacred Book." Benedict XVI, General Audience (June 4, 2008). See the discussion of this dimension of Benedict's thought in Scott Hahn, *Covenant and Communion: The Biblical Theology of Pope Benedict XVI* (Grand Rapids, Mch.: Baker Brazos Press, 2009), 190–92. Note that the Catholic Church very rarely defines the meaning of a given scripture passage through the exercise of the extraordinary Magisterium, but when this occurs it demands the Catholic exegete's assent. Pius XII, *DAS* §47.

might add in the spirit of St. Thomas that they are not necessarily to be proven to unbelievers but rather defended against objections.[10] In other words, for the Christian exegete the true task is not to prove deductively that scripture is inerrant or to prove the validity of the church's interpretation of scripture. There is a real sense in which these truths are recognizable only to those who already believe them, those who have committed themselves to Christ and have entered into his path through the church.[11] Given this situation, the Method C exegete's work begins by making clear his premise that scripture is from God and that the church guarantees its truth with infallible certitude. It is from here that he may seek a way to explain how the Bible is inerrant by answering objections against it. This has been the particular task of the theology of scripture in the preceding chapters. I have attempted to show how a Method C approach accounts for problems in the Bible's portrait of God's nature, the nature of good and evil, and the afterlife, and I have proposed that such an endeavor sheds light on the nature of Scripture itself. We have addressed very specific issues, but my hope for the future is that others will broaden this endeavor to make up for its shortcomings.

I wish to conclude by reiterating the ultimate goal of a Method

10. Aquinas states, "Sacred Scripture, since it has no science above itself, can dispute with one who denies its principles only if the opponent admits some at least of the truths obtained through divine revelation; thus we can argue with heretics from texts in Holy Writ, and against those who deny one article of faith, we can argue from another. If our opponent believes nothing of divine revelation, there is no longer any means of proving the articles of faith by reasoning, but only of answering his objections—if he has any—against faith. Since faith rests upon infallible truth, and since the contrary of a truth can never be demonstrated, it is clear that the arguments brought against faith cannot be demonstrations, but are difficulties that can be answered." *ST*, I, q.1, a.8.

11. To use the words of Pope Benedict, "The Christian faith is not a system.... It is a path, and it is characteristic of a path that it only becomes recognizable if you enter on it and start following it." *Truth and Tolerance: Christian Belief and World Religions*, translated by Henry Taylor (San Francisco: Ignatius Press, 2004), 145. For an illuminating discussion of the "practical realist" view that one can have warranted belief in the scriptures in the absence of absolute proofs for its veracity, see Kenton Sparks, *Sacred Word, Broken Word: Biblical Authority and the Dark Side of Scripture* (Grand Rapids, Mich.: Eerdmans, 2011), 72–88. An insightful consideration of how to approach this matter can also be found in Michael Bergmann, "Rational Religious Belief without Arguments," in Louis Pojman and Michael C. Rea, *Philosophy of Religion: An Anthology* (Boston, Mass.: Wadsworth/Cengage Learning, 2012), 534–49.

C theology of scripture. At the end of the day, and at the end of our lives, such a project has achieved its *telos* only if the improved reading of scripture it provides actually brings us closer to God—if it enables us to see the divine pedagogy leading the chosen people along the arduous path to hope in the resurrection not merely as someone else's instruction but as our own, as well. Throughout his pontificate, Pope Benedict has made it a priority to teach Christians how to achieve this goal in their own lives so as to bring about "a rediscovery of God's word in the life of the Church" and a "wellspring of constant renewal."[12] As the pontiff teaches, this is to take place through the practice of *lectio divina* or "divine reading." Although there are many ways to practice *lectio*, the essence of these endeavors is the same in that it puts believers into communion with God by means of their loving contemplation of scripture. Benedict drew attention to this form of meditation multiple times in his recent apostolic exhortation *Verbum Domini*, where he even took time to teach believers how to follow five steps of *lectio* in a practical manner.[13] Thankfully, Christians enjoy two thousand years of tradition to guide us in our journey of biblically-centered prayer. However, we must avail ourselves of the church's treasures if we earnestly desire to see renewal in ourselves, our church, and our society. If we do this, our Holy Father is convinced it will bring about a new springtime:

I would like in particular to recall and recommend the ancient tradition of *lectio divina*: the diligent reading of Sacred Scripture accompanied by prayer brings about that intimate dialogue in which the person reading hears God who is speaking, and in praying, responds to him with trusting openness of heart. If it is effectively promoted, this practice will bring to the Church—I am convinced of it—a new spiritual springtime.[14]

If we allow ourselves to enter into the mystery of the divine pedagogy through a prayerful encounter with scripture, by the grace of God we just may learn to love God more fervently, to overcome evil in our own lives, and to hope confidently in the Lord's promised gift of eternal life.

---

12. *VD* §1.   13. Cf. *VD* §§86–87.

14. Benedict XVI, Address to the Participants in the International Congress Organized to Commemorate the Fortieth Anniversary of the Dogmatic Constitution on Divine Revelation, *Dei Verbum* (September 16, 2005).

BIBLIOGRAPHY

BENEDICT XVI/JOSEPH RATZINGER
AND SCRIPTURE

Benedict XVI. *Theological Highlights of Vatican II*. New York: Paulist Press, 1966.

———. *Daughter Zion: Meditations on the Church's Marian Belief*. San Francisco: Ignatius Press, 1983.

———. "Sources and Transmission of the Faith." *Communio* 10, no. 1 (1983): 17–34.

———. *Behold the Pierced One: An Approach to a Spiritual Christology*. Translated by Graham Harrison. San Francisco: Ignatius Press, 1986.

———. *Feast of Faith: Approaches to a Theology of the Liturgy*. San Francisco: Ignatius Press, 1986.

———. *Eschatology: Death and Eternal Life*. Translated by Michael Waldstein. Washington, D.C.: The Catholic University of America Press, 1988.

———. "Biblical Interpretation in Crisis: On the Question of the Foundations and Approaches of Exegesis Today." In *Biblical Interpretation in Crisis: The Ratzinger Conference on Bible and Church*, edited by Richard John Neuhaus, 1–23. Grand Rapids, Mich.: Eerdmans, 1989.

———. Preface to *The Interpretation of the Bible in the Church*. 1994. www.ewtn.com/library/curia/pbcinter.htm

———. *In the Beginning: A Catholic Understanding of the Story of Creation and the Fall*. Translated by Boniface Ramsey. Grand Rapids, Mich.: Eerdmans, 1995.

———. *The Nature and Mission of Theology: Approaches to Understanding Its Role in the Light of Present Controversy*. Translated by Adrian Walker. San Francisco: Ignatius Press, 1995.

———. "On the 'Instruction Concerning the Ecclesial Vocation of the Theologian.'" In *The Nature and Mission of Theology: Approaches to Understanding Its Role in Light of the Present Controversy*, translated by Adrian Walker, 101–20. San Francisco: Ignatius Press, 1995.

———. Preface to *The Jewish People and Their Sacred Scriptures in the Christian Bible*. 2001. www.vatican.va

———. *God and the World: A Conversation with Peter Seewald*. San Francisco: Ignatius Press, 2002.

———. *Introduction to Christianity*. San Francisco: Ignatius Press, 2004.

———. *Truth and Tolerance: Christian Belief and World Religions* Translated by Henry Taylor. San Francisco: Ignatius Press, 2004.

———. Address to the Participants in the International Congress Organized to Commemorate the Fortieth Anniversary of the Dogmatic Constitution on Divine Revelation. In *Dei Verbum*. September 16, 2005. www.vatican.va

———. General Audience. November 30, 2005.

———. *On the Way to Jesus Christ*. Translated by Michael Miller. San Francisco: Ignatius Press, 2005.

———. *Pilgrim Fellowship of Faith: The Church as Communion* Translated by Henry Taylor. San Francisco: Ignatius Press, 2005.

———. "Faith, Reason and the University: Memories and Reflections." September 12, 2006. www.vatican.va

———. General Audience. May 30, 2007.

———. *Jesus of Nazareth*. Translated by Adrian J. Walker. New York: Doubleday, 2007.

———. *Saved in Hope* [*Spe salvi*]. 2007. www.vatican.va

———. *Angelus*. October 26, 2008. www.vatican.va

———. "Biblical Interpretation in Conflict: On the Foundations and the Itinerary of Exegesis Today." In *Opening Up the Scriptures: Joseph Ratzinger and the Foundations of Biblical Interpretation*, edited by José Granados, Carlos Granados, and Luis Sánchez-Navarro, 1–29. Grand Rapids, Mich.: Eerdmans, 2008.

———. "Exegesis and the Magisterium of the Church." In *Opening Up the Scriptures: Joseph Ratzinger and the Foundations of Biblical Interpretation*, edited by José Granados, Carlos Granados, and Luis Sánchez-Navarro, 126–36. Grand Rapids, Mich.: Eerdmans, 2008.

———. General Audience. June 4, 2008.

———. *The God of Jesus Christ: Meditations on the Triune God*. San Francisco: Ignatius Press, 2008.

———. Address to Academics of the Pontifical Biblical Institute on the Occasion of the 100th Anniversary of Its Foundation. October 26, 2009. www.vatican.va

———. *Credo for Today: What Christians Believe*. San Francisco: Ignatius Press, 2009.

———. *Principles of Catholic Theology: Building Stones for a Fundamental Theology*. San Francisco: Ignatius Press, 2009.

————. *Light of the World: the Pope, the Church, and the Signs of the Times*. San Francisco: Ignatius Press, 2010.

————. *The Word of God in the Life and Mission of the Church* [*Verbum Domini*]. 2010. www.vatican.va

————. Address to Participants in the Plenary Meeting of the Pontifical Biblical Commission. May 2, 2011. www.vatican.va

————. *Jesus of Nazareth: Holy Week: From the Entrance into Jerusalem to the Resurrection*. San Francisco: Ignatius Press, 2011.

Benedict XVI and Vittorio Messori. *The Ratzinger Report: An Exclusive Interview on the State of the Church*. Translated by Salvator Attanasio and Graham Harrison. San Francisco: Ignatius Press, 1985.

Benedict XVI, John F. Thornton, and Susan B. Varenne. *The Essential Pope Benedict XVI: His Central Writings and Speeches*. New York: HarperSanFrancisco, 2007.

Hahn, Scott. *Covenant and Communion: The Biblical Theology of Pope Benedict XVI*. Grand Rapids, Mich.: Baker Brazos Press, 2009.

Pursell, Brennan C. *Benedict of Bavaria: An Intimate Portrait of the Pope and His Homeland*. North Haven, Conn.: Circle Press, 2008.

Rahner, Karl, and Joseph Ratzinger. *Revelation and Tradition*. Translated by W. J. O'Hara. New York: Herder, 1966.

Stallsworth, Paul T. "The Story of an Encounter." In *Biblical Interpretation in Crisis: The Ratzinger Conference on Bible and Church*, edited by Richard John Neuhaus, 102–90. Grand Rapids, Mich.: Eerdmans, 1989.

MAGISTERIUM AND SCRIPTURE

Bechard, Dean Philip. *The Scripture Documents: An Anthology of Official Catholic Teachings*. Collegeville, Minn.: Liturgical Press, 2002.

Benedict XV. *On Saint Jerome* [*Spiritus Paraclitus*]. 1920. www.vatican.va

Catechism of the Catholic Church. Translated by United States Catholic Conference. Washington, D.C.: Libreria Editrice Vaticana, 1994.

John Paul II. *On the Relationship between Faith and Reason* [*Fides et ratio*]. 1998. www.vatican.va

Leo XIII. *On the Study of Holy Scripture* [*Providentissimus Deus*]. 1893. www.vatican.va

Pius XI. *On the Church and the German Reich* [*Mit brennender sorge*]. 1937. www.vatican.va

Pius XII. *Promotion of Biblical Studies* [*Divino afflante Spiritu*]. 1943. www.vatican.va

Pontifical Biblical Commission. *Instruction on the Historical Truth of the Gospels* [*Sancta Mater Ecclesia*]. 1964. http://www.ewtn.com/library/curia/pbcgospl.htm.

————. *The Jewish People and Their Sacred Scriptures in the Christian Bible*. 2001. www.vatican.va

Vatican Council II. *Lumen gentium*. 1964. www.vatican.va

————. *Dei verbum*. 1965. www.vatican.va

CONTEMPORARY WORKS PERTINENT
TO THEOLOGY OF SCRIPTURE

Alonso-Schokel, Luis. *The Inspired Word: Scripture in the Light of Language and Literature* [*La palabra inspirada*]. Translated by Francis Martin. New York: Herder and Herder, 1965.

Barthélemy, Dominique. *God and His Image: An Outline of Biblical Theology* Translated by Dom Aldhelm Dean, OSB. San Francisco: Ignatius Press, 2007.

Bea, Augustin. *De Scripturae Sacrae inspiratione*. Rome: Pontificio Instituto Biblico, 1935.

————. *De inspiratione et inerrantia Sacrae Scripturae*. Rome: Pontificio Instituto Biblico, 1954.

Benin, Stephen. *The Footprints of God: Accommodation in Jewish and Christian Thought*. Albany: State University of New York Press, 1993.

Benoit, Pierre. "Note complémentaire sur l'inspiration." *Revue Biblique* 63 (1956): 416–22.

————. "Révélation et Inspiration selon la Bible, chez Saint Thomas et dans les discussions modernes." *Revue Biblique* 70 (1963): 321–70.

————. *Aspects of Biblical Inspiration*. Translated by J. Murphy-O'Connor, OP and S. K. Ashe, OP. Chicago: The Priory Press, 1965.

Blandino, Giovanni. *La rivelazione e l'ispirazione della Sacra Scrittura*. Rome: Edizioni ADP, 1998.

Burtchaell, James Tunstead. *Catholic Theories of Biblical Inspiration since 1810: A Review and Critique*. London: Cambridge University Press, 1969.

Chesterton, G. K. *The Collected Works of G. K. Chesterton*. San Francisco: Ignatius Press, 1986.

Congar, Yves. *Sainte Église: études et approches ecclésiologiques*. Paris: Éditions du Cerf, 1963.

————. *The Meaning of Tradition*. San Francisco: Ignatius Press, 2004.

Dulles, Avery. *Models of Revelation*. Maryknoll, N.Y.: Orbis Books, 1992.

Enns, Peter. *Inspiration and Incarnation*. Grand Rapids, Mich.: Baker Academic, 2005.

————. *The Evolution of Adam: What the Bible Does and Doesn't Say about Human Origins*. Grand Rapids, Mich.: Brazos Press, 2012.

Farkasfalvy, Denis. "How to Renew the Theology of Biblical Inspiration?" *Nova et Vetera* 4 (2006): 231–53.

————. "Inspiration and Interpretation." In *Vatican II: Renewal within Tradition*, edited by Matthew W. Lamb and Matthew Levering, 77–100. New York: Oxford University Press, 2008.

———. *Inspiration and Interpretation: A Theological Introduction to Sacred Scripture*. Washington, D.C.: The Catholic University of America Press, 2010.

Hahn, Scott. "For the Sake of Our Salvation: The Truth and Humility of God's Word." *Letter and Spirit* 6 (2010): 21–46.

Healy, Mary. "Behind, in Front of … or through the Text? The Christological Analogy and the Last Word of Biblical Truth." In *Behind the Text: History and Biblical Interpretation*, edited by Craig Bartholomew, C. Stephen Evens, Mary Healy, and Murray Rae, 181–95. Grand Rapids, Mich.: Zondervan, 2003.

Holmes, Jeremy. "Biblical Scholarship New and Old: Learning from the Past." *Nova et Vetera* 1 (2003): 303–20.

Ker, Ian. Foreword to *An Essay on the Development of Christian Doctrine*, by John Henry Newman. Notre Dame, Ind.: University of Notre Dame Press, 1989.

Kreeft, Peter. *Three Philosophies of Life*. San Francisco: Ignatius Press, 1989.

Lamb, Matthew. *Eternity, Time, and the Life of Wisdom*. Naples, Fla.: Sapientia Press of Ave Maria University, 2007.

Lamb, Matthew, and Matthew Levering. "Introduction." In *Vatican II: Renewal within Tradition*, edited by Matthew W. Lamb and Matthew Levering, 3–22. New York: Oxford University Press, 2008.

Levering, Matthew. *Participatory Biblical Exegesis: A Theology of Biblical Interpretation*. Notre Dame, Ind.: University of Notre Dame Press, 2008.

———. "The Inspiration of Scripture: A *Status Quaestionis*." *Letter and Spirit* 6 (2010): 281–314.

Lewis, C. S. *Reflections on the Psalms*. London: Harvest Books, 1964.

———. *Miracles, a Preliminary Study*. New York: Macmillan, 1978.

———. *The Weight of Glory, and Other Addresses*. Edited by Walter Hooper. New York: Macmillan, 1980.

Lubac, Henri de. *La révélation divine*. Paris: Cerf, 1983.

Martin, Francis. *Sacred Scripture: The Disclosure of the Word*. Naples, Fla.: Sapientia Press of Ave Maria University, 2006.

———. "Joseph Ratzinger, Benedict XVI, on Biblical Interpretation: Two Leading Principles." *Nova et Vetera* 5 (2007): 285–314.

———. "Revelation and Its Transmission." In *Vatican II: Renewal within Tradition*, edited by Matthew W. Lamb and Matthew Levering, 55–75. New York: Oxford University Press, 2008.

Newman, John Henry. *On the Inspiration of Scripture*. Edited by J. Derek Holmes and Robert Murray. Washington, D.C.: Corpus Books, 1967.

———. *The Theological Papers of John Henry Newman on Biblical Inspiration and on Infallibility*. Edited by J. Derek Holmes. Oxford: Clarendon Press, 1979.

———. *An Essay in Aid of a Grammar of Assent*. New York: Clarendon Press, 1985.

———. *An Essay on the Development of Christian Doctrine*. Notre Dame, Ind.: University of Notre Dame Press, 1989.

———. "The Theory of Developments in Religious Doctrine." In *Fifteen Sermons Preached before the University of Oxford*, 312–51. Notre Dame, Ind.: University of Notre Dame Press, 1998.

Newman, John Henry, and Charles Kingsley. *Newman's Apologia Pro Vita Sua, The Two Versions of 1864 & 1865; Preceded by Newman's and Kingsley's Pamphlets*. London: H. Frowde, 1913.

Pontifical Council for Inter-Religious Dialogue. *Dialogue and Proclamation* (1991). www.vatican.va.

Rahner, Karl. *Inspiration in the Bible*. Translated by Charles H. Henkey. New York: Herder, 1964.

Schneiders, Sandra M. "Faith, Hermeneutics, and the Literal Sense of Scripture." *Theological Studies* 39 (1978): 719–36

Sparks, Kenton. *God's Word in Human Words: an Evangelical Appropriation of Critical Biblical Scholarship*. Grand Rapids, Mich.: Baker Academic, 2008.

Tromp, Sebastian. *De revelatione christiana*. Rome: Apud Aedes Universitatis Gregorianae, 1950.

———. *De sacrae scripturae inspiratione*. Rome: Apud Aedes Universitatis Gregorianae, 1953.

Vall, Gregory. "Psalm 22: *Vox Christi* or Israelite Temple Liturgy?" *The Thomist* 66 (2002): 175–200.

Work, Telford. *Living and Active: Scripture in the Economy of Salvation*. Grand Rapids, Mich.: Eerdmans, 2002.

Wright, N. T. *The New Testament and the People of God*. Minneapolis: Fortress Press, 1992.

———. *The Resurrection of the Son of God*. Minneapolis: Fortress Press, 2003.

———. *Scripture and the Authority of God: How to Read the Bible Today*. New York: HarperOne, 2011.

Wykstra, Stephen. "Toward a Sensible Evidentialism: On the Notion of 'Needing Evidence.'" In William Rowe and William Wainright, *Readings in the Philosophy of Religion*, 481–91. Fort Worth: Harcourt Brace Publishers, 1998.

Zerafa, Peter Paul. "The Limits of Biblical Inerrancy." *Letter and Spirit* 6 (2010): 359–76.

Zia, Mark J. *What Are They Saying about Biblical Inspiration?* New York: Paulist Press, 2011.

THE EXEGESIS AND THEOLOGY OF
SCRIPTURE OF THOMAS AQUINAS

Aquinas, Thomas. *Commentary on Saint Paul's Epistle to the Ephesians.* Translated by Matthew Lamb. Albany, N.Y.: Magi Books, 1966.

———. S. *Thomae Aquinatis Opera Omnia; ut sunt in Indice Thomistico, additis 61 scriptis ex aliis medii aevi auctoribus.* Edited by Robert Busa. 6 vols. Stuttgart-Bad Cannstatt: Frommann-Holzboog, 1980. www .corpusthomisticum.org/iopera.html

———. *Summa Theologica* [*Summa theologiae*]. Translated by the Fathers of the English Dominican Province. Westminster, Md.: Christian Classics, 1981.

Armitage, J. Mark. "Aquinas on the Divisions of the Ages: Salvation History in the *Summa.*" *Nova et Vetera* 6 (2008): 253–70.

Chenu, Marie-Dominique. *La théologie comme science au XIIIe siècle.* Paris: Librairie Philosophique, 1969.

Elders, Leo. "Aquinas on Holy Scripture as the Medium of Divine Revelation." In *La doctrine de la révélation divine de saint Thomas d'Aquin: actes du Symposium sur la pensée de saint Thomas d'Aquin, tenu a Rolduc, les 4 et 5 novembre 1989,* edited by Leo Elders, 132–52. Vatican City: Libreria Editrice Vaticana, 1990.

Journet, Charles. *The Meaning of Grace* [*Entretiens sur la grâce*]. Translated by Geoffrey Chapman, Ltd. New York: P. J. Kenedy and Sons, 1960.

———. *What Is Dogma?* [*Le dogme chemin de la foi*]. Translated by Mark Pontifex, OSB. New York: Hawthorn Books, 1964.

———. *L'Église du Verbe incarné.* Vol. 3, *Essai de théologie de l'histoire du salut.* Paris: Desclée De Brouwer, 1969.

Lonergan, Bernard. "St. Thomas' Theory of Operation." *Theological Studies* 3 (1942): 375–401.

———. "St. Thomas' Thought on *Gratia Operans.*" *Theological Studies* 3 (1942): 533–78.

Pinckaers, Servais. "Recherche de la signification véritable du terme 'spéculatif.'" *Nouvelle Revue Théologique* 81 (1959): 673–95.

Reyero, Maximino Arias. *Thomas von Aquin als Exeget: Die Prinzipien seiner Schriftdeutung und seine Lehre von den Schriftsinnen.* Einsiedeln: Johannes Verlag, 1971.

Seckler, Max. *Das heil in der geschichte.* Munich: Kösel, 1964.

Synave, Paul, and Pierre Benoit. *Prophecy and Inspiration: a Commentary on the Summa Theologica II–II, Questions 171–178.* New York: Desclee Co., 1961.

Torrell, Jean-Pierre. "La traité de la prophétie de S. Thomas d'Aquin et la théologie de la révélation." In *La doctrine de la révélation divine de saint*

Thomas d'Aquin: actes du Symposium sur la pensée de saint Thomas d'Aquin, tenu a Rolduc, les 4 et 5 novembre 1989, edited by Leo Elders, 171–95. Vatican City: Libreria Editrice Vaticana, 1990.

———. "Le savoir théologique chez saint Thomas." *Revue thomiste 96* (1996): 355–96.

———. *Saint Thomas Aquinas*. Vol. 1, *The Person and His Work*. Translated by Robert Royal. Washington, D.C.: The Catholic University of America Press, 2005.

———. *Saint Thomas Aquinas*. Vol. 2, *Spiritual Master*. Translated by Robert Royal. Washington, D.C.: The Catholic University of America Press, 2005.

———. "Saint Thomas et l'histoire: état de la question et pistes de recherches." *Revue Thomiste 105* (2005): 355–409.

———. "St. Thomas Aquinas: Theologian and Mystic." Translated by Therese C. Scarpelli. *Nova et Vetera 4* (2006): 1–16.

———. "Saint Thomas et les non-chrétiens." *Revue thomiste 106* (2006): 17–49.

PATRISTIC AND MEDIEVAL EXEGESIS
(OTHER THAN AQUINAS)

Athanasius. *On the Incarnation of the Word*. Crestwood, N.Y.: St. Vladimir's Seminary Press, 2000.

Augustine. *The City of God* [*De civitate Dei*]. Translated by Marcus Dods. In vol. 2 of *Nicene and Post-Nicene Fathers, First Series*, edited by Philip Schaff. Buffalo, N.Y.: Christian Literature Publishing Co., 1888.

———. *The Confessions* [*Confessiones*]. Translated by J. G. Pilkington. In vol. 1 of *Nicene and Post-Nicene Fathers, First Series*, edited by Philip Schaff. Buffalo, N.Y.: Christian Literature Publishing Co., 1888.

———. *Exposition on the Psalms* [*Enarrationes in psalmos*]. Translated by J. E. Tweed. In vol. 8 of *Nicene and Post-Nicene Fathers, First Series,* edited by Philip Schaff. Buffalo, N.Y.: Christian Literature Publishing Co., 1888.

———. *On the Catechising of the Uninstructed* [*De catechizandis rudibus*]. Translated by S. D. F. Salmond. In vol. 3 of *Nicene and Post-Nicene Fathers, First Series*, edited by Philip Schaff. Buffalo, N.Y.: Christian Literature Publishing Co., 1888.

———. *On Christian Teaching* [*De doctrina christiana*]. Translated by James Shaw. In vol. 2 of *Nicene and Post-Nicene Fathers, First Series*, edited by Philip Schaff. Buffalo, N.Y.: Christian Literature Publishing Co., 1888.

———. *The Teacher. The Free Choice of the Will. Grace and Free Will.* Washington, D.C.: The Catholic University of America Press, 1968.

Bonaventure. *Expositio in Ecclesiasten*. In *Opera omnia; Sixti V., pontificis maximi jussu Diligentissime*. Vol. 9, edited by Adolpho Carolo Peltier. Paris: Ludovicus Vivès, 1864.

Clement of Alexandria. *The Instructor* [*Paedagogus*]. In vol. 2 of *The Ante-Nicene Fathers*, edited by Alexander Roberts and James Donaldson. Buffalo, N.Y.: Christian Literature Publishing Co., 1885.

Cyril of Jerusalem. *Catechetical Lectures*. Translated by Edwin Hamilton Gifford. In vol. 7 of *Nicene and Post-Nicene Fathers, Second Series*, edited by Philip Schaff. Buffalo, N.Y.: Christian Literature Publishing Co., 1894.

Jerome. *Letter 108*. Translated by W. H. Fremantle, G. Lewis and W. G. Martley. In vol. 6 of *Nicene and Post-Nicene Fathers, Second Series*, edited by Philip Schaff. Buffalo, N.Y.: Christian Literature Publishing Co., 1893.

John Chrysostom. *Commentary on the Psalms*. Vol. 1, translated by Robert Charles Hill. Brookline, Mass.: Holy Cross Orthodox Press, 1998.

Lubac, Henri de. *Medieval Exegesis*. Vol. 1, *The Four Senses of Scripture*. Translated by Marc Sebanc. Grand Rapids, Mich.: Eerdmans, 1998.

Oden, Thomas C. *Ancient Christian Commentary on Scripture. Old Testament*. Downers Grove, Ill.: InterVarsity Press, 2001.

Origen. *Against Celsus* [*Contra Celsum*]. Translated by Frederick Crombie. In vol. 4 of *The Ante-Nicene Fathers: Translations of the Writings of the Fathers down to A.D. 325*, edited by Rev. Alexander Roberts and James Donaldson, 239–384. Grand Rapids, Mich.: Eerdmans: 1989.

———. *On First Principles* [*De principiis*]. Translated by Frederick Crombie. In vol. 4 of *The Ante-Nicene Fathers: Translations of the Writings of the Fathers down to A.D. 325*, edited by Rev. Alexander Roberts and James Donaldson. Grand Rapids, Mich.: Eerdmans: 1989.

———. *Homilies on Joshua*. Translated by Barbara J. Bruce and Cynthia White. Washington, D.C.: The Catholic University of America Press, 2002.

THE AFTERLIFE

Boadt, Lawrence. "Ezekiel, Book of." In vol. 2 of *The Anchor Bible Dictionary*, edited by David Noel Freedman, 711–22. New York: Doubleday, 1992.

Johnston, Phillip S. *Shades of Sheol: Death and Afterlife in the Old Testament*. Downers Grove, Ill.: Intervarsity Press, 2002.

Collins, John J. "Daniel, Book of." In vol. 2 of *The Anchor Bible Dictionary*, edited by David Noel Freedman, 29–37. New York: Doubleday, 1992.

———. "The Afterlife in Apocalyptic Literature." In *Judaism in Late Antiquity*, edited by Alan J. Avery-Peck and Jacob Neusner, 119–39. Boston: Brill Academic Publishers, 2000.

Davies, Jon. *Death, Burial, and Rebirth in the Religions of Antiquity*. London: Routledge, 1999.

Day, Jon. "The Development of Belief in Life after Death in Ancient Israel." In *After the Exile*, edited by J. Barton and D. J. Reimer, 231–56. Macon, Ga.: Mercer University Press, 1996.

Friedman, Richard, and Shawna Bolansky Overton. "Death and Afterlife:

The Biblical Silence." In *Judaism in Late Antiquity*, edited by Alan J. Avery-Peck and Jacob Neusner, 35–59. Boston: Brill Academic Publishers, 2000.

Goldingay, John. "Death and Afterlife in the Psalms." In *Judaism in Late Antiquity*, edited by Alan J. Avery-Peck and Jacob Neusner, 61–85. Boston: Brill Academic Publishers, 2000.

Lang, Bernhard. "Afterlife: Ancient Israel's Changing Vision of the World Beyond." *Bible Review* 4 (1988): 12–24.

Lewis, Theodore J. "Dead, Abode of the." In vol. 2 of *The Anchor Bible Dictionary*, edited by David Noel Freedman, 101–5. New York: Doubleday, 1992.

Martin-Achard, Robert. *From Death to Life: A Study of the Development of the Doctrine of the Resurrection in the Old Testament*. Translated by John Penney Smith. London: Oliver and Boyd, 1960.

———. "Resurrection (OT)." In vol. 5 of *The Anchor Bible Dictionary*, edited by David Noel Freedman, 680–84. New York: Doubleday, 1992.

Millar, William R. "Isaiah 24–27 (Little Apocalypse)." In vol. 3 of *The Anchor Bible Dictionary*, edited by David Noel Freedman, 488–90. New York: Doubleday, 1992.

Murphy, Roland. "Death and Afterlife in the Wisdom Literature." In *Judaism in Late Antiquity*, edited by Alan J. Avery-Peck and Jacob Neusner, 102–15. Boston: Brill Academic Publishers, 2000.

Nichols, Terence. *Death and Afterlife: A Theological Introduction*. Grand Rapids, Mich.: Baker Academic, 2010.

Nickelsburg, George. "Judgment, Life-after-Death, and Resurrection in the Apocrypha and the Non-Apocalyptic Pseudepigrapha." In *Judaism in Late Antiquity*, edited by Alan J. Avery-Peck and Jacob Neusner, 141–62. Boston: Brill Academic Publishers, 2000.

Pitard, Wayne. "Afterlife and Immortality." In *The Oxford Companion to the Bible*, edited by B. M. Metzger and M. D. Coogan, 15–16. New York: Oxford University Press, 1993.

Rea, Michael. "Divine Hiddenness, Divine Silence." In Louis Pojman and Michael Rea, *Philosophy of Religion: An Anthology*, 266–75. Boston, Mass.: Wadsworth/Cengage Learning, 2012.

Richards, Kent Harold. "Death (OT)." In vol. 2 of *The Anchor Bible Dictionary*, edited by David Noel Freedman, 108–10. New York: Doubleday, 1992.

Schmidt, Brian. "Memory as Immortality: Countering the Dreaded 'Death after Death' in Ancient Israelite Society." In *Judaism in Late Antiquity*, edited by Alan J. Avery-Peck and Jacob Neusner, 88–100. Boston: Brill Academic Publishers, 2000.

Spong, John Shelby. *Resurrection: Myth or Reality?* New York: Harper, 1994.

Spronk, Klaas. *Beatific Afterlife in Ancient Israel*. Neukirchen-Vluyn: Neukirchener Verlag, 1986.

Wächter, L. "שְׁאוֹל." In vol. 14 of *Theological Dictionary of the Old Testament*, edited by Johannes G. Botterweck and Helmer Ringgren, 240–48. Grand Rapids, Mich.: Eerdmans, 1974.

THE NATURE OF GOD

Byrne, Brendan. "Sons of God." In vol. 6 of *The Anchor Bible Dictionary*, edited by David Noel Freedman, 156–59. New York: Doubleday, 1992.

Dawkins, Richard. *The God Delusion*. Boston: Houghton Mifflin, 2006.

Fossum, Jarl. "Son of God." In vol. 6 of *The Anchor Bible Dictionary*, edited by David Noel Freedman, 128–37. New York: Doubleday, 1992.

Fretheim, Terrence. "Word of God," In vol. 6 of *The Anchor Bible Dictionary*, edited by David Noel Freedman, 961–68. New York: Doubleday, 1992.

Horn, F. W. "Holy Spirit." Translated by Dietlinde Elliott. In vol. 3 of *The Anchor Bible Dictionary*, edited by David Noel Freedman, 260–80. New York: Doubleday, 1992.

Johnson, Elizabeth. *She Who Is: The Mystery of God in Feminist Theological Discourse*. New York: Crossroad, 1992.

Levering, Matthew. *The Betrayal of Charity: The Sins that Sabotage Divine Love*. Waco, Tex.: Baylor University Press, 2011.

Mansini, Guy. "The Voices of the Trinity in Scripture." In *Wisdom and Holiness, Science and Scholarship: Essays in Honor of Matthew L. Lamb*, edited by Michael Dauphinais and Matthew Levering, 173–204. Ave Maria, Fla.: Sapientia Press, 2007.

Matthews, Victor Harold, and Don C. Benjamin. *Old Testament Parallels: Laws and Stories from the Ancient Near East*. New York: Paulist Press, 1991.

Newsome, Carol. "Angels." In vol. 1 of *The Anchor Bible Dictionary*, edited by David Noel Freedman, 248–53. New York: Doubleday, 1992.

Penchansky, David. *What Rough Beast? Images of God in the Hebrew Bible*. Louisville, Ky.: Westminster John Knox Press, 1999.

———. *Twilight of the Gods: Polytheism in the Hebrew Bible*. Louisville, Ky.: Westminster John Knox Press, 2005.

Sanders, James A. *Canon and Community: A Guide to Canonical Criticism*. Philadelphia: Fortress Press, 1984.

Scullion, John. "God (OT)." In vol. 2 of *The Anchor Bible Dictionary*, edited by David Noel Freedman, 1041–48. New York: Doubleday, 1992.

Smith, Mark S. *The Origins of Biblical Monotheism: Israel's Polytheistic Background and the Ugaritic Texts*. New York: Oxford University Press, 2004.

THE NATURE OF GOOD AND EVIL

Bergmann, Michael, Michael J. Murray, and Michael C. Rea. *Divine Evil? The Moral Character of the God of Abraham.* Oxford: Oxford University Press, 2011.

Collins, John. "The Zeal of Phineas: The Bible and the Legitimation of Violence." *Journal of Biblical Literature* 122 (2003): 3–21.

Copan, Paul. *Is God a Moral Monster? Making Sense of the Old Testament God.* Grand Rapids, Mich.: Baker Books, 2011.

Dever, William G. "Archaeology and the Israelite 'Conquest.'" In vol. 3 of *The Anchor Bible Dictionary,* edited by David Noel Freedman, 546–58. New York: Doubleday, 1992.

Earl, Douglas. "The Christian Significance of Deuteronomy 7." *Journal of Theological Interpretation* 3 (2009): 41–62.

———. *The Joshua Delusion? Rethinking Genocide in the Bible.* Eugene, Ore.: Cascade, 2010.

Ehrman, Bart. *God's Problem: How the Bible Fails to Answer Our Most Important Question: Why We Suffer.* New York: HarperOne, 2008.

Foerster, Werner. "διάβολος." In vol. 2 of *Theological Dictionary of the New Testament,* edited by Gerhard Kittel and Gerhard Friedrich, 71–81. Grand Rapids, Mich.: Eerdmans, 1971.

Forsyth, Neil. *The Old Enemy: Satan and the Combat Myth.* Princeton, N.J.: Princeton University Press, 1987.

Hahn, Scott. *The Kingdom of God as Liturgical Empire: A Theological Commentary on 1–2 Chronicles.* Grand Rapids, Mich.: Baker Academic, 2012.

Hamilton, Victor. "Satan." In vol. 5 of *The Anchor Bible Dictionary,* edited by David Noel Freedman, 985–89. New York: Doubleday, 1992.

Hitchens, Christopher. *God Is Not Great.* New York: Twelve, 2007.

Holliday, William. *The Psalms through Three Thousand Years: Prayerbook of a Cloud of Witnesses.* Minneapolis: Fortress Press, 1993.

Lohfink, Norbert. "חֵרֶם." In vol. 5 of *Theological Dictionary of the Old Testament,* edited by Johannes G. Botterweck and Helmer Ringgren, 180–99. Grand Rapids, Mich.: Eerdmans, 1974.

Pagels, Elaine H. *The Origin of Satan.* New York: Vintage Books, 1996.

Sparks, Kenton. *Sacred Word, Broken Word: Biblical Authority and the Dark Side of Scripture.* Grand Rapids, Mich.: Eerdmans, 2011.

Trible, Phyllis. *Texts of Terror: Literary-Feminist Readings of Biblical Narratives.* London: SCM Press, 2002.

Watson, Duane. "Devil." In vol. 2 of *The Anchor Bible Dictionary,* edited by David Noel Freedman, 183–84. New York: Doubleday, 1992.

OTHER WORKS

Bergmann, Michael. "Rational Religious Belief without Arguments." In Louis Pojman and Michael Rea, *Philosophy of Religion: An Anthology*, 534–49. Boston, Mass.: Wadsworth/Cengage Learning, 2012.

Brown, Raymond Edward. *The Critical Meaning of the Bible.* New York: Paulist Press, 1981.

———. *An Introduction to the New Testament.* New Haven, Conn: Yale University Press, 2007

Brown, Raymond Edward, and Raymond F. Collins. "Canonicity." In *The New Jerome Biblical Commentary*, edited by Raymond Edward Brown, Joseph A. Fitzmyer, and Roland Edmund Murphy, 1034–54. Englewood Cliffs, N.J.: Prentice-Hall, 1990.

Brown, Raymond Edward, D. W. Johnson, and Kevin G. O'Connell. "Texts and Versions." In *The New Jerome Biblical Commentary*. Edited by Raymond Edward Brown, Joseph A. Fitzmyer, and Roland Edmund Murphy, 1083–112. Englewood Cliffs, N.J.: Prentice-Hall, 1990.

Brown, Raymond Edward, Pheme Perkins, and Anthony J. Saldarini. "Apocrypha; Dead Sea Scrolls; Other Jewish Literature." In *The New Jerome Biblical Commentary*, edited by Raymond Edward Brown, Joseph A. Fitzmyer, and Roland Edmund Murphy, 1055–82. Englewood Cliffs, N.J.: Prentice-Hall, 1990.

Brown, Raymond Edward, and Sandra Schneiders. "Hermeneutics." In *The New Jerome Biblical Commentary*, edited by Raymond Edward Brown, Joseph A. Fitzmyer, and Roland Edmund Murphy, 1146–65. Englewood Cliffs, N.J.: Prentice-Hall, 1990.

Butterfield, Herbert, and Adam Watson. *The Origins of History.* New York: Basic Books, 1981.

Clifford, Richard J. "Second Isaiah." In vol. 3 of *The Anchor Bible Dictionary*, edited by David Noel Freedman, 490–501. New York: Doubleday, 1992.

Crenshaw, James. "Ecclesiastes, Book of." In vol. 2 of *The Anchor Bible Dictionary*, edited by David Noel Freedman, 271–80. New York: Doubleday, 1992.

———. "Job, Book of." In vol. 3 of *The Anchor Bible Dictionary*, edited by David Noel Freedman, 858–68. New York: Doubleday, 1992.

Davies, W. D., and Dale C. Allison. *A Critical and Exegetical Commentary on the Gospel According to Saint Matthew.* Edinburgh: T.&T. Clark, 1988.

Dhorme, Edouard. *A Commentary on the Book of Job.* Translated by Harold Knight. Nashville: Thomas Nelson Publishers, 1984.

Ehrman, Bart. *Jesus, Interrupted.* New York: Harper, 2009.

Fitzmyer, Joseph A. *The Interpretation of Scripture: In Defense of the Historical-Critical Method.* New York: Paulist Press, 2008.

Frankfort, Henri, Henriette Antonia Groenewegen Frankfort, John Albert Wilson, Thorkild Jacobsen, and William Andrew Irwin. *The Intellectual Adventure of Ancient Man: An Essay on Speculative Thought in the Ancient Near East.* Chicago: University of Chicago Press, 1946.

Gnilka, Joachim. *Jesus of Nazareth: Message and History.* Peabody, Mass.: Hendrickson Publishers, 1997.

Gunton, Colin. *Christ and Creation.* Grand Rapids, Mich.: Eerdmans, 1992.

Jepsen, Alfred. ".אָמַת" In vol. 1 of *Theological Dictionary of the Old Testament*, edited by Johannes G. Botterweck and Helmer Ringgren, 309–23. Grand Rapids, Mich.: Eerdmans, 1974.

Kittel, Rudolf, Karl Elliger, Wilhelm Rudolph, Hans Peter Rüger, G. E. Weil, and Adrian Schenker. *Biblia Hebraica Stuttgartensia.* Stuttgart: Deutsche Bibelgesellschaft, 1997.

Kraus, Hans-Joachim. *Psalms 1–59: A Commentary.* Minneapolis: Augsburg, 1988.

———. *Theology of the Psalms.* Translated by Keith R. Crim. Minneapolis: Augsburg, 1986.

Kselman, John S., and Ronald D. Witherup. "Modern New Testament Criticism." In *The New Jerome Biblical Commentary*, edited by Raymond Edward Brown, Joseph A. Fitzmyer, and Roland Edmund Murphy, 1130–45. Englewood Cliffs, N.J.: Prentice-Hall, 1990.

Marshall, I. Howard. *Beyond the Bible: Moving from Scripture to Theology.* Grand Rapids, Mich.: Baker, 2004.

McKenzie, John L. "Aspects of Old Testament Thought." In *The New Jerome Biblical Commentary*, edited by Raymond Edward Brown, Joseph A. Fitzmyer, and Roland Edmund Murphy, 1284–315. Englewood Cliffs, N.J.: Prentice-Hall, 1990.

Meier, John. *A Marginal Jew: Rethinking the Historical Jesus.* New York: Doubleday, 1991.

Metzger, Bruce. *The New Testament: Its Background, Growth, and Content.* Abingdon: Nashville, 1991.

Nestle, Eberhard, Erwin Nestle, Barbara Aland, Kurt Aland, and Barclay Moon Newman. *Novum Testamentum Graece.* Stuttgart: Deutsche Bibelgesellschaft, 2001.

Peters, Melvin. "Septuagint." In vol. 5 of *The Anchor Bible Dictionary*, edited by David Noel Freedman, 1093–104. New York: Doubleday, 1992.

Quell, G. "ἀλήθεια." In vol. 1 of *Theological Dictionary of the New Testament.* Edited by Gerhard Kittel and Gerhard Friedrich, 232–37. Grand Rapids, Mich.: Eerdmans, 1971.

Reiser, Marius. *Bibelkritik und Auslegung der Heiligen Schrift: Beiträge zur Geschichte der biblischen Exegese und Hermeneutik.* Tübingen: Mohr Siebeck, 2007.

Seow, C. L. "Hosea, Book of." In vol. 3 of *The Anchor Bible Dictionary*, edited by David Noel Freedman, 87–100. New York: Doubleday, 1992.

Spinoza, Baruch. *Theological-Political Treatise*. Cambridge: Cambridge University Press, 2007.

Suelzer, Alexa, and John S. Kselman. "Modern Old Testament Criticism." In *The New Jerome Biblical Commentary*, edited by Raymond Edward Brown, Joseph A. Fitzmyer, and Roland Edmund Murphy, 1113–29. Englewood Cliffs, N.J.: Prentice-Hall, 1990.

Vanhoozer, Kevin. *The Drama of Doctrine: A Canonical-Linguistic Approach to Christian Theology*. Louisville: Westminster John Knox Press, 2005.

Wright, Addison G. "Ecclesiastes." In *The New Jerome Biblical Commentary*, edited by Raymond Edward Brown, Joseph A. Fitzmyer, and Roland Edmund Murphy, 489–95. Englewood Cliffs, N.J.: Prentice-Hall, 1990.

Würthwein, Ernst. *The Text of the Old Testament: An Introduction to the Biblia Hebraica*. Grand Rapids, Mich: Eerdmans, 1995. ^^Ramage. frst index^^

SCRIPTURE INDEX

GENERAL INDEX

Accuser, 37–38, 185. *See also* Satan
affirmation, 132, 152–53, 176–77
afterlife, 8, 40–48, 75–76, 144–45, 196–273
Allison, Dave, 42
angel, 20, 24–26, 29–30, 31–32, 161–63,
    166–67
angel of the Lord, 172–73
Aquinas, Thomas, 10–13, 92–113, 114–25,
    127–31, 150–51, 173, 191, 202, 221–22,
    250–51, 256–67, 278
assertion. *See* affirmation
Athanasius, 67, 276n6
Atrahasis, 23
Augustine of Hippo, 14, 59n11, 60n15, 67,
    72n46, 74, 160–63, 180, 184–85, 276
authorship, 94–95, 115, 119–25, 126–34;
    instrumental, 126–29, 235–37, 144

Baal, 163–64, 169, 174–75, 212–14
Babylon, 23, 175, 182–83, 194, 212, 216, 228
ban, 33–34, 188
Barthélemy, Dominique, 237n80, 239n82
Benedict XV, 58n9
Benedict XVI, 3–16, 120n11, 123–24,
    113–34, 139–41, 156, 172–73, 178, 180,
    192–94, 197, 207–9, 214–15, 243–33,
    252–53, 274–77
Benoit, Pierre, 56n5, 117–38, 147–56,
    194n43, 235–38, 248–49n97, 272
Bernard of Clairvaux, 54, 65
Bonaventure, 240–42, 244
Book of Jubilees, 190n39
Burtchaell, James, 57n7, 117n6, 141–44
Byrne, Brendan, 18n3, 21–22, 166

canon, 62–68
Christological analogy, 56–58
Chrysostom, 54, 199–200
Collins, John J., 187n36, 226n62
Congar, Yves, 63–64, 70n39, 71, 121–23
contradictions, 114–54
Cyril of Jerusalem, 201

David, 25, 38, 44, 59–60, 106, 115, 124, 132,
    149, 186, 206, 262–65, 270–73
Davies, W. D., 42
Dawkins, Richard, 158–59
death, 37, 40–48, 75, 106, 145, 175, 184,
    197–235, 239–71
Dei Verbum, 4, 9, 56, 64, 68, 82, 88n79,
    110, 134, 279
development, 92–114, 214
Devil, 76. *See also* Satan
divine council 18, 20–28, 37, 49–50,
    161–63, 165–68, 175–76
divine pedagogy, 4–8, 15–16, 100–113,
    133–34, 141–42, 157–58, 163–68, 173–74,
    202, 204, 210–11, 237–39, 244–46,
    250–52, 269

Ecclesiastes, 17, 47–48, 50–51, 144–46, 197,
    237–49
Ehrman, Bart, 198
Elihu, 240n83, 253–54
Enns, Peter, 24n7, 28, 138n44
Enuma Elish, 23
environmental glitch, 145–46, 175, 192
Erasmus lecture, 11, 14, 53, 78, 90
error, 134–39, 143–45, 153–54, 192

*Dark Passages of the Bible: Engaging Scripture
with Benedict XVI & Thomas Aquinas* was
designed in Minion by Kachergis Book Design
of Pittsboro, North Carolina. It was printed on
60-pound Natures Book Natural and bound by
McNaughton & Gunn of Saline, Michigan.